PSYCHOLOGY
for A S Level

PSYCHOLOGY
for A S Level

Michael W. Eysenck
and Cara Flanagan

Psychology Press
a member of the Taylor & Francis group

First published 2000 by Psychology Press Ltd
27 Church Road, Hove, East Sussex, BN3 2FA

http://www.psypress.co.uk

Simultaneously published in the USA and Canada
by Taylor & Francis Inc
325 Chestnut Street, Suite 800, Philadelphia, PA 19106

Psychology Press is part of the Taylor & Francis Group

© 2000 by Psychology Press Ltd

British Library Cataloguing in Publication Data
A catalogue record for this book is available from the British Library

Library of Congress Cataloging in Publication Data

ISBN 0-86377-665-5 (pbk)

Cover design by Hurlock Design, Lewes, East Sussex
Typeset in Great Britain by Facing Pages, Southwick, West Sussex
Printed in Hong Kong by Midas Printing Limited

Dedication

To Our Families, With Love

Contents

Acknowledgements

We have benefited from the advice and guidance of a number of people: our thanks to Di Dwyer, Anthony Curtis, and Evie Bentley, who very painstakingly read the final manuscript; Viv Ward, Alison Dixon, Mike Forster, and Tanya Sagoo at Psychology Press, for their enthusiasm and good lunches; and finally to our many colleagues for their support, perhaps most importantly Paul Humphreys, whose E-mails are always a joy, and Liz Hey, an ever-cheerful examinations officer who copes magnificently.

About the Authors

Michael W. Eysenck is one of the best-known British psychologists. He is Professor of Psychology and head of the psychology department at Royal Holloway University of London, which is one of the leading departments in the United Kingdom. His academic interests lie mainly in cognitive psychology, with much of his research focusing on the role of cognitive factors in anxiety in normal and clinical populations.

He is an author of many titles, and his previous textbooks published by Psychology Press include *Psychology: A Student's Handbook* (2000), *Simply Psychology* (1996), *Cognitive Psychology: A Student's Handbook* (1995, with Mark Keane), *Perspectives on Psychology* (1994), *Individual Differences: Normal and Abnormal* (1994) and *Principles of Cognitive Psychology* (1993). He has also written the research monographs *Anxiety and Cognition: A Unified Theory* (1997), and *Anxiety: The Cognitive Perspective* (1992), along with the popular title *Happiness: Facts and Myths* (1990). He is also a keen supporter of Crystal Palace and Wimbledon football clubs.

Cara Flanagan has worked for many years as a GCSE and A-level examiner, team leader and assessor for various examination boards. She has recently been appointed the Reviser for one of the new psychology specifications and, in that capacity, will be closely involved in setting all the new examination papers. As an experienced examiner, she knows intimately the intricacies of the examination system and what is needed by students to do well in examinations.

Cara has also written extensively for A-level psychology. Her textbooks include, most recently, the *Letts AS Level Revision Guide* (2000), *Early Socialisation* (1999), and *Practicals for Psychology* (1998). She is co-editor of the highly successful Routledge modular series of psychology books. She also contributes regularly to *Psychology Review*, has written various teacher packs, and speaks at student conferences. She looks after three children and a husband, and enjoys walking in the Scottish Highlands where she lives.

1

Starting Psychology

Welcome to psychology. Presumably you are reading this book because you have elected to study AS-level psychology, and what a good choice. The AS-level course should give you some fundamental and lasting insights into human behaviour which will enable you to cope better with your own life and in your interactions with the people around you.

It is very important to read this first chapter of the book because it sets the scene for all that follows. You might be asking some of the following questions:

"What is psychology?"

"Is psychology just common sense?"

"What do psychologists do?"

"How do they explain behaviour?"

"What kind of exam will I take?"

"How is it marked?"

This first chapter of the book is divided into three sections to look at these questions:

- *Section 1: Introducing psychology*. A brief look at what psychology is, and how it is more than just common sense. We also take a look at what psychologists do.
- *Section 2: Psychological explanations*. Psychologists have a "toolkit" that contains a set of explanations (tools) which they use to explain behaviour. This section has a look at that toolkit.
- *Section 3: Studying and taking examinations*. You are probably using this book because you are taking a course in AS-level psychology and therefore, from the start, you should be aware of how you will be examined. Study skills are also important—all too often students realise, too late, that they haven't been studying effectively.

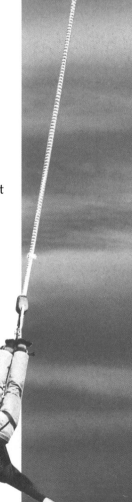

Taking a course in psychology will change your life. Besides learning about human behaviour, you should also learn how to express yourself coherently, how to challenge information, how to be confident about yourself, and to be a better friend, employee, and member of society!

SECTION 1
Introducing Psychology

These animals are "behaving"—they are sleeping and sleep is a behaviour, something we all experience. Psychology is the science of behaviour and experience.

What is Psychology?

Psychology is the science of behaviour and experience.

The term "science" refers to the objective study of something. Psychologists study *behaviour*—what people (and other animals) *do*. "Behaviour" includes being aggressive or kind, thinking and seeing, breathing and walking, growing up and getting old, being a friend or a parent, and so on. These are all examples of "behaviour".

Psychologists are also interested in "experience". If we want to understand behaviour we also need to consider what the experience is like for the individual doing the behaving. For example, if we want to study aggression, it matters what the person who is behaving aggressively *feels like*.

Psychology is concerned with the study of all animals, humans and non-humans alike. In this book, however, we will focus on the study of human behaviour.

Is Psychology Just Common Sense?

Many people say "Well, isn't psychology no more than common sense?" Everyone is an "armchair psychologist". We all have views about why people behave as they do and, in a sense, these are "theories of psychology". For example, your friend might say "Those football fans act like that because they're hooligans". By saying "they're hooligans" your friend is presumably offering an explanation for the fans' behaviour, such as "they have no care for the feelings of others". But how do we *know* this explanation is correct? That's the starting point for psychological research. Psychologists observe behaviour, formulate an explanation or theory to account for the behaviour, and then conduct a test to see if their theory is correct. Consider the following example:

Common sense can be contradictory: "Look before you leap" vs. "He who hesitates is lost".

> *Several years ago, a young woman was stabbed to death in the middle of a street in a residential section of New York City. Although such murders are not entirely routine, the incident received little public attention until several weeks later when the New York Times disclosed another side to the case: at least 38 witnesses had observed the attack—and none had even attempted to intervene. Although the attacker took more than half an hour to kill Kitty Genovese, not one of the 38 people who watched*

from the safety of their own apartments came out to assist her. Not one even lifted the telephone to call the police. (From A.M. Rosenthal, 1964, Thirty-eight witnesses. New York: McGraw Hill.)

Two psychologists John Darley and Bibb Latané (1968) read this report, and it made them wonder, "Why *do* bystanders in an emergency fail to offer assistance?" The *common sense* answer, given by the *New York Times*, was that city dwellers were a callous and uncaring lot of people. Darley and Latané came up with a different explanation. They thought that perhaps the reason was related to the number of bystanders, in this case there were "38 silent witnesses". Could it be that each individual witness assumed someone else was taking action to end the emergency situation and therefore they personally did not need to do anything?

Up to this point you might say that Darley and Latané's thinking was not necessarily more than common sense (although it was an unusual explanation). But what they did next is what distinguishes psychology from common sense. They set up an experiment to test their opinions—they arranged for students to discuss personal problems with each other over an intercom. Except that there was only one actual student involved: the other participants were confederates of the experimenter. During the conversation one of the "students" appeared to have an epileptic fit. If the real student was under the impression that five people were listening to the conversation it took them three times as long before they offered help than if the student thought there were just two people having the discussion.

The findings from this study appear to demonstrate that it is the number of people present that affects how likely one is to offer help in an emergency situation. This is psychology—the attempt to explain why people behave in the way they do, and to support these explanations with objective evidence.

You still might think "I knew it all along", but this is called **hindsight bias**—the tendency to be wise after the event. Two psychologists, Fischhoff and Beyth, conducted a study to demonstrate hindsight bias in action (see the Key Study overleaf).

Research

Darley and Latané's study, described earlier, is an example of one kind of psychological research. It is an **experiment**. Psychologists use other methods of research besides the experiment, and we will look at these in Chapter 7 of this book. Some of the methods are rather less "artificial" and more like real life. For example,

Have you ever been in a situation where someone was in trouble and you did nothing? Can you explain why you did not help?

Key terms in bold are explained in the glossary at the back of the book.

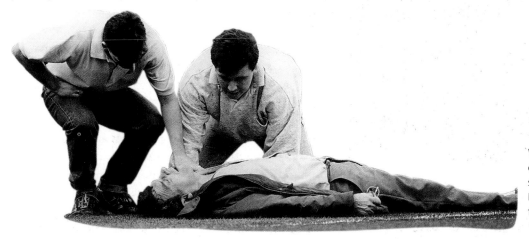

We expect bystanders to help in emergency situations, but sometimes they don't. Why is this? Psychological research has tried to find clear answers to this so-called "bystander behaviour."

Demonstrating hindsight bias

Two psychologists, Fischhoff and Beyth (1975), asked American students to estimate the probability of various possible outcomes on the eve of President Nixon's trips to China and Russia. After the trips were over, the students were asked to do the same task, but without taking into account their knowledge of what had actually happened. In spite of these instructions, participants did use the benefit of hindsight and gave events that had actually happened a much higher probability than they had done before the events had occurred. The participants had added their knowledge of what had happened to what they already knew in such a way that they could not remember how uncertain things had looked before the trips. This tendency to be wise after the event is known as hindsight bias.

Slovic and Fischhoff (1977) carried out a similar study involving predictions about the results of a series of scientific experiments. Some of the participants were told what had happened in the first experiment of the series, but they were told not to use this information when making their predictions. However, participants thought a given outcome was much more likely to occur in future experiments if it had already been obtained. This is another example of hindsight bias.

Hindsight bias seems to be very strong, and is hard to eliminate. In another study, Fischhoff (1977) told his participants about hindsight bias, and encouraged them to avoid it. However, this had little or no effect on the size of the hindsight bias. Hindsight bias poses a problem for teachers of psychology, because it produces students who are unimpressed by almost everything in psychology!

Discussion points

1. Can you think of any ways in which we could try to eliminate hindsight bias?
2. When you think about the views you used to have about psychology, is it possible that you have shown hindsight bias?

When there are more than two authors of a research paper we use "et al.", which means "and others", to refer to all the other researchers.

in another study of bystander behaviour, Piliavin, Rodin, and Piliavin (or Piliavin **et al.**, 1969) arranged for someone to "collapse" on an underground train and timed how long it took for people on the train to offer help.

If research is like "real life" we say it has greater **ecological validity**—it is more true to life and therefore perhaps it will tell us more about "real" behaviour. The problem is that the more like real life the research, the less easy it is to control other factors that might influence the particular behaviour we want to study (called the "target behaviour")—in our example the extent of helping behaviour. Consider the case of Kitty Genovese. This situation was very like real life—in fact it was real life. But just observing what happened did not allow us to know for sure why the witnesses didn't respond. We have to narrow down the possibilities to determine if it was the number of people that was the cause. There may be other explanations as well, and to find them out we would need to conduct other research. In each research study we have to control irrelevant factors to demonstrate the effect of the one we are interested in. We will consider ecological validity again, later in the book.

What Do Psychologists Do?

Do you have to remember all the names of psychologists? No, but it helps. Knowing the name of a researcher can be like a key that unlocks a memory—but the description of the study is more important than the name.

If you don't quite understand what psychology is, then maybe another way to approach it is to ask "What do psychologists do?" (For instance, if you want to understand what the study of law involves, then it might make more sense to find out what lawyers do.) Some psychologists conduct research into psychology, whereas other psychologists apply this research in areas such as health, business, crime, and education. Research psychologists focus on different branches of psychology. These branches include the core areas of cognitive, developmental, physiological, individual differences, and social psychology.

Cognitive psychology

The word "cognitive" is derived from a Latin word *cognitio* meaning "to apprehend" or understand. Cognitive psychologists look at topics such as memory, perception, thought, language, attention, and so on. In other words they are interested in mental processes and seek to explain behaviour in terms of these mental processes.

There are many applications of cognitive psychology, ranging from suggestions about how to improve your memory (useful for examination candidates), to how to improve performance in situations requiring close attention (such as air traffic control).

Developmental psychology

Developmental psychologists study the changes that occur over a person's lifetime, starting from conception and infancy through to adolescence, adulthood, and finally old age. This approach has also been called lifespan psychology. Changes can be related to maturing and ageing. Developmental psychologists focus on how particular behaviours change as individuals grow older. In children, they look at the changes in the way children think, and how they acquire language. They also look at moral, social, and gender development. Developmental psychologists might also consider changes such as coping with retirement or coping with loss of memory.

Physiological psychology

"Physiology" refers to bodily processes. Physiological psychologists are interested in how to explain behaviour in terms of bodily processes. They look at topics such as how the nerves function, how hormones affect behaviour, and how the different areas of the brain are specialised and related to different behaviours.

Individual differences

The study of "individual differences" is literally the study of the ways that individuals differ in terms of their psychological characteristics. Individuals differ *physically* in terms of, for example, height and hair colour. They differ psychologically in terms of intelligence, aggressiveness, willingness to conform, masculinity and femininity, and just about every behaviour you can think of.

An important individual difference can be found in the degree to which a person is mentally healthy. This is specifically referred to as the study of abnormal behaviour and is the remit of **abnormal** or **atypical psychology**. Psychologists study childhood and adult disorders such as dyslexia, autism, schizophrenia, and

The experiences we have during childhood have a great impact on our adult lives.

Physiological and psychological explanations

Neurology and biochemistry underlie all behaviour. What happens when a person sees a sunset? The physiological explanation would be that light reflected from the landscape forms an image on the retina, which is converted into a neural signal and transmitted to the brain, and so on. No-one disputes that this is true, and the process is absolutely essential, but does it give a full and adequate explanation of what is going on? A psychological explanation would probably include the personal and social relevance of the experience, which many would argue are of equal value.

Social psychology looks at our relationships with other people and society.

depression, seeking to find explanations for the causes of such difficulties and to find valid methods of treatment.

Social psychology

"Social" refers to any situation involving two or more members of the same species. Social psychologists are interested in the way people affect each other. They look at, for example, interpersonal relationships, group behaviour, leadership, conformity, obedience to those in authority, and the influence of the media. Social psychology differs from sociology in placing greater emphasis on the individual as a separate entity; sociologists are interested in the structure and functioning of groups, whereas social psychologists look at how these processes influence the individual members of a social group.

Other branches of psychology

The five core areas just described form the basis of this book, but there are other areas of psychology as well. For example, **comparative psychology** is the study of non-human animals. It is called "comparative" because psychologists make comparisons between animals of different species to find out more about human behaviour. The study of **animal behaviour** is a field of study in its own right and straddles psychology and biology.

Comparative psychologists study non-human animals and make comparisons between them and humans. How much can the study of chimpanzee behaviour tell us about the relationship between human parents and their children?

SECTION 2
Psychological Explanations

How Do Psychologists Explain Behaviour?

In discussing the issue of what psychologists do, we have touched on the question of how they explain behaviour. For example, physiological psychologists clearly explain behaviour in terms of bodily processes, and social psychologists explain behaviour in terms of the interactions between people. In the case of the "hooligans" mentioned earlier, a physiological explanation might be that they have high levels of **hormones** which make them more aggressive; whereas a social explanation would be that they are influenced by the people they are with—everyone else in the group behaves in an anti-social manner and the "hooligan" conforms to the group behaviour. These are some of the ways that psychologists explain behaviour, and they are explored in later sections of the book.

There are a few kinds of explanation that are more general to all areas of psychology, such as learning theory, psychoanalytic theory, social learning theory, cognitive or information processing theory, and evolutionary theory. For example, if we think of our hooligan again, a learning theory explanation would be that he (or she) had learned to behave in this way because other people admired them more for behaving like that. We will now consider all these more general kinds of explanation.

Psychologists use similar explanations for all kinds of behaviour. In a way their set of explanations is like a toolkit and, when faced with having to explain a behaviour, they try out all their various tools to see which ones do the job best. It is usual to find that they need more than one tool!

Learning Theory

One way to explain behaviour is in terms of **learning**. This form of explanation is called **learning theory** and is based on the principles of **conditioning**.

Classical conditioning

The origins of behaviourism lie in Ivan Pavlov's work as a physiologist. He was conducting research into the digestive system, which required that his experimental

Have you ever noticed how a cat comes running as soon as it hears the cupboard door opening? Classical conditioning can explain this.

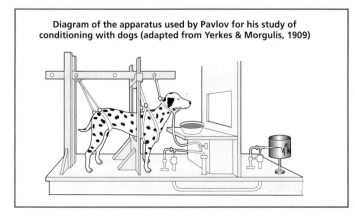

Diagram of the apparatus used by Pavlov for his study of conditioning with dogs (adapted from Yerkes & Morgulis, 1909)

Ivan Pavlov (1849–1936), a Russian physiologist.

Classical conditioning

US ➔ UR

NS + US paired

NS (now CS) ➔ UR (now CR)

The concepts of classical and operant conditioning are important elements in the psychologist's toolkit. It is important that you try to learn the terminology that is used.

dogs were connected to a machine that collected saliva. When the dogs were offered food, saliva production increased. But he also noticed something particularly interesting—this salivation started to increase as soon a researcher opened the door to bring them the food. The dogs had learned that "opening door" signalled "food coming soon". It was in their nature to salivate when they smelled food. This is a reflex response. But the dogs had now *learned* a link between "door" and their reflex response (salivation). This is **classical conditioning**.

Food is an unconditioned stimulus (US) and salivation is an unconditioned response (UR). No learning is required for this stimulus–response (S–R) link, which is why both stimulus and response are described as "unconditioned".

The sound of the door opening is a neutral stimulus (NS). There is no inborn reflex response to hearing a door open.

If an NS and US occur together repeatedly they become associated, until eventually the NS also causes the UR—now the NS is called a conditioned stimulus (CS) and the UR becomes a conditioned response (CR) to this. The CS on its own will produce the CR. A new **S–R link** has been learned.

Operant conditioning

Edward Thorndike (1874–1949) extended classical learning theory to include **instrumental learning**. Thorndike suggested that learning could take place through *trial and error*, rather than just by association as in classical conditioning. He demonstrated this by placing a hungry cat in a "puzzle box" with a fish hanging nearby. The cat scratched and clawed and meowed to try to get out of the box, and eventually, by accident, tripped the latch of the box and jumped out. The next time the cat was placed in the box, it went through the same sequence of somewhat random behaviours but took less time to escape from the cage. After a few more trials the cat had learned what to do and, each time it was imprisoned, would release the catch immediately. This led Thorndike to state his "Law of Effect": acts that are followed by a positive state of affairs are more likely to recur than acts followed by an annoying state of affairs.

How do classical and operant conditioning differ?

- Positive effects (rewards) led to the *stamping in* of a behaviour.
- Negative effects (punishments) led to the *stamping out* of a behaviour.

This theory of instrumental conditioning was further developed by B.F. Skinner (1904–1990) into **operant conditioning**. Thorndike's and Skinner's approaches

B.F. Skinner, 1904–1990.

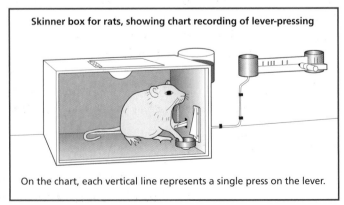

Skinner box for rats, showing chart recording of lever-pressing

On the chart, each vertical line represents a single press on the lever.

were similar in that they concentrated on the *effects* of behaviour, in contrast with Pavlov's focus on the behaviours themselves.

The essence of operant conditioning can be seen in Skinner's (1938) experiments with rats. A rat is placed in a cage with a lever (bar) sticking out on one side. If the lever is pressed, a pellet of food will be delivered. At first the rat presses the lever by accident but soon learns that there is a link between lever pressing and food appearing. Skinner stated that the rat *operated* on the environment. When there was a reward (food) this **reinforced** the likelihood of the behaviour occurring again. When an animal performs a behaviour (or operates on the environment) there are four possible consequences:

"Well, I simply trained them to give me fish by pressing this over and over again."

- *Positive reinforcement* is pleasurable and therefore increases the likelihood of a behaviour occurring again. For example, receiving food.
- *Negative reinforcement* refers to the avoidance of an unpleasant stimulus, but the result is that it is also pleasurable (like positive reinforcement) and thus increases the likelihood of a behaviour. For instance, if the floor of the cage was electrified and pressing the lever stopped this, then the rat would be more likely to press the lever.
- *Positive punishment* such as receiving an electric shock decreases the likelihood of a behaviour. For example, if the rat received a shock every time it pressed the lever it would stop doing it.
- *Negative punishment* such as removing some food (removing a pleasant stimulus), decreases the likelihood of a behaviour. An example in human terms might be being grounded for staying out late. The removal of a desirable option (going out) reduces the likelihood of staying out late.

A mother learns that if she shouts loudly her children will stop misbehaving. In what way is this an example of negative reinforcement?

A child learns that he can avoid being hit by his father if he smiles. Which kind of reinforcement is this: positive or negative?

John Watson and behaviourism

John Watson was very impressed with the principles of conditioning and felt that they offered psychology a way to become a more objective science. Up until the end of the 19th century psychology was still quite close to philosophy and most research relied on **introspection**, investigating human behaviour by asking well-trained participants to report what was going on in their mind. Watson founded behaviourism, based on the principles of learning outlined by Pavlov and Thorndike. This approach rejected the idea of the mind. Behaviourists felt that there was no need to explain what went on in the mind, or as they called it, the "black box". It was sufficient to talk in terms of a stimulus and a response.

Assumptions of the behaviourist approach
- Behaviourists think that behaviour is all that matters: the stimulus and the response.
- It doesn't matter what goes on inside the "black box".
- All behaviour is learned.
- The same laws apply to all animal behaviour, including humans. This can be justified in terms of the **theory of evolution** which shows that human and non-human animals are quantitatively not qualitatively different.

Evaluation of learning theory

A great deal has been written about behaviourism, some of it negative. First of all you should note that no psychologists today claim that we can explain *all* behaviour

Note that reinforcement always makes behaviour more likely.

in terms of learning theory. And all psychologists agree that *some* aspects of behaviour can be explained using learning theory. So, learning theory is an important part of our toolkit.

One of the criticisms of the theory is that it was developed through work with non-human animals (such as dogs, cats, and rats). Learning theory may explain the behaviour of these animals but it may not be appropriate for more complex human behaviours, such as learning to use language. These more complex behaviours are probably governed more by "mental processes", such as memory and reasoning. This means that we do need to know what is going on inside the "**black box**".

There are ethical concerns about behaviourist explanations. A central aim of behaviourists is the prediction and control of behaviour. Both Watson and Skinner had a desire to use their principles to produce a better society. Indeed behaviourist approaches are used in this way, for example in some prisons, schools, and psychiatric institutions—to train people to behave in "desirable" ways. Some people regard this as a good thing, while others feel it is unethical. The issue of ethics will be considered later in this book.

Psychoanalytic Theory

A "Freudian slip" is a mistake that betrays the concerns of the unconscious mind. Think of a time when you might have called someone by the wrong name. In what way might this have been a Freudian slip?

In the 19th century another form of psychological explanation grew out of Sigmund Freud's theory of personality development. Freud practised as a psychiatrist in Vienna and collected a body of data from his patients about their feelings and experiences, especially those related to early childhood. He developed his ideas into a theory (**psychoanalytic theory**) and a form of therapy (**psychoanalysis**).

Psychoanalytic theory seeks to explain human development in terms of an interaction between **innate** drives (such as the desire for pleasure) and early experience (the extent to which early desires were gratified). Individual personality differences can be traced back to the way the early conflicts between desire and experience were handled. These conflicts remain with the adult and exert pressure through unconsciously motivated behaviour. In order to understand this we need to look briefly at Freud's description of development.

The structure of the personality

Sigmund Freud, 1856–1939.

Freud assumed that the mind is divided into three parts. First, there is the **id**. This contains innate sexual and aggressive instincts, and is located in the unconscious mind. The sexual instinct is known as libido. The id works in accord with the **pleasure principle**, with the emphasis being on immediate satisfaction. Second, there is the **ego**. This is the conscious, rational mind, and it develops during the first two years of life. It works on the **reality principle**, taking account of what is going on in the environment, i.e. in reality. Third, there is the **superego**. This develops at about the age of 5 and embodies the child's conscience and sense of right and wrong. It is formed when the child adopts many of the values of the same-sexed parent (the process of identification).

Freud also assumed that there were three levels of the mind: the conscious; the preconscious; and the unconscious. The conscious consists of those thoughts that are currently the focus of attention. The preconscious consists of information and ideas that could be retrieved easily from memory and brought into consciousness. The unconscious consists of information that is either very hard or almost impossible to bring into conscious awareness.

Defence mechanisms

An important part of Freud's theory was the notion that there are frequent *conflicts* among the id, ego, and superego. Conflicts are perhaps most common between the id and the superego, because the id's demands for instant gratification clash with the superego's sense of right and wrong (i.e. morals or conscience) and the ego's sense of reality, as well as the superego's sense of ideal self (the person that the individual wants to be). Conflicts cause the individual to experience anxiety, and this leads the ego to devote much time to trying to resolve these conflicts. The ego protects itself by using a number of **defence mechanisms**, which are strategies designed to reduce anxiety. Some of the main defence mechanisms are as follows:

1. *Repression*. Keeping threatening thoughts out of consciousness. For example, a person may not remember a dental appointment because it is going to be painful.
2. *Displacement*. Unconsciously moving impulses away from a threatening object and towards a less threatening object. For example, someone who has been made angry by their boss may go home and kick the cat.
3. *Projection*. An individual may attribute their undesirable characteristics to others. For example, someone who is very unfriendly may accuse other people of being unfriendly.
4. *Denial*. Refusing to accept the existence or reality of a threatening event. For example, patients suffering from life-threatening diseases often deny that these diseases are affecting their lives.
5. *Intellectualisation*. Thinking about threatening events in ways that remove the emotion from them. An example would be responding to the sinking of a car ferry with considerable loss of life by thinking about ways of improving the design of ferries.

Psychosexual development

One of Freud's key assumptions was that adult personality depends very much on childhood experiences. In his theory of **psychosexual development**, Freud assumed that all children go through five stages as shown in the box below.

> **Useful mnemonic**
> To help you remember Freud's stages of psychosexual development, the following mnemonic is made from the initial letter of each stage: Old Age Pensioners Love Greens!

FREUD'S STAGES OF PSYCHOSEXUAL DEVELOPMENT

1. *Oral stage*: this occurs during the first 18 months of life. During this stage, the infant obtains satisfaction from eating, sucking, and other activities using the mouth.
2. *Anal stage*: this occurs between about 18 and 36 months of age. Toilet training takes place during this stage, which helps to explain why the anal region becomes so important.
3. *Phallic stage*: This occurs between 3 and 6 years of age. The genitals become a key source of satisfaction during this stage. At about the age of 5, boys acquire the **Oedipus complex**, in which they have sexual desires for their mother and therefore want to get rid of their father, who is a rival. They then also fear their father who might realise what they are thinking. This complex is resolved by identification with their father, involving adopting many of their father's attitudes and developing a superego. Jung (a follower of Freud) suggested that a similar process operates in girls called the **Electra complex**, in which girls desire their fathers. Freud's own view was that, during the genital stage, girls come to recognise that they don't have a penis and blame their mother for this. The girl's father now becomes her love-object and she substitutes her "penis envy" with a wish to have a child. This leads to a kind of resolution and ultimate identification with her same-sex parent.
4. *Latency stage*: this lasts from 6 years of age until the onset of puberty. During this stage, boys and girls spend very little time together.
5. *Genital stage*: this starts from the onset of puberty and continues throughout adult life. During this stage, the main source of sexual pleasure is in the genitals.

Freud suggested that adult personality types could be linked with fixations during each stage of development.

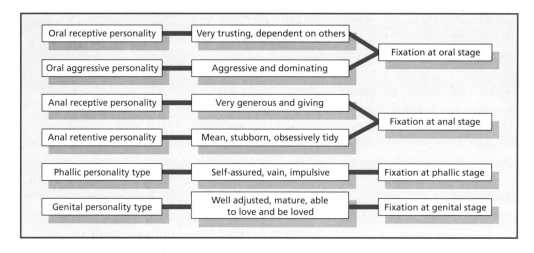

Oral receptive personality	Very trusting, dependent on others	Fixation at oral stage
Oral aggressive personality	Aggressive and dominating	
Anal receptive personality	Very generous and giving	Fixation at anal stage
Anal retentive personality	Mean, stubborn, obsessively tidy	
Phallic personality type	Self-assured, vain, impulsive	Fixation at phallic stage
Genital personality type	Well adjusted, mature, able to love and be loved	Fixation at genital stage

Personality theory

Note that the term "sexual" is roughly equivalent to "physical pleasure".

Freud coupled the theory of psychosexual development with a theory of personality. If a child experiences severe problems or excessive pleasure at any stage of development, this leads to **fixation**, in which basic energy or libido becomes attached to that stage for many years. Later in life, adults who experience very stressful conditions are likely to show **regression**, in which their behaviour becomes less mature, and more like that displayed during a psychosexual stage at which they fixated as children. According to Freud, these processes of fixation and regression play important roles in determining adult personality. Some personality types are shown in the box above, along with descriptions and a link to the stage of psychosexual development at which fixation may have occurred.

Evaluation of psychoanalytic theory

Freud and his psychoanalytic theory have had an enormous impact on psychology. Williams (1987) commented that

Freud developed his Oedipus complex at a time when lone-parent families were very rare. What bearing do you think this had on his theorising?

> *psychoanalysis has been society's most influential theory of human behaviour … it profoundly altered Western ideas about human nature and changed the way we viewed ourselves and our experience.*

Freud's work was largely with middle-class women in Vienna in the 1890s and 1900s. How relevant do you think his ideas are to other cultures, particularly given the social changes during the 20th century?

On the other hand, some psychologists object outright to Freud's theory, more so than any of the other approaches considered in this chapter.

Freud's method of investigation was to focus on the individual, observing particular "cases" in fine detail. In some ways this is to his credit—giving an in-depth understanding of the way people think and feel. However, many people see this approach as a drawback, mainly because Freud's observations were largely based on a rather narrow sample of people: white, middle-class Victorian Viennese women. The theory may not be universally applicable, yet certain key concepts have endured, namely, the emphasis on childhood and on the influence of the unconscious.

It has been suggested that Freud may have overemphasised sex because he developed his theory at a historical time of great sexual repression. Understandably this may have caused sex to be something that was repressed in many minds (Banyard & Hayes, 1994). There are a number of neo-Freudians who have adapted Freud's explanation and incorporated more social rather than sexual influences.

> **Assumptions of the psychoanalytic approach**
> * Development is the result of an interaction between innate drives and early experience.
> * Childhood experiences are of fundamental importance.
> * Early conflicts result in unconscious forces that drive many aspects of adult behaviour.

Considering that Freud was working in a strict Victorian society, why was sexual behaviour so strongly emphasised in his theory of development?

Social Learning Theory

Albert Bandura was one of the first psychologists to propose an alternative to learning theory that incorporated mental processes. Psychoanalytic theory used the concept of identification and this reappeared in **social learning theory**. Bandura suggested that behaviour was learned but not always through direct conditioning. There are many occasions when we learn by watching what other people do. If they appear to be rewarded for their actions then we are likely to imitate them. This is called **vicarious reinforcement** because we are reinforced second-hand or vicariously. If we identify with a person, then we are also likely to imitate his or her behaviour.

A key difference between *social* learning theory and learning theory is the introduction of mental states. In order to imitate someone's behaviour there must be an intervening cognitive state. Behaviourists rejected the concept of mind, saying there was no need for it—one could explain behaviour without it. Social learning theorists introduced a role for cognition as well as the influence of social factors. The classic study that is used to support Bandura's theory is described in the Key Study on the next page.

A theory is basically an organised collection of related statements that seek to explain observed phenomena.

Evaluation of social learning theory

The social learning explanation is found throughout psychology and is an important one. It is a neo-behaviourist ("new behaviourist") account because it still emphasises the role of learning as a way of explaining why people behave as they do, but with the additional involvement of cognitive (mental) and social factors. Children learn many of their behaviours by observing others and modelling their own behaviour on what they have seen. Likely models include parents, friends, people of the same sex, film stars, rock stars and, of course, model models.

However there are limitations to the social learning approach. Behaviour does not depend only on observational learning. People's internal emotional state, their interpretation of the current situation, and their personality are other important factors that need to be taken into account.

The social learning of aggression

According to Bandura's theory, observational learning or modelling is of great importance in producing aggressive behaviour. **Observational learning** is a form of learning in which the behaviour of others is imitated or copied. Bandura, Ross, and Ross (1961) carried out a classic study on observational learning or modelling. Young children watched as an adult behaved aggressively towards a Bobo doll. The adult punched the doll and hit it with a hammer. After 10 minutes the children were moved to another room where there were some toys, including a hammer and a Bobo doll. The children had to walk some distance before they got to the room. This was done to create a sense of frustration. Once in the room, they were watched through a one-way mirror and rated for their aggression. The children who had watched an adult behaving aggressively were more violent and imitated exactly some of the behaviours they had observed, as compared with children who either had seen no model or watched an adult (model) behaving in a non-aggressive manner.

Bandura (1965) carried out another study on aggressive behaviour towards the Bobo doll. One group of children simply saw a film of an adult model kicking and punching the Bobo doll. A second group saw the same aggressive behaviour performed by the adult model, but this time the model was rewarded by another adult for his aggressive behaviour by being given sweets and a drink. A third group saw the same aggressive behaviour, but the model was punished by another adult, who warned him not to be aggressive in future.

Those children who had seen the model rewarded, and those who had seen the model neither rewarded nor punished, behaved much more aggressively towards the Bobo doll than did those who had seen the model punished. It could be argued that the children who had seen the model being punished remembered less about the model's

---

KEY STUDY EVALUATION — Bandura

In spite of the successes of social learning theory, there are reasons for arguing that Bandura exaggerated the extent to which children imitate the behaviour of models. Children are very likely to imitate aggressive behaviour towards a doll, but they are generally much less likely to imitate aggressive behaviour towards another child. Bandura consistently failed to distinguish between real aggression and playfighting, and it is likely that much of the aggressive behaviour observed by Bandura was only playfighting (Durkin, 1995).

The Bobo doll is of interest to young children, because it has a weighted base and so bounces back up when it is knocked down. Its novelty value is important in determining its effectiveness. Cumberbatch (1990) reported that children who were unfamiliar with the doll were five times more likely to imitate aggressive behaviour against it than were children who had played with it before.

Finally, there is the problem of **demand characteristics**. These are the cues used by participants to work out what a study is about. In an experiment, participants will try to guess what it is they should be doing. This leads them to search for cues that might help them and they use these cues, or demand characteristics, to direct their behaviour. Because experiments aim to have the same conditions for all participants, all participants will be using the same cues and therefore they all end up behaving in ways that are predictable from the set up of the experiment. As Durkin (1995, p.406) pointed out:

Where else in life does a 5-year-old find a powerful adult actually showing you how to knock hell out of a dummy and then giving you the opportunity to try it out yourself?

The Bobo doll experiment provided cues that "invited" the participants to behave in certain predictable ways.

Does this study have ecological validity? In other words, to what extent can we generalise the findings obtained in this study to real life?

Children watched adults behaving aggressively with a "Bobo" doll.
Afterwards they were filmed imitating this behaviour.

behaviour than did the other groups of children. However, this was shown not to be the case by Bandura. All the children were rewarded for imitating as much of the model's aggressive behaviour as they could remember. All three groups showed the same good ability to reproduce the model's aggressive behaviour. Thus, the children in all three groups showed comparable levels of observational learning, but those who had seen the model punished were least likely to apply this learning to their own behaviour.

Discussion points

1. What are some of the limitations of this famous research by Bandura?

2. How important do you think observational learning is with respect to producing aggressive behaviour?

Cognitive or Information Processing Theory

One of the main reasons why cognitive psychology developed in the 1950s was a growing dissatisfaction with the behaviourist approach. Suppose that we wish to understand cognitive abilities, such as our mastery of language or the processes involved in problem solving. It is very hard to do this from the behaviourist perspective, with its emphasis on observable behaviour. What is also needed is a focus on internal processes, and this is what cognitive psychologists tried to do.

Another reason for the emergence of the cognitive approach was the arrival of the computer revolution. Psychologists have often tried to understand the complexities of human cognition by comparing it with something simpler and better understood. The computer system provided an ideal analogy and a good basis for understanding human cognition. So, cognitive psychologists seek to explain human cognition in terms of an information processing system. The brain is a processor and data is both input to it and output from it. Some processing may occur in parallel, whereas other processing is serial. Parts of the brain may form a network. These are all information-processing concepts.

Cognitive explanations are in part inspired by information-processing concepts, using terms like "input", "processing", and "networks".

Evaluation of the cognitive theory

Cognitive explanations tend to be as mechanistic, or machine-like, as behaviourist ones. They lack the human element, often ignoring the role of emotion or the influence of other people. This is obviously going to be the case if we base our explanations on the behaviour of a machine. As the philosopher A.J. Ayer pointed out, it is hard to "allow machines an inner life, to credit them with feeling and emotion, to treat them as moral agents."

The greatest limitation of cognitive explanations is that the research on which they are based is often rather artificial. This occurs because most experiments are carried out under highly controlled conditions in a laboratory. As a result, such experiments often lack ecological validity, meaning that they cannot be applied to everyday settings.

If we can model human thinking processes on a computer, does this mean that humans process information in the same way as computers?

Evolutionary Theory

Charles Darwin presented the most influential theory of evolution. It is important to recognise that evolution

Whereas the behaviourists reduced psychology to stimulus and response (S–R), cognitive psychologists have added an extra dimension. Instead of dismissing the internal cognitive processes and the issue of how the stimulus provokes the response, they have focused on this middle, internal stage (stimulus–information processing–response).

Charles Darwin, 1809–1882.

Can you think of everyday examples of artificial selection (e.g. animals on the farm)?

is a fact. Darwin composed a theory to account for the fact that animal species have evolved and continue to evolve (i.e. change their characteristics). The essential principles of this theory are:

- Environments are always changing, or animals move to new environments.
- Living things are constantly changing. This happens partly because of sexual reproduction where two parents create a new individual by combining their **genes**. It also happens through chance **mutations** of the genes. In both cases new traits are produced.
- Those individuals who possess traits that are best adapted to the environment are more likely to survive to reproduce (it is reproduction rather than survival that matters); or, to put it another way, those individuals who best "fit" their environment survive (survival of the *fittest*); or, to put it still another way, the *genes* of the individuals with these traits are naturally selected.

In order to understand the concept of **natural selection** consider this example. A farmer chooses which males and females have the best characteristics for milk production or for increased reproduction (giving birth to lots of twins), and mates these individuals. This is selective breeding or artificial selection. In nature, no-one does the selecting—it is natural pressures that do it, thus it is called "natural selection".

All dogs have the same distant ancestors, but selective breeding (artificial selection) has resulted in major variations.

The end result is that physical characteristics and behaviours that are **adaptive**, i.e. help the individual to better fit its environment, are the ones that survive. Those traits that are non-adaptive disappear, as do the individuals with those traits. However, it should be emphasised it is not the individual but their genes that disappear. A classic example of this role of the genes can be seen in the tendency for parents to risk their lives to save their offspring. This is described as **altruism**. Darwin could not explain this behaviour because, according to his theory, it is only the *individuals* who survive that count. If a parent dies saving their offspring this would appear to be a non-adaptive behaviour. However, altruism is adaptive at the level of the genes. A parent who dies in order to save his or her offspring is ensuring that their **genetic** line survives. Therefore altruism can be seen to be adaptive behaviour.

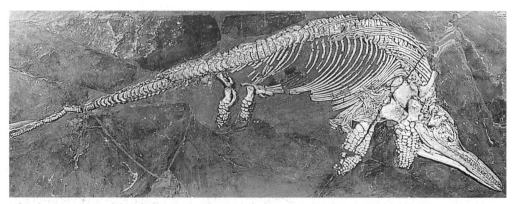

It has been suggested that the reason the dinosaurs died out was that they were not able to evolve quickly enough to continue to "fit" the environmental changes that were taking place.

Evaluation of evolutionary theory

The theory of natural selection offers a good account of the facts, but we can only point to fossil records and the evidence from a few species who have changed before our eyes, seemingly in response to environmental demands. Probably the best known case of this is the peppered moth described in the **case study** on the right.

One criticism is that the theory of evolution offers mainly *post-facto* (after the fact) evidence. It is hard to know whether a behaviour is actually beneficial, and that's why it remained, or whether it was simply neutral, and was never selected against.

Approaches in Psychology

All of these different kinds of explanation can also be called "approaches" or "perspectives". They are ways to approach the problem of explaining behaviour. Different psychologists prefer different approaches, in the same way that you may be politically liberal whereas someone else is politically conservative. We all find that different things make sense. In terms of psychology, the situation is not as straightforward as in politics, because most people might favour one kind of approach when explaining, say, aggression, whereas they might favour another approach when offering an account of why some individuals develop mental disorders. In politics, individuals tend to stick with one perspective.

No single explanation is "right" and no explanation is right for every behaviour. Each of them is appropriate in different contexts and many of them can be used together. They form part of the psychologists "toolkit". You must choose the psychological explanations which make best sense to you in the context of different behaviour.

CASE STUDY: *The Peppered Moth*

What has often been regarded as fairly direct support for some of the assumptions of Darwin's theory was obtained by Kettlewell (1955). He studied two variants of the peppered moth, one of which was darker than the other. The difference in colour is inherited, with the offspring of the darker type being on average darker than those of the lighter type. Both types of peppered moth are eaten by birds such as robins and redstarts that rely on sight to detect them. Kettlewell observed the moths when they were on relatively light lichen-covered trees and when they were on dark, lichen-less trees in industrially polluted areas. The lighter-coloured moths survived better on the lighter trees and the darker-coloured moths survived better on the darker trees.

According to Darwin's theory, the number of darker moths should increase if there is an increase in the proportion of dark trees. Precisely this happened in England due to the industrial revolution, when pollution killed the lichen and coated the trees with sooty deposits. The proportion of peppered moths that were dark apparently went from almost nil to over half the resident population in a period of about 50 years. However, the baseline evidence that there were few dark peppered moths before the industrial revolution comes from moth collections. As Hailman (1992, p.126) pointed out, "Those collections were not scientific samples but were made by amateurs … Perhaps they did not like ugly black moths."

■ Activity: Divide the class into five groups and give each group one of the approaches covered: behaviourist, psychoanalytic, cognitive, social learning, evolutionary. They should draw up a list of the advantages and disadvantages of their approach. Each group should give a brief presentation of their approach and, at the end of the lesson, let everyone decide which approach gets their vote for being the most valuable.

"I just love this view of the Firth—does it make you feel as exhilarated?" When psychologists view human behaviour they each have their own perspective.

SECTION 3
Studying and Taking Examinations

In theory psychology students should find it easier to develop good study skills because psychological principles are at the heart of study skills.

This is a section which you are likely to refer back to as you go through the book—but at least you know it is here. You can start being a serious student of psychology by reading the evidence now!

Study Skills

Students of psychology should find it easier than other students (at least in theory!) to develop good study skills. This is because psychological principles are at the heart of these skills. For example, study skills are designed to promote effective learning and remembering, and learning and memory are key areas within psychology. Study skills are also concerned with motivation and developing good work habits, and these also fall very much within psychology, although they are not part of your AS-level course. Most of what is involved in study skills is fairly obvious. As a result, we will focus on detailed pieces of advice rather than on vague generalities (e.g. "Work hard"; "Get focused").

Motivation

Most people find it hard to maintain a high level of motivation over long periods of time. We all know what happens. You start out with high ideals and work hard for the first few weeks. Then you have a bad week and/or lose your drive, and everything slips.

What can you do to make yourself as well motivated as possible? One psychological theory of motivation (Locke, 1968) suggested the following seven ways to set appropriate goals and maintain motivation:

1. You must set yourself a goal that is hard but achievable.
2. You need to commit yourself as fully as possible to attaining the goal, perhaps by telling other people about your goal.
3. You should focus on goals that can be achieved within a reasonable period of time (e.g. no more than a few weeks). A long-term goal (e.g. obtaining an upper second class degree in psychology) needs to be broken down into a series of short-term goals (e.g. obtaining an excellent mark on your next essay).
4. You should set yourself clear goals, and avoid very vague goals such as simply doing well.
5. You should do your best to obtain feedback on how well you are moving towards your goal (e.g. checking your progress with a teacher or friend).
6. You should feel pleased whenever you achieve a goal, and then move on to set slightly harder goals in future.
7. You should try to learn from failure by being very honest about the reasons why you failed: was it really "just bad luck"?

One motivational strategy is to reward yourself at regular intervals. For example, having a biscuit after you have read 10 pages, or worked for an hour. Make sure your rewards are for easily achievable goals—but not too easy!

Your attempts to motivate yourself are only likely to be successful if you make use of all seven points. If you set yourself a very clear, medium-term goal, and obtain feedback, but the goal is impossible to achieve, then you are more likely to *reduce* rather than *increase* your level of motivation.

Reading skills

You will probably spend a fair amount of time reading psychology books (or at least reading this book), and it is obviously important to read in as effective a way as possible. Morris (1979) described the **SQ3R** approach, which has proved to be very useful. SQ3R stands for Survey, Question, Read, Recite, Review, and these represent the five stages in effective reading. We will consider these five stages with respect to the task of reading a chapter.

Survey

The Survey stage involves getting an overall view of the way in which the information in the chapter is organised. If there is a chapter summary, this will probably be the easiest way to achieve that goal. Otherwise, you could look through the chapter to find out what topics are discussed and how they are linked to each other.

Question

The Question stage should be applied to fairly short parts of the chapter of no more than six pages. The essence of this stage is that you should think of relevant questions to which you expect this part to provide answers.

Have you got any questions? Always question everything you read by saying, for example, "Does this explain my own knowledge of the world?" or "Do I understand all the words?"

Read

The Read stage involves reading through each part identified at the Question stage. There are two main goals at this stage. First, you should try to answer the questions that you thought of during the previous stage. Second, you should try to integrate the information provided in the part of the chapter with your pre-existing knowledge of the topic.

Recite

The Recite stage involves you in trying to remember all the key ideas that were contained in the part of the chapter you have been reading. If you cannot remember some of them, then you should go back to the Read stage.

Review

The Review stage occurs when you have read the entire chapter. If all has gone well, you should remember the key ideas from the chapter, and you should be able to combine information from different parts into a coherent structure. If you cannot do these things, then go back to earlier stages in the reading process.

The most important reason why the SQ3R approach works so well is because it ensures that you do not simply read in a passive and mindless way. Instead, it encourages you to engage with the reading material in a very *active* and *proactive* way. However, there is another important reason why the SQ3R approach is effective. If you read a chapter in a book in a passive way, you may convince yourself that all is well when the material in it seems familiar. However, there is a big difference between *recognising* information as familiar and being able to produce it during an anxiety-inducing examination.

In order to succeed in examinations, you must be able to recall the information you need. The Recite and Review stages of the SQ3R approach are designed to achieve precisely that.

Time management

What do you do with the 100 or so hours a week during which you are awake? Probably the honest answer is that you only have a vague idea where most of the time goes. As time is such a valuable commodity, it is a good idea to make the most efficient use of it. Here are some suggestions on how to achieve that goal:

- Create a timetable of the time that is available over, say, a whole week. Indicate on it also times that are *not* available. You will probably be surprised at how much time there is, and how much you tend to waste. Now indicate on your timetable those subjects that are going to be given study time on different days, and how much time within each day you are going to spend on any subject.
- Decide what is, for you, a reasonable span of attention (possibly 30–40 minutes). Set aside a number of periods of time during the week for study. Make a commitment to yourself to use these periods for study.
- Note that the more of a habit studying becomes, the less effortful it will be, and the less resistant you will be to making a start.
- No-one has limitless concentration. After initially high levels of concentration, the level decreases until the end is in sight. Regular breaks are needed to bring you to a fresh peak of concentration. So make sure that the time you commit to studying is realistic. You can probably improve your level of concentration by including short (10-minute) rest periods. Remember to avoid distractions like the television in your study area (don't kid yourself that you can watch TV *and* study—reward yourself later with half an hour slumped in front of the TV).
- During these study times, there will be a tendency to find other things to do (e.g. have a drink). This is where the hard part begins. You must try to be firm and say to yourself that this is time you have committed to studying, and that is what you are going to do. However, you will have time available later for other things. It is hard to do on the first occasion, but it gets easier.

Planning fallacy

We are almost all familiar with the **planning fallacy**, even though we may never have heard it called that. It was first systematically studied by Kahneman and Tversky (1979). They defined the planning fallacy as "a tendency to hold a confident belief that one's own project will proceed as planned, even while knowing that the vast majority of similar projects have run late." In other words, we all kid ourselves that it will be easy despite knowing that, on previous occasions, we and other people have not managed to fulfil our planned intentions.

As we are psychologists, we might be interested to know whether there is evidence to support this planning fallacy, and indeed there is. Buehler, Griffin, and Ross (1994) found that, on average, students submitted a major piece of work 22 days later than they had predicted. The tendency to underestimate the time to completion was just as great among those students who were specifically told that the purpose of the study was to examine the accuracy of people's predictions. Buehler et al. found that students were much more accurate at predicting completion times for other students than for themselves. The reason for this is that they were more likely to use what is called "distributional" information when making predictions about other students, whereas they tended to use "singular" information when making predictions about themselves. Singular information is that which is related to the current task. Distributional information comes from knowledge about similar tasks completed in the past.

Why do many people fail to achieve work targets, despite the fact that they really should know better?

Taking Examinations

We don't want to spoil your enjoyment of psychology by reducing it to a set of examinations—but ultimately your pleasure will be increased by being able to use what you know to achieve a good mark in the examinations.

The TEE approach

We have used the **TEE approach** throughout this book: starting with a theory (T), moving on to evidence (E), and then concluding with evaluation (E).

> **Coping with stress in examinations**
> In Chapter 4 you will be studying stress and how to manage it. Here is some advice from that chapter:
> - Increase your sense of control, think *positively*: "I can only do my best".
> - Avoid ego defence mechanisms such as denial: recognise the feeling of stress and intellectualise your problem.
> - Relax. At intervals during the examination have a break and think pleasant thoughts unrelated to the exam.
> - Social support: think about comforting people or things.
> - Physical exercise and emotional discharge: go for a run before the exam, stretch your legs, find some means of discharging tension during the exam (that doesn't disturb anyone else).

What is "evaluation"? We have already noted that the term means "determining the value of something". When evaluating something you might ask whether the explanation is useful, or whether it can account for real-life behaviour. Evaluation mostly involves considering the various strengths and limitations of the theories or ideas that have been discussed, but there are other ways to evaluate, such as:

- Applications. If a theory can be applied to some real-life situation, this informs us of its value.
- Empirical evidence (evidence found by conducting a study). If a theory is supported by an empirical study then it is more likely to be a "good" theory.
- Commentary. Perhaps this isn't really "evaluation", but it's equally important. "Commentary" means offering a comment about the meaning of a theory or piece of evidence. For example, you might say "This theory suggests that all babies should remain with their mothers at all times".
- Analysis. To determine the separate strands of an argument. This helps us to see what value there is in the theory.

When in doubt, try writing a sentence that starts "This suggests that …" or "Therefore, one can conclude …".

The TEE approach reflects the way that AS-level examinations are marked. There are two so-called "skill clusters": AO1 and AO2.

Skill AO1

Skill AO1 is knowledge and understanding of psychological theories, terminology, concepts, studies, and methods, and the ability to communicate this knowledge and understanding of psychology in a clear and effective manner.

Examinations are an opportunity for you to demonstrate your knowledge to an examiner. It isn't just a question of what you know, but you have to convince the examiner that you really do understand it. You should not just mention psychological terms, but should show you know what they mean. For example, you might have heard the phrase "learning theory" but is that all you know? Don't just name a theory or concept, explain it as well.

The kind of questions you will be asked are:

Describe one *theory explanation of forgetting in short-term memory.*

Describe one *study that demonstrates the long-term effects of privation.*

Give two *criticisms of this study.*

Describe how personality can play a role in how people respond to stress.

Describe two *attempts to define psychological abnormality.*

Skill AO2

Skill AO2 requires you to analyse and evaluate psychological theories, concepts, studies, and methods. We have considered analysis and evaluation earlier.

The kind of questions you will be asked are:

Evaluate any two *explanations for conformity.*
To what extent have attempts to explain attachment taken account of cultural variation?
Critically consider the usefulness of stress management techniques.

You will find more examples of all of these questions at the end of each chapter of this book.

How are examinations marked?

Avoid "common-sense" answers: you must convince the examiner that your answer is drawn from what you have learned, not from everyday knowledge.

Examiners are given marks schemes to enable them to work out how many marks to award to an answer. Some marks schemes are based on skill cluster AO1 and others are based on cluster AO2. The mark schemes are shown below, and are applied here in some examination answers.

AO1-style question

Question: Describe one *study of short-term memory. (6 marks)*

Candidate's answer: Peterson and Peterson did a study where participants were shown three-letter consonants. They then were asked to recall them either after 3 seconds, 12, 15 or 18 seconds. The longer the interval, the less good their recall.

Mark scheme for AQA specification AS-level examinations		
Skill cluster AO1		
• Band 3	5–6 marks	The description is *accurate* and *detailed*.
• Band 2	3–4 marks	The description is *limited*. It is *generally accurate* but *less detailed*.
• Band 1	1–2 marks	The description is *basic, lacking detail* and may be *muddled*.
	0 marks	The description is *inappropriate* or the description is *incorrect*.
Where an answer is marked out of 3, then the marks are changed accordingly.		
Skill cluster AO2		
• Band 3	11–12 marks	There is an *informed commentary* and *thorough analysis* of the relevant psychological studies/methods. Material has been used in a *highly effective* manner.
	9–10 marks	There is an *informed commentary* and *reasonably thorough analysis* of relevant psychological studies/methods. Material has been used in an *effective* manner.
• Band 2	7–8 marks	There is a *reasonable commentary* and *slightly limited analysis* of the relevant psychological studies/methods. Material has been used in an *effective* manner.
	5–6 marks	There is a *reasonable commentary*, but *limited analysis* of the relevant psychological studies/methods. Material has been used in a *reasonably effective* manner.
• Band 1	3–4 marks	There is *superficial commentary* and *rudimentary analysis* of the relevant psychological studies/methods. There is *minimal interpretation* of the material used.
	1–2 marks	Commentary is *just discernible*. Analysis is *weak* and *muddled*. The answer may be *mainly irrelevant* to the problem it addresses.
	0 marks	Commentary is *wholly irrelevant* to the problem it addresses.

Examiner's comment: The candidate has included some details, such as who did the study and what they did. The findings have been treated rather briefly and certain other details were omitted (such as what the participants did while they were waiting to recall the digits). Therefore this answer would be described as "limited" and would get 4 out of 6 marks.

AO2-style question

Question: "People who witness a crime want to be able to provide useful information to the police to help them catch the criminal." With reference to psychological research, consider the extent to which it is possible for eyewitnesses to provide useful information. (12 marks)

Candidate's answer: Psychological research has investigated many areas of memory which are relevant to eyewitness testimony.

The first area I will consider is Loftus' research on the way the language used in questioning the eyewitness will affect recall. In her experiment it was found that, if people were asked "About how fast were the cars going when they smashed into each other?", they estimated the cars' speed as being faster than if the word "hit" was used in the question. This shows that the accuracy of their recall is very much influenced by the way they are asked questions.

Another line of evidence has looked at flashbulb memories. It has been suggested that certain events are printed in our memories because they occur at times of high emotion, such as when Princess Diana died, and you remember exactly what you were doing at the time. The same thing might be true of a crime scene so that you can see a picture of what actually happened. However, research into flashbulb memories suggests that they are not as accurate as people think. McCloskey et al. interviewed people shortly after the explosion of the space shuttle *Challenger* and then re-interviewed the same people nine months later. McCloskey et al. found that the participants did forget elements. We should also consider evidence which shows that high emotion may led to poorer recall. Freud suggested that people repress memories which create anxiety and there is evidence to support this.

This research on flashbulb memories and emotion suggests that eyewitness recall may be less accurate than people like to think it is.

Another kind of evidence is that people often don't remember things until they have their memory jogged. Psychologists have shown that a lot of forgetting can be explained in terms of not having the right cues (Tulving & Psotka, 1971). This is why it is good for police to stage reconstructions of a crime scene to help witnesses recall what happened.

Finally we should consider face recognition. It is very hard to recognise an unfamiliar face and one that is still rather than moving.

Remember: there are no right answers, only answers that are well informed, well constructed, well argued, and in which the material used is well selected.

Remember that quantity doesn't equal quality. Stick to the point and organise your answer clearly so the examiner can follow your argument.

Examiner's comment: The candidate has presented a very well-structured answer to the question. It is all relevant and there has been good use of evidence ("informed commentary"). An especially good feature is the way that the candidate has not just presented evidence but has also explained what it demonstrates ("effective use of material"). Some of the points have not been backed up by specific references but they continue to demonstrate that the candidate is "psychologically informed". Perhaps there is slightly too much reliance on description and not enough analysis and evaluation, in other words the answer is "reasonably thorough" rather than "thorough". Therefore this would get 9 out of 12 marks.

CHAPTER SUMMARY

Introducing psychology

❖ Psychology is the science of behaviour and experience.

❖ Psychology is more than common sense because it uses research-based evidence to support its theories. It is not sufficient to rely on what people think, as is demonstrated by hindsight bias.

❖ Psychological research aims to achieve a balance between ecological validity and good control of irrelevant factors.

❖ What do psychologists do? Psychologists conduct research or apply that research. The core areas of psychology are cognitive, developmental, physiological, individual differences, and social psychology. Cognitive psychology examines mental processes; developmental psychology is concerned with changes that occur in relation to age; physiological psychology looks at bodily processes; individual differences includes the study of differing degrees of mental health; social psychology considers the way that individuals of the same species affect each other.

Psychological explanations

❖ Psychologists use a variety of different explanations or "tools". For example, physiological psychologists explain behaviour in terms of bodily processes. There are some more general explanations that are used more or less throughout psychology.

❖ Learning theory is based on conditioning. Classical conditioning occurs when a neutral stimulus is paired with an unconditioned stimulus, eventually producing a conditioned stimulus and response. Operant conditioning is the result of reinforcement or punishment, which either increases or decreases the likelihood of a behaviour being repeated. It is not possible to explain all behaviour using learning theory but it is a key explanation in psychology, despite some ethical concerns about its application.

❖ Psychoanalytic theory is both an account of personality development and a therapy. The basic principle is that early experiences may result in unconscious conflicts which motivate adult behaviour. Freud described the personality in terms of three structures: the id, ego, and superego, which are likely to come into conflict because they are motivated by different principles. Conflicts create anxieties which are coped with by defence mechanisms such as: repression, displacement, projection, denial, and intellectualisation. Freud also described five stages in development: the oral, anal, phallic, latency, and genital stages. At each of these stages the child may develop a fixation and this can be linked to their later adult personality. Freud's research has been criticised in terms of bias, but has had enormous influence.

❖ Social learning theory explains learning in terms of conditioning *and* observation. One route for learning is vicarious reinforcement, which is learning through indirect reinforcement. Additionally learning may occur because you identify with a person and therefore wish to imitate them. This is identification or modelling. Social learning theory is a powerful explanation but, like all explanations, is not sufficient on its own.

❖ Cognitive explanations use the analogy of information processing systems. Inevitably this is a mechanistic explanation of behaviour.

❖ Evolutionary explanations describe behaviour in terms of adaptiveness. Any physical or psychological characteristic that enhances reproduction is more likely to be perpetuated than those that do not. Natural selection passively chooses those genes that are desirable. Altruism is a good example. Criticism relates to the available evidence for the theory.

❖ No one explanation or approach is "right". They are all used as part of the psychologists' "toolkit".

❖ Psychological research can inform us about better studying methods. Motivation can be increased by setting appropriate goals that are sufficiently challenging but also achievable. You should reward yourself. The SQ3R method of reading represents five stages in effective reading, which should encourage you to read actively and check your understanding. Time management is important to avoid trying to do too much, or too little. You should avoid the planning fallacy trap.

Studying and taking examinations

❖ Good examination performance depends on communicating your knowledge and understanding of psychological topics to the examiner, as well as being able to evaluate the material. Ensure that you understand the mark scheme and write your answers with this in mind. Remember that there are no right answers, only ones that are well explained and supported by research. The examination is marked in terms of two skill clusters: AO1 (description) and AO2 (analysis and evaluation).

FURTHER READING

Two useful books on perspectives are C. Tavris and C. Wade (1997) *Psychology in perspective* (New York: Longman), and W.E. Glassman (1995) *Approaches to psychology* (Milton Keynes, UK: Open University Press). Books written more specifically for AS and A-level include M.W. Eysenck (1994) *Perspectives on psychology* (Hove, UK: Psychology Press), and A.E. Wadeley, A. Birch, and A. Malim (1997) *Perspectives in psychology (2nd Edn.)* (Basingstoke, UK: Macmillan). For a general introduction to psychology you could try J.C. Berryman, D.J. Hargreaves, C.R. Hollin, and K. Howells (1987) *Psychology and you* (Leicester, UK: BPS Books). There is also an amusing series of introductory books written by Nigel Benson (1998), including *Introducing psychology* and *Introducing Freud* and *Introducing evolutionary psychology* (Duxford, UK: Icon Books).

Revision Questions

This first chapter of the book is not directly examined, so it would be unrealistic to set exam-style questions. But here are a few multiple choice questions to reassure you that you've understood what you read!

1. Common sense is different from psychology because:
   a. Psychology consists of a set of loosely related inconsistent ideas
   b. Psychology is based on research
   c. Psychology is about cognition
   d. Psychology is about emotions
   e. All of the above

2. Some of the areas involved in psychology are:
   a. Cognitive psychology
   b. Abnormal psychology
   c. Developmental psychology
   d. Physiological psychology
   e. All of the above

3. Physiological psychology attempts to understand human behaviour by studying:
   a. Non-human species
   b. The peripheral nervous system
   c. Physiological processes especially the brain
   d. Central nervous system
   e. b, c, & d

4. Abnormal psychology is centrally concerned with the study of:
   a. Mental disease
   b. Medical models
   c. Mental disorders
   d. Psychiatry
   e. Perception

5. Social psychology looks at:
   a. How people relate in society
   b. How the nervous system affects our functioning in society
   c. Stigmata
   d. Social cognition
   e. How social groups relate to each other

6. Cognitive psychology is concerned with:
   a. External processes
   b. Internal processes
   c. External cognition
   d. Internal inhibition
   e. All of the above

7. Developmental psychology is concerned mainly with:
   a. Lifespan development
   b. Brain development
   c. Infant development
   d. Old age
   e. Animal development

8. Reinforcement leads to:
   a. A sense of pleasure
   b. A conditioned response
   c. The stamping-in of a behaviour
   d. The stamping-out of a behaviour
   e. a & c

9. According to the psychodynamic approach, which part of the mind is the conscious, rational part?
   a. The ego
   b. The id
   c. The superego
   d. All of these
   e. a & c

10. Examples of defence mechanisms are:
   a. Protection
   b. Displacement
   c. Denial
   d. a & b
   e. b & c

11. Goal setting is most effective when:
   a. You set a goal that is hard but achievable
   b. You commit yourself to attaining it
   c. The goals are clear
   d. After achieving a goal you feel pleased and set a harder one
   e. All of the above

12. The reason why the SQ3R approach works is because:
   a. It ensures that you are not passive in the process
   b. It engages you proactively
   c. It forces you to recall
   d. It uses recognition as its strength
   e. a, b, & d

13. You should ensure your answers always contain:
   a. Common-sense material
   b. Knowledge of psychological concepts
   c. Understanding of psychological concepts
   d. All of the above
   e. b & c

14. TEE stands for:
   a. Theory, Evidence, and Evaluation
   b. Treisman, Eysenck, and Ericson
   c. Thematic apperception, Evolution, and Evidence
   d. Teishman, Erlbaum, and Edwards
   e. None of the above

The answers are:
1. (b) 2. (e) 3. (e) 4. (c) 5. (a) 6. (b) 7. (a) 8. (e) 9. (a) 10. (e) 11. (e) 12. (b) 13. (e) 14. (a)

Cognitive psychology is an approach or perspective in psychology. The material in this chapter is intended as an example of the way that cognitive psychologists explain behaviour.

Cognitive psychologists are interested in internal mental (cognitive) processes such as those of perceiving, thinking, talking, and attention. Behaviour and experience are explained in terms of these internal processes rather than in terms of external influences. The emphasis is on how we perceive and think about a stimulus rather than the stimulus itself. Essentially cognitive psychology is the study of how the mind works and how it influences our behaviour and experience.

2

Cognitive Psychology
Human Memory

Remember riding a bicycle, then a famous date: Is the process the same?

My friend Mavis was standing at a bus stop when a bright green car careered around the corner. She was terrified because it mounted the kerb and only just missed her. Just afterwards a police car sped by. By the time Mavis got home she had calmed down a bit but she described the car and driver to me in every detail.

In an ideal world we might remember every detail of things that happen, especially when they are important. Except—if we did remember everything our memories would be very full. What makes some things memorable, and others forgettable?

This chapter explores one topic in cognitive psychology—human memory. How important is memory? Imagine if we were without it. We would not recognise anyone or anything as familiar. We would not be able to talk, read, or write, because we would remember nothing about language. We would be like newborn babies.

We use memory for numerous purposes. It allows us to keep track of conversations, to remember telephone numbers while we dial them, to write essays in examinations, to make sense of what we read, and to recognise people's faces. There are many different *kinds* of memory, which suggests that we have a number of memory systems. This chapter explores in detail some of the sub-divisions of human memory, as well as the reverse side of the coin—forgetting.

- *Section 4: Short-term memory and long-term memory.* Short-term memory (STM) is the division of memory where information is initially stored. Information that we remember is held in long-term memory (LTM). This section will examine research into the nature and structure of memory, including the capacity and duration of both STM and LTM. What causes memories to be moved from STM to LTM? The answer is offered by various models of memory.
- *Section 5: Forgetting.* Why do we forget? Why do some memories cease to be accessible? In this section we will consider explanations of forgetting in STM and LTM. We will also consider the role of emotional factors in forgetting, including flashbulb memories and repression.
- *Section 6: Critical issue—Eyewitness testimony.* We will also look at one practical application of memory research. Police and solicitors rely on reports of crimes from eyewitnesses. This may involve identifying suspects or describing what happened when a crime was committed. How reliable are eyewitnesses when they try to recall what happened or to describe a person's face? In particular we will consider reconstructive memory (schema theory), Loftus' research on leading questions, and the problem of face recognition.

Short-term Memory and Long-term Memory

What is Memory?

Memory is the process of retaining information after the original thing is no longer present. There are close links between **learning** and **memory**. Something that is learned is lodged in memory. The two terms are almost synonymous, although learning theorists—behaviourists—would dismiss the concept of memory, because the concept of memory is more than just learning, implying the involvement of cognitive processes.

Memory and learning can most clearly be demonstrated by good performance on a memory test. Memory tests typically involve giving someone a list of words for a specified period of time, removing the list, and at a later time asking them to recall the list. When learning and memorising the words in the list, there are three stages:

What is the difference between learning and memory? Are they different?

1. **Encoding**. When the person is given the list they encode the words. They place the words in memory. The term "encoding" means to put something into a code, in this case the code used to store it in memory—some kind of chemical **memory trace**.
2. **Storage**. As a result of encoding, the information is stored within the memory system.
3. **Retrieval**. Recovering stored information from the memory system. This is known as "recall" or "remembering".

Psychologists who are interested in learning focus on encoding and storage, whereas those interested in memory concentrate on retrieval. However, all these processes depend on each other.

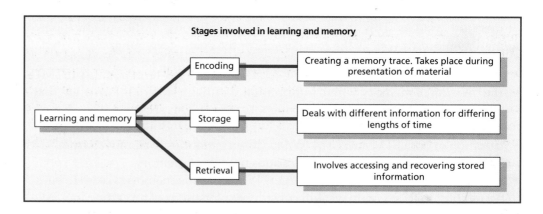

Short-term and long-term memory

Most psychologists agree that there is a distinction between two kinds of memory: short- and long-term memory. One lasts for only a short time, while the other lasts theoretically forever or at least for a long time.

Trying to remember a telephone number for a few seconds is an everyday example of the use of the **short-term memory**. It illustrates two of its key features:

1. Short-term memory has a very limited **capacity** (it doesn't hold very much).
2. Short-term memory has very limited **duration** (it doesn't last for very long).

Long-term memory, on the other hand, has unlimited capacity and lasts (potentially) forever. As an example, you might think of your childhood memories.

We will look at capacity and duration, as well as other features of both short- and long-term memory, and then consider explanations relating to how memory is transferred between short- and long-term memory.

Testing memory

Psychologists use various methods to test recall or learning.

- Free recall. Give participants some words to learn and then ask them to recall the words in any order.
- Cued recall. After presenting the material to be learned, provide cues to help recall. For example, saying that some of the items are minerals.
- Recognition. Giving a list of words which includes some of those in the initial presentation. Participants are asked to identify those in the original list.
- Paired-associate learning. Participants are given word pairs to learn and then tested by presenting one of the words and asking them to recall the other word.
- Nonsense syllables. Participants are asked to memorise meaningless sets of letters. These may be trigrams (three letters).

Short-term Memory

Capacity of short-term memory

It is not as easy as you might think to estimate the capacity of short-term memory. Psychologists have devised two main strategies: span measures, and the recency effect in free recall.

Span measures

Span measure is an assessment of how much can be stored in short-term memory at any time. For example, we might consider how many digits can be remembered—this would be digit span, in which participants have to repeat back immediately a list of random digits in the correct order. According to Miller (1956) it has been generally found that the span of immediate memory is "seven, plus or minus two", whether the units are numbers, letters, or words. As three words will always contain more than three letters, one might think that a person should remember fewer words than letters. However Miller reported that the key issue is **chunks** (integrated pieces or units of information). About seven chunks of information can be held in short-term memory at any time. The question of what constitutes a "chunk" depends on your personal experience. For example, "IBM" is one chunk—as long as you are familiar with the company name International Business Machines. If you are not familiar with this abbreviation, then "IBM" would be three chunks. Miller's study is reported in the Key Study on the next page.

■ Activity: Read quickly through the following list of digits once. Cover the list and try to write the digits down in the correct order.

7 3 5 1 5 6 9 8 2 7 4

How many did you remember in the correct order? This is one way of measuring your memory span. Now try the following digits:

1 9 3 9 1 0 6 6 1 8 0 5 1 2 1 5

More digits, but if you recognised the "chunks" you should have remembered them all:

    1939 Start of Second World War
    1066 Battle of Hastings
    1805 Battle of Trafalgar
    1215 Signing of the Magna Carta

Did you find any primary or recency effects when you tried to recall the list of digits? Try the test again (with different data) with this in mind.

Why would lists of people's names be unsuitable material for use in research into memory processes? Why is it better to use nonsense syllables?

The recency effect

A familiar example of the **recency effect** is the observation that a pop group is only as good as their last hit song. People remember things better if they have happened most recently. In relation to short-term memory, the recency effect can be measured using free recall. This is where participants are shown a list of words or syllables, and asked to recall them in any order immediately after the list was presented. The recency effect is demonstrated by the fact that the last few items in a list are usually much better remembered than items from the middle of the list.

Glanzer and Cunitz (1966) found that counting backwards for only 10 seconds between the end of list presentation and the start of recall virtually eliminated the

If you were shown these ten words: cat, butter, car, house, carpet, tomato, beer, river, pool, tennis; and then asked to recall them immediately in any order, what words are likely to be best remembered?

The magic number seven plus or minus two

Why are there so many things that come in sevens—such as seven wonders of the world, seven deadly sins, seven primary colours, seven notes of the musical scale, and seven days of the week? Miller (1956) reviewed psychological research to see what had been discovered. Investigations into various cognitive abilities have found that people can easily distinguish three musical tones, but when they are asked to distinguish between five or more tones they become progressively more confused. If research participants are shown an arrangement of dots, flashed onto a screen, they can count five or six of them easily. More than that number, and accuracy deteriorates. Such findings suggest that our span of absolute judgement (e.g. distinguishing musical tones) and of immediate memory (e.g. counting dots) is for about five or six items.

This would lead us to expect that, if you have to remember a string of letters, seven letters might be the maximum that could be held in short-term memory. But what if the letters were C-A-T-W-A-L-L? In this case the seven letters make two chunks of data ("CAT" and "WALL"). All words consist of bits of information—in the case of "catwall" there are seven bits altogether, but there are only two chunks of information. If memory was limited by the "bits" of information it could handle, then we can predict that it would be possible to remember twice as many five-letter words as ten-letter ones. Miller found that this wasn't true.

Research has demonstrated that people can remember about seven words, no matter how many bits of information are in the word. It is the chunks of data that limit memory. Miller called chunking "the very lifeblood of the thought processes". It improves the capacity of memory, although it may reduce accuracy.

KEY STUDY EVALUATION — Miller

This research has useful applications. For example phone numbers are chunked to make them easier to remember when making a phone call. However, later research didn't completely confirm Miller's conclusion. For example, Simon (1974) found that the number of bits in a chunk did have an effect on memory. Participants in his study had a shorter span for larger chunks such as eight-word phrases, than for smaller chunks such as one-syllable words. Therefore immediate memory span is related to chunking but the number of chunks remembered depends how big the chunks are!

Some psychologists, such as Case (1974), have used the idea of chunking to explain how children become capable of more complex mental tasks as they get older. Case suggests that M-space (which is roughly equivalent to short-term memory) is used to hold information required while you are thinking. The restricted size of this space acts as a limit to cognitive processing. As one gets older the space increases a little, but more importantly we also become more efficient at using it. An example of this would be playing chess. Inexperienced players have to hold the rules in M-space while they are playing. As one becomes more experienced these rules become more automatic, having been incorporated in higher-order units—a process akin to chunking. This form of chunking leaves more space in M-space for mental activities.

Discussion points

1. Why might adults be better than children when given tasks that involve chunking (such as trying to remember a list of abbreviations or a list of fruits)?
2. Does this research have **ecological validity**?

recency effect, but otherwise had no effect on recall. In other words, people could remember a similar number of words from earlier in the list but not the few at the end. This can be explained by the fact that the two or three words at the end of the list were in a fragile state (not well encoded) and therefore were easily wiped out by the task of counting backwards (called an **interference** task because it interferes with the process of creating a memory). In contrast, the other list items were in the long-term store, and so were unaffected by the interference task.

In Glanzer and Cunitz's experiment the participants recalled the first few items much better than those from the middle of the list. This is known as the **primacy effect**. Why is there a primacy effect? The words at the start of the list are rehearsed more than those from the middle. This was shown by Rundus and Atkinson (1970), who asked their participants to rehearse out loud any of the words they wanted to during list presentation.

The recency effect suggests that the capacity of the short-term store is about two or three items. However, span measures indicate a capacity of about seven items. Why do these two techniques produce different results? One reason relates to different patterns of rehearsal. Participants carrying out a span task rehearse as many items as possible, whereas those asked to learn a list for free recall rehearse only a few items at a time. The recency effect and span measures both indicate that the capacity of short-term memory is strictly limited. In contrast, no effective limits on the capacity of long-term memory have been discovered.

Duration in short-term memory

How long does a short-term memory last? This was demonstrated in an experiment by Peterson and Peterson (1959) using a method that became known as the Brown-Peterson technique. Participants were shown a trigram (three consonants such as BVM or CTG). They were then asked to recall the trigram either after 3 seconds, 6 seconds, 9, 12, 15, or 18 seconds. Participants were given an interference task between the initial presentation of the trigram and the time when they were asked to recall it. The reason for including an interference task was to prevent them rehearsing the trigram—rehearsal might have improved their performance. The interference task was to count backwards in threes from a three-digit number. (Try it and you'll find that it stops you thinking of anything else!)

Peterson and Peterson found that participants were quite able to recall the trigrams after 3 seconds, they recalled fewer trigrams after 6 seconds, and after 18 seconds recall was very poor—only about 10% of the trigrams were recalled correctly whereas after 3 seconds participants were able to recall about 80% correctly (see the graph on the right).

The conclusion is that memory trace in short-term memory has just about disappeared after 18 seconds. It's as if the information is written on a magic slate and, as time passes, the writing fades away. Of course, if you rehearse the information (repeat it over and over) you can remember it for longer.

> ■ Activity: Recency and primacy effects
>
> You can demonstrate these effects by asking people to learn a list of words or nonsense syllables. You should use two conditions:
>
> 1. Ask some participants to free recall the words immediately after presentation.
>
> 2. Ask others to do an interference task (such as counting backwards in threes from a three-digit number) for 10 seconds after presentation of the list.
>
> Which condition will show the recency effect? Which condition should show a primacy effect? Why do you think it is important to use "free recall" to test memory?

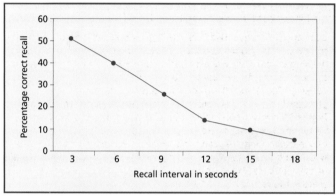

The graph shows a steady decline in short-term memory recall after longer retention intervals (from Peterson & Peterson, 1959).

EVALUATION — Peterson and Peterson

Participants in this experiment were required to remember a rather artificial kind of data: trigrams. It might be that STM is longer lasting when the material to be remembered is more meaningful. On the positive side, the simple nature of the experiment means we can clearly identify the effect of the independent variable (time delay) on the dependent variable (recall).

Encoding in short-term memory

The idea that short-term memory has less capacity and shorter duration is fairly commonplace knowledge. The concept of "encoding" will probably be less familiar. When psychologists talk about "encoding" they are referring to the way the information is stored in memory. One of the ways to compare encoding is in terms of acoustic or semantic coding. "Acoustic" refers to the sound of a word, and "semantic" refers to the meaning of a word. The words "cap" and "can" are acoustically similar whereas "cap" and "hat" are semantically similar. One can remember words by the way they sound (acoustic) or by their meaning (semantic).

It seems that short- and long-term memory differ in the way that information is coded. Baddeley (1966, see Key Study on the next page) found that if participants were asked to recall words immediately (from short-term memory) they did not confuse words that had the same meaning (such as "big" and "large") but they often confused words that sounded similar (for example, remembering "cat" instead of

Are the words "stream" and "river" acoustically or semantically similar?

Acoustic, semantic, and visual coding

If you have to remember something for a short time, such as a phone number, you probably repeat it over and over. You repeat it acoustically. What is interesting is that people do this whether they heard the information (someone told you the number) or saw it (you looked it up in the phone book). This suggests that short-term memory may encode information acoustically.

Conrad (1964) investigated this by comparing performance with acoustically and visually presented data. He presented participants with six letters at a time, displaying each of them for 0.75 of a second. The participants had to recall the letters in the order that they were presented. When the letters sounded alike, even though they were visually presented, errors were made in terms of sound confusions, for example S was recalled instead of X.

In a different experiment, Baddeley (1966) contrasted coding in short-term and long-term memory, and found that long-term memory was more likely to rely on semantic coding. He gave participants four sets of words to recall:

KEY STUDY EVALUATION — Conrad

Later research (Posner, 1969) demonstrated that visual codes do in fact exist in STM, at least some of the time. In Posner's experiment participants were shown two letters, where the second letter was either identical to the first letter (e.g. AA), or the same but a different form (e.g. Aa), or different (e.g. AB). The letters were displayed one at a time, separated by a 2-second interval. Participants had to say whether the letters were the same or different. Reaction time was longer for Aa than AA which suggests that participants were processing the data visually rather than acoustically ("A" and "a" sound the same but look different).

- Set A (acoustically similar: words that sound the same) e.g. man, cap, can, cab, mad, max, mat, cat, map.
- Set B (acoustically dissimilar) e.g. pit, few, cow, pen, sup, bar, day.
- Set C (semantically similar: words that have similar meaning) e.g. great, large, big, huge, broad, long, tall, fat, wide, high.
- Set D (semantically dissimilar) e.g. good, huge, hot, safe, thin, deep, strong, foul.

If participants were using their short-term memory (in other words they were asked to recall the word list immediately) then they did less well with the words that sounded alike (set A) than those that sounded different (set B). This supports the view that short-term memory codes are mainly acoustic.

When participants were using their long-term memory (they were asked to recall the word lists after an interval), they performed the same on lists A and B, the words that were acoustically similar and dissimilar. However there were pronounced differences between the words that had the same or different meanings. This indicates that long-term memory is using semantic codes

Discussion points

1. What was the research aim of Conrad's experiment?

2. Identify the **independent** and **dependent variables** in these studies.

"cap"). The opposite was true for long-term memory. This suggests that short-term memory largely uses an acoustic code, storing words in relation to how they sound, and long-term memory mainly uses a semantic code, storing words according to their meaning.

■ Activity: You could test the effects of semantic and acoustic recall by using Baddeley's word lists and asking for immediate or delayed recall.

Construct four word lists: acoustically similar, acoustically dissimilar, semantically similar, and semantically dissimilar.

Divide participants into two groups—immediate recall (short-term memory) and longer-term recall. Participants should be randomly allocated to conditions to ensure that both groups of participants are equivalent.

For each group, which lists are they best at recalling and which lists do they perform least well on?

Evidence about short-term memory from studies of brain damage

Probably the strongest evidence for a distinction between short-term and long-term memory has come from the study of brain-damaged patients. You may be familiar with the idea of **amnesia**. This is when a person has lost much of their long-term memory, often due to an accident that has caused brain damage. Such patients usually have almost normal short-term memories. In contrast there are other patients with brain damage who have no problem with their long-term memories, but their short-term memory is disabled. Shallice and Warrington (1970) studied KF, who suffered brain damage as a result of a motorcycle accident. KF had no problem with long-term memory, but his digit span was only two items (in other words he could only remember two digits at a time whereas, on average, people remember seven digits in short-term memory). These findings suggest that different parts of the brain are involved in short-term and long-term memory.

The evidence from the study of KF provided additional insights into short-term memory. Warrington and Shallice (1972) found that KF's short-term forgetting of auditory letters and digits (things that were heard) was much greater than his forgetting of visual stimuli. They also found that KF's short-term memory deficit was limited to verbal materials (e.g. letters, words), and did not extend to meaningful sounds (e.g. cats mewing), in other words he couldn't remember the things like words, but could remember meaningful sounds. This suggests that there is not just one short-term memory but a number of different stores, each represented in different parts of the brain. According to Shallice and Warrington (1974), KF's problems centred on what they called the "auditory-verbal short-term store". These distinctions within short-term memory are important and we will return to them later.

Evaluation of studies of brain-damaged patients

When we consider the effects of brain damage, we must remember that it may not be reasonable to make generalisations from such individuals' behaviour to that of "normal" individuals.

Ecological validity of short-term memory research

Before we move on to long-term memory, it is worth considering the fact that all of the research considered so far has been *experimental* and conducted in *laboratories*. In some ways this might seem quite an appropriate way to study memory, because it appears to be a behaviour that lacks emotion or is not likely to be influenced by others. However, this isn't true. Your emotional state and social circumstances influence your memory considerably, and therefore it may be that we are studying one particular *kind* of memory and not all kinds of memory. This is especially true of studies of long-term memory. The conclusion must be that generalisation from these studies to all situations may not be reasonable.

Long-term Memory

The concept of long-term memory describes all those things that we remember for a long time. The long-term storage space in your brain is unlimited in capacity and the duration of these memories is also thought to be unlimited. The main differences between short- and long-term memory are summarised in the box on the next page.

CASE STUDY: *The Man Who Never Got Older*

In the 1950s a man known as "HM" sought medical help for his epileptic seizures. He had been forced to give up his job because the seizures had became so frequent and severe, and it was not possible to control them with drugs. In desperation the doctors decided to remove a structure called the hippocampus from both hemispheres of his brain because this was the seat of his seizures. No-one quite knew what the outcome would be. The operation did reduce his epilepsy but it also had a dramatic effect on his memory.

His personality and intellect remained the same, but his memory was severely affected. Some aspects of his memory were fairly intact: he could still talk and recall the skills he knew previously (semantic memory), he continued to be able to form short-term memories, but was unable to form any new long-term ones. For example, given the task of memorising a number he could recall it 15 minutes later but, after being distracted, he had no recollection. He could read the same magazine over and over again without realising that he had read it before.

HM moved house after his operation and had great difficulty learning his new route home. After 6 years he was finally able to at least find his way around the house. This shows that he did have some memory capacity and, intellectually, he was quite "intact" so he did have some awareness of his predicament.

For many years he reported that the year was 1953 and he was 27 years old. As time went on he clearly realised this could not be true and he started to guess a more appropriate answer. In other words he tried to reconstruct his memories, although not very successfully.

You have just finished the first six pages of this section. The SQ3R approach suggests that now would be an appropriate time to think of some questions to which you would expect this section to provide answers. What questions might an examiner set on this part of the book?

Comparing STM and LTM	Short-term memory	Long-term memory
Duration (how long it lasts)	Short (seconds)	Long, potentially forever
Capacity (how much it holds)	Limited by duration	Unlimited
Encoding differences	Acoustic	Semantic
Serial position effect	Recency effect (last material is better remembered because of interference)	Primacy effect (earlier material is better remembered because it is better rehearsed)
Brain damage	Some patients only lose short-term memory whereas others only lose long-term memory.	

Capacity of long-term memory

The capacity of the human brain for storing information is enormous, even in comparison with computers (Solso, 1991). People are able to remember a vast amount of information—especially when you consider the kind of information that is stored in memory: the route you take to get home, what your primary school looked like, the names of all the people you know and other things about those people, how to eat and what food you like, the letters of the alphabet and the rules of arithmetic, what you learned in psychology class today … the list is endless. Presumably there is some physical limit in terms of the actual brain cells available, but it seems likely that we never reach this upper limit in long-term memory. It is not a limited-capacity store, whereas short-term memory is.

Duration in long-term memory

How can one assess how long a memory lasts? This is difficult because, even if you can't remember something at this moment, it is hard to prove that it is not there somewhere, but you simply cannot bring it into your conscious mind. If you can remember something, it may be an inaccurate memory and one you have "confabulated" from relevant cues. To confabulate means to make up details.

However, psychologists have conducted research into "very-long-term memory" (VLTM). It is said that the elderly never lose their childhood memories and many skills, such as riding a bicycle, are never forgotten. Bahrick, Bahrick, and Wittinger (1975) produced a clever demonstratation of VLTM using photographs from high-school yearbooks (an annual publication in American High Schools where everyone's picture is shown with their name and other details). Bahrick et al. asked 392 ex-high-school students of various ages to free recall the names of any of their classmates, and also showed them a set of appropriate photographs and asked them to identify individuals. Even after 34 years ex-students were still able to name 90% of the photographs of their classmates. This supports the view that people do have very long-term memories that are not confabulated.

Further support comes from a study by Shepard (1967) who showed that people have remarkably long-term memories for pictures. Shepard selected 612 memorable pictures, such as advertisements, and showed them one at a time to participants. When the participants were shown another set of pictures later, which contained 68 of the original ones, they had

Some memories never fade. One study found that people were still able to remember most of the names of their high-school classmates after 34 years.

almost perfect recognition after two hours, and 120 days later they were still able to recognise 50% of the photographs. This again demonstrates that some memories do last.

Varieties of long-term memory

There is an enormous wealth of information stored in long-term memory, including such different things as the knowledge that Emma Thompson is a film star, that 2 + 2 = 4, that we had fish and chips for lunch yesterday, and information about how to deal a pack of cards. It seems improbable that all this knowledge is stored within a single long-term memory store. This is important because it could be, for example, that different kinds of memory have greater duration or are affected by forgetting in different ways.

If there is more than one long-term store, we need to work out the number and nature of long-term stores that we possess. Some of the main suggestions are considered briefly next.

The idea that there is a single long-term memory store has been questioned. Imagine how difficult it could be to retrieve a specific item from the confusion shown here, let alone to retrieve your knowledge of it from all the varied memories you have stored in your life.

Episodic and semantic memory

Tulving (1972) argued for a distinction between two types of long-term memory: **episodic memory** and **semantic memory**. Episodic memory has an autobiographical flavour. It contains the memories of specific events or episodes occurring in a particular place at a particular time. Memories of what you did yesterday or what you had for lunch last Sunday are examples of episodic memory.

In contrast, semantic memory contains information about our knowledge of the world. It includes knowledge of the rules and the words of our language, about how to calculate percentages and how to fill your car with petrol, about what is the capital of France, and who starred in *Star Wars, Episode I*.

Tulving (1989) obtained some support for the distinction between episodic and semantic memory. A small dose of radioactive gold was injected into the bloodstream of volunteers, including Tulving himself. They thought about personal events or about information in semantic memory (e.g. the history of astronomy). Blood flow in different areas of the brain was recorded. Increased blood flow indicated that a certain part of the brain was active. When participants were using their episodic memory parts of the frontal cortex were active, whereas semantic memory was associated with a high level of activation in the posterior or back regions of the cortex. The fact that different parts of the brain were most active during retrieval of episodic and semantic memories fits the view that there are at least partially separate episodic and semantic memory systems.

Evaluation. How useful is the distinction between episodic and semantic memory? It is clear that there is a difference in *content* between the information in episodic and semantic memory. However, it is less clear that there is a difference in the *processes* involved. Episodic and semantic memory depend heavily on each other. For example, remembering what you had for lunch last Sunday basically involves episodic

I remember that hot day when my ice-cream melted faster than I could eat it. EPISODIC MEMORY

Ice-cream melts unless it is kept cold. SEMANTIC MEMORY

memory. However, semantic memory is also involved, in that your knowledge of the world is needed to identify the different kinds of food you ate.

Explicit and implicit memory

How would you test participants' recognition memory for a word list?

The memory tests discussed in this chapter (e.g. free recall, cued recall, recognition) all involve the use of direct instructions to the participants to retrieve specific information. Such memory tests are tests of **explicit memory**, which "is revealed when performance on a task requires conscious recollection of previous experiences". Explicit memory can be contrasted with **implicit memory**, which "is revealed when performance on a task is facilitated in the absence of conscious recollection" (Graf & Schachter, 1985, p.501). The term "explicit" means to be stated directly or plainly, whereas implicit means that something is implied or assumed but no-one tells you specifically. An example of an explicit memory would be being shown a list of things and asked to memorise them, for subsequent recall. An example of implicit memory would be being asked to write a list of all the pubs you have visited—you know the pub names not because you were told to learn them but because you have learned them in the natural course of events. Tulving et al. demonstrated how these two kinds of memory differ. This research is described in the Key Study below.

What is the difference between cued recall tests and free recall tests?

Evaluation. The distinction between explicit and implicit memory is clearly important when considering the value of memory research because such research often involves only explicit memory.

Testing explicit and implicit memory

Tulving, Schachter, and Stark (1982) carried out a study on explicit and implicit memory. Their participants learned a list of rare words (e.g. "toboggan"). One hour or one week later, their memories were tested in two ways.

1. *Implicit memory.* They were asked to "fill in the blanks" to make words (e.g. _ O _ O _GA _). Half of the solutions were words from the original list, but the participants were not told this. Tulving et al. found that the participants were better able to complete these fragments for the words that were in their original list as opposed to the words that were not in their list. The participants must have been using their implicit memory for this task because they were not consciously recalling the words.

KEY STUDY EVALUATION — Tulving et al.

It could be argued that the fragment-completion task was actually testing explicit not implicit memory because participants deliberately searched through the original lists. However this cannot be the explanation because it does not explain why there was a difference in performance after the retention interval on implicit and explicit memory.

2. *Explicit memory.* The participants were given a list of words and asked to identify the words that were on their original list. This tested explicit memory because they had to consciously recall the words they learned.

Recognition memory was much worse after one week than after one hour, whereas fragment-completion performance did not change significantly over time. This demonstrates a difference between the two kinds of memory. The study also demonstrates implicit memory in action.

Discussion points

1. The participants were given certain words to learn. Why did the researchers use rare words?

2. Memory was tested using recognition. How else might memory have been tested and what would the relative advantages have been?

The distinction is also useful because it explains the behaviour of brain-damaged patients suffering from amnesia. These patients have severe problems with long-term memory. What is important here is that these problems are mainly with explicit memory rather than implicit memory. This can be seen in a story told by Claparède (1911). He hid a pin in his hand before shaking hands with an amnesic patient. After that, she was reluctant to shake hands with him, but was embarrassed that she could not think of any reason for her reluctance. Her behaviour indicated implicit memory, but this occurred in the absence of explicit memory of the incident.

Was Claparède's method of conducting research ethical?

Declarative and procedural knowledge systems

Cohen and Squire (1980) argued that long-term memory is divided into two memory systems: **declarative knowledge** and **procedural knowledge**. This distinction is related to that made by Ryle (1949) between "knowing that" and "knowing how". Declarative knowledge corresponds to knowing that. Thus, for example, we know *that* we had roast pork for Sunday lunch, and we know *that* Paris is the capital of France. Procedural knowledge corresponds to knowing how, and refers to the ability to perform skilled actions (e.g. *how* to ride a bicycle, *how* to play the piano) without the involvement of conscious recollection. Explicit memory depends largely or wholly on the declarative knowledge system, whereas implicit memory depends on the procedural knowledge system.

Evaluation. Evidence for the existence of a separate declarative and procedural system comes from research into brain structures. Squire et al. (1992) used PET scans (which take images of the active brain) and found that blood flow in the right hippocampus was much higher when the participants were performing a declarative memory task (cued recall) than a procedural memory task (word-stem completion). It has proved harder to identify the brain structures involved in procedural or implicit memory, because implicit memory consists of a large collection of skills and processes such as learning, perception, skills, facts, and so on.

The three "varieties" of long-term memory: episodic and semantic, explicit and implicit, and declarative and

> ■ Activity: State whether the following involve procedural or declarative knowledge.
>
> • Your name
> • Driving a car
> • The capital city of Japan
> • The value of m^2 when $m = 6$
> • Balancing on one leg
>
> Think of some other examples of procedural and declarative knowledge.

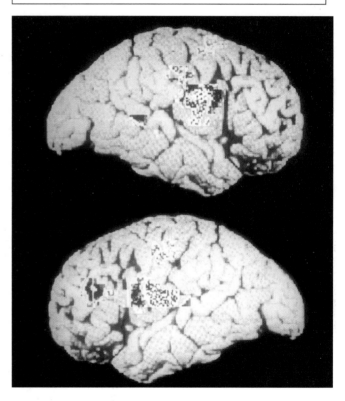

PET scans record the areas of the brain that are active when the brain is engaged in certain behaviours. In a PET scan the active areas of the brain are coloured—in this picture they show up as textured.

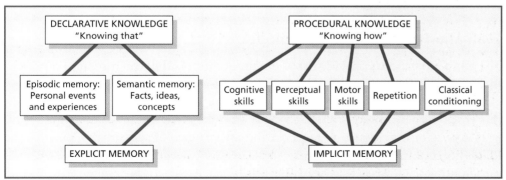

procedural knowledge, all enable us to better understand some of the different kinds of memory performance. For example, it may be that procedural memories are very long-term but the same is not true of all explicit memories. Understanding the different kinds of memory enables us to appreciate the research findings better, especially because memory tests are most likely to test certain kinds of memory rather than others (e.g. declarative rather than procedural).

Models of Memory

How and why does information get passed from short- to long-term memory? You meet someone and they tell you their name. Minutes later, you can't recall it! The information has disappeared from short-term memory because short-term memory is limited in duration, and the information has not been placed in long-term storage. But why not? **Models** or theories of memory aim to explain how the transfer happens, and why it doesn't happened every time.

The multi-store model of memory

You may be familiar with the following experience: your mother is talking to you and she says "Are you listening to me?" You weren't listening, but remarkably you are able to repeat the last few things she said. This is because that information is in a sensory memory store, where it is held for a few seconds before entering short-term memory.

Atkinson and Shiffrin (1968) argued that there are three memory stores: a sensory store, a short-term store, and a long-term store. According to the theory, information from the environment is initially received by the sensory stores. Some of this information is attended to, and processed further, by the short-term store. In turn, some of the information processed in the short-term store is transferred to the long-term store.

In the **multi-store model** the reason given for the transfer between short- and long-term memory is because it is *rehearsed* or repeated verbally. The more something is rehearsed, the stronger the memory trace. The main emphasis of this model is on the structure of memory and on rehearsal.

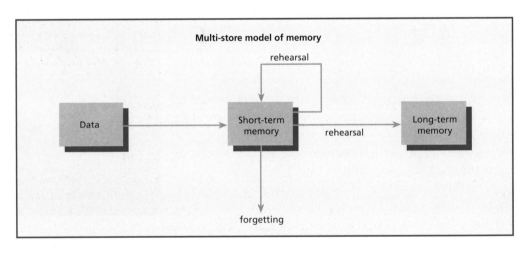

Evaluation of the multi-store model

The multi-store model provides a systematic account of the structures and processes involved in human memory. The notion that there are at least two qualitatively different kinds of memory store is supported by the evidence described earlier in this chapter on duration, storage capacity, and the effects of brain damage.

There is also evidence to support the importance of rehearsal. Consider the following example given by Henderson (1999): if an experimenter slows down the presentation of words, this would allow the participant to rehearse the words more and therefore we would expect to see an increased primacy effect (the words earlier in the list receive more rehearsal). This is what happens. And if rehearsal is prevented, for example by asking the participant to count backwards in threes, the primacy effect disappears—participants remember words at approximately equal frequency throughout the list. This demonstrates the importance of rehearsal.

However, there are also criticisms of the model. The two main ones are as follows: first, the multi-store model proposes that the transfer of information from short- to long-term memory is through rehearsal. However, in day-to-day life most people devote very little time to active rehearsal, even though they are constantly storing away new information in long-term memory. Rehearsal may describe what happens when psychologists conduct experiments in laboratories but this isn't true to life. Consider the Key Study below (which *was* conducted in a laboratory).

Second, the multi-store model is oversimplified. It assumes there is a *single* short-term store and a *single* long-term store. These assumptions have been disproved. For example, the evidence we examined from brain-damaged patients suggested that there were several different short-term stores. There is similar evidence for long-term memory, as we have also seen. This evidence indicates that the single long-

Incidental learning

If participants are given a list of words and told that they are going to be asked to recall them, they will probably be tempted to "memorise" the words, for example, by repeating them over and over again. What happens if you don't tell the participants you are going to test their recall? This would be a test of **incidental learning**, unconscious storage in long-term memory. One method that has been used to study incidental learning is to present participants with a list of words and ask them to do something with the words, such as count the number of letters in each word.

This is what Hyde and Jenkins (1973) did. They gave different groups of participants the same list of nouns to learn. Some groups were not told that there would be a memory test given at the end (*incidental* learning) whereas others were pre-warned (*intentional* learning). Different groups of participants were given different tasks and all were then given a free recall test:

KEY STUDY EVALUATION — Hyde and Jenkins

Of course, we should carefully consider the ethics of deceiving participants about the purpose of an experiment. However, this can be overcome to some extent by asking the participants after the study whether the deception had caused them any distress. If so, the study could be stopped. In reality, however, it is unlikely that the minor deception involved in incidental learning would be distressing to anyone.

- Rating the words for pleasantness.
- Estimating the frequency with which each word is used in the English language.
- Detecting the occurrence of the letters "e" and "g" in the list of words.
- Deciding whether the words fitted into certain sentences.
- Deciding the part of speech (noun, verb, etc.) appropriate to each word.

If participants were asked to rate pleasantness or rate frequency of usage they must have used some kind of semantic processing (processing of meaning), whereas those participants doing the other three tasks did not have to think about the meaning of the words while processing them. When the list of words was unrelated, recall was 51% higher after the semantic tasks than the non-semantic tasks. When the list of words were related recall was even higher for the semantic tasks—there was 83% recall. This demonstrates that what matters is the nature of the processing activity.

Surprisingly, incidental learners recalled the same number of words as intentional learners. Thus, we can conclude that one does not have to consciously remember words to be able to recall them. Rehearsal may not be necessary but meaning may be the key.

Discussion points

1. What are the advantages and disadvantages of conducting laboratory experiments?

2. Try to think of some real-life examples of incidental and intentional learning.

Which type of memory (procedural or declarative) is likely to be tested in a memory experiment?

term store proposed by Atkinson and Shiffrin (1968) needs to be replaced by at least two separate long-term memory systems. One of these systems is concerned with declarative knowledge, and the other with procedural knowledge. Retrieval from the declarative knowledge system typically involves explicit memory. Retrieval from the procedural knowledge system typically involves implicit memory.

The working memory model

Perhaps a more accurate representation of short-term memory would be given by a multi-store model of short-term memory. Baddeley and Hitch (1974) described such a model of short-term or "working" memory (that area of memory which is used while working on things). According to them, the **working memory system** consists of three components:

- **Central executive**: a modality-free component. It has a limited capacity and is like attention.
- **Articulatory-phonological loop**: the loop is divided into a phonological store, which is directly concerned with speech *perception*, and an articulatory process, which is linked to speech *production*.
- **Visuo-spatial sketch pad** (sometimes called a scratch pad): this is specialised for spatial and/or visual coding, a kind of writing pad for visual data.

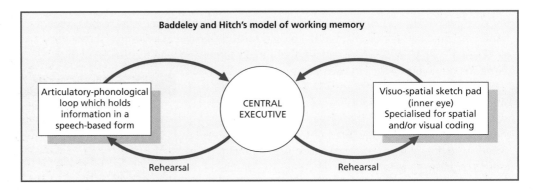

Baddeley and Hitch's model of working memory

Articulatory-phonological loop which holds information in a speech-based form

CENTRAL EXECUTIVE

Visuo-spatial sketch pad (inner eye) Specialised for spatial and/or visual coding

Rehearsal

Rehearsal

Most is known about the articulatory loop, which was studied by Baddeley, Thomson, and Buchanan (1975). They asked their participants to recall sets of five words immediately in the correct order. Participants' ability to do this was better with short words than with long ones, i.e. recall was a function of word length. Further investigation of this *word-length effect* showed that the participants could recall as many words as they could read out loud in two seconds. This suggested that the capacity of the articulatory loop is determined by how long it takes to perform something.

What is the articulatory or phonological loop used for in everyday life? It is used in reading difficult material, making it easier for readers to retain information about the order of words in text. For example, Baddeley and Lewis (1981) gave their participants sentences to read and asked them to say whether the sentences were meaningful. Some of the sentences were not meaningful because two words in a meaningful sentence had been switched round (e.g. "The tree flew up into the birds"). When the participants were prevented from using the articulatory loop by saying something meaningless repeatedly, their ability to decide whether sentences were meaningful was reduced because they could not re-examine the sentences repeatedly.

Evaluation of the working memory model

The working memory model is an advance over the account of short-term memory provided by the multi-store model in various ways. First, the working memory system is concerned with both active processing and the brief storage of information. Thus, it is relevant to activities such as mental arithmetic, verbal reasoning, and comprehension, as well as to traditional short-term memory tasks.

Second, the working memory model accounts for many findings (e.g. those of Hitch and Baddeley, see Key Study below) which are hard to explain within the multi-store approach.

Third, the working memory model views verbal rehearsal as an *optional* process that occurs within the articulatory or phonological loop. This is more realistic than the central importance of verbal rehearsal in the multi-store model.

Testing the working memory model

The working memory model can be used to predict whether or not two tasks can be performed successfully at the same time. Every component of the working memory system has limited capacity, and is relatively independent of the other components. Two predictions follow:

1. If two tasks make use of the same component, they cannot be performed successfully together.

2. If two tasks make use of different components, it should be possible to perform them as well together as separately.

Hitch and Baddeley (1976) tested these predictions. Their participants carried out a verbal reasoning task, which involved deciding whether each in a set of sentences provided a true or a false description of the letter pair that followed it (e.g. participants were told "B is followed by A" and then shown "BA", they then had to state if this was a true or false description of what they had been told). It was assumed that this task would make extensive use of the central executive.

At the same time, the participants had to do one of four things: say "the" repeatedly, say the sequence "one two three four five six" over and over again, repeat a different random string of digits out loud every trial, or there was no additional task. They were given this additional task before the reasoning task was presented. It was assumed that saying "the" or "one two three four five six" repeatedly would involve only the articulatory loop, because little thought or attention is involved. In contrast, saying six random digits involves the central executive as well as the articulatory loop. Thus, saying six random digits should interfere with performance on the verbal reasoning task, but saying six digits in sequence or saying "the" should not. As predicted, reasoning performance was slowed down by the additional task only when it involved using the central executive (i.e. six random digits).

Discussion points

1. Do you think all the assumptions made by Hitch and Baddeley are justified?

2. In what ways does this research go beyond research on short-term memory designed to test Atkinson and Shiffrin's multi-store model?

KEY STUDY EVALUATION — Hitch and Baddeley

Working memory was proposed by Baddeley and Hitch as an alternative to the model of short-term memory described by the multi-store model. Baddeley and Hitch carried out research using the dual-task technique. The assumption that lies behind this technique is that each of the processors has only a limited capacity to process information. If two tasks using the same processor are carried out concurrently, performance on one or both of the tasks will be impaired. This research is an example of how theorising about a concept such as working memory can lead to the development of a hypothesis and controlled research.

Intuitively this research may make sense to us, by suggesting that there are different ways of dealing with different forms of information. The concept of working memory is an active rather than a passive process, and can be used to explain real-life situations, such as reading and doing mental arithmetic. It can also explain short-term memory problems experienced by brain-damaged patients. However, there are always difficulties in using research from patients with brain damage to support a theory (as, for example, in Shallice & Warrington's study of KF). It is difficult, if not impossible, to assess precisely what the short-term memory function of a person would have been prior to the event or accident that leads to them being assessed by psychologists.

■ Activity: Try the dual-task technique yourself. Read a page in a book you have not read before. You should find that you have understood what was being written about, and could explain what you have read to another person. Now turn to a different page and try to read it while saying "the, the, the" aloud repeatedly. You may find that you have some difficulty in understanding the text, and your reading rate may have been reduced. Can you explain what you have read to someone else this time? If you can, how would you explain this?

On the negative side, little is known about the central executive. It has limited capacity, but this capacity has not been measured accurately. It is argued that the central executive is "modality-free" (i.e. it does not rely on any manner of receiving information, such as sound or vision) and used in many different processing operations, but the precise details of its functioning are not known.

Levels of processing theory

In what way are processed peas "processed"?

Craik and Lockhart (1972) put forward an alternative to the multi-store model of memory, called the **levels of processing theory**. They argued that the concept of rehearsal is not sufficient to account for long-term memory. There is evidence to show that the cognitive processes that are operating at the time of learning determine what is stored in long-term memory. More specifically, Craik and Lockhart proposed that it is the *level* of **processing** that determines whether something is stored in long-term memory. If you process information a lot, or "deeply", then it will be stored. If you only process something rather superficially then it won't be stored in long-term memory. Rehearsal is a kind of processing, so it could be explained by this theory, but there are other forms of processing such as depth of analysis, elaboration, organisation, and distinctiveness.

■ Activity: Try to construct a list of words that have approximately the same frequency of usage. Now think of questions to ask that will involve deep processing (e.g. Is this the opposite of …?) or shallow processing (e.g. Does this word include the letter G?). It will be easier if your questions have yes/no answers. Divide the list in half, give each half to a naive participant, such as a member of your family, and ask the questions. Take the list away and give the participant a blank piece of paper for a free recall test. Your findings should be in line with those of Craik and Lockhart: deep processing should lead to better recall.

Depth of analysis

"Depth" is a crucial concept for this theory, as Craik and Lockhart first and foremost predicted that:

- The **depth of processing** of a stimulus has a substantial effect on its memorability, i.e. how well it is remembered.
- Deeper levels of analysis produce more elaborate, longer-lasting, and stronger memory traces than do shallow levels of analysis.

Craik (1973, p.48) defined depth as "the meaningfulness extracted from the stimulus rather than in terms of the number of analyses performed upon it." In this sense, rehearsal or repetition is not a form of deep processing because it only involves a repeated "number of analyses", and not an extraction of meaningfulness.

In a classic piece of research to demonstrate the levels of processing theory, Craik and Tulving (1975, see Key Study on the next page) used **semantic processing** to represent deep processing and the physical analysis of a stimulus to represent more **shallow processing**. As the theory would predict, participants remembered those words that were deeply processed better than those processed more shallowly. The findings of Hyde and Jenkins (1973, see Key Study on page 43) also support this theory.

However, it became apparent that the concept of "depth" alone was an over simplification, and so various other forms of processing were included to extend the concept of "processing".

Elaboration

Craik and Tulving's (1975) classic study (see Key Study on page opposite) also looked at how the **elaboration of processing** can lead to greater recall. In a further

Depth of processing

Craik and Tulving (1975) conducted a series of experiments to provide support for the levels of processing theory. The research aim was again to demonstrate that memory is an automatic by-product of semantic processing. If information has more meaning, then it should be more memorable. In one experiment, participants were shown a list of words (five-letter concrete nouns such as "table") and asked a question for each. For each question the answer was "yes" or "no". The questions were of three types:

- Case (shallow processing), such as "Is the word in capital letters?"
- Rhyme (phonemic processing), such as "Does the word rhyme with 'able'?"
- Sentence (semantic or deep processing), such as "Would the word fit in the sentence 'They met a —— in the street'?"

Some of the participants were tested on incidental learning (unexpected test of recall) whereas others were pre-warned about the memory test (intentional learning). Craik and Tulving found that those words that had been processed semantically were recalled best and those processed phonemically were processed second best (see graphs below). The intentional learners did better than the incidental learners but in both conditions semantic processing produced the highest result for that condition.

Discussion points

1. The words used for each kind of question were varied, so that, for example, the word "train" was sometimes processed shallowly, sometimes phonemically, and sometimes semantically. Why was it necessary to do this in order to get a valid result?

2. Why do you think that participants usually had better recall for the "yes" words than the "no" words?

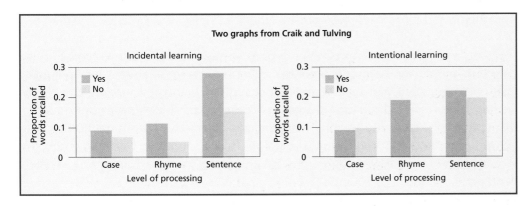

The graphs show recall for all three conditions with incidental and intentional learning. You can see that deeper processing produced better recall in both kinds of learning, and that learning was not greater when participants were pre-warned. The graphs also show the differences between recall when the questions had a "yes" answer (better recall).

experiment, the participants were presented on each trial with a word and a sentence containing a blank. They were again asked to decide whether the word fitted into the incomplete sentence. Elaboration was manipulated by varying the complexity of the sentence between the simple (e.g. "She cooked the ——") and the complex (e.g. "The great bird swooped down and carried off the struggling ——"). Recall was twice as high for words accompanying complex sentences, suggesting that elaboration benefits long-term memory. Remember that longer time spent processing questions requiring **phonemic processing** (e.g. "Does the word fit the pattern CCVCV?") did *not* result in better recall. There is a difference between elaboration, as in the *complexity* of the sentence, and time spent on a task, as in the phonemic processing. Depth of processing involves elaboration.

Organisation

Organisation is another form of deep processing. Research has shown that, like semantic processing, organisation creates a lasting memory. No conscious processing needs to take place (i.e. this is implicit rather than explicit memory). Mandler (1967) demonstrated this in an experiment. He gave participants a pack of 52 picture cards, each of which had a word printed on it. Participants were asked to sort the cards into piles, using anything from two to seven categories, according to any system they wished. They were asked to repeat the sorting until they had achieved two identical sorts. If anyone was still trying to achieve this after 1¼ hours they were excluded from the experiment! Most participants took about six sorts to gain 95% consistency. At this point they were given an unexpected free recall test. Mandler found that recall was poorest for those who had decided to use only two categories, and best for those who used seven categories. According to Mandler, those participants who used several categories in sorting were imposing more organisation on the list than were those who used only a few. Mandler (1967, p.328) concluded that "memory and organisation are not only correlated, but organisation is a necessary condition for memory."

> ■ Activity: Organisation and memory
>
> You can demonstrate that organisation aids memory by constructing two lists of the same words. List 1 will be a categorised word list containing a number of words belonging to several categories (e.g. four-footed animals, sports, flowers, articles of furniture). List 2 will consist of the same words but presented in a random order (e.g. golf, rose, cat, tennis, carnation, and so on). To avoid bias you should allocate participants to conditions (list 1 or list 2) on a random basis. Give them a set time to study the list. After an interval (they could count backwards in threes to prevent rehearsal), give them a test of free recall. You should find that the participants in condition 1 were able to recall more words and that the words were recalled category by category. The experiment shows how organisation aids memory.

Distinctiveness

Memory traces that are distinctive or unique in some way will be more memorable than memory traces closely resembling others. Eysenck and Eysenck (1980) tested this theory by using nouns having irregular grapheme–phoneme correspondence (i.e. words not pronounced in line with pronunciation rules, such as "comb" with its silent "b"). The participants were asked to perform the shallow (non-semantic) task of saying such words as if they were regular (e.g. pronouncing the "b" in "comb"). This resulted in a unique memory trace, so that this was the non-semantic, distinctive condition. In the non-semantic, non-distinctive condition, nouns were simply pronounced in their normal fashion. In the semantic, distinctive and the semantic, non-distinctive conditions, nouns were processed in terms of their meaning.

On an unexpected test of recognition memory, words in the non-semantic, distinctive condition were much better remembered than those in the non-semantic, non-distinctive condition. Indeed, they were remembered almost as well as the words in the two semantic conditions. These findings show the importance of distinctiveness.

> ■ Activity: It would be fairly easy to manipulate distinctiveness in a similar manner to the "Smith" example and to observe its effects on long-term memory, if you wanted to carry out an experiment in this area.

Distinctiveness depends in part on the context in which a given stimulus is processed. For example, the name "Smith" if presented in the list "Jones, Robinson, Williams, Baker, Smith, Robertson" would not be distinctive, but it would stand out in the following list:

"Zzitz, Zysblat, Vangeersadaele, Vythelingum, Smith, Uwejeyah" (for which we are indebted to the London Telephone Directory).

Evaluation of levels of processing theory

Processes occurring at the time of learning have a major impact on long-term memory. That sounds obvious, but few studies before 1972 considered learning processes and their effects on memory. The view then was that memory could be explained in terms of structure and rehearsal. The depth of processing theory offered a model that could be applied to improving memory. If you find it hard to remember someone's name, don't just repeat it over and over again—elaborate on it or make the memory distinctive. This enhances the depth of processing and will make it more memorable.

However, the theory is not without criticism. First of all, it is hard to decide whether a particular task involves shallow or deep processing. This problem occurs because of the lack of any independent measure of processing depth. Craik and Tulving (1975) assumed that semantic processing involved greater "depth" than phonemic processing, but they had no real evidence for this assumption—only the fact that semantic processing resulted in more memorability. This is a circular argument: memorability relies on depth therefore semantic processing must be deep, but our only evidence for depth is that the material is more memorable.

A related point is that participants may not stop at the expected level of processing. For example, if you were asked to count the numbers of "e"s and "g"s in your own name, it is likely that you would think about yourself in a meaningful way as well as doing the task. So who knows exactly what task any participant is actually doing.

Some evidence does not support levels of processing theory. Morris, Bransford, and Franks (1977) found that stored information is remembered only if it is *relevant* to the memory test. Participants who were tested with a rhyming recognition test recalled words that had been processed in terms of their sound rather than those that had been processed for meaning. This disproves the prediction of levels of processing theory that deep processing is always better than shallow processing. The reason is that processing the meaning of the list words was of little help when the memory test required the identification of words rhyming with list words. The information acquired from the shallow rhyme task was far more relevant, and so memory performance was higher in this condition.

A final criticism of the levels of processing approach is that it *describes* rather than *explains*. Craik and Lockhart (1972) argued that deep processing leads to better long-term memory than shallow processing. However, they failed to provide a detailed account of *why* deep processing is so effective. Why would something that is elaborated or more distinctive be more likely to result in long-term storage? It does happen (a description) but *why*?

From what you have learned so far about recall, what advice would you give to doctors about how to improve their patients' recall of medical advice?

SECTION 5
Forgetting

When we considered the evidence related to the *capacity* of short- and long-term memory we overlooked the issue of **forgetting**. The reason a memory is no longer present may *not* be due to the capacity of the store, but because it has been forgotten. We all know, only too well, the experience of forgetting but in the spirit that psychology is more than common sense we should ask whether there is actually evidence that people do forget. A classic study by Ebbinghaus (1885, see Key Study below) established it as a fact.

People do forget

It may seem obvious to you that people forget things, but what evidence have you got for this belief? How do you know that a memory for what happened in the past tends to become worse as time goes by? Hermann Ebbinghaus (1885) produced the first clear experimental evidence for increased forgetting over time. In his studies, Ebbinghaus was both the experimenter and the only participant. He learned a list of meaningless items known as nonsense syllables (e.g. MAZ, TUD) until he could recall all of them. If he tested himself after a short period of time, his recall was good, but this decreased as the retention interval (the time between learning and recall) increased. There was a large increase in forgetting over the first hour after learning, after which forgetting increased more slowly.

KEY STUDY EVALUATION — Ebbinghaus

The participant in this case study (Ebbinghaus) may not, of course, have been representative of people generally. He was an extremely intelligent individual who may have had an especially good memory. He was also both experimenter and participant which could mean that the data he collected were biased. Might his expectations have influenced his performance?

Ebbinghaus also made another discovery. He tried to re-learn the list until he could again recall all of the words. Ebbinghaus measured his level of remembering in terms of "savings". Each time he re-learned the list he recorded the number of trials that were necessary to get back to having full recall. He found that each time he re-learned the list fewer trials were required. He called this re-learning "savings". It suggests that each time you learn something, some kind of "trace" is left which may not be sufficient for complete recall, but makes subsequent learning quicker.

How might this concept of "savings" be used to explain successful revision techniques?

Discussion points

1. Why is it necessary to actually demonstrate that people do forget?

2. Why do you think that Ebbinghaus used nonsense syllables?

All memory experiments rely on retrieving information from memory, and assume that, if it can't be retrieved, then it must be forgotten. The concept of "forgetting" suggests that something has disappeared from memory (it is not available). Or it could be that the memory is simply "mislaid" (it is not accessible). We can consider the problem of forgetting in terms of these two features of recall:

- Is the memory not available, i.e. has it ceased to exist?
- Is the memory just not accessible, i.e. might we find it given time or the right clues?

Forgetting in short-term memory is likely to be due to a failure of availability because it is a limited-capacity store—it is unlikely that in a limited-capacity store one is unable to find something. Forgetting in long-term memory may be due to a lack of availability and/or a lack of accessibility. We will consider explanations of forgetting in short-term memory first.

Forgetting in Short-term Memory

Trace decay

In the study by Peterson and Peterson (see page 35) it was found that recall dropped from 80% after 3-second recall to under 20% when the retention interval was 18 seconds. What caused this drop to occur? One possibility is that the memory trace simply disappears if it is not rehearsed. (In the Brown-Peterson technique, participants were required to count backwards in threes to prevent rehearsal.) This is called **trace decay theory** and is based on the idea that memories have a physical basis (a "trace") and that this will decay in time unless the trace is passed to long-term memory. The trace disappears just like a photographic image that is not fixed with chemicals. Information in short-term memory certainly does disappear but it may not be because of spontaneous decay—it may be the result of interference.

Interference

Another possible explanation for the Peterson and Peterson findings is that the interference task caused **retroactive interference**. This occurs when a second set of information (counting backwards in threes) "pushes out" earlier material from the memory store. It is most likely to happen when the two sets of information are sufficiently similar. Evidence supporting that point of view was reported by Reitman (1971). The participants carried out either a syllable detection task or a tone detection task during the retention interval. Those who performed the syllable detection task had much lower recall than those who performed the tone detection task, presumably because syllables interfered much more than tones. Evidence on the effects of interference is considered again later.

Diversion of attention

However, in the Brown-Peterson task the two sets of information were different (letters and numbers). Another possibility is that forgetting occurs because attention is diverted away from the to-be-remembered information. This explanation is rather similar to decay theory, because it assumes that forgetting can occur simply because of the passage of time. Watkins et al. (1973) obtained evidence favouring the diversion of attention theory. Some of their participants had to listen to musical notes, then hum them, and finally identify them, whereas others simply had to listen to the notes. Those who had to hum and identify the notes showed much forgetting, whereas those who merely listened showed no forgetting. Watkins et al. argued that forgetting occurred because the requirements to hum and identify the notes diverted attention away from the to-be-remembered information.

Conclusion

In sum, forgetting in short-term memory probably depends mainly on decay-like processes based on attention being diverted away from the material to be remembered. In addition, interference is likely to be a factor.

Is forgetting always a bad thing? Do we need to remember everything?

Forgetting in Long-term Memory: Availability

Trace decay theory

Forgetting might also be due to the gradual physical decay of the memory traces in long-term memory, as has been suggested for short-term memory. It has proved hard to study these physical or physiological changes directly. As a result, tests of trace decay theory have been somewhat indirect. The assumption is that if a person does nothing during the time of initial learning and subsequent recall (called the retention interval) and they forget the material, then the only explanation can be that the trace has disappeared.

Jenkins and Dallenbach (1924) asked two students to recall **nonsense syllables** at intervals between one and eight hours. The students were either awake or asleep during the retention interval. There was much less forgetting when the students were asleep during the retention interval than when they were awake. If trace decay theory was correct we would expect the same amount of forgetting whether they were asleep or awake. The fact that they forgot more when they were awake suggests that the interference from other activities was responsible for the increased forgetting, rather than decay. The fact that *some* forgetting took place when the participants were asleep could be explained in terms of interference from dreams, or perhaps there may indeed have been some trace decay.

What were the independent and dependent variables in the Jenkins and Dallenbach study? Were there any confounding variables?

Evaluation of trace decay theory

Jenkins and Dallenbach's experiment was flawed because there was no control over what was happening when the participants were awake or asleep. In addition, there were other differences between the two conditions. In the asleep condition, the students learned the material in the *evening*, whereas their learning usually occurred in the *morning* in the awake condition. Thus, the high level of forgetting in the awake condition could have occurred either because the students were awake throughout the retention interval, or because learning is worse in the morning. Hockey, Davies, and Gray (1972) tested the effects of morning versus evening learning. They found that the rate of forgetting was rapid during daytime sleeping, suggesting that forgetting depends mostly on the time at which learning occurs.

In sum, there is very little support for trace decay theory. If all memory traces are subject to decay, it is surprising how well we can remember many events that happened several years ago and which are rarely thought about or rehearsed. For example, most people remembered in detail for some years what they were doing when they heard the news of Mrs Thatcher's resignation in 1990 (Conway et al., 1994). Accurate and long-lasting memories for very significant events are known as flashbulb memories (discussed later in this section). However, trace decay may play some causal role in forgetting, but it is by no means the main explanation.

Interference theory

After reorganising the contents of kitchen cupboards, you may find yourself looking for something in its old location, even weeks after everything has been moved. This is an example of interference—memory for the old location is interfering with memory for the new one.

If you had asked psychologists during the 1930s, 1940s, or 1950s what caused forgetting, you would probably have received the answer "interference". It was assumed that one set of learning in some way interferes with another set and wipes out the memory. When previous learning interferes with later learning and retention, this is known as **proactive interference**. When later learning disrupts memory for earlier learning, this is known as retroactive interference (which was the kind of interference proposed for short-term memory).

Interference theory has been tested by means of **paired-associate learning**. The participants are initially presented with several pairs of words (e.g. cat–tree, candle–table). The first word in each pair (e.g. cat or candle) is known as the stimulus term, and the second word (e.g. tree or table) is the response term. Learning continues until the participants can recall each response term when presented with the stimulus term. The participants then learn a second list of paired associates.

- *Proactive interference*: Past experience interferes with current recall. Participants' recall is tested for the second list of paired associates. Performance of the experimental group (who learned both lists) is compared with a control group (who learned only the second list). Proactive interference should mean that the experimental group do less well than the control group.
- *Retroactive interference*: Subsequent experience interferes with recall of material learned earlier. Participants' recall is tested on the first list of paired associates. Performance of the experimental group (learned both lists) is compared with the control group (learned only the first list). Retroactive interference should mean that the experimental group do less well.

There is strong evidence for both proactive and retroactive interference when the same stimulus terms are used in both lists of paired associates (list A would contain cat–tree and list B would contain cat–book, the same stimulus word "cat" appears in both lists). However, little proactive or retroactive interference is found when different stimulus terms are used in the two lists (Underwood & Postman, 1960). Read through the activity on the right if you are still feeling confused!

Lists of paired associates: words that could be used to test proactive and retroactive interference

List A:		List B:	
	cat–tree		cat–glass
	candle–table		candle–whale
	book–tractor		book–revolver
	apple–lake		apple–sadness
	doll–kettle		doll–pedal
	glacier–poster		glacier–cane
	locker–cigar		locker–bullet
	jelly–moss		jelly–time
	hammer–monk		hammer–pencil
	ankle–blister		ankle–head

■ Activity: You could try testing interference yourself. Arrange for one group of participants (group 1) to learn list A until they can remember all the response terms when you say the stimulus term.

Then ask them to learn list B in the same way.

Ask another group (group 2) to just learn list B.

Afterwards test both groups on list B. Group 1 should do less well, in terms of number of items correctly recalled, than group 2 because of proactive interference.

Test group 1 on list A. They should do less well, in terms of number of items correctly recalled, than group 2 did for list B. This is retroactive interference.

Try the experiment again using the following list instead of the original list B (and use a new set of participants):

      hostage–glass
      bandage–whale
      pear–revolver
      pin–sadness
      trumpet–pedal
      day–cane
      soup–bullet
      money–time
      mast–pencil
      toy–head

Are your findings any different? Why?

Evaluation of interference theory

It is unlikely that interference theory has much applicability to everyday life. It is rare that two different responses are attached to the same stimulus and therefore much of our forgetting is unlikely to be due to interference. But it does happen occasionally in everyday life. Consider for example the case of the 19th-century German psychologist Hugo Munsterberg, who moved his pocket-watch from one pocket to another. When asked "What time is it?" (this is the recurrent stimulus), Munsterberg would often fumble about in confusion, and put his hand into the wrong pocket (proactive interference because past experience is interfering with current recall).

The most significant criticism of interference theory is that the effects disappear when cued recall rather than free recall is used. This is clarified in the Key Study by Tulving and Psotka (1971), described on the next page.

Cue-dependent forgetting and interference

Endel Tulving conducted a number of studies on cue-dependent forgetting. In one study Tulving and Psotka (1971) compared the cue-dependent explanation of forgetting with the interference theory of forgetting. In this experiment participants were given word lists. There were six different word lists, each with 24 words. Each set of words was divided into six different categories of four words (therefore 36 categories in all of the six word lists). The words were presented in category order so that the organisation and the categories were quite obvious. For example, one list could be: cat, tiger, dog, whale, ruby, diamond, sapphire, emerald, chair, table, sofa, bed, apple, pear, orange, lemon, oak, maple, birch, elm, lake, river, sea, pond.

> **KEY STUDY EVALUATION — Tulving and Psotka**
>
> There is the possibility that improved performance on the cued-recall task might be due to a **practice effect**. The participants had completed at least two free recall tests before doing the cued recall and this may have led to better recall. However this cannot explain all the results, such as why recall was the same for all lists no matter how many were given.

Some of the participants only learned one list, some learned two lists, and so on … some learned as many as all six lists. Words were shown one at a time. After each list had been presented, the participants free-recalled as many words as possible. That was the original learning. After all the lists had been presented, the participants tried to recall the words from all the lists that had been presented. That was total free recall. Finally, all the category names were presented, and the participants tried again to recall all the words from all the lists. That was total free *cued* recall (cued because they were given the category names).

There were two main findings:

1. There was apparently strong evidence for retroactive interference in the total free recall condition. Participants who were only given one or two lists to recall were able to recall a higher percentage of their words than those who had more lists. In other words, recall decreased as retroactive interference increased. This finding would be interpreted within interference theory as the unlearning of the earlier lists due to interference from subsequent lists.

2. When the participants were given the cued recall test, the effects of retroactive interference disappeared. No matter how many lists the participants were given, recall was the same for each list (about 70%) when they were given category names as cues. This means that interference had not caused unlearning, it only *appeared* to have this effect. The memories were available but not accessible. Thus, the forgetting observed in total free recall was basically cue-dependent forgetting.

Discussion points

1. How could you apply these results to your methods of revision?
2. This experiment used a **repeated measures design**. Could an **independent measures design** have been used, and what would have been the advantages and drawbacks?

Forgetting in Long-term Memory: Accessibility

Cue-dependent forgetting

Mary says to Susan: "Do you remember what that boy was called?"

Susan: "No, it was something like 'Ted' or 'Frank' or something like that."

Mary: "Oh that's it, it was Fred!"

Cue-dependent forgetting is a classic example of forgetting because of lack of *accessibility*. The information is in memory, but just cannot be accessed until an appropriate cue is given and suddenly, up it pops! Such information is said to be available (i.e. it is still stored) but not accessible (i.e. it cannot be retrieved). Evidence of the importance of cue-dependent forgetting was provided by in the Key Study by Tulving and Psotka (1971), described above. Participants were given a long list of words to remember. The words belonged to several different categories (e.g. articles of furniture, four-footed animals). The participants were tested twice. On the first occasion they were asked for free (non-cued) recall, i.e. to write down all of the words they could remember. The second time they were given category names as cues, and were again asked to write down the list words. This is called **cued recall**. Perhaps you may be surprised to hear that they were now able to remember a lot more words, up to four times as many. The relatively better performance with cued recall occurred because the participants were better able to *access* their memory. The words they had forgotten on the first (non-cued) test were available but temporarily "forgotten". This is cue-dependent forgetting.

Some psychologists have argued that all forgetting is cue-dependent forgetting. They claim that we store all, or almost all, information *permanently*. The problem is being able to find a way to access it. The difficulty in trying to research this hypothesis is that it is not possible to *disprove* the idea that long-term memory is permanent. It *is* possible that information is still stored somewhere in long-term memory, even if it cannot be retrieved. At present, the most appropriate conclusion is probably that most (but not all) forgetting is cue-dependent.

Can you apply Tulving and Psotka's research to your study of psychology? Try to think of "cues" that you can use to organise recall.

Encoding specificity principle

Remembering something hinges on having the right cues. Tulving (1979) used this notion to put forward his **encoding specificity principle**: this is the idea that the closer the retrieval cue is to the information stored in memory, the greater the likelihood that the cue will be successful in retrieving the memory. For example, in the example given earlier, "Ted" was a good cue for the information stored in memory ("Fred") because they rhyme. "Frank" would also have been a good cue because it starts with the same sound. Even "Flintstone" might have been helpful!

The encoding specificity principle is also hard to test, because we do not usually know how much "informational overlap" there is between retrieval cue and memory trace. For some people "Ted" might be a good cue, but is it better than "Frank"?

Do you have to remember the names of researchers when describing a study? No, but the name may act as a useful cue for recall.

In addition, according to the encoding specificity principle, retrieval (or its opposite, forgetting) occurs fairly rapidly and with little thinking involved. However, retrieval often involves problem-solving activities which take time and conscious thought. For example, if asked what you were doing last Friday, you might reply: "Let's see, on Friday I usually play badminton, but last week was half-term, and so I went to see *Titanic* with a friend."

The role of context

Tulving's studies of cue-dependent forgetting involved *external* cues (e.g. presenting category names). However, cue-dependent forgetting has also been shown with *internal* cues (e.g. mood state). This can be seen amusingly in the film *City Lights*, in which Charlie Chaplin saves a drunken millionaire from attempted suicide, and is befriended in return. When the millionaire sees Charlie again he is sober, and fails to recognise him. However, when the millionaire becomes drunk once again, he catches sight of Charlie, treats him like a long-lost friend, and takes him home with him. The next morning, when the millionaire is sober again, he forgets that

The film *City Lights* illustrates the concept of mood-state-dependent memory.

Charlie is his invited guest, and gets his butler to throw him out. This is called **mood-state-dependent memory**. People tend to remember material better when there is a *match* between their mood at learning and at retrieval. The effects are stronger when the participants are in a positive mood than a negative mood (Ucros, 1989).

How might one make more effective television advertisements using the knowledge about mood-state-dependent memory (remember that people recall more when they are in a better mood)?

These internal cues are a form of context. They place the memory in a context and the context serves as the retrieval cue. An experimental study of the effects of external context was conducted by Abernethy (1940). A group of psychology students were given a set of tests before their course began. The course lasted four weeks, all students had the same lecturer and all lessons were in the same room. At the end of each week they were all tested. Some were tested in the same room by their usual lecturer, or by a different lecturer. Others were tested in a different room either by their normal lecturer or a different one. Those students tested in their usual room by their usual lecturer did best of all on the tests. It was presumed that the context (same room, same lecturer) must have acted as a cue to recall. Perhaps the students looked around the room when they couldn't think of an answer and something they saw jogged their memory, acting as a retrieval cue. This has obvious applications to your own studies.

Emotional factors in forgetting: Repression

A further reason for lack of accessibility is that emotionally threatening material is repressed, that is, it is held from conscious awareness. You may remember from Chapter 1 Section 2 of this book that Freud (1915) suggested that material which caused anxiety may be dealt with in a number of ways that will reduce one's feelings of anxiety. **Repression** is one of these methods of **ego defence**.

The concept of repression can be used to explain forgetting. A simple example would be of someone who dislikes going to the dentist. If they told you that they "forgot" their appointment, you might think of this as a repressed memory—the anxiety caused by the memory in some way made it inaccessible to conscious thought.

It is hard to test Freud's theory, and therefore to disprove the validity of the concept of repressed memories. However there have been attempts to conduct experiments to demonstrate the phenomenon of repression. These typically involve creating anxiety to produce forgetting or repression. After that, the anxiety is removed to show that the repressed information is still in long-term memory (referred to as the "return of the repressed").

Such experimental procedures are ethically questionable—is it right to expose anyone to anxiety-producing situations in order to study the effects on their memory? One way to do this is to give participants "failure feedback" (telling the participants their memory-task performance is poor). It is presumed that this will create a sense of anxiety. Then removal can be achieved by telling the participants that the failure feedback was false (this might be stressful as well!). Failure feedback often leads to impaired memory, but in fact it is not clear that repression is involved. As Holmes (1990) has pointed out, the participants may think about their failure and the reasons for it rather than devoting all their efforts to the memory test. So the experimenter isn't truly assessing repression.

More convincing evidence for repression has come from "repressors", individuals who have low scores on trait anxiety (a personality factor relating to how likely you are to become anxious) and high scores on defensiveness (the tendency to protect oneself from anxiety or embarrassment). Myers and Brewin (1994) conducted a natural experiment to compare repressors with other personality types, such as individuals high on both trait anxiety and defensiveness (defensive high-anxious). Myers and Brewin measured the length of time taken for participants to recall negative childhood memories. Repressors were much slower than other personality types. They also found that the "repressors" were the ones who reported having experienced the most indifference and hostility from their fathers. Therefore, the finding suggests that individuals with anxiety-provoking memories are also more likely to repress such memories.

How does a natural experiment differ from a laboratory experiment?

The concept of repression is related to the idea of recovered memories. Some adults seem to have repressed memories for sexual abuse which they suffered in childhood. For example, Herman and Schatzow (1987) found that 28% of a group of female incest victims reported severe memory deficits from childhood, and such repressed memories were most frequent among women who had suffered violent abuse. However, there is often no concrete evidence to confirm the accuracy of repressed memories. Brewin, Andrews, and Gotlib (1993, p.94) discussed the issues involved, and came to the following conclusion: "Provided that individuals are questioned about the occurrence of specific events or facts that they were sufficiently old and well placed to know about, the central features of their accounts are likely to be reasonably accurate." However, it must be borne in mind that the whole issue of recovered memories of abuse is very sensitive. It raises major ethical and legal issues concerning the therapist's responsibilities, the effects of accusations on other members of the family, and so on.

How much do such studies as Myers and Brewin (1994) tell us about other repressed childhood memories? Do such studies have "ecological validity"?

Flashbulb Memories

On the other hand, emotion may also cause stronger memories rather than repressing them. The term **flashbulb memory** describes long-lasting and vivid memories of highly important and dramatic events. Brown and Kulik (1977) first

What were you doing when you heard about Princess Diana's fatal accident? Why do so many people have a vivid memory for this and other extremely emotional and important events?

coined the term "flashbulb memories". They noticed that many people were able to vividly recall what they were doing at the time of President Kennedy's assassination. More recent examples include the fact that millions of people have flashbulb memories of the death of Diana, Princess of Wales, remembering clearly where and how they learned of her death. It is as if a flash photograph was taken at the very moment of the event and every detail indelibly printed in memory. One eyewitness described his memory of the Oklahoma bombing as being *"engraved on his memory"* (Cahill & McGaugh, 1998). Flashbulb events don't have to be negative or to concern international events. Happy events can create a "photographic" image, such as a wedding, or a special night out, or the birth of a child.

Clearly, the emotional nature of such events contributes to the way they remain in memory. Brown and Kulik suggested that flashbulb memories were distinctive because they were both enduring and accurate. The concept of flashbulb memories seems to contradict the notion that thorough processing in the short-term store is needed for good long-term memory, and to support the idea that distinctiveness and emotional factors are important in memory.

What causes a flashbulb memory?

Brown and Kulik suggested that a special neural mechanism might be responsible for flashbulb memories. Other psychologists have suggested that flashbulb memories are so memorable because they are repeated so often, on occasions when people recall these emotionally significant life events.

A more recent theory has been developed by Cahill and McGaugh (1998). They suggest that it is easy to see why it would not be desirable to be able to remember every detail of every experience. On the other hand, it would be useful to have a biological mechanism that could regulate the degree to which something was remembered by somehow ranking the importance of events and experiences. This would be a form of **adaptive** behaviour.

What personal "flashbulb memories" have you got?

Cahill and McGaugh propose that what happens is that, at times of high emotional arousal, **hormones** are produced which have a two-fold effect. In the short-term, emotional hormones create a sense of arousal that helps the animal to respond to an emotionally charged situation (in simple terms, the animal is ready to respond). These same hormones have a long-term function in terms of their effect on memory. Future responses to the same emotional (important) situation will be enhanced because the events surrounding the original emotional experience are well remembered.

This was demonstrated in an experiment with rats, where they were injected with a stimulant drug (like a hormone) just after the rats learned something new. The drug successfully enhanced the rats' abilities to recall the task.

Are flashbulb memories accurate?

How do you know that your flashbulb memories are accurate?

A second question is whether such memories are actually as reliable as they have been described. You might report that you were sitting eating Weetabix when you heard the news of Diana's death, but how can we reliably confirm this? McCloskey, Wible, and Cohen (1988) did test the reliability of flashbulb memories. They interviewed people shortly after the explosion of the space shuttle *Challenger* and then re-interviewed the same people nine months later. McCloskey et al. found that the participants did forget elements of the event, and they also showed some inaccuracies in their recall (there were discrepancies between their initial and later recall). And this was despite the fact that they may have enhanced their memories during the initial interview. This finding suggests that flashbulb memories are subject to forgetting in the same way that other memories are.

Conway et al. (1994) disagreed with this. They felt that the *Challenger* explosion was not a particularly good example of a flashbulb memory because it did not have important consequences in the lives of those interviewed, and therefore lacked one of the central criteria for a flashbulb memory. Conway et al. looked at reactions to the resignation of Mrs Thatcher—an event that was surprising and consequential to most people in the UK (or so Conway et al. claimed), and therefore one that should produce a flashbulb memory. They tested people a few days after the event and again later, and found that 86% of their UK participants still had flashbulb memories after 11 months compared to 29% in other countries. The UK memories were very detailed and quite consistent over time. This suggests that when an event has a distinctive meaning it will be more memorable. Flashbulb memories are considered further in the next section, on page 63.

> ■ Activity: You might try asking people if they have special public or personal flashbulb memories, and ask them to describe the event that these memories are associated with. What conclusions might you draw?
>
> As a long-term project you might identify a highly emotional event that has recently occurred and ask people to say what they were doing at the time. Return a few months from now and ask them to report again what they were doing. Did they give similar answers? [Note that you should consider how you might score "similarity."]

SECTION 6   CRITICAL ISSUE
Eyewitness Testimony

Much of the research that we have considered in this section on human memory may have seemed to be of little relevance to everyday life. In this section, our focus will be on a major practical application of our knowledge of human memory—eyewitness testimony.

Brown (1986, p. 258) suggested that there is a paradox to eyewitness testimony, which is: "judges, defense attorneys and psychologists believe it to be just about the least trustworthy kind of evidence of guilt, whereas jurors have always found it *more* persuasive than any other sort of evidence." Brown's concerns were confirmed in a study by Wells, Liepe, and Ostrom (1979). Participants in this experiment were told to wait in a cubicle before the study started. In the cubicle there was a calculator and, while the participant sat there a **confederate** of the experimenter appeared and popped it into her purse. When the participants were asked to identify the "thief" from a set of six photographs, only 58% were correct. However, even more worryingly, when the same participants were asked to "testify" at a mock trial, 80% of them were believed by the jury.

Wells et al.'s study involved deceiving the participants. Do you feel this is acceptable?

The Devlin report (1976) to the British Home Secretary found that, in the year 1973, there were 850 cases where eyewitness testimony was the only evidence of guilt. In 74% of them, the accused was found guilty by a jury. The Devlin committee considered the evidence about the **reliability** of such testimony and advised that no jury should convict on eyewitness testimony alone. Why is eyewitness testimony so unreliable, and what can we do to improve it?

Eyewitness testimony has been found by psychologists to be extremely unreliable, yet jurors tend to find such testimony highly believable. This is very worrying. What can we do about it?

Unreliable Evidence

In a study by Allport and Postman (1947) participants were shown this picture. Later they were more likely to recall that the black man was holding the razor, presumably because this fitted in with the stereotype at the time.

There are a variety of explanations for the unreliability of eyewitness testimony. For example, people often don't have total recall for events and they fill in the gaps in their memory on the basis of what they *think* might have happened. This is called reconstructive memory. Reconstructive memory relies on the stereotypes people have about people. For example, you might expect that, if a crime was committed, it wasn't done by a little old woman wearing a suit and this might lead you to "recall" that it was a man rather than a woman. If you have to "reconstruct" your memory, it will be affected by your stereotypes.

A further issue is the effects of language. If you are asked "What was the doctor wearing?" it would lead you to give a different answer from "What was the woman wearing?" The language used when questioning eyewitnesses may lead them to give certain answers.

Reconstructive nature of memory

The concept of reconstructive memory is related to **schema theory**. During the course of life we develop schemas. A **schema** is an organised package of information that stores your knowledge about the world. Schemas are stored in long-term memory. Your schemas tell you that if you were wearing a short-sleeved shirt it was likely to be summer and that last names are more likely to be "Thatcher" than "Roofer". Bower, Black, and Turner (1979) demonstrated that most people share similar schemas, such as for a restaurant meal. They asked several people to list the most important events associated with having a restaurant meal, and found that most included the following events in their list: sitting down, looking at the menu, ordering, eating, paying the bill, and leaving the restaurant.

Schema theory offers a rather different view of memory and learning from the one we have looked at so far. Most memory research presents the view that memories are things that are stored, and then accessed. Bartlett (1932, see Key Study opposite) suggested that the process of remembering things is an *active* reconstruction of the bits that are stored. When you learn something, it is actually only elements of the experience that are stored.

So reconstructions are made by combining the real elements of a memory with your knowledge of the world—these things that are called schemas. Schema theory indicates that prior expectations will influence our perceptions. This means that our prejudices and stereotypes will influence what we think we have seen, and how we subsequently recall the information, as we shall see in a moment. Before that, let us briefly consider the nature of stereotypes.

■ Activity: In small groups, write your own schemas for the following:

• Catching a train
• Buying a newspaper
• Starting school

How easy was it to agree on a uniform pattern of events? Were any of the themes easier to agree on than the others? Why might this be?

Stereotypes

In Bartlett's classic study he showed how our cultural expectations or **stereotypes** lead to predictable changes in memory. Stereotypes are schemas that summarise large amounts of data. Like schemas, stereotypes influence memory. If you are told that a target person

Testing Bartlett's theory

How can we show the impact of prior knowledge (schemas) on memory? Bartlett (1932) asked people to learn a piece of prose text. The text was selected to produce a conflict between its contents and the reader's own knowledge of the world. This would mean that the reader might impose his or her own schemas on the contents, and this would result in some distortion of the material. For example, if people read a story taken from a different culture, then this would contain words and concepts that were foreign. It would be likely that the reader's prior knowledge would affect the way this information was remembered, making it more conventional and acceptable from the standpoint of their own cultural background.

In one study, Bartlett asked English participants to read a North American Indian folk tale called "The War of the Ghosts", after which they tried to recall the story. Part of the story was as follows:

One night two young men from Edulac went down the river to hunt seals, and while they were there it became foggy and calm. Then they heard war-cries, and they thought: "Maybe this is a war-party." They escaped to the shore, and hid behind a log. Now canoes came up, and they heard the noise of paddles, and saw one canoe coming up to them. There were five men in the canoe, and they said: "What do you think? We wish to take you along. We are going up the river to make war on the people."

What did Bartlett find? When he asked participants to recall the story after 20 hours the story was considerably changed:

Two men from Edulac went fishing. While thus occupied by the river they heard a noise in the distance. "It sounds like a cry", said one and presently there appeared some men in boats who invited them to join the party on their adventure.

The participants" recall distorted the content and style of the original story. The story was shortened, and the phrases were changed to be more similar to our own language and concepts (e.g. "boats" instead of "canoe").

Bartlett asked his participants to recall the story many times, even a year later. He found that the distortions increased over successive recalls. Most of the recall errors were in the direction of making the story read more like an ordinary English story and to make it more coherent. Bartlett used the term "rationalisation" to refer to this type of error. Other distortions of memory included flattening (failing to recall unfamiliar details) and sharpening (elaboration of certain details). These changes make the story more easily remembered.

Bartlett's expectation was that participants' successive reproductions would eventually become fixed. In fact he found that the reproductions just went on evolving: they very soon become fairly fixed but gradual transformations went on indefinitely. In other words memory was forever being reconstructed.

Discussion points

1. Why do you think that Bartlett's research has been so influential in the study of memory?

2. Do you think that the kinds of errors and distortions observed by Bartlett would be found with other kinds of material?

KEY STUDY EVALUATION — Bartlett

One of the main criticisms of Bartlett's schema theory is that he used stories from an unfamiliar culture to find good evidence of systematic distortions in memory. Support for Bartlett (1932) has come from several studies. Sulin and Dooling (1974) asked their participants to read a story, having told them it was about either Adolf Hitler or Gerald Martin (a fictitious character). Afterwards, they were given a test of recognition memory, and asked to decide whether each sentence in the test had been presented in the story. The key sentences were those that had not been presented, but which referred to well-known facts about Adolf Hitler. Those participants who had been told the story was about Hitler were much more likely to claim mistakenly that these key sentences had been in the original story. Thus, their prior knowledge about Hitler produced distortions in their recall.

Another criticism of Bartlett's work was that his approach to research lacked objectivity. Some psychologists believe that well-controlled experiments are the only way to produce objective data. Bartlett's methods were somewhat casual. He simply asked his group of participants to recall the story at various intervals and there were no special conditions for this recall. It is possible that other factors affected their performance, such as the conditions around them at the time they were recalling the story.

On the other hand, one could argue that his research is more ecologically valid than those studies that involve the recall of syllables or list of words. In recent years there has been an increase in the kind of research conducted by Bartlett, looking at more "everyday memory".

Think back to the case study of HM on page 37. In what way did HM make use of reconstructive memory?

We all use stereotypes, usually without even thinking about them, e.g. "Essex girl", "trainspotter", "teacher". Think of some other examples in common use. Are stereotypes always necessarily negative or inaccurate?

A stereotypical image of an Italian matriarch which gives rise to many expectations of what she is likely to wear, say, do, and so on.

is a waitress rather than a librarian, this may influence your recall of that person. Cohen (1981) showed participants a 15-minute video of a man and woman eating a meal, and celebrating a birthday. The woman was either described as a waitress or a librarian. Later participants were asked to describe the woman's behaviour, appearance, and personality. Participants were more likely to recall information that was consistent with the stereotype than information that was inconsistent. (Consistent traits were established in a pilot study.)

Furthermore, if the "occupational information" was provided before the videotape then later recall was more accurate than if participants were told the woman's occupation *after* watching the video. The pre-tape information served to generate expectations which enhanced recall. Bartlett (1932) argued that schemas affect the retrieval process rather than initial storage, but Cohen's study shows that schemas and stereotypes are important at both stages of memory: initial storage and retrieval.

Influence of schemas on learning

Schemas and stereotypes are likely to affect the way information is initially perceived and stored, providing eyewitnesses with mistaken memories from the start. One way to study these initial processes is to consider the comprehension process—understanding what you read. Bransford and Johnson (1972) asked participants to answer question on a passage that began as follows:

> *The procedure is actually quite simple. First you arrange items into different groups. Of course one pile may be sufficient depending on how much there is to do. If you have to go somewhere else due to lack of facilities, that is the next step; otherwise you are pretty well set. It is important not to overdo things. That is, it is better to do too few things rather than too many. In the short run this may not seem too important but complications can easily arise. A mistake can be expensive as well …*

After hearing this passage, participants were asked to recall the essential ideas of the passage. Those participants who were told "The passage you will hear will be about washing clothes" before reading the passage had much better recall than those given the title afterwards. The schema "washing clothes" enabled them to organise the incoming data more efficiently and enhanced storage for later recall. Thus, schemas are important in comprehension and this obviously affects subsequent recall. So, in terms of your prior expectations, stereotypes and schemas affect what you observe at the crime scene, and thus what is initially stored in memory.

The influence of schemas on recall

When eyewitnesses are *later* asked to recall information, schema theory also has implications. People may incorporate information received subsequent to the crime. They might hear details of the crime on television and these details are woven into their own memory for the event, or they might discuss the crime with others present. Memon and Wright (1999) described how the testimony of some of the eyewitnesses to events leading up to the Oklahoma bombing became erroneous. The bombers visited a garage two days before the bombing to hire a van. One eyewitness at the garage recalled seeing two men, but in fact one of the men described was another customer. The other two eyewitnesses at the garage originally only recalled one man, but days later they came to "remember" the second man as a result of hearing the first eyewitness's recall, i.e. information received subsequent to the crime influenced their memory.

Evaluation of the reconstructive nature of memory

Schemas influence the way data are stored and can explain how data are actively retrieved. However, some psychologists believe that schema theory goes too far in the direction of claiming that memory is usually inaccurate. We often remember accurately the personal remarks that others make about us, and actors and actresses need to remember their lines perfectly. Such phenomena are not easily explained by schema theory, with its emphasis on the ways in which schemas change what has been presented in systematic ways.

High emotion

In the last section we considered the ways in which memory is affected by emotion. Presumably an eyewitness will be in a state of high emotion at the time the crime is committed, and the psychological evidence suggests this may well influence their recall—for good or ill.

Flashbulb memories

Flashbulb memories are created at times of high emotion. Many people claim that such memories are very accurate and there is some evidence to support this view. For example, Sheingold and Tenney (1982) found that adults could recall details of the birth of a sibling, such as what time of day they were told, who told them, and so on. Other studies have found that such accounts do remain consistent over time, but we have no way of knowing whether the memories are accurate because most studies are retrospective. In other words the researchers ask people at a later date to say what they recall about the original event and then, after a further time interval, retest recall. The accounts may have remained consistent over the test period but that does not tell us anything about how consistent or accurate they were in the first place.

Some studies have attempted to overcome this weakness by using an experimental design. Johnson and Scott (1978) arranged for witnesses to overhear a violent fight taking place in a neighbouring room. In one condition a confederate emerged from the room carrying a letter-opener covered in blood (high stress condition). In the other condition (low stress) the confederate ran through the room holding a pen and covered in grease. The high emotion condition was intended to be sufficiently stressful to arouse a flashbulb memory but the results were mixed. The participants were asked later to identify the culprit. Some participants in the high emotion condition did have better recall but it was not true for all participants. The link between high emotion and flashbulb memory remains unproven but popular.

Are there ethical concerns related to Johnson and Scott's research?

Repressed memories

By no means all emotional experiences produce good recall. For example there are many emotional experiences for which people have very poor memory, and many crime victims remember no details of the crime. This could be because emotion actually caused the memory to be repressed. For this reason hypnosis is sometimes used to try to access memories that cannot be brought to consciousness. Freud used hypnosis as a means of uncovering the painful memories of some of his clients. However, in the end he preferred to use dream analysis to tap the unconscious because he found that memories produced under hypnosis were often unreliable, in the sense that it was not clear that the events remembered had actually happened.

The media have reported numerous cases in which hypnosis seems to have been remarkably effective in bringing forgotten memories to light. For example, the

Israeli National Police Force and many other police forces have used hypnosis to collect relevant evidence from eyewitnesses about matters such as car number plates and the physical features of wanted criminals. The term **hypermnesia** has been used to refer to the enhanced memory allegedly created by hypnosis.

Hypermnesia

Does hypermnesia really exist? In general terms, the hypnotic method is nothing like as effective in enhancing memory as has been claimed. The hypnotised individual is less cautious than normal in his or her reported memories. For example, hypnotised individuals will confidently "recall" events from the future! However, the reduced cautiousness of the hypnotised individual means that some genuine memories that could not otherwise be recalled come to light under hypnosis. The obvious problem is to tell which of the memories reported by hypnotised individuals are genuine and which are false.

Relevant evidence was reported by Putnam (1979). He showed people a videotape of an accident involving a car and a bicycle. They were then asked a series of questions, some of which contained misleading information. Some of the participants were asked these questions while hypnotised, whereas others were not hypnotised. The hypnotised participants made more errors in their answers than did the non-hypnotised ones, and this was especially the case with the misleading questions. These findings led Putnam (1979, p.444) to conclude that participants are "more suggestible in the hypnotic state and are, therefore, more easily influenced by the leading questions."

In recent unpublished work, Green and Lynn asked hypnotised individuals whether they had heard any loud noises during a good night's sleep. In fact, it had previously been ascertained that practically none of them had actually heard a loud noise. Some of the participants were warned while still hypnotised that hypnosis can cause people to misremember what has happened, whereas the others were not. Afterwards, when they were no longer hypnotised, the participants were asked whether they had heard a loud noise. Of those who had not been warned, 44% reported hearing a loud noise; in contrast, only 28% of those warned did so. These findings suggest that false memories can be planted in the mind, and that specific warnings can reduce the likelihood of such "memories" occurring.

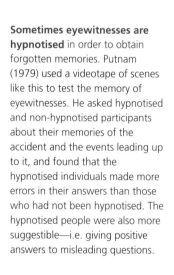

Sometimes eyewitnesses are hypnotised in order to obtain forgotten memories. Putnam (1979) used a videotape of scenes like this to test the memory of eyewitnesses. He asked hypnotised and non-hypnotised participants about their memories of the accident and the events leading up to it, and found that the hypnotised individuals made more errors in their answers than those who had not been hypnotised. The hypnotised people were also more suggestible—i.e. giving positive answers to misleading questions.

Leading questions

An eyewitness's testimony about an event can be affected by the questions that are asked. If the experimenter asks, "Did you see the broken headlight?" rather than "Did you see a broken headlight?", the use of "the" suggests there was a broken headlight and therefore the participant goes on to build up a memory for that headlight (Loftus & Zanni, 1975). The language used in questioning eyewitnesses may alter what they remember. Loftus has conducted a number of studies that demonstrate this (see the Key Study below). This shows that leading questions affect post-event information. That is, information provided after the event has occurred and then changes the actual memory you have stored. Lindsay (1990) showed that the actual memory had genuinely changed in an experiment where participants were later told that the post-event information was wrong. Memory for the incident was still distorted by the post-event information, suggesting that this information had indeed changed memory.

There have been other experimental demonstrations of the effects of language on memory. A classic study was conducted by Carmichael et al. (1932). They showed their participants a series of drawings, and told them that each drawing resembled some well-known object. For example, one drawing which was of a segment of a circle was labelled either as a crescent moon or the letter "C" (see the

Do you think different cultures think differently as a consequence of their different beliefs about the world? How might this affect memory?

The effects of language on recall

Some studies have focused on the unreliability of eyewitness memories and the ways in which such memories can be distorted after the incident. Loftus and Palmer (1974) showed their participants a series of projected slides of a multiple-car accident. The participants then answered specific questions. Some were asked "About how fast were the cars going when they smashed into each other?", whereas for others the verb "hit" was substituted for "smashed into". The estimated speed was affected by the verb used, averaging 41 mph when the verb "smashed" was used, versus 34 mph when "hit" was used. Thus, the information implicit in the question affected memory, even though the questions apparently only differed slightly.

KEY STUDY EVALUATION — Loftus and Palmer

A major limitation of most studies on the effects of post-event information is that they have focused on memory for peripheral details (e.g. presence or absence of broken glass). As Fruzzetti et al. (1992) pointed out, it is harder to distort eyewitnesses' memory by misleading post-event information for key details (e.g. the murder weapon) than for minor details.

The studies by Loftus were well-controlled experiments, although as is common, students were used as participants and it could be argued that students are not necessarily representative of the general population.

The experiment also lacks ecological validity, in that the participants only witnessed a video clip, and it could be said that this would lack the emotional effects of witnessing a real-life accident.

One week later, all the participants were asked the following question: "Did you see any broken glass?" There was actually no broken glass, but 32% of the participants who had been asked previously about speed using the verb "smashed" said they had seen broken glass. In contrast, only 14% of the participants asked using the verb "hit" said they had seen broken glass. Thus, the change of only one word in a question heard a week earlier had a major effect on the participants' memory!

Loftus later showed that even small differences in the way in which a question is asked can have a marked effect. Loftus and Zanni (1975) showed their participants a short film of a car accident. Some of them were asked "Did you see a broken headlight?', whereas others were asked "Did you see the broken headlight?" There was no broken headlight in the film, but the latter question implies there was. Only 7% of those asked about a broken headlight said they had seen it, against 17% of those asked about the broken headlight.

Discussion points

1. How confident can we be that such laboratory-based findings resemble what would be found in the real world?

2. What are some of the practical implications of this research?

■ Activity: Test out the research by Carmichael et al. by showing the pictures to people. For some participants, use the word list on the left, and for other people use the word list on the right. Test recall after a few days by asking them to draw what they remember. If you show the drawings to an independent judge, are the pictures more like the original drawing or more like one of the words on the list? Are they most like the words the participants were given?

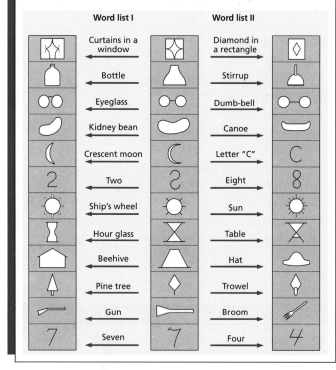

activity on the left). The participants' subsequent reproductions from memory were influenced by the verbal labels provided for each object.

Face recognition

Much eyewitness testimony involves identifying a person glimpsed in poor conditions. The data are often incomplete and therefore recall is prone to be influenced by schemas and stereotypes. Under normal conditions, how do people recognise faces?

Object recognition

The process of object recognition generally has been a matter of interest for psychologists. Template theorists suggest that we have a store of templates for different patterns and these are matched with the incoming stimulus. The problem with this explanation is that one would need a huge number of templates, and it would take a long time to find the right match. Feature detection is an alternative model which proposes that we look for certain features of an object. For instance, when searching a list of letters for an "A" we look for straight lines. It is therefore easier to find an "A" in a list of rounded letters (such as "O" and "G") than in a list of letters with similar features (such as "M" and "H"). Indeed, this is what Neisser (1964) found.

When you see an object such as a table, information from your senses will tell you its size, shape, and colour, but you will need to add meaning to this sensory information to know what the object is used for.

The difference between recognising an object and a face

There is evidence that the process of face recognition differs from object recognition in major ways. There is evidence from studies of people with brain damage that the two processes are governed by different areas of the brain. Patients with *prosopagnosia* cannot recognise familiar faces but they can identify familiar objects. This is not because prosopagnosic patients cannot make the fine discriminations necessary for face recognition. DeRenzi (1986) studied one patient and found that he was quite good at, for example, recognising his own handwriting as different from someone else's, but was unable to recognise relatives by sight (he could recognise their voices). This does suggest that there is a special area of the brain involved in face recognition.

Configuration

When recognising faces there is evidence that people do use information about individual features (such as eye colour) but they also use information about the overall arrangement of the features. In fact configuration may be more important for recognition of faces. Young, Hellawell, and Hay (1987) constructed faces by combining the top half of a famous person's face with the bottom half of another famous person. When these combined pictures were aligned as closely as possible, participants found it harder to identify the two contributing people than when they were not as closely aligned. Presumably the close alignment produced a new configuration which interfered with face recognition.

Identikit pictures

In eyewitness identification the police often use Identikit pictures of faces. This involves constructing a face on a feature-by-feature basis. The fact that this is a "features" rather than a "configuration" approach may lessen its value because, as we have seen, face recognition relies more on the latter. A further problem for Identikit faces is that they are motionless whereas our usual interaction with faces is when they are in motion, showing emotional states for example. The importance of these changes was shown in research by Bruce and Valentine (1988). They arranged for participants to see only the motion in faces rather than the features. They did this by attaching lights to a face and filming the face in the dark. Participants could identify the facial expressions (e.g. smiling or frowning) and sometimes could identify the person on the basis of the movements only. This may explain why people appear to perform better in general studies of face recognition than they do in eyewitness identification experiments, because studies of face recognition use the same stimuli (i.e. photographs) at both acquisition and testing. For real identification, eye witnesses have to match Identikit pictures to the real thing, and there is a less good match.

Unfamiliar faces

Perhaps most important of all is the distinction between familiar and unfamiliar faces. In eyewitness testimony, an individual is usually asked to recognise an unfamiliar face. People have excellent memories for familiar faces. As we have seen earlier, Bahrick et al. (1975) demonstrated that people can still recognise the school photographs of their classmates 35 years later. But this is different from recognising the face of someone you have only seen once. Bruce and Young (1986) have proposed a model for face recognition which suggests that there are two different mechanisms for familiar and unfamiliar face recognition. There is again evidence from the study of brain-damaged patients to support this idea. It has been suggested that the recognition of unfamiliar faces involves feature detection (as in Identikit photographs) whereas familiar face recognition involves configural recognition (Yin, 1969).

How Can Evidence Be Made More Reliable?

Many innocent people have been put in prison purely on the basis of eyewitness testimony. Mistakes by eyewitnesses may occur because of what happens at the time of the crime or incident, or because of what happens thereafter. Perhaps the most obvious reason for mistaken testimony is that the eyewitness was not paying enough attention to the incident and has used subsequent information to "enhance" their recollection.

Implications for police procedures

It follows from the research we have discussed that the questions asked during a police interview may distort an eyewitness's memory, and thus reduce its reliability. What happened until fairly recently in the United Kingdom was that an eyewitness's account of what had happened was repeatedly interrupted. The interruptions made it hard for the eyewitness to concentrate fully on the process of retrieval, and thus reduced recall. As a result of psychological research, the Home Office issued guidelines recommending that police interviews should proceed from free recall to general open-ended questions, concluding with more specific questions.

Are there any other changes that have been (or should be) introduced to improve eyewitness testimony? Geiselman et al. (1985) argued that interview techniques should take account of some basic characteristics of human memory:

- Memory traces are complex, and contain various features and/or kinds of information.
- The effectiveness of a retrieval cue depends on the extent to which the information it contains overlaps with information stored in the memory trace, this is the encoding specificity principle (see page 55).
- Various retrieval cues may permit access to any given memory trace, for example, if the name of an acquaintance cannot be retrieved, it may be recalled if other information is used as a retrieval cue (e.g. forming an image of him or her, thinking of the names of the person's friends). Re-enactments of crimes are a means of providing cues to retrieve memories.

What empirical evidence demonstrated the value of retrieval cues?

Geiselman et al. used these considerations to develop the basic **cognitive interview**. The eyewitness tries to recreate mentally the context that existed at the time of the crime, including environmental and internal (e.g. mood state) information. The eyewitness then simply reports everything he or she can think of relating to the incident, even if the information is fragmented. In addition, the eyewitness reports the details of the incident in various orders, and from various perspectives (e.g. that of another eyewitness).

Geiselman et al. compared the effectiveness of the basic cognitive interview with that of the standard police interview. The average number of correct statements produced by eyewitnesses was 41.1 using the basic cognitive interview, compared to only 29.4 using the standard police interview. Fisher et al. (1987) devised an enhanced cognitive interview, and showed that it was even more effective than the basic cognitive interview. The enhanced cognitive interview includes the main aspects of the basic cognitive interview. However, it also makes use of the following recommendations (Roy, 1991, p.399):

One method used to produce lots of ideas is called "brainstorming", where all ideas are received without criticism. How reliable would such evidence be?

> *Investigations should minimise distractions, induce the eyewitness to speak slowly, allow a pause between the response and next question, tailor language to suit the individual eyewitness, follow up with interpretive comment, try to reduce eyewitness anxiety, avoid judgmental and personal comments, and always review the eyewitness's description of events or people under investigation.*

Expert witnesses

In important criminal cases psychologists are sometimes asked to explain the reliability of eyewitness testimony to the jury. They are called in as **expert witnesses**. Elizabeth Loftus, mentioned earlier, acted as an expert witness at the trial of José Garcia who was accused of robbing a liquor store in California and killing one of two clerks in the store. The only evidence of Garcia's guilt was the eyewitness testimony of the surviving clerk, Joseph Melville. Loftus was called in to help the jury decide how much weight to give to Melville's testimony. For example, she was questioned about the fact that Melville was only asked to identify the attacker two weeks after the incident. What effect might a two-week interval have on Melville's recall? Loftus answered that people do forget over time. Another question was about the relationship between stress and memory. Loftus answered that situations of high stress can lead to impaired memory. She was also asked about the fact that Garcia was a Mexican-American; could his race have aroused a stereotyped perception by Melville? Loftus answered that people have been found to be less good at cross-racial identification and memory is influenced by stereotypes (Loftus, 1979).

In the case of this trial, the jury could not agree on a verdict and Garcia was acquitted. Presumably they were not convinced about the accuracy of the eyewitness testimony. One note of criticism: The evidence presented by Loftus was based on laboratory experiments and may not be valid in real life.

> You have reached the end of the chapter on cognitive psychology. Cognitive psychology is an approach or perspective in psychology. The material in this chapter has exemplified the way that cognitive psychologists explain behaviour. They look at behaviour in terms of the way that it can be explained by reference to mental (cognitive) processes. This is sometimes regarded as a rather "mechanistic" approach to the study of behaviour because it focuses on machine-like processes and tends to exclude the influence of social or emotional factors.

CHAPTER SUMMARY

Short-term memory and long-term memory

❖ Memory and learning involve the retention of information but the *study* of memory focuses on cognitive processes and retrieval. Memory tests assess learning. Psychologists distinguish between short-term and long-term memory in terms of capacity and duration.

❖ Short-term and long-term memory differ in terms of capacity and duration. Span measures indicate a capacity of about seven items for short-term memory. This can be increased by chunking. Capacity for short-term memory can also be seen in recency effects, caused by higher recall for the last few items in a list. The Brown-Peterson technique is a means of demonstrating duration of short-term memory. If rehearsal is prevented there is little recall beyond 18 seconds. Short-term memory uses a mainly acoustic code unlike long-term memory which is more semantically coded. Evidence from studies of brain-damaged individuals also supports a distinction between short- and long-term memory, as well as for different kinds of short-term memory. This research may lack ecological validity. The same problem may apply to all memory research.

❖ Long-term memory is coded differently from short-term memory, and has unlimited capacity. Its duration has been demonstrated in studies of very long-term memories (VLTMs). It is useful to distinguish between different varieties of long-term memory. Episodic memory is concerned with events, and semantic memory contains knowledge about the world. Memory research often tests explicit memory rather than implicit memory, when you learn something in the absence of a direct instruction. Declarative knowledge is about "knowing that" whereas procedural knowledge is "knowing how". The latter typically involves implicit memory. These distinctions are important for criticising the validity of memory research.

❖ Models of memory offer accounts of how information is transferred from short- to long-term memory. The multi-store model, which supports the distinction between three separate stores (sensory, short- and long-term stores), suggests that transfer occurs by means of verbal rehearsal. The model is supported by research but may be an oversimplification and less true of real-life memory performance.

❖ The working memory model offers a more accurate representation of short-term memory. It consists of: a central executive, an articulatory-phonological loop, and a visuo-spatial sketch pad. This model has the benefit of accounting for empirical findings, such as different kinds of short-term memory, as well as representing more active processing.

❖ The third model is the levels of processing theory which proposes that material that is processed more deeply will be better remembered. "Depth" can be provided through meaning, elaboration, organisation, or distinctiveness. This theory also has some empirical support but may do little more than describe rather than explain memory processes Another problem is that the concept of depth is circular.

Forgetting

❖ Forgetting may be due to a lack of availability or a lack of accessibility.

❖ In short-term memory the three most likely explanations are trace decay, interference, and diversion of attention, which are all examples of lack of availability.

❖ Lack of availability in long-term memory could also be due to trace decay and interference. However, trace decay is unlikely to be a major factor in long-term forgetting. Proactive and retroactive interference account for forgetting in long-term memory when stimulus material is similar, but may not apply to real life.

❖ Lack of accessibility can be explained in terms of cue-dependent forgetting and emotional factors, such as repression. The encoding specificity principle states that the closer cues are to the actual memory the more effective they are. Internal context (e.g. mood) and external context (e.g. a room) can also act as cues. Repression occurs as a result of increased anxiety and may explain forgetting.

❖ Emotion may lead to increased memorability, as in flashbulb memories. Such memories may be more accurate and longer-lasting because of hormones produced at times of high emotion. This might suggest that such memories have an adaptive function.

Critical issue—
Eyewitness testimony

❖ Eyewitness testimony tends to be unreliable yet many jurors find it highly persuasive. This unreliability can be explained in terms of the reconstructive nature of memory (schema theory) and the effects of language on memory (leading questions). Schema theory offers a different perspective on memory that describes memory retrieval as a process of active reconstruction relying on, and being biased by, schemas and stereotypes. Schemas affect recall because they affect both initial learning (comprehension) and subsequent retrieval. The weakness in schema theory is that it cannot account for occasions when memory is extremely accurate.

❖ Unreliability may also be due to the emotional state of the eyewitness at the time of the crime. The concept of flashbulb memory suggests that recall may be improved because of high emotion. Alternatively emotion may create repressed memories, which can be accessed by hypnosis. Enhanced memories (hypermnesia) may bring out inaccessible memories but such recall tends to be influenced by leading questions.

❖ Leading questions are a third explanation for lack of reliability of eyewitness testimony. When eyewitnesses are questioned after an event (post-event information) the language used may affect the way information is stored and thus affect later recall. There is general evidence that language effects recall. The research on leading questions, however, is based on laboratory studies and may not apply to real life.

❖ Face recognition is an important and often unreliable element of eyewitness testimony. Identikit pictures may not be effective because they are based more on feature detection than configuration and they are motionless.

Recognition for unfamiliar faces probably involves quite a different mechanism from the one involved in detection of familiar faces. Altogether this means that research on face recognition may not always apply to eyewitness testimony.

❖ There are implications from psychological research for improvements in the collection and use of eyewitness testimony. Police might develop the basic cognitive interview by increasing contextual cues to enhance recall, minimising distractions and reducing eyewitness anxiety. Psychologists can be used as expert witnesses in criminal trials to advise jurors on the reliability of eyewitness testimony.

FURTHER READING

Nearly all the topics discussed in this chapter are dealt with in Chapter 4 of M.W. Eysenck (1993) *Principles of cognitive psychology* (Hove, UK: Psychology Press). A much fuller account of human memory is contained in M.W. Eysenck and M.T. Keane (1995) *Cognitive psychology: A student's handbook (3rd Edn.)* (Hove, UK: Psychology Press). Several key topics in memory are discussed in an accessible way in J.A. Groeger (1997) *Memory and remembering: Everyday memory in context* (Harlow, UK: Addison Wesley Longman). There is an interesting discussion of eyewitness testimony in Chapter 6 of R. Brown (1986) *Social psychology: The second edition* (London: Free Press).

Revision Questions

The examination questions aim to *sample* the material in this whole chapter. For advice on how to answer such questions, refer to Chapter 1 Section 3.

Whenever you are asked to describe a study try to include some or all of the following details: research aim(s), participants, research method (e.g. experiment or observation), procedure, findings, and conclusions.

You will always have a choice of two questions in the AQA AS-level exam and 30 minutes in which to answer the question you choose:

Question 1
a. Outline *two* explanations of forgetting in long-term memory. (3 marks + 3 marks)
b. For *one* of these explanations describe a relevant research study. (6 marks)
c. Give *two* criticisms of this study. (3 marks + 3 marks)
d. "Some psychologists believe there are two different memory stores: short-term memory and long-term memory." To what extent does research support this view? (12 marks)

Question 2
a. Describe *two* ways that short-term memory differs from long-term memory. (3 marks + 3 marks)
b. Outline *one* theory or model of memory. (6 marks)
c. Describe *one* research study that supports the theory/model you have described. (6 marks)
d. "It is clear that eyewitness testimony is entirely unreliable." To what extent does psychological research support this view of eyewitness testimony? (12 marks)

Developmental psychology is an approach or perspective in psychology. The material in this chapter will exemplify the way that developmental psychologists explain behaviour.

Developmental psychology is concerned with the way people change as they get older. Some of these changes are innate. For example, puberty occurs as a result of a hormonal surge. This is biologically driven and innate, although it happens late in childhood. Many of the changes that occur during development, however, are a result of experience. For example, a girl learns many aspects of feminine behaviour by modelling herself on women around her. Therefore it is most accurate to say that developmental changes occur as a result of an *interaction* between innate factors and experience: these two forces are called nature and nurture. For example, your height is in part determined by your genetic make-up (nature), and partly due to the quality of your diet (nurture).

A developmental psychologist wants to describe *how* children (and adults) develop and also explain *why* they develop as they do.

3

Developmental Psychology
Attachments in Development

"I really love your new trainers."
"Yes, I do too, I have become quite attached to them."

People develop attachments to all sorts of things—footwear, favourite restaurants, friends, lovers, and parents. You form attachments throughout your life but possibly the most important ones are those that are formed early in development.

> *Think of parent swans and their cygnets swimming along in single file. It is as if they were joined by an invisible piece of string.*

> *Think of a mother sitting on a park bench on a warm spring day. Her two-year-old son toddles around on the grass. Every now and again he returns to his mother just to touch her knee or smile at her. He never wanders far. Again, it is as if there is an invisible tie between them.*

Psychologists suggest that the early attachment formed between an infant and his or her caregivers is fundamentally important for successful emotional development.

Attachment is like a piece of invisible string that binds individuals in a way that allows healthy development, as you will see in this chapter. The tie is *reciprocal*: parents are as attached to their children as the children are to their parents.

This chapter explores one topic in developmental psychology: attachment. We will consider how attachment develops and why it happens at all, as well as other related issues:

- *Section 7: The development and variety of attachments.* When do infants first become attached? We will consider the sequence of attachment development, individual differences, such as secure versus insecure attachment, and cultural variation. Finally we will discuss the theories that can account for why children form attachments, and why they become attached to one person rather than another.
- *Section 8: Deprivation and privation.* What happens when children are separated from their main caregivers? In the short term infants become anxious. We will examine how this subsequently affects the child's development, both in the short and long term. An important distinction has been made between deprivation (separation from caregivers) and privation (a lack of attachment).
- *Section 9: Critical issue—Day care.* Children in day care experience short-term separations from their main caregivers. How does this affect their emotional and cognitive development?

SECTION 7
The Development and Variety of Attachments

What is Attachment?

According to Shaffer (1993), an attachment is "a close emotional relationship between two persons, characterised by mutual affection and a desire to maintain proximity [closeness]." It is an emotional relationship that is experienced throughout the lifespan. When you are attached to someone, it makes you feel good to be in that person's company and also makes you feel anxious when they are not there. You may also experience a longing to be reunited. This is the "desire to maintain proximity."

There are other characteristics of attachment. Maccoby (1980) identified four key behaviours:

- Seeking proximity to primary caregiver. The infant tries to stay close to its caregiver or "attachment figure."
- Distress on separation. When caregiver and infant are separated, *both* experience feelings of distress.
- Pleasure when reunited. Attachment is demonstrated not just in the distress experienced on separation but also pleasure experienced when being reunited.
- General orientation of behaviour towards primary caregiver. The infant is aware of his or her caregiver at all times and may frequently make contact for reassurance.

Do these characteristics describe how you feel and behave towards someone you love (mother, father, boyfriend, or girlfriend)?

Attachment, as we said, occurs across the lifespan but the earliest attachment, between an infant and his or her caregivers, has a special role to play in development, as we will see.

It is important to recognise that all attachments are *reciprocal*. Both partners must be involved in order for the bond to be forged. Maurer and Maurer (1989) wrote "Attachments are not formed by a congenital glue held in limited supply: they are welded in the heat of interactions." In other words, attachments depend on interaction rather than two people just being together.

There are a number of questions that we can ask about the development of attachments. Why do infants form attachments? When does an infant begin to form an attachment? Who do infants become attached to?

Why Do Infants Form Attachments?

Attachment appears to serve a number of purposes, some of which are immediate whereas others are longer-term.

Immediate benefits

There are certain behaviours that characterise attachment: distress on separation, pleasure when reunited, seeking out the attachment figure and general orientation to each other.

Young animals are relatively helpless at birth and need caregivers to provide food and protection in order to ensure their survival. One can see why a young animal who is not cared for in this way would be much less likely to survive. This means that any animal who has an **innate** behaviour that will ensure closeness between itself and a caregiver will be more likely to survive. Attachment is just such a behaviour and the drive to become attached is found in both young animals and their caregivers. Attachment is likely to be an innate behaviour because it increases reproductive success.

Long-term benefits of attachment

In the short term, attachment helps a young animal to survive. In the long term, attachment provides a basis for emotional relationships. The early bond between caregiver and infant is the basis for all later emotional involvements. In other words, the infant is learning how to form an emotional or "love" relationship. According to Eibl-Eibesfeldt (1995) only warm-blooded animals form these bonds. Fish and reptiles may gather in groups but they form no bonds of love. Where animals care for their young, long-lasting affectionate bonds develop.

John Bowlby (1969) suggested that the means by which the early attachment relationship influences emotional development is via an **internal working model** about relationships. This model or schema represents the infant's knowledge about his or her relationship with the primary caregiver. The model generates expectations about other relationships so that whatever this child's primary relationship was like will lead the child to have expectations about other relationships. The model will predict how other people will behave and react to the child, about whether to trust other people, and so on—in short it is a template for all future relationships.

Bowlby's concept would lead us to expect a correlation between early attachment experiences and later relationships. There is evidence to support this expectation. For example, Hazan and Shaver (1987) found that romantic types were related to early styles of attachment (see Key Study on the next page). Grossmann and Grossmann (1991) found that children who were securely attached to their mothers as infants enjoyed close friendships later in childhood, whereas those who were avoidant or anxious reported either having no friends or few friends.

Who are you most attached to? How do you think this attachment has affected your development?

Perhaps even more importantly a relationship has been found between early attachment experiences and later styles of parenting. Quinton, Rutter, and Liddle (1988) studied women who had spent much of their early lives in institutions where they had little opportunity to form any attachments. Quinton and Rutter found that the women interacted poorly with their own children and concluded that the institutionalised women were less sensitive, less supportive, and less warm than a group of non-institutionalised women.

Evaluation of early attachments

The research evidence suggests that early attachments form a basis for later relationships because they act as a model for these relationships. However, there are many other factors that will also influence how an individual copes with later relationships, for example an experience of divorce during childhood. There are

Parenting is one of the most important relationships in adult life. A person's attachment to their own parents will influence their subsequent relationship with their own child.

The kind of lover you are may be related to the kind of attachment you had as an infant.

What is a "biased sample" and what effect does it have on Hazan and Shaver's research findings?

The love quiz

Could it be that early attachment type can be used to explain later styles of adult romantic love? Hazan and Shaver (1987) proposed that the reason adults experience different kinds of romantic relationships is because of their different experiences as infants. To test this hypothesis they devised a "love quiz", a questionnaire that could assess an individual's style of love as well as their attachment type. The quiz consisted of two components:

1. A measure of attachment style. A simple adjective checklist of childhood relationships with parents, and parents' relationships with each other.

2. The love experience questionnaire which assessed individuals' beliefs about romantic love, such as whether it lasted for ever, whether it was easy to find, how much trust there was in a romantic relationship, and so on.

The love quiz was printed in the *Rocky Mountain News*, a local newspaper, and readers were asked to send in their responses. The researchers analysed the first 620 replies received, from people aged between 14 and 82. Hazan and Shaver used the answers to (1) classify respondents as secure, ambivalent, or avoidant "types" based on their description of their childhood experiences, and (2) classify them on their adult style of romantic love. Hazan and Shaver found a consistent relationship between attachment "type" and adult style of love:

- Secure types described their love experiences as happy, friendly, and trusting. They emphasised being able to accept their partner regardless of any faults and their relationships tended to be more enduring.

- Anxious ambivalent types experienced love as involving obsession, a desire for reciprocation, emotional highs and lows, and extreme sexual attraction and jealousy. They worried that their partners didn't really love them or might abandon them.

- Avoidant lovers typically feared intimacy, emotional highs and lows, and jealousy. They believed that they did not need love to be happy.

These attachment "types" are based on research examined later in this section using the Strange Situation (see page 88).

KEY STUDY EVALUATION — Hazan and Shaver

One major problem with this study was the fact that some of the data were collected retrospectively. An individual's recall of their childhood experiences might not be very reliable and it might have been biased by subsequent relationship experiences.

A second problem is that other data were collected through self-report questionnaires. People don't always give truthful answers to questionnaires. They may prefer to present themselves in a desirable way rather than telling you their true feelings.

Finally, the sample was biased because the participants were self-selected. Only certain types of people complete and send in questionnaires. To balance this out, Hazan and Shaver conducted a second study using 108 undergraduates (which is also a biased sample). The results were very similar, although the association was not as strong. This may be because the younger participants had less experience of adult relationships.

Discussion points

1. Can you think of another way of explaining the correlation between attachment type and later love relationships?
2. What ethical issues are raised by this research?

also important individual differences. For example, Lewis et al. (1984) looked at behaviour problems in older children and found that there was a greater incidence of maladjustment in *boys* who had been classed as insecure at an earlier age, but the same was not true for girls. Therefore we must be very cautious about the generalisations that we make.

Perhaps more fundamentally, Harris (1998) suggested that the concept of one internal working model is just wrong. She claimed that the infant is well aware that the model is only of use with a particular person and will not function with, for example, an indifferent babysitter or a playful peer. So you can see that not everyone accepts that attachments are the basis for later relationships. The alternative would be that each of us has an innate **temperament** which determines how well we form relationships. If you are good at forming relationships this would explain why you had good early attachments and were also good at later relationships. Individuals who are innately less good at forming relationships will form poorer early attachments and poorer later relationships.

When Does An Infant Begin To Form An Attachment?

Stages in the development of attachment

The stage approach is a popular way to describe how children develop—to identify the ages at which certain typical changes occur, such as when an infant first crawls and then walks, and talks. Bowlby (1969) described four phases in the development of attachments, which are shown in a box on page 94.

Schaffer and Emerson (1964, see Key Study overleaf) also developed a stage theory of attachment, arguing that infants go through three stages in the early development of attachments to others:

1. *The asocial stage*, which lasts for about the first six weeks of life. During this stage, emotional behaviour such as smiling or crying does not seem to be directed specifically at any given individual.
2. The stage of *indiscriminate attachments*, which lasts between the ages of about six weeks and seven months. During this stage, the infant seeks attention from numerous different people, and is generally content when he or she receives attention from them.
3. The stage of *specific attachments*, which starts at about seven months of age and continues to eleven months. The infant in this stage typically forms a strong attachment to one individual, but good attachments to others often follow shortly thereafter.

STAGES OF ATTACHMENT		
Asocial stage	**Indiscriminate attachment**	**Specific attachments**
0–6 weeks	6 weeks–7 months	7–11 months
Smiling and crying, not directed at any special individuals	Attention sought from different individuals	Strong attachment to one individual. Good attachments to others often follow

Evaluation of Schaffer and Emerson's stage theory

This stage theory appears to be generally correct, in as much as infants are easily comforted by anyone but, as they get older, they are less willing to be separated from their mother-figure. If their caregiver does leave the infant, he or she will show **separation anxiety**. This is the main characteristic of being attached. We know when an infant is attached because he or she recognises the *absence* of an attachment figure and becomes anxious. Up until this point such an absence causes little concern.

In addition infants also start to show **stranger anxiety**—when a strange person comes close and tries to interact, the infant may withdraw and show signs of distress. Both of these forms of anxiety show that the infant now has formed

Schaffer and Emerson's study of Glasgow babies

Schaffer and Emerson (1964) designed a large-scale longitudinal study to find out more information about the development of attachment. Over a period of two years they followed 60 infants from a mainly working class area of Glasgow, keeping a detailed record of their observations. The infants were observed every four weeks until they were 1 year old and then again at 18 months. At the start of the investigation the youngest participant was 5 weeks and the oldest was 23 weeks old.

Attachment was measured in two ways:

- Using **separation protest** in seven everyday situations. The infant was left alone in a room, left with other people, left in his/her pram outside the house, left in his/her pram outside the shops, left in his/her cot at night, put down after being held by an adult, or passed by while sitting in his/her cot or chair.

- Using **stranger anxiety**. Every visit started with the researcher approaching the infant and noting at what point the infant started to whimper, thus displaying anxiety.

Separation protest and stranger anxiety are signs that an attachment has formed. Before this stage of specific attachments infants show neither of these behaviours.

Schaffer and Emerson found that:

1. Half of the children showed their first specific attachment between 25 and 32 weeks (6–8 months). Fear of strangers occurred about a month later in all the children.

2. The intensity of attachment peaked in the first month after attachment behaviour first appeared, as measured by the strength of separation protest. However there were large individual differences. Intensely attached infants had mothers who responded quickly to their demands (high responsiveness) and who offered the child the most interaction. Infants who were weakly attached had mothers who failed to interact.

3. Multiple attachment: soon after one main attachment was formed, the infants also became attached to other people. By 18 months very few (13%) were attached to only one person, 31% had five or more attachments, such as the father, grandparent, or older sibling. In 65% of the children the first specific attachment was to the mother, and in a further 30% the mother was the first joint object of attachment.

4. Time spent with infant: in 39% of the cases the person who usually fed, bathed, and changed the child was not the child's primary attachment object. In other words, many of the mothers were not the person who performed these tasks yet they were the main attachment object.

KEY STUDY EVALUATION — Schaffer and Emerson

This study remains one of the largest longitudinal study of infant attachment behaviour and a classic, despite the fact that it was conducted more than 35 years ago. Criticisms can be made about the methodology, perhaps most importantly about some of the data collection. The data were collected either by direct observation or from the record kept by mothers. These are both prone to bias and inaccuracy. Mothers were asked to record situations where separation protest was shown, and to whom these protests were directed. It is quite possible that a busy mother may have had to manufacture these records some days after the events and her memory would have been influenced by expectations. On the other hand, such data would have been more accurate than the retrospective recollections used in many studies, and would have had more ecological validity than data collected in laboratory observations (e.g. the Strange Situation).

Discussion points

1. In what way might the sample used here make it difficult to generalise from these data?

2. Compare the method of measuring attachment behaviour used here with the methods used in the Strange Situation (see page 88). Suggest at least one advantage and one disadvantage of the method used in Schaffer and Emerson's study.

schemas for known and unknown people, and has reached an emotional stage of development where the unknown creates a fear response.

However, the asocial stage may not be quite as asocial as Schaffer and Emerson presumed. Subsequent research has shown that very young infants actually do respond to one special person in a unique way. Carpenter (1975) demonstrated that two-week-old infants can recognise their mother's face and voice. He set up a

Infants distrust strangers and cling to familiar people.

situation in which infants looked at a face while hearing a voice. Sometimes the face and the voice belonged to the same person, and sometimes they did not. The infants looked at the face for the longest time when it was the mother's face, and when it was accompanied by her voice. More convincing evidence that the infants recognised their mother's face and voice was obtained when they were presented with their mother's face but an unfamiliar voice, or vice versa. Most of the infants found this distressing, and rapidly looked away from the face.

Might Carpenter have predicted that infants would become distressed by seeing their mother's face but hearing someone else's voice? If so, to what extent was this study ethical?

There are some problems of interpretation with Carpenter's study, because those rating the behaviour of the infants knew which condition was being used at any time. However, improved versions of Carpenter's design have been used successfully in several later studies and the findings have been supported by other research. For example, Bushnell, Sai, and Mullin (1989) presented *two-day-old* babies with the faces of their mother and a female stranger until they had spent a total of 20 seconds fixating on one of the faces. Almost two-thirds of them showed a preference for their mother over the stranger, indicating that they had some ability to recognise their own mother within a few days of birth.

How else could the problems of interpretation of Carpenter's study have been overcome?

A critical period

Another way to consider the question "When do attachments form?" is in terms of the concept of a **critical period**. This concept comes from the study of biological development. In the case of biological characteristics, development has to take place during a set period, otherwise it won't take place at all. For instance, in the development of the human embryo the arms begin to develop between day 24 and day 26. Any interference with development at this critical stage will permanently affect the limb's development—it won't happen.

Ethologists suggested that this principle of a critical period might apply to attachment. One ethologist, Konrad Lorenz, found that the young of some species of birds tended to follow the first moving object they saw on hatching, and they continued to follow it thereafter. This is known as **imprinting**. It only occurs during

Lorenz hatched some goslings and arranged it so that he would be the first thing that they saw. From then on they followed him everywhere and showed no recognition of their actual mother. The goslings formed a picture (imprint) of the object they were to follow.

The process of imprinting results in an "imprint", an indelible impression of that thing.

a short critical period in the bird's life. When imprinting has occurred, it tends to be irreversible, in the sense that the bird will continue to follow the object on which it is imprinted. Imprinting results in the formation of a bond between caregiver and its young. Like attachment, this **bonding** process is desirable because it means the offspring are more likely to survive and therefore the parents' genes are passed on.

The chief characteristics of imprinting are proposed to be:

1. It occurs during a critical period. If the infant is not exposed to a "mother" within a critical time window, then imprinting will not take place.
2. It is irreversible. Once an imprint is formed it cannot be changed.
3. It has lasting consequences. It has consequences in the short term for safety and food, but it also affects the individual in the long term because it acts as a template for future reproductive partners. For example, Immelmann (1972) arranged for zebra finches to be raised by Bengalese finches, and vice versa. In later years, when the finches were given a free choice, they preferred to mate with the species on which they had imprinted.

Imprinting

The BBC television series *Supernature* used imprinting as a means of obtaining spectacular close-up film of geese in flight. A member of the production company made sure he was the first thing a group of goslings saw when they hatched, and from then on the birds followed him everywhere, even into the office! When the geese were young adults, their adopted "parent" took to the skies as a passenger in a microlight aircraft. The geese followed and flew alongside, allowing him to film their flight to produce a truly breathtaking sequence for the television series.

Criticisms of imprinting

These characteristics of imprinting have been challenged to some extent. For example, Guiton (1966) found that he could reverse imprinting in chickens. Guiton's chickens were initially imprinted on some yellow rubber gloves. When the chickens matured, this early imprint acted as a mate template and the chickens tried to mate with the rubber gloves, which appears to support the claims made for imprinting. However, Guiton found that still later, after spending time with their own species, the chickens were able to engage in normal sexual behaviour with their own kind.

It may be that the idea of a critical period is rather too strong and it would be more appropriate to describe it as a **sensitive period**. This shift of emphasis has

CASE STUDY: *Amorous Turkeys*

Some psychologists were conducting research on the effects of hormones on turkeys. In one room there were 35 full-grown male turkeys. If you walked into the room, the turkeys fled to the furthest corner and if you walked towards them, the turkeys slid along the wall to maintain a maximum distance between you and them. This is fairly normal behaviour for wild turkeys. However, in another room, there was a group of turkeys who behaved in a very different manner. These turkeys greeted you by stopping dead in their tracks, fixing their eyes on you, spreading their tail into a full courtship fan, putting their heads down and ponderously walking towards you, all at the same time. Their intention was clearly one of mating. (Fortunately turkeys in mid-courtship are famously slow so it is easy to avoid their advances.)

What was the difference between these two groups? The first set were raised away from humans, whereas the second group had received an injection of the male hormone, testosterone, when they were younger. The hormone created an artificial sensitive period during which the turkeys imprinted on their companion at the time—a male experimenter. Subsequently, these turkeys showed little interest in female turkeys, however they were aroused whenever they saw a male human—displaying their tail feathers and strutting their stuff.

It has been suggested that the reason this learning was so strong and apparently irreversible was because it took place at a time of high arousal—when hormones were administered. In real life, hormones may be involved as well. Perhaps, for these birds, a moving object creates a sense of pleasure and this pleasure triggers the production of endorphins, opiate-like biochemicals produced by the body, which in turn create a state of arousal that is optimal for learning.

(From Howard S. Hoffman, 1996, *Amorous turkeys and addicted ducklings: A search for the causes of social attachment*. Boston, MA: Author's Cooperative.)

resulted from research which showed that, even though imprinting is *less* likely to occur outside a particular time window, imprinting does still occur at other times. The notion of a sensitive period is that imprinting takes place most easily at a certain time but still may happen at any time during development.

Applying imprinting to humans

Bowlby (1969) claimed that something like imprinting occurs in infants. He proposed that infants have an innate tendency to orient towards one individual—attachment. As attachment is innate, it is biological and like all biological mechanisms should have a critical period for its development. Bowlby argued that this critical period ends at some point between 1 and 3 years of age. After that, Bowlby claimed that it would no longer be possible to establish a powerful attachment to the mother or other person.

Klaus and Kennell (1976) were in general agreement with Bowlby (1958) that early contact between infant and mother is of great importance. In fact they argued that there is a *sensitive period* immediately after birth in which bonding (an initial part of the attachment process) can occur through skin-to-skin contact. Klaus and Kennell compared the progress of two groups of infants. One group only had routine contact with their mothers during regular feeding sessions throughout the first three days of life, whereas the other group had extended contact for several hours a day with their mothers over the same period.

Skin-to-skin contact immediately after birth may be very important in establishing a bond between mothers and infants. Klaus and Kennell proposed that this is a sensitive period in the development of attachments.

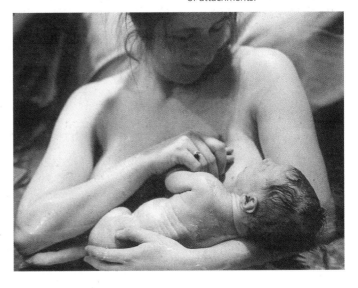

Do you think that there are any ethical issues related to studies such as Klaus and Kennell's?

When the mothers returned to the hospital one month later, there was evidence that more bonding had occurred in the extended contact group than in the routine contact group. During feeding, the extended-contact mothers cuddled and comforted their babies more, and they also maintained more eye contact with them. Even one year later, the extended-contact mothers still behaved in a more soothing and involved way with their infants.

Klaus and Kennell (1982) suggested that it is the **hormones** that are present around the time of birth which make both the mother and infant especially sensitive to bond formation. Indeed, Trevarthan (1979) found unusually high levels of certain hormones present in both mothers and their infants during and immediately after delivery. If a bond is not formed during this hormonal surge, then the mother and infant may less *easily* form a bond, in the same way that imprinting occurs less easily outside the sensitive period.

Evaluation of the skin-to-skin hypothesis

Later research generally failed to repeat the findings reported by Klaus and Kennell (1976). Durkin (1995) pointed out that most of the mothers in the original study were unmarried teenagers from disadvantaged backgrounds; therefore it may not be reasonable to generalise from this rather atypical sample. It is also true that the extended-contact mothers may have become more involved with their babies than the routine-contact mothers because of the special attention they received, rather than because of the hours of skin-to-skin contact they had with their babies.

What is an "atypical sample" and how might this problem be overcome?

Cross-cultural evidence supports these conclusions. Lozoff (1983) reported that mothers were no more affectionate towards their babies in **cultures** that encouraged early bodily contact between mother and baby. Furthermore, mothers in cultures in which early nursing is typical did not show greater bonding with their babies than did mothers in other cultures.

There has been, however, some support for the skin-to-skin hypothesis. De Chateau and Wiberg (1977) found that mothers who had skin-to-skin contact with their unwashed babies immediately after birth, and also immediately put the baby to their breast to suckle, engaged in significantly more kissing and embracing with their infants, and breastfed on average for 2½ months longer than "traditional contact" mothers.

Klaus and Kennell suggested that prolonged skin-to-skin contact between baby and mother gave rise to greater bonding. However, recent research, including cross-cultural studies, indicates that other forms of attention also promote bonding.

The general view nowadays is that the relationship between mother and baby develops and changes over time rather than being fixed shortly after birth, although early bonding experiences may be helpful.

To Whom Do Infants Become Attached?

Schaffer and Emerson's research gave us several answers to this question in the Key Study on page 78. One thing they noted was that infants usually become attached to one person first and this is then followed by attachments to many others. The concept of having one main attachment is called "monotropy". "Monotropy" means "learning towards one thing". Schaffer and Emerson also considered the amount of time spent with caregivers and questioned how this affected the attachment relationship. They found that attachments were not necessarily formed with the person who spent most time with the infant.

We will now consider further evidence.

Monotropy or multiple attachments?

There is considerable debate about whether infants become attached to one person or to many people. To some extent the debate stems from the claim made by Bowlby (1953) that infants have a hierarchy of attachments, at the top of which is one central caregiver. This is called the **monotropy hypothesis**. Many people mistakenly think that Bowlby said this one person was the infant's mother. He suggested that it would *often* be the mother but this was not invariable. When he used the terms "maternal" and "mothering" he did not mean that they were things that had to be done by a woman.

Therefore the importance of monotropy does not lie in the woman's role. The special significance of monotropy, or one primary attachment, is that it alone provides the experience of an intense emotional relationship which forms the basis of the **internal working model**, the **schema** a child has for forming future relationships. Bowlby (1988) said "it is because of this marked tendency to monotropy that we are capable of deep feelings."

Not everyone agrees with Bowlby. The disagreement is not about multiple attachments, as Bowlby said the infant has many attachments. The disagreement is about the relative importance of these attachments. Some psychologists feel that healthy psychological development is *not* best served by having one primary attachment. Thomas (1998) suggests that it might be more desirable to have a network of close attachments to sustain the needs of a growing infant who has a variety of demands for social and emotional interactions. This is certainly true in some cultures, such as Caribbean countries, and even in European culture infants do form several attachments and these are all beneficial probably exactly because of their qualitative differences. For example, fathers' style of play is more often physically stimulating and unpredictable whereas mothers are more likely to hold their infants, soothe them, attend to their needs and read them stories (Parke, 1981).

However, Bowlby (1969) argued that within these multiple attachments there was always a hierarchy, with a qualitatively different relationship at the top. There is **cross-cultural evidence** to support this. For example, Tronick, Morelli, and Ivey (1992) studied an African tribe, the Efe, from Zaire who live in extended family groups. The infants were looked after and even breastfed by different women but usually they slept with their own mother at night. Tronick et al. found that, by the age of 6 months, the infants still did show a preference for their mothers, a single primary attachment.

Quantity or quality?

Whether children form one or multiple attachments, the question remains as to *why* they become attached to any caregiver. Is it simply a consequence of the time spent with a person, i.e. *quantity* of care, or is it more related to the *quality* of care that is received?

Quantity of care
A study by Fox (1977) looked at the effects of time on the closeness of attachment between mother and child. This study involved children growing up in a kibbutz,

Cross-cultural research

There are several reasons for conducting cross-cultural research; that is, research that looks at the customs and practices of different countries and makes comparisons with our own cultural norms. First of all, such research can tell us about what might be universal in human behaviour. If the same behaviours are observed in many different cultures, all of which have different ways of socialising children, then the behaviour may be due to innate (universal) factors rather than learning. The second reason for conducting cross-cultural research is that it offers us insights into our own behaviour. Insights that we may not otherwise be aware of. Perhaps that is the appeal of watching programmes on the television that show foreign lands and different people.

There are some major weaknesses to cross-cultural research. First of all, any sample of a group of people may well be biased and therefore we may be mistaken in thinking that the observations made of one group of people are representative of that culture. Second, where the observations are made by an outsider, that person's own culture will bias how they interpret the data they observe. Finally, the psychological tools that are used to measure people, such as IQ tests and the Strange Situation, are designed in one particular culture and based on assumptions of that culture. They may not have any meaning in another culture.

Therefore cross-cultural research has the potential to be highly informative about human behaviour but also has many important weaknesses.

a kind of farming community in Israel where many things are shared including infant care. The children spent most time of their time in an infant house being cared for by a nurse or *metapelet*, and visiting their parents every evening. Fox found that the infants were nevertheless most strongly attached to their mothers. We should note, however, that the *metapelets* had to divide their attention among many children and had less interest in any one individual, which might explain why the children were usually less attached to their *metapelet* than their mothers.

Children who spend the majority of their waking days away from their parents in day care nevertheless remain more attached to their parents, as we will see later in Section 9. Perhaps food might be a more significant issue than time. It might be that children become most attached to the person who feeds them. However, Harlow's research (1959, see Key Study opposite) strongly showed that attachment was quite unrelated to feeding. In this study rhesus monkeys were "raised" by wire "mothers". The monkeys appeared to be more attached to the "mother" who was cloth-covered and thus offered contact comfort, rather than the mother who supplied food. We must consider the fact that this evidence is from non-human animals, but the results were so dramatic that it is hard to feel anything but convinced that feeding itself has nothing whatsoever to do with attachment. The study by Schaffer and Emerson (see Key Study on page 78) also found that infants were *not* most attached to the person who fed them.

Quality of care

Harlow's research pointed to another possibility. The monkeys' only attachment was with a mother who offered contact comfort but not interaction. These monkeys grew up to be quite maladjusted. Perhaps it is the responsiveness of the caregiver that is important. This could explain why the children on the Kibbutzim remained most strongly attached to their mothers. The *metapelets*, who had to look after many children, had less time to interact with each one individually and also may have had less interest because of their short-term commitment. In contrast, the mothers invested in a more intense emotional relationship during the quality time they had with their infants. Schaffer and Emerson (1964) also found that responsiveness from caregivers was important. In their study well-attached infants had mothers who responded most quickly to their demands (high responsiveness) and who offered the child the most interaction. The infants who were weakly attached had mothers who failed to interact.

The monkeys in Harlow's study appeared to be more attached to a cloth-covered artificial "mother" than to a wire version.

Love in infant monkeys

Harry Harlow was initially interested in the psychology of learning, and conducted experiments using rhesus monkeys. In order to reduce mortality rates in the experimental participants, Harlow found it best to separate them from their mothers after birth and raise them in sterile conditions. The monkeys were provided with a nappy on the floor of their cages because it had been observed that the monkeys liked to touch these, especially when feeding from a bottle. In fact, the monkeys appeared to become extremely attached to these nappy pads as indicated by the fact that they became very agitated when the pads were removed daily for cleaning.

This attachment reminded Harlow of a child's fondness for a special blanket or a cuddly toy, and suggested to him an idea for an experiment. Would the monkeys prefer the activity of feeding to that of bodily comfort? To test this Harlow (1959) arranged for very young rhesus monkeys to be taken from their mothers and placed in cages with two surrogate (or substitute) mothers, as shown in the picture. One of the "mothers" was made of wire and the other was covered in cloth. Milk was provided by the wire mother for some of the monkeys, whereas it was provided by the cloth mother for the others. The findings were clear-cut. The monkeys spent most of their time on the cloth mother even when she did not supply milk.

Although the wire mother on the left is where the baby monkey receives his food, he runs to the cloth mother for comfort, when he is frightened by the teddy bear drummer (Harlow, 1959).

The cloth mother provided "contact comfort" which was clearly preferable. If the monkeys were frightened they ran to their cloth mother. However the monkeys did not develop into normal adults. Later in life the monkeys were either indifferent or abusive to other monkeys and had difficulty with mating and parenting. This shows that contact comfort is preferable but not sufficient for healthy development. Presumably infants need a responsive caregiver, and an interactive relationship with this individual for healthy development.

Harlow conducted various further studies to investigate the effects of deprivation. Harlow and Harlow (1962) raised monkeys for lengthy periods in total isolation. When they were placed with other monkeys they remained withdrawn and extremely fearful. In comparison, monkeys raised with a cloth "mother" were much more able to engage in social activity. This shows that the cloth mother was better than nothing.

In another experiment four young monkeys were raised on their own, without any "mother". They spent the first few months huddled together but gradually developed more independence and finally appeared to have suffered no ill-effects. This suggests that the infant–infant affectional bond can be just as effective as mother–infant. (See Freud and Dann's study on page 102 for more on the effects of infant–infant bonding.)

Discussion points

1. Why should one be cautious in using these results from animal studies to explain human behaviour?

2. What can we conclude about the importance of "contact comfort"?

KEY STUDY EVALUATION — Harlow

Monkeys are social animals who usually live in quite large groups. This means that Harlow's studies could be criticised on two grounds: modern ethical considerations would make this experimental approach hard to justify, but the studies could also be methodologically flawed.

The rhesus monkeys were reared in isolation. These are monkeys who come from a highly social background. After the experiments were completed, the monkeys exhibited severely disturbed behaviour. At the time, the distress caused to the monkeys was seen as acceptable in the light of the possible benefits of understanding how attachment develops. However, it is unlikely that such a study would be allowed to proceed today because of stricter ethical guidelines for research using non-human participants.

The baby monkeys were doubly deprived of both maternal care and the company of others. Therefore we cannot be certain whether their maladjustment was due to maternal deprivation or social deprivation, or both.

"Attachments are not formed by a congenital glue held in limited supply: They are welded in the heat of interactions" (Maurer & Maurer, 1989). In other words, attachments depend on interaction, rather than two people just being together.

Ainsworth, Bell, and Stayton (1974) proposed a **caregiving sensitivity hypothesis**, suggesting that it is the *quality* of the relationship that matters most of all. Attachment depends on the warm and loving responsiveness of the mother-figure. There is considerable support for this. For example, Ainsworth et al. (1971) found that mothers who responded to their infants in a sensitive manner had securely attached children whereas mothers who were less responsive had insecurely attached children. Isabella, Belsky, and Von Eye (1989) also found that those mothers and infants who tended to be responsive to each other at one month were more securely attached to each other at twelve months. Those who had a more one-sided pattern of interaction tended to have insecure relationships.

Individual Differences in Attachment

Most psychological theories are written in a way which suggests that everyone is the same. However, it is fairly obvious that each one of us is different. For example, Schaffer and Emerson found that some babies like cuddling whereas others may prefer not to be touched. We have also seen in this same study that some infants are attached to one person, whereas others have multiple attachments (remember that, at 18 months, 13% of the children were attached to only one person).

These are **individual differences**. The same can be said about differences between **cultures**. There are differences both within a culture and between cultures. In the next part of this section we will look at cross-cultural differences. First of all we will consider individual differences within our culture.

All normal children are attached to a caregiver, even those children who have been neglected or abused (see box on Abuse and attachment, below). The main individual difference lies in the degree to which a child is attached, known as secure and insecure attachment.

Secure and insecure attachment

When we describe a child as "being attached" this implies a **secure attachment**. Not all children are as securely attached as others. Some are rather insecurely attached. Mary Ainsworth provided us with a way of measuring this aspect of attachment, called the **Strange Situation**, as a means to test the quality of an infant's attachment to its caregiver (see the Key Study on page 88). The Strange Situation has been used

Resistant attachment is shown when a baby resists contact with his or her mother after being left. The baby cries and tries to twist away from the mother.

Abuse and attachment

Harris (1998) notes that it is a "sad and paradoxical fact that abuse may actually increase a child's clinginess." A number of studies have investigated the consequences of neglect or abuse on the bonds that form between caregiver and infant. In one of Harlow's studies of rhesus monkeys, the cloth "mother" blasted the infant monkey with a strong current of compressed air (Rosenblum & Harlow, 1963). The findings were that these abused monkeys appeared to be *more* strongly attached to their "mother" than the other monkeys. This is confirmed by a report from a researcher studying imprinting in ducklings. He found that when he accidentally stepped on the foot of one of the ducklings who had already imprinted on him, then the duckling followed him more closely than ever (Harris, 1998).

However, this link between abuse and attachment may not extend to humans. Lynch and Roberts (1982) suggested that abuse leads to bonding failure rather than stronger attachment. One example is seen in mothers described as "primary rejectors" (Jones et al., 1987). These tend to be middle-class women who have had an unwanted child, a difficult pregnancy, and/or experienced early separation from their infant due to problems at the time of birth. The mothers may have good relationships with other children. Rejection starts from the time of birth and the mother–infant relationship never recovers. It is possible that children who experience this "primary rejection" go on to suffer from reactive attachment disorder, which is described on page 104. These children do not appear to be attached to their rejecting caregiver, and in fact are unable to form any attachments. Therefore, this suggests that abuse does not create a stronger bond in humans.

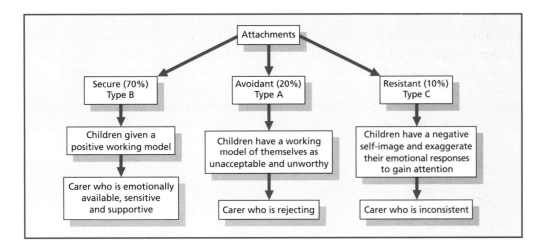

Ainsworth and Bell proposed three attachment types (A, B, and C). Main and Soloman proposed a fourth category, Type D, which they described as "Insecure: Disorganised".

in many studies of attachment—in fact it is the main means of assessing attachment. Studies using this form of assessment have found that there are four types of attachment: **secure** (also called type B), **avoidant** (type A), **resistant** (type C), and **disorganised** (type D). All the last three are examples of insecure attachment. Only secure attachment is likely to be related to healthy emotional and social development.

The Strange Situation consists of seven 3-minute episodes:
1. Parent (or caregiver) and infant enter a room.
2. Stranger joins parent and infant.
3. Caregiver leaves.
4. Caregiver returns, stranger leaves.
5. Caregiver leaves.
6. Stranger returns.
7. Caregiver returns, stranger leaves.

Evaluation of the Strange Situation assessment

Studies that have used the Strange Situation have found that it is both reliable and valid. The question of **reliability** is determined by seeing if the same child, tested at different times, produces the same result. In order for the Strange Situation to be a reliable measure of attachment we would expect this to be the case. Main, Kaplan, and Cassidy (1985) assessed infants in the Strange Situation before the age of 18 months with both their mothers and fathers. When the children were retested at the age of 6, the researchers found that 100% of the secure babies were still classified as secure, and 75% avoidant babies remained in the same classification. When differences occur, these are often associated with changes in the form of care, such as separation of parents (Melhuish, 1993). Therefore, the evidence suggests that the Strange Situation reliably measures attachment.

The issue of **validity** concerns the extent that the Strange Situation measure is "true" or measures something that is real. One way of assessing validity is by using criterion validity, for example in the case of an intelligence test we would expect that someone who did well on a test would do well in exams. Therefore exam performance acts as a criterion for assessing the test. In terms of attachment, if the Strange Situation assessment is valid, then we would expect that securely attached infants should be better socially and emotionally adjusted at later ages than an insecurely attached child. The evidence is mixed. Bates, Maslin, and Frankel (1985) found that attachment style at 12 months did not predict the presence of behaviour problems at 3 years of age. However, Sroufe (1983) reported that infants rated as secure in their second year have been found later to be more popular, having more initiative, being higher in self-esteem, less aggressive, and social leaders. Secure children were also rated as more popular by other children. On the whole, the evidence does support the hypothesis that early attachment behaviour predicts later social and emotional development.

The Strange Situation

In order to develop a full understanding of infants' attachment behaviour, we need to have good ways of measuring it. Ainsworth and Bell (1970) developed the Strange Situation procedure to measure an infant's attachment type. An infant (normally aged between 12 and 18 months) is observed during a sequence of seven short episodes (see box on previous page). For some of the time, the infant is with its caregiver. At other times, it is with its caregiver and a stranger, or just with a stranger, or on its own. Overall, the key observations that are made relate to the child's reactions to the stranger (stranger anxiety), to separation from the caregiver (separation anxiety), and to being reunited with its caregiver.

The infant's reactions to these episodes allow one to categorise the infant's attachment type.

1. **Secure attachment**: the infant is distressed by the caregiver's absence. However, he or she rapidly returns to a state of contentment after the caregiver's return, immediately seeking contact with the caregiver. There is a clear difference in the infant's reaction to the caregiver and to the stranger. Ainsworth et al. (1978) reported that 70% of American infants show secure attachment.

2. **Resistant attachment**: the infant is insecure in the presence of the caregiver, and becomes very distressed when the caregiver leaves. He or she resists contact with the caregiver upon return, and is wary of the stranger. About 10% of American infants were found to be resistant.

3. **Avoidant attachment**: the infant does not seek contact with the caregiver, and shows little distress when separated. The infant avoids contact with the caregiver upon return. The infant treats the stranger in a similar way to the caregiver, often avoiding him or her. About 20% of American infants were avoidant.

Why do some infants have a secure attachment with their caregiver, whereas others do not? According to Ainsworth's (1982) caregiving hypothesis, the sensitivity of the caregiver is of crucial importance. Ainsworth et al. (1971) found that most of the caregivers of securely attached infants were very sensitive to their needs, and responded to their infants in an emotionally expressive way. In contrast, the caregivers of resistant infants were interested in them, but often misunderstood their infants' behaviour. Of particular importance, these caregivers tended to vary in the way they treated their infants. As a result, the infant could not rely on the caregiver's emotional support.

Finally, there are the caregivers of avoidant infants. Ainsworth et al. (1971) reported that many of these caregivers were uninterested in their infants, often rejecting them, and tending to be self-centred and rigid in their behaviour. However, some caregivers of avoidant infants behaved rather differently. These caregivers act in a suffocating way, always interacting with their infants even when the infants did not want any interaction. What these two types of caregivers have in common is that they are not very sensitive to the needs of their infants.

Discussion points

1. What are the strengths of the experimental approach used by Ainsworth?
2. What factors determine infants' attachment style?

It appears that the Strange Situation is both a reliable and a valid form of assessment. However, there is one fundamental flaw to the procedure. The essential concept of the Strange Situation assessment is that one is testing something about the child, some aspect of their personality—how securely (or insecurely) attached they are. But this may not be the case. One may be testing the *relationship* between the infant and their caregiver, rather than the resulting attachment type. Main and Weston (1981) did find that children behaved differently depending on which parent they were with in the Strange Situation, which suggests that attachment type is not a consistent individual difference. The fact that some studies, such as Main et al. and Sroufe, have found consistent and long-term patterns may be explained in terms of the fact that *most* children tend to have the same relationships throughout childhood and so it *appears* that this is their attachment type. This line of argument suggests that the whole basis of the Strange Situation assessment is flawed and meaningless.

Studies that look at the association between two variables have the drawback that they appear to demonstrate cause and effect, whereas all they really show is whether a correlation exists.

The temperament hypothesis

An alternative way to explain the correlation between early attachment type and later development is by using the **temperament hypothesis**. Kagan (1984) proposed that an infant's relationships, both attachments with primary caregivers and those later in life, can be explained in terms of the infant's innate temperament. Some people are innately good at forming relationships whereas others aren't. We have already considered this argument on page 77.

Kagan further argued that the caregiving sensitivity hypothesis (see page 86) overemphasises the role played by the caregiver in the development of attachment and ignores the part played by the infant's temperament or personality in determining his or her attachment to the mother. Evidence that the infant's temperament may be important was reported by Belsky and Rovine (1987). Newborns who showed signs of behavioural instability (e.g. tremors or shaking) were less likely to become securely attached to their mother than were newborns who did not. In other words, it was their innate personality that was the key factor in the formation of an attachment.

Evaluation of the temperament hypothesis

Much of the evidence fails to support Kagan's temperament hypothesis. For example, infants' temperament as assessed by their parents is not usually associated with their attachment type as determined by the Strange Situation assessment (Durkin, 1995).

It is probable that neither relationship (caregiver sensitivity) nor temperament is wholly responsible for the development of attachment, but that there is an interaction between them (Belsky & Rovine, 1987). Supporting evidence was reported by Spangler (1990) in a study of German mothers. These mothers' responsiveness to their infants was influenced by their perceptions of the infants' temperament.

Cross-cultural Variation in Attachment

If attachment is an innate behaviour then we would expect attachment behaviours to be very similar across the world.

Secure and insecure attachment

Infant attachment styles in various cultures have been studied using the Strange Situation test. Findings for infants in the United States, Israel, Japan, and Germany were reported by Sagi, van Ijzendoon, and Koren-Karie (1991). Their findings for the American infants were similar to those reported by Ainsworth and Bell (1970): 71% of them showed secure attachment, 12% showed anxious and resistant attachment, and 17% were anxious and avoidant.

Israeli and American children
The Israeli infants behaved rather differently from the American ones. Secure attachment was shown by 62% of them, 33% were anxious and resistant, and only 5% were anxious and avoidant. These infants lived in a kibbutz or collective farm, and were looked after much of the time by adults who were not part of their family. However, they had a close relationship with their mothers, and so tended not to be anxious and avoidant.

Israeli and Japanese children
Japanese infants are treated very differently from Israeli infants. Japanese mothers practically never leave their infants alone with a stranger. In spite of the differences in child-rearing practices in Japan and Israel, the Japanese infants showed similar attachment styles to the Israeli ones. Two-thirds of them (68%) had a secure attachment, 32% were anxious and resistant, and none was anxious and avoidant.

However, the Israeli and Japanese children probably showed anxious and resistant attachment for rather different reasons. Israeli children are accustomed to being separated from their mother, but they rarely encounter complete strangers. Thus, their resistant behaviour was perhaps due to the presence of the stranger. In contrast, Japanese children are practically never separated from their mother, and this would be the main cause of their resistant attachment behaviour.

German children
Finally, the German infants showed a different pattern of attachment from the other three groups of infants. Only 40% of them were securely attached, which was less

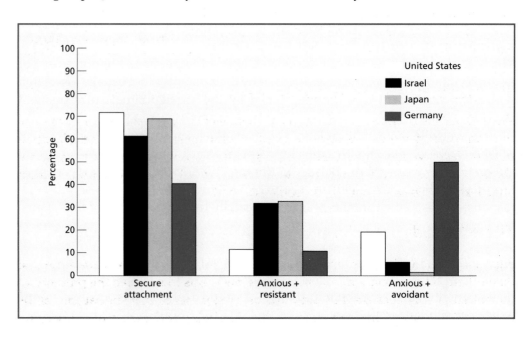

Children from different countries vary in their attachment types. The graph summarises research from Sagi et al. (1991) and Ainsworth and Bell (1970).

than the number of infants (49%) who were anxious and avoidant. The remaining 11% were anxious and resistant. Grossmann et al. (1985) obtained very similar findings. They suggested that German culture requires keeping some interpersonal distance between parents and children. As Grossmann et al. (1985, p.253) expressed it, "the ideal is an independent, nonclinging infant who does not make demands on the parents but rather unquestioningly obeys their commands."

Evaluation of cross-cultural attachment studies

Van IJzendoorn and Kroonenberg (1988) compared the results of cross-cultural studies using the Strange Situation (see the table below that summarises their data). One of their key findings was that the variation of attachment *within* cultures was 1½ times greater than the variation *between* cultures. This suggests that it is false to think of one culture as consisting of the same practices. The idea that there is a *single* British or American culture is undoubtedly an oversimplification: in fact, there are several sub-cultures within most large countries. Therefore the idea of making cross-cultural comparisons may lack validity.

A further problem lies in the actual measurement used to assess attachment. The principle behind the Strange Situation comes from the belief in our culture that attachment is related to anxiety on separation. As we have seen, in other countries children have very different early experiences and therefore the fact that they become anxious in the Strange Situation may *not* be due to secure or insecure attachment. The Strange Situation measurement assumes that the behaviour of all children in all cultures means the same thing, whereas for Japanese children separation was an unusual experience and therefore did not have the same meaning that it had for American children.

Therefore we can see that the Strange Situation is based on cultural assumptions. This is called an **imposed etic**, the use of a technique developed in one culture to study another culture. This means that the cross-cultural evidence is inherently flawed by the use of an invalid measuring tool. The same conclusion may be true for sub-cultures within America and Britain.

Infant behaviour in the Strange Situation, from studies in different cultures

Country	Number of studies	Percentage of each attachment type (to the nearest whole number)		
		Secure	Avoidant	Resistant
West Germany	3	57	35	8
Great Britain	1	75	22	3
Netherlands	4	67	26	7
Sweden	1	74	22	4
Israel	2	64	7	29
Japan	2	68	5	27
China	1	50	25	25
United States	18	65	21	14
Overall average		65	21	14

(From Van Ijzendoorn & Kroonenberg, 1988.)

Explanations of Attachment

We will now consider some of the major theories of attachment. A theory aims to offer an account of the facts, so a theory of attachment should offer an explanation of those facts we have considered. A theory also aims to explain the facts, so we should be able to use these theories to explain why and how infants form attachments, and to whom they become attached.

The psychodynamic approach

Sigmund Freud (1924) put forward a simple account of the infant's attachment to its mother: "The reason why the infant in arms wants to perceive the presence of its mother is only because it already knows by experience that she satisfies all its needs without delay." In other words, babies like being with their mothers because the mother is their source of food, comfort, and warmth. This explanation is sometimes referred to as being "cupboard love".

Freud's views on early attachment stemmed from his theory of development, described on pages 12 to 15. According to this theory adult personality depends very much on childhood experiences. Childhood can be divided into five stages of psychosexual development, stages during which the child is biologically driven to seek pleasure in certain ways. The first stage of psychosexual development is the oral stage when pleasure is derived orally, for example sucking at the mother's breast. The result is an attachment to the mother because she is associated with the satisfaction of pleasure. This first attachment has long-lasting effects. Freud argued that the mother's status was "established unalterably for a whole lifetime as the first and strongest love-object and as the prototype of all later love-relations" (1924, p.188).

Evaluation of the psychodynamic approach

Freud's theory suggests that attachment behaviour in babies will be related to feeding but we have seen that this is not the case. For example, Harlow's research with young monkeys (see page 85) showed that food alone could not explain attachment. It could be argued that Harlow's work on monkeys is not relevant to the study of human attachment because non-human animal behaviour is more affected by innate behaviour patterns. However, research with humans has supported Harlow's finding. For example, Schaffer and Emerson (1964, this research is described on page 78) found with about 40% of human infants that the adult who fed, bathed, and changed the infant was not the person to whom the infant was most attached. Thus, there is not the simple link between food and attachment behaviour that was assumed by Freud. Infants were most likely to become attached to adults who were responsive to them, and who provided them with much stimulation in the form of touching and playing.

Do you think that there are problems with generalising from the behaviour of one species to another?

Learning theory

The basic principle of **learning theory** is that all behaviour has been learned (it is not innate). Learning theorists (also called "behaviourists") believe that learning is the result of conditioning—either **classical conditioning** or **operant conditioning** (see Chapter 1 Section 2). A reminder of these processes is shown in the box below.

An infant is born with reflex responses. The stimulus of food (an unconditioned stimulus) produces a sense of pleasure (an unconditioned response). The person providing the food (usually mother) becomes associated with this pleasure and therefore becomes a conditioned stimulus which independently will produce the unconditioned stimulus (pleasure). The food-giver then becomes a source of pleasure independent of whether or not food is supplied. This, according to learning theory, is the basis of the attachment bond.

Dollard and Miller (1950) offered a further learning theory explanation for the development of attachments. This explanation focuses on motivation, the explanation of what it is that drives behaviour. According to Dollard and Miller, all humans possess

---

Classical conditioning

- Unconditioned stimulus (US) e.g. food ➜ causes ➜ reflex response e.g. salivation.
- Neutral stimulus (NS) e.g. bell ➜ causes ➜ no response.
- NS and US are paired in time (they occur).
- NS (e.g. bell) is now a conditioned stimulus (CS) ➜ which produces ➜ a conditioned response (CR) [a new stimulus–response link is learned, the bell causes salivation].

Operant conditioning

- A behaviour that has a positive effect is more likely to be repeated.
- Negative reinforcement (escape from aversive stimulus) is agreeable.
- Punishment is disagreeable.

various primary motives or drives, such as hunger and thirst. A person will be "driven" to seek food to satisfy hunger. Obtaining food results in drive reduction which is rewarding. According to the principles of operant conditioning anything that is rewarding is more likely to be repeated and therefore this behaviour is repeated (learned).

In the context of attachment, hunger and thirst are the primary drives. The mother (or person doing the feeding) provides the food which reduces the drive. Therefore the mother becomes a **secondary reinforcer**. From then on the infant seeks to be with this person because they are now a source of reward in themselves. The infant has thus become attached.

Mothers also learn to be attached to their infants because of reinforcement. For example, mothers may be rewarded when they make their offspring smile or stop crying.

Evaluation of learning theory

However, as we have just seen, infants often become attached to adults who are *not* involved in feeding or basic care-giving (Schaffer & Emerson, 1964), therefore learning theory cannot be the whole explanation.

Learning theory is generally criticised for being **reductionist**. This means it "reduces" the complexities of human behaviour to over-simple ideas such as stimulus, response, and reinforcement. It then uses these ideas as building blocks to explain complex human behaviours such as attachment. It may be that these ideas are too simple to explain a complex behaviour such as attachment.

Social learning theory

Social learning theory is a more sophisticated version of this type of theory. Learning theory proposes that conditioning takes place *directly*, there is no intervening mental process—you do something and you are rewarded (or punished). Social learning theory, on the other hand, suggests that we also learn by imitating others—you see someone else rewarded for doing something and you imitate their behaviour; you have learned a new behaviour. This indirect or **vicarious reinforcement** (also described on page 15) requires some intervening mental processing.

Hay and Vespo (1988) used social learning theory to explain attachment. They suggested that attachment occurs because parents "deliberately teach their children to love them and to understand human relationships" (p.82). How do parents achieve these goals? Some of the main ways are as follows:

- Modelling: children learn to imitate the affectionate behaviour shown by their parents.
- Direct instruction: parents teach their children in a direct and explicit way to attend to them and to show affection.
- Social facilitation: parents watch their children carefully and provide assistance as and when necessary. (The parents are "social" and they help or facilitate the new behaviour.)

Some psychologists think of attachment behaviour as something that is learned because it is reinforced. Young children may learn about human relationships by imitating the affectionate behaviours of their parents.

Evaluation of social learning theory

The greatest strength of the social learning approach is that it has led to a detailed consideration of the interactional processes that occur between parents and children. In addition, at least some of the attachment learning shown by infants does depend on processes such as modelling, direct instruction, and social facilitation. On the negative side, as Durkin (1995) pointed out, the strong emotional intensity of many parent–child attachments is not really explained by social learning theorists.

Bowlby's theory of attachment

John Bowlby (1907–1990) was a child psychoanalyst whose main interest was in the relationship between caregiver and child. According to Holmes (1993) Bowlby's theory of attachment theory appeared to him as a flash of insight: Freud's views of the importance of maternal care could be combined with the ethological concept of imprinting to produce a new theory. This theory has had a profound effect on the way psychologists think about attachment and infant development.

The fundamental principle of Bowlby's theory is that attachment is an innate and **adaptive** process, for both infant and parent. Attachment behaviour has evolved and endured because it promotes survival, as proposed by Darwin's **theory of evolution**. If you recall from Chapter 1 Section 2, the argument is that any behaviour which promotes successful reproduction makes it more likely that the genes for that behaviour remain. The genes help the individual to be better adapted to its living conditions.

Bowlby's proposed phases in the development of attachment

Bowlby proposed that an infant is born with a set of behavioural systems that are ready to be activated, for example crying, sucking and clinging (all called "social releasers'), and an ability to respond to the "stimuli that commonly emanate from a human being"—sounds, faces and touch. Shortly thereafter other behaviours appear which are equally innate though not present at birth, such as smiling and crawling. From these small beginnings, sophisticated systems soon develop.

In the table below, four phases in the development of attachments are described, with very approximate ages.

Phase 1 Birth–8 weeks	Orientation and signals towards people without discrimination of one special person	Infants behave in characteristic and friendly ways towards other people but their ability to discriminate between them is very limited, e.g. they may just recognise familiar voices
Phase 2 About 8/10 weeks–6 months	Orientation and signals directed towards one or more special people	Infants continue to be generally friendly but there is beginning to be a marked difference of behaviour towards one mother-figure or primary caregiver
Phase 3 6 months through to 1–2 years old	Maintenance of proximity to a special person by means of locomotion as well as signals to that person	The infant starts to follow his or her mother-figure, greet her (him) when she (he) returns, and use her (him) as a base from which to explore. The infant selects other people as subsidiary attachment figures. At the same time the infant's friendly responses to other people decrease and the infant treats strangers with increasing caution
Phase 4 Starts around the age of 2	Formation of a goal-corrected partnership	The child develops insight into the mother-figure's behaviour and this opens up a whole new relationship where the infant can consciously influence what she (or he) does. This is the beginning of a real partnership

Adapted from J. Bowlby (1969), *Attachment and love, Vol. 1: Attachment*. London: Hogarth.

Attachment promotes survival in many ways:

1. *Safety.* Attachment results in a desire to maintain proximity and thus ensure safety. Both infant and caregiver experience feelings of anxiety when separated and this creates a proximity-seeking drive.

2. *Emotional relationships.* Attachment enables the infant to learn how to form and conduct healthy emotional relationships. Bowlby used the concept of the **internal working model** to explain how this happens. The internal working model, as we have seen, is a set of conscious and/or unconscious rules and expectations regarding our relationships with others. This model develops out of the primary attachment relationship and is what it sounds like, a model or **schema** that is used as a template for future relationships.

3. *A secure base for exploration.* Attachment also provides a safe base for exploration, a process that is fundamentally important for mental development. A child uses their attachment figure(s) as the pivot for their roving. The child often returns periodically to "touch base". An insecurely attached child is less willing to wander. Exploration is very important for cognitive development, as shown in a study by Bus and van IJzendoorn (1988). They assessed the attachment types of children aged 2 years old, using the Strange Situation. Three years later the children were assessed in terms of their reading interests and skills, and their pre-school teachers also completed a questionnaire about preparatory reading and intelligence. Bus and van IJzendoorn found that the securely attached children showed more interest in written material than did the insecurely attached children, regardless of their intelligence and the amount of preparatory reading instruction.

The attachment between a child and his or her caregiver serves many important functions. According to Bowlby, it maintains proximity for safety, the caregiver acts as a secure base for exploration, and the attachment relationship acts as a template for all future relationships.

The role of social releasers

In order to be successful, attachment must be innate and reciprocal. If it wasn't innate, the infant or parent might not show it. It is reciprocal because both infant

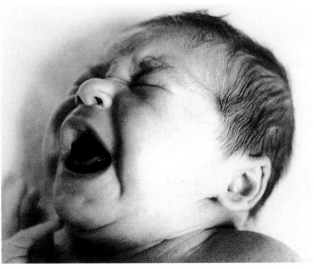

The features of a baby face are very appealing. They act as a "social releaser", a social stimulus that "releases" a desire to offer caregiving.

and caregiver must actively take part: the infant innately elicits caregiving from its mother-figure by means of **social releasers**, behaviours such as smiling or crying which encourage a response. Other humans are innately programmed to respond to these social releasers.

Most people feel uncomfortable when they hear an infant, or an adult, crying. This is no accident because it helps to ensure that someone will respond. Some adults suggest that an infant who is crying is somehow being "very clever" and "manipulating you". But it is a mechanism that has evolved exactly because it does just that, and thus maximises survival by keeping the caregiver(s) close. These innate behaviours and innate responses are a fundamental part of the process of forming an attachment.

How should you respond when you hear a baby cry?

Evaluation of Bowlby's theory

Why do infants become attached? Bowlby explains the purpose of attachment in terms of adaptation. To whom do infants become attached? Bowlby would say that the primary caregiver will be the individual who is most responsive to the infant's social releasers, and enters into mutual interactions.

There have been many criticisms of Bowlby's theory but first and foremost one should recognise the enormous influence of the theory. It has generated a great deal of research—studies that have tried to prove or disprove it, and theories that have modified it. It has also had important practical applications, as we will see in the next two sections.

On the negative side, we have seen the problems with Bowlby's view of attachment as a template for future relationships. This would lead us to expect children to form similar relationships with others but the correlations among a child's various relationships are actually quite low (Main & Weston, 1981). There has been evidence that links attachment style to later relationships (e.g. Hazan & Shaver, see page 76) but this is not a universal finding. For example, Howes, Matheson, and Hamilton (1994) found that parent–child relationships were not always positively correlated with child–peer relationships. In addition, even if there are positive correlations between the main attachment relationship and later relationships, there are other ways to explain this. It could be that some infants are simply better than others at forming relationships. Children who are appealing to their parents are likely to be appealing to other people, so that a child who does well in one relationship is likely to do well in others (Jacobson & Wille, 1986).

There have been various other criticisms which relate to information throughout this chapter, such as Bowlby's views on a critical period for the development of attachment (see page 81), his argument about bad homes versus good institutions (see page 105), and perhaps most fundamentally research related to the effects of separation (discussed in the next section).

■ Activity: List all the theories of attachment covered in this section. For each of them, suggest how the following questions would be answered: Why do attachments form? With whom are attachments formed? What is the major drawback of this explanation?

One final point we should note regards the evolutionary argument, which is not accepted by everyone. It is a *post hoc* (after the fact) assumption rather than proven fact. In other words, we are making the judgement looking backwards and arguing that a behaviour must be adaptive because it persists. We cannot *know* that natural selection works, but we assume that it is likely. It could be that the value of a behaviour that endures is simply neutral rather than positive, and that is why it has remained.

SECTION 8
Deprivation and Privation

In the last section we considered the development of attachments. In the real world, of course, there are circumstances such as divorce between parents or the death of a parent, that can disrupt the child's attachments, or even prevent them from being formed at all. If attachment is critical to healthy psychological development, then Bowlby's theory would predict that any disruption to this process should result in the opposite effect—unhealthy psychological development. One way of determining the validity of Bowlby's theory is to consider the effects of such disruption.

In this section, we will discuss the effects on the young child of being separated from one or more of the most important adults in his or her life. Most studies have focused on the long-term effects of deprivation. However, we will first consider some of the short-term effects.

Some people may be more likely to become depressed at an older age because of early experiences of separation from an attachment figure.

Short-term Effects of Separation

Even fairly brief separation from a primary caregiver has severe emotional effects on the child. Robertson and Bowlby (1952) studied young children who were separated from their mother for some time, often because she had gone into hospital. They found that there were three stages in the child's response to separation, called the protest-despair-detachment (PDD) model:

1. Protest, which is often very intense. The child cries much of the time, and sometimes seems panic-stricken.
2. Despair, involving a total loss of hope. The child is often apathetic and shows little interest in its surroundings.
3. Detachment, during which the child seems to behave in a less distressed way. If the mother reappears during this stage, she is not responded to with any great interest.

It used to be thought that children in the third stage of detachment had adjusted fairly well to separation from their mother. However, it seems that the calm behaviour shown by the child often hides underlying distress. The indifference shown by the child when its mother reappears is a disguise for true feelings but most children will re-establish an attachment to the mother over time.

Evaluation of the PDD model

Barrett (1997) suggests that the PDD model does not take individual differences into account. For example, a securely attached child may show little initial protest and cope relatively well, whereas an ambivalent or avoidant child would be plunged more immediately into protest and despair and become quite disoriented.

We should also ask whether it is inevitable that short-term separation will produce these negative effects. Evidence reported by Robertson and Robertson (1971) suggests that it is not inevitable. They looked after, in their own home, a number of young children who had been separated from their mothers, and took various steps to minimise any distress the children might experience. First, they ensured that the children visited their home some time before the actual separation,

Separation from the mother can have severe emotional effects on a child. The first stage of the child's response to the separation is known as protest: an intense period during which the child cries for much of the time.

so that they could become familiar with their new surroundings. Second, they did their best to provide the children with the kind of daily routine with which they were familiar. Third, they discussed the children's mothers with them. This approach proved successful, with the children showing much less distress than do most separated children. The Robertsons also studied other children who were separated from their mothers but who spent the time in a residential nursery. These children did not cope as well as those looked after by the Robertsons. The nursery children received good physical care but lacked emotional care. The Robertsons said that the nursery children experienced **bond disruption** whereas the others did not because they were offered substitute mothering. Therefore, we might conclude that separation need not lead to **deprivation** but it may if it is accompanied by bond disruption.

Long-term Effects of Separation

In Section 7 we discussed Bowlby's (1969) theory of attachment. Prior to the development of this theory, Bowlby had proposed an earlier version called the **maternal deprivation hypothesis** (1953). This hypothesis focused more on the effects of deprivation rather than the benefits of attachment.

Maternal deprivation hypothesis

According to this hypothesis, breaking the maternal bond with the child during the early years of its life is likely to have serious effects on its intellectual, social, and emotional development. Bowlby also claimed that many of these negative effects of maternal deprivation would be permanent and irreversible. In other words, this hypothesis focused on the negative effects of attachment—what might happen when the process was interrupted. At the time this theory was first proposed, at the beginning of the 1950s, the ideas were quite revolutionary. Most professionals then felt that adequate physical provision was all that was necessary and psychological care was like the icing on the cake. Bowlby produced an astonishing claim, "prolonged deprivation of a young child of maternal care may have grave and far reaching effects on his character ... similar in form ... to deprivation of vitamin(s) in infancy" (Bowlby, 1953).

Bowlby formed his hypothesis on the basis of his own study which is described in the Key Study opposite, and other studies of institutionalisation conducted around the time of the Second World War, which are described next. All of this research pointed to the fact that early separations were associated with severe consequences.

Institutionalisation

Important evidence came from the work of Spitz (1945) and Goldfarb (1947). Spitz visited several very poor orphanages and other institutions in South America. Most of the children in these orphanages received very little warmth or attention from the staff, as a result of which they became apathetic. Many of the children appeared to suffer from **anaclitic depression**, a state involving resigned helplessness and loss of appetite. This was attributed to their lack of emotional care, and separation from their mothers. Spitz and Wolf (1946) studied 100 apparently normal children who became seriously depressed after staying in hospital. They observed that the children generally recovered well if the separation lasted less than three months. Longer separations were rarely associated with complete recovery.

How might the findings from the Robertson and Robertson study be applied to helping children in institutional care?

Remember that the term "maternal" meant mothering, which could be done by anyone not just the infant's mother.

In what way were Bowlby's theory of attachment and maternal deprivation hypothesis different?

Forty-four thieves

John Bowlby (1946) conducted his own research with clients from the child guidance clinic where he worked. He interviewed the children and their families and was able to build up a record of their early life experiences. He found that some of the children had experienced "early and prolonged separations from their mothers". He also found that some of the children were emotionally maladjusted, in other words their emotional development was not normal. In particular he diagnosed the condition of **affectionless psychopathy** in some of the children, a disorder involving a lack of guilt and remorse. Could it be that there was a link between this form of emotional maladjustment and early separations?

Bowlby focused on a group of 44 children who had been referred to the clinic because they were stealing (these were the "thieves"). He selected another group of 44 children to act as "controls". These were individuals who had been referred to the clinic because of emotional problems but had not committed any crimes. The thieves were children who lacked a social conscience whereas the control group were children who were disturbed but emotionally functional. He found that:

- 32% of the thieves could be described as affectionless psychopaths. None of the control group were affectionless psychopaths.

- 86% of those "thieves" diagnosed as affectionless psychopaths had experienced early separation—separation for at least a week before the age of 5. In contrast, only 17% of the thieves *without* affectionless psychopathy had been maternally deprived.

These findings suggested that maternal deprivation can lead to a lack of emotional development (affectionless psychopathy).

Discussion points

1. What other differences might there have been between the "thieves" and the control group?

2. How might individual differences be important in the development of affectionless psychopathy?

KEY STUDY EVALUATION — Bowlby

There are a number of flaws in this research. First, the data on separation were collected retrospectively and may not be reliable. Second, some of the children had been separated for very short periods and it is difficult to see how this might be the cause of such a serious condition. Third, Bowlby made the diagnosis of affectionless psychopathy himself and his own expectations might have influenced this diagnosis. Finally, the evidence is *correlational*, which means that we can only say that separation and affectionless psychopathy are linked, not that one caused the other. Therefore the evidence offers questionable support for the maternal deprivation hypothesis.

Goldfarb (1947) compared two groups of infants from a poor and inadequately staffed orphanage. One group had spent only the first few months of their lives there before being fostered. The other group consisted of infants who had spent three years at the orphanage before fostering. Both groups were tested at various times up to the age of 12. Those children who had spent three years at the orphanage did less well than the other on intelligence tests. They were less socially mature, and they were more likely to be aggressive.

In the 1950s orphanages in the UK gradually began to disappear and therefore research into separation was limited. More recently there has been a new opportunity to study orphans—children from Romania. For example, Rutter and the ERA Study Team (1998) have followed 111 Romanian orphans adopted in the UK before the age of 2. When the orphans first arrived in the UK they were physically and mentally underdeveloped, but by the age of 4 all of them had improved, presumably as a result of the

---

CASE STUDY: *The Riley Family*

Jean Riley (54) and her husband Peter (58) adopted two children from Romania who are now aged 17 and 9. Cezarina, when they first saw her, was cross-eyed, filthy, and about four years behind in her physical development. First Cezarina's physical problems had to be sorted out, but from then on she made good progress. However, Cezarina is "laid back" about things that seem important to Jean and Peter. Jean understands this attitude, though, because clearly examinations seem less important when a child has had to struggle to survive.

According to Jean, Cezarina is bright, but needs to have information reinforced over and over again. She has also struggled to understand jokes and sarcasm, although this may be due to difficulties with learning the language. Jean sees Cezarina as naive and emotionally immature. Cezarina says herself that initially she was frustrated because she couldn't communicate. She does see herself as being different from other girls, although she likes the same things, such as fashion and pop music. Jean runs The Parent Network for the Institutionalised Child, a group for people who have adopted such children. Cezarina has partly recovered from her poor early experiences.

(Account based on an article in *Woman*, 21 September 1998.)

News reports in the 1980s highlighted deprivation in Romanian orphanages, with many children demonstrating anaclitic depression, having received basic sustenance but little human warmth or contact.

Are deprivation and separation the same thing?

What are the disadvantages associated with conducting longitudinal research?

improved care they were receiving. Those children who were adopted latest showed the slowest improvements, which appears to support the view that the poorer the early experience the more there is to recover from. However the evidence does show that recovery is possible given good subsequent care.

Evaluation. The findings reported here provide less support for the maternal deprivation hypothesis than Bowlby assumed. The institutional experience was deficient in several ways, the children were not simply deprived of maternal care but also suffered from a general lack of stimulation and attention. As a result, we cannot interpret the findings: they may be due to absence of the mother (lack of emotional care), or they may be due to presence of poor institutional conditions (poor physical care), or to some combination of both factors.

There is, however, some evidence that supports the importance of emotional care. Widdowson (1951) recorded the case of a group of orphanage children who were physically underdeveloped, a condition called **deprivation dwarfism**. A regime of dietary supplements did not lead to weight gain but a change in supervisor did. Their original supervisor had been harsh and unsympathetic. Therefore improved emotional, rather than physical, care appeared to be the cause of their physical improvements.

A further consideration of the effects of institutional care is given in Tizard's Key Study on page 105. The discussion of this study is included later.

Hospitalisation

Children experience separation as a result of being hospitalised. When children have to be hospitalised for prolonged periods this may lead to the breaking of attachment bonds (deprivation) and later maladjustment. A study by Douglas (1975) analysed used data collected as part of the National Survey of Health and Development, a longitudinal study of 5000 children born during one week in 1946. The children were assessed at regular intervals up to the age of 26. Douglas found that children who had spent more than a week in hospital, or had experienced repeated admissions under the age of 4, were more likely to have behaviour problems in adolescence and to be poor readers. Quinton and Rutter (1976) also found that repeated hospital admissions were associated with later problems whereas children admitted only once rarely had later difficulties.

Evaluation. Clarke and Clarke (1976) suggested that this apparent relationship between hospitalisation and later difficulties may be due to a third factor, namely general home problems. It could be that children from disadvantaged homes were more likely to need hospital treatment because of poor living conditions and that their disadvantaged homes might explain the maladjustment as well. Therefore the maladjustment was not the result of separation.

There is another way to interpret Douglas's findings. The experience of being in hospital is likely to create anxiety and the lack of caregiving at such a critical time may cause long-term problems. So it is not separation alone that has long-term effects but the anxiety created by the hospital situation, which is not helped by being alone. Bowlby et al. (1956) conducted a study of children who were hospitalised for long periods. The children had tuberculosis and spent between 5 and 24 months in a sanatorium outside London. The children were all under the age of 4 when they were first hospitalised. They did not receive substitute mothering by the hospital staff but most of them were visited weekly by their families (i.e. bond disruption was minimised). When the TB children were assessed later by their teachers and a psychologist, it was found that there were very few differences between them and their school peers in terms of later intellectual development and emotional adjustment. Therefore, it would appear that hospitalisation does not inevitably have harmful effects, possibly as long as bond disruption is minimised.

Evaluation of the maternal deprivation hypothesis

The evidence examined here, in relation to institutionalisation and hospitalisation, suggests that early separations can have important consequences in certain circumstances but that this is not necessarily the case. The maternal deprivation hypothesis has similarities with the concept of imprinting and can therefore be subject to similar criticisms. There may be a sensitive period in the development of attachments but probably not a critical period, and the damage caused by deprivation may be reversible.

The importance of the maternal deprivation hypothesis, and the research related to it, is that it changed our attitudes towards infant care and influenced the way children are looked after, in hospitals, in institutions, and at home. Thirty years *before* Bowlby, the behaviourist J.B. Watson wrote a book called *The psychological care of infant and child* (1928) where he recommended that parents should avoid displays of affection towards their children. Thirty years after Bowlby, Western attitudes are considerably changed—children are now accompanied by their parents while they are in hospital, institutional care has been largely replaced by fostering, and child-centred child care is the rule. A more recent child care book says "make [your baby] feel good and let him make you feel good too. You have everything to gain and nothing to lose" (Leach, 1985, p.195).

Do you feel that we live in a more caring society nowadays?

The most major criticisms of the maternal deprivation hypothesis were put forward by Rutter (1972) in a book entitled *Maternal deprivation reassessed*, which we will consider next.

Distinguishing Separation, Deprivation, and Privation

Rutter pointed out that Bowlby had assumed that all experiences of deprivation were the same whereas in fact there are some quite key differences. Children may experience very short-term separations, as in the Robertsons' studies, or they may have repeated and prolonged separations. Children may experience separation without bond-disruption, as with Bowlby's sanatorium study, or children may have no adequate substitute maternal care. Finally, children may experience deprivation as a result of never having formed any attachments. Rutter suggested that there was a key difference between deprivation and privation. **Deprivation** occurs when a child has formed an important attachment, but is then separated from the major attachment figure. In contrast, **privation** occurs when a child has never formed a close relationship with anyone. Many of Bowlby's juvenile delinquents had experienced several changes of home and of principal caregiver during their early childhood. This indicated to Rutter (1981) that their later problems were due to privation rather than deprivation. Rutter argued that the effects of privation are much more severe and long-lasting than those of deprivation.

Studies of privation

A few researchers have looked at the effects of very extreme privation and isolation on children. It is surprising how resilient these children seem to be. Koluchová (1976) studied identical twins who had spent most of the first seven years of their lives locked in a cellar. They had been treated very badly, and were often beaten. They were barely able to talk, and relied mainly on gestures other than speech. The twins were fostered at about the age of 9 by a pair of loving sisters. By the time they were 14, their behaviour was essentially normal. By the age of 20, they were of above average intelligence and had excellent relationships with the members of their foster family (Koluchová, 1991).

What ethical issues might be involved in the case study of Genie? Do these outweigh any understandings gained from this study?

Curtiss (1989) reported the **case study** of Genie, who spent most of her childhood locked in a room at her home in Los Angeles. She had had very little contact with other members of her family, and was discouraged from making any sounds. She was found in 1970 when she was 13½ years old. She had not been fed adequately, could not stand erect, and had no social skills. At that time, she did not understand language and could not speak. Genie was given a considerable amount of education and assistance in the years after she was found. Her ability to perform tasks that did not depend on language improved rapidly, and she reached normal levels on several perceptual tasks (Curtiss, 1989). Unfortunately, Genie's language skills failed to reach normal adult levels. She developed a fairly large vocabulary, but she generally spoke in short, ungrammatical sentences, and did not understand sentences that were complex grammatically. Her social skills remained limited, in part because her language was poor but also because she seemed uninterested in people (Rymer, 1993).

In what way might Genie be described as suffering from affectionless psychopathy?

Not all children who experience privation may experience permanent emotional damage. Freud and Dann (1951) provided evidence that young children who form strong attachments with other young children can avoid the severe damage resulting from privation. They studied six war orphans whose parents had been murdered in a concentration camp when they were only a few months old. The infants lived together in a deportation camp for about two years until the age of 3, and had very distressing experiences such as watching people being hanged. In this camp, they were put in the Ward for Motherless Children, and had very limited contact with anyone other than each other. After the camp was liberated at the end of the Second World War, they were flown to England. When they were freed from the camp, the children had not yet developed speech properly, they were underweight, and they expressed hostility towards adults. However, they were greatly attached to each other. According to Freud and Dann (1951, p.131): "The children's positive feelings were centred exclusively in their own group … They had no other wish than to be together and became upset when they were separated from each other, even for short moments."

As time went by, the six children became attached to their adult carers. In addition, they developed rapidly at a social level and in their use of language. It is hard to say whether their early experiences had any lasting adverse effects. One of them (Leah) received psychiatric assistance, and another (Jack) sometimes

Case studies

Some of the studies of privation described in this chapter are case studies. The advantage of such research is that it produces rich data that can be used by a researcher to develop new theoretical ideas. Case studies can provide information about exceptional types of behaviour or performance that had been thought to be impossible.

However, we need to be very careful when interpreting the evidence from a case study. The greatest limitation is the typically low reliability. The findings that are obtained from one unusual or exceptional individual are unlikely to be repeated in detail when another individual is studied. Thus, it is often very hard to generalise from a single-case study. Second, many case studies involve the use of lengthy, fairly unstructured interviews which may produce subjective information. Third, researchers generally only report some of the data they obtained from their interviews with the participant. They may be unduly selective in terms of what they choose to report or to omit.

Children in concentration camps experienced terrible early privation. The children in this picture are awaiting release from Auschwitz in January 1945. Freud and Dann studied six such children who only had each other for companions throughout their early lives.

felt very alone and isolated (Moskovitz, 1983). However, it would not be exceptional to find similar problems in six adults selected at random.

Evaluation of studies of privation

In sum, the evidence indicates that most of the adverse effects of maternal deprivation or privation can be reversed, and that children are more resilient than Bowlby believed. Clarke and Clarke (1998) note that early experience represents "no more than an initial step on the ongoing path of life". In other words, for most people early experience is very much related to what happens later on. Bad experiences are often likely to be followed by more of the same. However, where severely bad experiences are followed by much better ones the outcome may well be good. The Czech twins went to a loving home whereas Genie experienced a series of difficult carers, ending in a foster home where she was once again abused. There is one set of children for whom this may not be true, children with reactive attachment disorder, as described in the box on the next page.

It is important to consider the methodology of these studies. They are very small samples and it may not be reasonable to generalise from them. It is possible that the children were abnormal from birth—we only have a retrospective history of their experience and abilities. In fact, Genie's father thought she was retarded and that is why he locked her away.

Better evidence comes from Tizard's longitudinal research (see Key Study on page 105). On the one hand this study appears to support our conclusion that both deprivation and privation can be recovered from, given good subsequent care. However, Tizard's research also suggests a rather different conclusion, which is that recovery is only possible within the context of a loving relationship. Outside that relationship, children who have been deprived (or privated) may be unable to recover. Tizard and her colleagues found that those children who went on to have good relationships at home coped well *at home* but all the ex-institutional children found relationship difficulties *outside* the home. In some way they lacked an adequate model for future relationships. This would appear to support Bowlby's attachment theory.

Reactive attachment disorder

Consider a child in the early months of life. The child is hungry, or wet. What does the child do? He screams out for attention, and in the rage he expresses, the mother comes to the child's aid and feeds or changes the child. Day after day, week after week, the closeness of eye contact, touch, movements, and smiles creates a bond of trust between the child and its mother.

But what happens if this cycle is broken? What if the mother doesn't want to respond to the demanding needs of the child? What if there was an undiagnosed condition in the child, that was never appropriately responded to and comforted? In these instances, the child does not learn to trust, does not learn to bond, and proceeds on with the next lesson to learn in life.

This leads to a condition called "reactive detachment disorder". Children with attachment disorders have trouble trusting others. Trusting means to love, and loving hurts. They attempt to control everyone and everything in their world. Lack of a conscience appears to be caused by their lacking trust in anyone. They become so dependent on themselves, that they ignore the needs of others to the point that they will steal, damage, and destroy anything that they feel hinders their control. In short, they do not trust any caregiver or person in authority.

As a relatively new diagnosis to the **DSM-IV** manual, reactive attachment disorder is often misunderstood, and relatively unknown. All too often these individuals grow up untreated and become **sociopaths** without conscience and without concern for anyone but themselves. This condition was made popular by the recent academy award winning movie *Good Will Hunting*. But unlike the movie, the hero, or heroine, rarely drives off into the sunset to have a happy-ever-after life. More realistically, parental dreams are lost, and the children grow up uncaring and without social conscience.

(Adapted from http://members.tripod.com/~radclass/index.html)

In what way is reactive attachment disorder similar to affectionless psychopathy?

Reasons for Deprivation

Rutter's main criticism of Bowlby was that he had muddled together various kinds of separation. He also made a second criticism. Bowlby (1951) had argued that deprivation was the *cause* of long-term difficulties. In contrast, Rutter (1981) suggested that it might simply *appear* to be deprivation that was causing later difficulties, whereas in fact the difficulties were due to factors associated with the deprivation. For example, in the case of hospitalisation, as we have seen, the cause of maladjustment was probably poor living conditions rather than separation *per se*. The same may be true for the effects of maternal deprivation due to divorce. It might be that the discord and stress surrounding divorce is what might cause maladjustment rather than any maternal deprivation, as Bowlby would have predicted.

To test this hypothesis, Rutter conducted his own study of young boys (The Isle of Wight study, Rutter et al., 1976). Over 2000 boys living on the Isle of Wight, aged between 9 and 12, were questioned and their families were interviewed as well. Rutter et al. looked at the relationship between separation and delinquency. They found that if the separation was due to the physical illness or death of the mother, there was no correlation with delinquency. However, if the separation was due to psychiatric illness or discord within the family, then the boys were four times more likely to become delinquent. This suggests that it is mostly family discord, rather than separation as such, that causes difficulties and maladjustment in children.

This finding was supported by more recent research by Cockett and Tripp (1994). They found that children from homes where there was conflict suffered in terms of health, school performance, and **self-esteem** when compared with children who experienced minimal conflict at home.

Separation, Deprivation, and Privation: A Conclusion

Rutter made two important qualifications to Bowlby's maternal hypothesis. He also made a third point, which was that some, if not many, children recover quite well and perhaps this is where our focus should be. We should consider why some children are able to be quite resilient whereas others never recover.

Ultimately Rutter's contribution was not to cause people to reject Bowlby's hypothesis but to change the emphasis of this hypothesis. Maternal deprivation should be seen as a "vulnerability factor" (Brown & Harris, 1978) which raises the likelihood of a child becoming disturbed but not a factor that *necessarily* implies that maladjustment will follow.

Try to recall all three of Rutter's criticisms.

A longitudinal study of privation

Bowlby (1951) argued that the negative effects of maternal deprivation could not be reversed or undone. However, much of the available evidence does not support his argument, and indicates that even privation does not always have permanent effects. Some of the most thorough evidence on this issue was reported in a series of studies by Barbara Tizard and colleagues (Hodges & Tizard, 1989; Tizard, 1977; Tizard & Hodges, 1978; Tizard & Rees, 1985). They followed a group of 65 children who had been taken into care before they were 4 months old. The children were unable to form any consistent relationships in the institution, having an average of 50 different caregivers by the time they were 4 years old. The lack of a strong, continuous relationship with any one adult meant that they suffered from maternal deprivation. In spite of this, the children had a mean IQ of 105 at the age of 4½. Thus, the maternal deprivation did not appear to hold back the children's cognitive development.

By the age of four, 24 of the institutionalised children had been adopted, 15 had returned to their natural homes, and the rest remained in the institution. This natural experiment allowed the researchers to examine the effects of early deprivation on later development and compare the effects of the children's different attachment experiences. The children were assessed at age 4, 8, and 16.

At both later ages (8 and 16) it was found that most of the adopted children had formed close relationships with their adoptive parents. This was less true of the children who returned to their own families, possibly because their parents were often not sure they wanted to have their children back. One of Bowlby's predictions was that a bad home was better than a good institution because of the potentially better emotional care that can be offered. This research shows otherwise.

Perhaps a key finding was that, despite the adopted group doing better at home, both groups (adopted and restored to home) experienced difficulties at school. According to Tizard and Hodges (1978, p.114), they had "an almost insatiable desire for adult attention, and a difficulty in forming good relationships with their peer group." They were less likely than other children to have a special friend or to regard other adolescents as sources of emotional support.

The conclusion was that the adopted and restored groups differed in terms of their relationships *within* their families. However there were similarities in the behaviour of the two groups *outside* the family, when interacting with other adults and peers. Clarke and Clarke (1979) put forward a transactional model to explain this. It may be that the adopted children got on well within their families because the families made special efforts to love them, whereas they did not experience this outside the home and thus were unable to form relationships as easily or well. This would suggest that the children's ability to form relationships was affected by their early privation, and reminds us of the reciprocal nature of relationships.

The early effects of institutionalisation can be overcome by subsequent attachments but there are also lasting effects.

Discussion points

1. How has the research of Tizard added to our knowledge of the effects of deprivation?

2. How might we account for the different patterns of behaviour shown by adopted children and children who returned to their families?

KEY STUDY EVALUATION — Tizard

One of the criticisms of this study is that some of the children had "dropped out" before the end of the study. This left a biased sample because those children who could not be traced or were not willing to take part may well have been different from those who were left in the study. In fact Hodges and Tizard reported that those adopted children who were left in the study were the ones who, at age 4, had fewer adjustment problems. In contrast the restored children who remained in the study had earlier shown somewhat more adjustment problems than the restored children who dropped out. This left a "better" sample of adopted children and might explain why they did better.

It is also important to note that there were considerable individual differences within each group: some of the restored children actually had good family relations and some of the adopted children didn't. This reminds us that individual differences are important and that early attachment experiences are not the only cause of later maladjustment.

How does a natural experiment differ from a laboratory experiment?

SECTION 9   CRITICAL ISSUE
Day Care

Some people interpreted Bowlby's maternal deprivation hypothesis as meaning that day care was a bad thing. Separation would harm the child's emotional development if he or she spent time away from a primary caregiver. However, this is only an interpretation put on Bowlby's views. Bowlby himself did not specifically suggest that women should stay at home to look after their children but it seemed logical to argue that, if absent mothers create unhappy children, then mothers need to be present full-time. It is even possible that Bowlby's views were popularised by the post-war government to encourage women to stay at home—a cheaper alternative than having to provide universal child-care facilities. Bowlby argued that the quality of substitute care that is offered should be improved, as exemplified in the research he did with the Robertsons.

On the other side of the coin, there were those who argued for the *benefits* of day care, at least for *certain* children. In America in the 1960s there was a move towards providing pre-school care for disadvantaged children to enable them to start school on a par with their more middle-class peers. The best known project of this kind was called Headstart, which involved half a million children in its first year. Kagan, Kearsley, and Zelazo (1980) asked whether there wasn't some kind of dual standard. It was thought that lower-class children might benefit from day care as a source of intellectual enrichment but it was not desirable for middle-class children who would be harmed because of maternal deprivation.

Many parents have little choice about day care for economic reasons, and some parents wish to work because they otherwise feel trapped at home. Therefore the question of the effects of day care is of great practical concern. We have seen that there are arguments for and against it. We should first of all see to what extent day care does affect the social and cognitive development of children and then ask what can be done to improve the quality of day care.

Kinds of Day Care

There are many different kinds of day care and many ages at which children are in day care. In this book we will consider pre-school children and two main forms of care: day nurseries and childminding.

Day nurseries

Why do you think that it might be significant that the staff at the Boston school had responsibility for a small number of children, and maintained close emotional contact with them?

Kagan et al. (1980) studied nursery care by setting up their own nursery school in Boston. The school had a fairly mixed intake from middle- and lower-class families and from various ethnic groups. The staff at the school each had special responsibility for a small group of children, thus ensuring close emotional contact. The study focused on 33 infants who attended the nursery full-time from the age of 3½ months, and compared them with a matched home control group. Kagan et al. assessed the children throughout the two years they were at the nursery school. The researchers measured attachment, cognitive achievements, and general sociability, finding no consistently large differences between the nursery and home children. They did, however, find large variability among all the children, but it was not related to the form of care. So this underlines individual differences in attachment, which may be due to temperamental or home factors, or both. The study also shows that day care need not have harmful effects on a child's development.

A larger-scale longitudinal study of day nurseries was conducted by Andersson (1992) in Sweden. This is described in the Key Study on the next page. The conclusion again was that day care had few negative effects, in fact some children appeared to *benefit* from the care offered. One interesting point is that day care in Sweden is generally of a higher quality than in the UK because it is better funded by the government. This would lead us to conclude, again, that high-quality care at least has no negative effects.

Operation Headstart in the USA also involved day care. The programme was designed to reverse the effects of what was seen as social disadvantage by providing intensive pre-school education for certain children. When the children did start school, they showed IQ gains in comparison to those disadvantaged children who had not attended day care programmes but these differences soon disappeared. Later studies of the same children did find benefits, for example Lazar and Darlington (1982) reported that in adolescence the Headstart children were less likely to be placed in special classes, were more likely to go to college and, in terms of social benefits, were less likely to need welfare assistance or become delinquent. This evidence is important because, aside from the potential detrimental effects of day care, we find that there are some benefits, although they are not very clear or certain. The lack of large-scale success may be due to the variety of other factors that influence children's scholastic success. The Headstart effects have been found to be stronger when the pre-school programme had been followed up with later interventions.

Childminders

Childminding is an alternative form of day care which some people feel is preferable because it is more similar to the care that a child might get in their own home. Or at least it appears to be more similar. Mayall and Petrie (1983) studied a group of London children aged under 2 and their mothers and childminders. They found that the quality of care offered to these children varied considerably. They found that some childminders were excellent but others provided a rather unstimulating environment and the children in their care were failing to thrive.

Bryant, Harris, and Newton (1980) also studied childminding and found that some of the children were actually disturbed. Bryant et al. suggested that it may be that many minders feel they do not have to form emotional bonds with the children nor do they have to stimulate them. They found that minders rewarded quiet behaviour therefore encouraging passivity and understimulation.

Effects on Social and Cognitive Development

Having explored the effects of certain kinds of care on development generally, we should specifically consider the way day care may affect social and cognitive development. We should also consider emotional development, as it was this feature of development that Bowlby focused on, saying that *emotional* development would be irrevocably harmed by separation from a primary caregiver.

Child care may affect **sociability**—either positively or negatively. Various studies have found that children who go more often to a day nursery become more active, outgoing, and playful, and less aggressive. For example, Shea (1981)

What are the likely features of high-quality day care?

How might you use this evidence to advise parents on which form of child care to use?

Day care in Sweden

Early research into the effects of day care focused on the question of whether it was a good or bad thing. As research progressed psychologists realised that this question was too simplistic. Research should focus on what *features* of the day care situation lead to positive experiences and what factors lead to negative outcomes. More recent research has also looked at the long-term effects of the day-care experience as opposed to more immediate outcomes.

One example of this is a longitudinal study by Andersson (1992) conducted in Sweden. A sample of over 100 children were studied from both lower- and middle-class homes as well as one-parent families. The families were first contacted when the children were aged between 3 and 4. At this time their early child-care arrangements were recorded, most importantly the age that they first started in day care.

The children were assessed at age 8 and 13. Cognitive and socioemotional competence was rated by their classroom teachers and IQ test data were collected. Andersson found that school performance was rated highest in those children who entered day care before the age of 1. School performance was lowest for those who did not have any day care. This suggests that day care is not harmful in terms of development and may even be beneficial.

There is one important factor. Those children who did enter day care before the age of 1 also came from families with higher socioeconomic status. This means that the reason such children did better was possibly related to their socioeconomic status (better-off families are better educated and produce more well-adjusted children). Nevertheless the day-care experience could have been detrimental, but it was not.

Discussion points

1. This research was conducted in Sweden. How well do you think the findings can be applied to our culture (i.e. in what ways might our culture be different from theirs)?

2. What were the strengths of this research study?

What special ethical considerations should be taken into account when conducting work with young children?

Children attending nursery school are more likely to develop proper social behaviour in relation to other infants. One example of this is that nursery school children are more likely to engage in non-aggressive rough-and-tumble play.

videotaped 3- and 4-year-olds in the playground during their first 10 weeks at nursery school, and found that sociability increased over that time. The children's behaviour was assessed on five dimensions: aggression, rough-and-tumble play, frequency of peer interaction, distance from the teacher, and distance from the nearest child. There were clear indications that the children became more sociable over time. There was a decrease in the distance from the nearest child and in aggression, and an increase in rough-and-tumble play, frequency of peer interaction, and in distance from the teacher. The increases in sociability were greater in those attending the nursery school for five days a week than in those attending for only two days, indicating that it was the experience of nursery school rather than maturation that was producing most of the changes.

Clarke-Stewart, Gruber, and Fitzgerald (1994) also found that peer relationships were more advanced in day-care children. This study looked at 150 children from Chicago, aged between 2 and 3 and from various social backgrounds. The children in day care had more advanced peer relationships due, no doubt, to their extensive experience coping with peers in the day-care setting. They learned earlier how to cope in social situations and how to negotiate with peers. This is useful experience for later years at school.

However, this is not true for all children. When children are shy and unsociable, the nursery experience can be threatening which may have a negative effect on their school career (Pennebaker et al., 1981).

Once they start school, children who have attended pre-school classes have a range of advantages over children who have not.

Cognitive development

There is much evidence that day care can have positive effects on cognitive development for *all* children. For example, Burchinal, Lee, and Ramey (1989) tested the IQ of children entering school and found that those who had been in day care usually did better than those who had been at home with their mothers, which suggests that children benefit from the stimulation received at nursery. Broberg et al. (1997) in a study of 146 Swedish children compared children in day care with those looked after by a childminder and those who remained at home. When these children were assessed at the age of 8, the children who had been in day care were consistently better than the other groups on tests of verbal and mathematical ability. Moreover, the longer the children had been in day care the higher their scores. Childminding again came out worst. Andersson's study (see the Key Study opposite) found that all children, but especially boys, benefited from day care in terms of school achievement, in particular if they started before the age of 1 year. Clarke-Stewart et al. (1994) also found that children in day care had benefited from their enhanced amount of educational stimulation, although there was evidence that being in day care for more than six hours a day was not good for such young children.

On the other hand, Tizard (1979) found evidence that, irrespective of social class, the conversations between mother and child were more complex than between nursery teacher and child. Teachers had fewer exchanges and elicited less from the children, which may be due to the teacher's inevitably divided attention and less intimate relationship with the child. Such differences in conversation could be expected to affect cognitive progress.

Emotional development

Bowlby's attachment theory made especial claims for the effects of separation on emotional development. There is some support for this. For example, Belsky and Rovine (1988) found that there was an increased risk of an infant developing insecure attachments if they were in day care for at least four months and if this had begun before their first birthday.

However, there is considerable evidence that day care does not effect emotional development. Clarke-Stewart et al. (1994) investigated the relationship between time spent in day care and quality of attachment in over 500 children. They found that 15-month-old children who experienced "high-intensity" child care (30 hours or more a week from age 3 months) were equally distressed when separated from their mothers in the Strange Situation as "low-intensity" children (less than 10 hours a week). This suggests that attachment was not affected by the experiences of separation. Roggman et al. (1994) also found no ill-effects from early day care when they looked at behaviour in the Strange Situation. They compared infants who were cared for at home with those who attended day care before the age of 1. Both groups were equally securely attached to their mothers.

Individual differences

It is worth considering the fact that some children may benefit from day care whereas others don't, and that this will be related to individual differences. Consider the following study. Egeland and Hiester (1995) studied at about 70 children, about half of whom entered day care before the age of 1 and the rest remained at home with their mothers. All the children came from poor backgrounds. The children were assessed at age 1 and again at 3½ years, using the Strange Situation procedure. Day care appeared to have a negative effect for secure children but had a positive influence for insecure children.

This may be because insecurely attached children *needed* compensatory education, and therefore benefited from day care, whereas the securely attached children did not need this extra attention and therefore the separation effects alone were apparent. However, later reports on socioemotional development found no differences in the two groups. These findings suggest, again, that what appears to matter is not the day-care experience but the *conditions* under which it may be positively beneficial.

Another study focused on differences in the mothers. The National Institute of Child Health and Human Development (NICHD) Study of Early Child Care (1997) examined over 1000 infants and their mothers at age 6 months and again at 15 months. The mothers were interviewed and the infants were observed at home and, where possible, in day care. The study found no differences between the two groups of children in terms of emotional adjustment but it did find effects if maternal sensitivity and responsiveness were taken into account. Those infants whose mothers were low in sensitivity/responsiveness were less secure if the infants were experiencing poor day-care arrangements. So the two factors—maternal sensitivity and poor-quality care—did affect development.

Do you think the fact that all the children came from poor background's may have biased Egeland and Hiester's results?

What method was probably used by the NICHD to assess emotional adustment?

Recommendations for Improved Day Care

When day care is associated with a poor outcome this may be related to the *quality* of care rather than separation. Bowlby's arguments, as we have mentioned, could be interpreted as favouring *improved* child care. He suggested that separation could be compensated for by adequate bond substitution, where the child's emotional needs are placed foremost. For many parents there is little choice about day care— it is an economic necessity. Therefore the question is "What can we do to improve the potential emotional harm?" Andersson's descriptions of high-quality child care in Sweden suggest that we need to develop higher quality care worldwide. Schaffer

(1998) felt that we need to focus on consistency of care, as well as quality, to improve day care.

Consistency of care

A number of the studies that we have already examined point to the importance of consistency of care. For example, in Tizard's study of institutional care (see Key Study on page 105) it was noted that one of the reasons the children did not form attachments was because they had an average of 50 different caregivers before the age of 4. In contrast, in Kagan et al.'s study of day care, one of the key criteria was that the children received consistent emotional support. The NICHD study (1997) reported that the highest infant-to-caregiver ratio should be 1:3 in order to ensure that infants had sensitive and positive interactions. In order to improve consistency a day-care facility needs to find some way of ensuring minimal turnover of staff, and to arrange that each child is assigned to one specific individual who is more or less constantly available and feels responsible for that child. It may also be important to establish consistent routines and physical environments.

Quality of care

Schaffer notes that it is very difficult to define "quality of care" although we can identify some features of day care that contribute to it. One important characteristic of high-quality care is the amount of verbal interaction between caregiver and child. We have already noted Tizard's (1979) evidence that mothers had more complex conversations with their children than teachers did, which is likely to be due to the fact that teachers have to divide their attention between more individuals.

A second way to improve the quality of day care is by increasing the availability of suitable toys, books, and other playthings. This is clearly important for cognitive development in order to provide sufficient stimulation.

Third, and perhaps most important, is the issue of providing sensitive emotional care. The NICHD study found that just over one-quarter of the infant care providers gave highly sensitive infant care, half of them provided moderately sensitive care, but worryingly another one-fifth of the caregivers were "emotionally detached" from the infants under their care. Where day care lacks emotional involvement we have seen that infant development will suffer.

It may be possible to improve the quality of care that is offered by day-care providers. Howes, Galinsky, and Kontos (1998) found that a modest intervention programme which aimed at improving the caregiving practices of caregivers in child care did improve the attachment security of children within child care. They arranged for a number of caregivers to receive in-service training aimed to increase their sensitivity. Six months after training Howes et al. found that the children (aged around 2 years) became more secure and the caregivers were rated as more sensitive after training. There was a control group of caregivers who received no training. The attachment of the children in their care and their own sensitivity remained unchanged.

The effects of separation on parents

One issue that is frequently overlooked is the reciprocal nature of the separation. Parents may themselves suffer when separated from their children, and this may affect their ability to give quality care when they are with their children. For many

You have reached the end of the chapter on developmental psychology. Developmental psychology is an approach or perspective in psychology. The material in this section has exemplified the way that developmental psychologists explain behaviour. They look at behaviour in terms of the way that people change as they grow older, and the forces which create this change. Many of the changes, as we have seen, are due to inherited factors (nature). However, a major contribution also comes from to the influence of other people and the physical environment (**nurture**). Development doesn't stop when you leave childhood, it continues through the lifespan. If you go on to study psychology, you will consider this wider area of developmental, or lifespan, psychology.

parents work is an economic necessity. In addition parents are often made to feel guilty about leaving children in day-care facilities. It might be helpful to provide more interlinking between home and day care, for example providing such services at the workplace.

Furthermore, it might help to relieve some of the guilt to recognise that day care is not necessarily associated with negative effects. For some children there are actually benefits of having parents who work. For example, Brown and Harris (1978) found that women who don't work and have several young children to care for are more likely to become seriously depressed; and Shaffer (1993) reported that children of working mothers tend to be more confident in social settings than those who have remained in their mother's care. It might be that going out to work enables some women to be *better* mothers.

CHAPTER SUMMARY

The development and variety of attachments

❖ Attachment is shown by a desire to maintain proximity and general orientation towards an attachment figure. Distress on separation and joy at reunion are also characteristic. Why do infants form attachments? Attachment behaviour is adaptive because, in the short term, it promotes survival. In the long term it may be important as a template (internal working model) for adult relationships. There is some debate about whether the facts can be better explained in terms of innate temperament rather than early attachments. When do infants form attachments? Bowlby described four phases. Schaffer and Emerson described three stages: asocial, indiscriminate, and specific attachments. Both separation and stranger anxiety signify the onset of specific attachments. One point of criticism concerns the extent to which infants are asocial at an early age, and incapable of distinguishing between different categories.

❖ Attachments may occur at a critical or sensitive period in development, in the same way that imprinting and bonding takes place in birds. The claims made for imprinting have been criticised. It is probable that imprinting describes a kind of learning that takes place most easily, but not exclusively, during a certain stage of development: a sensitive rather than a critical period. The skin-to-skin hypothesis suggests that infants also have a sensitive period in development during which attachment bonds form most easily, perhaps because of a hormonal surge. There is mixed support for this hypothesis.

❖ To whom do infants become attached? Bowlby suggested that infants are most attached to a primary caregiver (monotropy) who is at the top of a hierarchy. This would be important for healthy emotional development. Others have disputed the concept of monotropy, and suggested that multiple equivalent attachments are more healthy. However many attachments are formed, it appears that the caregiver's sensitivity is a prime factor in the development of attachment. In other words, quality (responsiveness) rather than quantity (time or feeding) is most important.

❖ Individuals differ in terms of the quality of their attachment. Four attachment types have been identified using the Ainsworth Strange Situation: secure attachment and three kinds of insecure attachment—resistant, avoidant, and disorganised. The Strange Situation procedure has been found to be reliable and valid; however it may be measuring an infant's different relationships rather than a fixed feature of their personality. An alternative is to explain security of attachment in terms of innate temperament.

❖ Cross-cultural studies of secure and insecure attachment find general agreement for the classification of attachment types, although again there are questions about the validity of the Strange Situation assessment. The same behaviour (e.g. separation) may mean something different in different cultures, which invalidates the procedure.

❖ Explanations of attachment should account for the facts and explain why and how attachments form, and to whom. The psychodynamic approach suggests that an infant becomes attached to its mother because she gives pleasure to the infant through feeding. The mother is the first love object. Learning theory also suggests that attachment occurs through feeding. Attachment is a learned drive and the mother (or person doing the feeding) is a secondary reinforcer. Learning explanations are reductionist and we know that feeding on its own cannot explain attachment. Social learning theory suggests that attachment, and relationships generally, are learned through imitation.

❖ Bowlby's theory of attachment is of enduring importance. He argued that attachment is innate, adaptive, and reciprocal. The primary attachment relationship (monotropy) creates proximity-seeking behaviour, provides an internal working model for all later relationships, and offers a secure base for exploration. Social releasers are a fundamental part of this process. The value of the theory is to some extent undermined by some of Bowlby's claims. He may not have been right about the critical period for attachment, or about the importance of the internal working model. Research on the effects of separation also challenges his theory.

❖ The short term effects of deprivation have been described in the PDD (protest-despair-detachment) model. There may be important individual differences in how children respond, and the short-term effects of separation can be moderated if bond disruption is avoided. The long-term effects of separation were predicted by Bowlby's maternal deprivation hypothesis, in particular affectionless psychopathy and anaclitic depression. Evidence that supports such effects includes Bowlby's own "44 thieves" study, as well as studies of the effects of institutional life and hospitalisation. Poor outcome from institutional care may be due to physical rather than emotional deprivation, although deprivation dwarfism suggests otherwise. Maladjustment has been associated with prolonged early hospitalisation but both may be due to poor living conditions. Minimising bond disruption may help children cope with the anxiety of hospitalisation and thus avoid subsequent maladjustment.

Deprivation and privation

❖ Rutter distinguished between different kinds of separation, suggesting that the complete lack of early attachments (privation) *may* have permanent consequences. Studies of children who have experienced extreme privation are hard to interpret but appear to suggest that recovery is possible. However, Tizard's research indicates that recovery is only possible within the context of supportive relationships. Without that support, privated children may not have the ability to sustain emotional relationships. Children with reactive attachment disorder appear to be permanently affected by early privation.

❖ Rutter also pointed out that Bowlby confused correlation with cause. Bowlby proposed that maternal deprivation was the cause of maladjustment, whereas the evidence suggests that the two are related but both may be caused by a third factor such as poor living conditions or family discord.

❖ In addition, Rutter suggested that heed should be taken of the fact that some children *are* quite resilient. Rutter did not disagree with Bowlby's basic concept. He simply suggested that there were important refinements to be made.

Critical issue—Day care

❖ Day nurseries appear to offer a good standard of care but childminding may be less desirable when only routine care is offered. Day care has been shown to improve cognitive development in disadvantaged children, especially where intervention continues through childhood.

❖ It is suggested that social, cognitive, and emotional development may be affected by day care. In terms of social development, it seems that many children benefit from attending day care although children who are by nature shy may find the experience is harmful to their development. In general the research also indicates that day care has a positive effect on cognitive development although it is likely that children receive less personal attention and therefore less stimulation when having to share the attention of a caregiver. This could affect their cognitive development. Finally, the same picture is true for emotional development. Children seem to be equally attached to their primary caregivers whether or not they are in day care.

❖ The effects may be better understood in terms of individual differences. It is likely that some children do, and some children do not, benefit from day care. Those who are insecurely attached and lacking in cognitive stimulation at home may benefit, as well as those whose mothers lack sensitivity. Equally, where the quality of day care is low, children may not thrive.

❖ This leads us to recommend improving the quality of day care through more consistent care as well as better interactions with infants, more stimulating environments, and more sensitive care. It may be possible to improve sensitivity through in-service training. Finally, the effects of day-care separation on parents should not be overlooked, if primary caregivers are to continue to give quality care when they are with their children and bond disruption should be minimised.

FURTHER READING

Chapter 3 in K. Durkin (1995) *Developmental social psychology: From infancy to old age* (Oxford, UK: Blackwell) contains a good account of theory and research on attachment behaviour and maternal deprivation. An accessible account of early development is provided by J.C Berryman, D. Hargreaves, M. Herbert, and A. Taylor (1991) *Developmental psychology and you* (Leicester, UK: BPS Books). The early development of sociability and attachment is discussed fully in Chapter 11 of D.R. Shaffer (1998) *Developmental psychology: Childhood and adolescence (5th Edn.)* (Pacific Grove, CA: Brooks/Cole). Studies of day care and other attachment issues are considered in H.R. Schaffer (1998) *Making decisions about children (2nd Edn.)* (Oxford, UK: Blackwell).

Revision Questions

The examination questions aim to *sample* the material in this whole chapter. For advice on how to answer such questions, refer to Chapter 1, Section 3. You will always have a choice of two questions in the AQA AS-level exam and 30 minutes in which to answer the question you choose:

Question 1
a. Explain what psychologists mean by the terms "deprivation" and "privation".   (3 marks + 3 marks)
b. Outline *one* psychological explanation of attachment.   (6 marks)
c. Describe *one* strength and *one* weakness of this explanation.   (3 marks + 3 marks)
d. "Some mothers choose to stay at home to look after their children while other mothers have little choice in the matter and may feel quite worried about the effects of day care." To what extent does day care affect the social and cognitive development of children?   (12 marks)

Question 2
a. Outline the development of attachment.   (6 marks)
b. Describe *one* research study that has investigated cross-cultural variations in attachments.   (6 marks)
c. Give *two* criticisms of this study.   (6 marks)
d. "A child who experiences early separation from caregivers may suffer permanent damage in terms of his or her social and/or cognitive development." To what extent have deprivation and privation been shown to influence later development?   (12 marks)

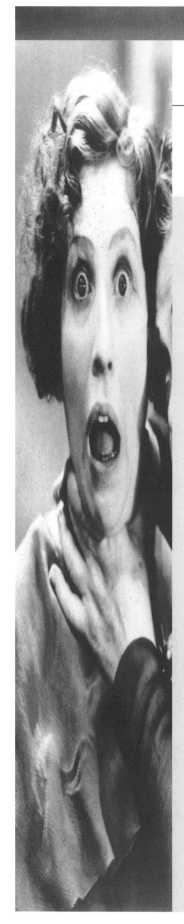

Physiological psychology is an approach or perspective in psychology. The material in this chapter is intended as an example of the way that physiological psychologists explain behaviour.

Physiological psychology is concerned with explanations of behaviour that refer to the body systems—cells, muscles, blood, hormones, and the nervous system.

I could tell I was hungry because my tummy was rumbling.

The jet screeching overhead made my heart pound.

People feel sleepy when a certain substance is released into their body from their brain.

These are all physiological explanations of behaviour and experience. There is no doubt that much of human behaviour can be explained in terms of our body systems, or physiology. However, it may not be possible to explain higher activities, such as problem solving, in this way. Even a relatively "basic" behaviour, such as emotion, might seem rather simplistic when described in terms of the flow of hormones and the rate of your heart. For this reason psychologists often combine physiological explanations with psychological and sociological ones—this is called the biopsychosocial approach.

4

Physiological Psychology
Stress

Physiological response: getting a shock may make your heart pound.

"I simply can't cope any more, the stress of the job is getting to me."

"When I run in a race, I manage to get my best scores because I do well when performing under stress."

This chapter explores a topic in physiological psychology—stress. Stress is an example of a behaviour and experience that can be explained in **physiological** and psychological terms. Stress is something with which we are all familiar. If the media are to be believed, the pressures of everyday life are so great that most of us are highly stressed much of the time. No-one denies that millions of people suffer stress. However, people may have become too concerned about it. For example, some people who spend a lot of money on the National Lottery have received stress counselling because their failure to win is making them poor. Others receive counselling because of the stress associated with winning large sums of money! Stress is all around us.

In this chapter we consider the processes involved in stress and the management of stress:

- *Section 10: Stress as a bodily response.* Stress is a healthy and adaptive response to certain situations. The bodily response is mediated through the autonomic nervous system and can be described by the General Adaptation Syndrome. Prolonged stress may result in lack of health such as cardiovascular disorders. This can be explained in terms of the effects of stress on the immune system.
- *Section 11: Sources of stress.* This section looks at sources of stress such as life changes and work place stressors. When considering stressors it is important to remember that different people respond quite differently. Therefore we will consider the role of individual differences, such as personality, culture, and gender.
- *Section 12: Critical issue—Stress management.* The study of stress can be used to suggest ways of managing stress. There are physiological methods of stress management, such as using drugs or biofeedback. There are also psychological approaches to stress management, such as Meichenbaum's stress inoculation therapy and Kobosa's concept of increasing hardiness.

117

Defining Stress

We will make a start by considering the meaning of the term **stress**. Selye (1950) defined stress as "the nonspecific response of the body to any demand." In other words, stress is a generalised reaction to a demand placed on the body. Interestingly, the term "stress" had not been used in relation to behaviour until Selye (1936) suggested using the term to describe what happened when an organism was exposed to a noxious (unpleasant) stimulus.

It might help to think of stress in engineering terms, where the term means "a force that causes some significant modification of form to a system." Engineers worry about the effects of stress on, for example, a bridge. Stress might cause a bridge to crack. In terms of the human body, the "force" is the demand placed on the body and stress is the response to it.

"Demands" are called **stressors**—events that throw the body out of balance and force it to respond. Examples include environmental factors such as noise, cold, pain, or viruses. The stress response is useful in situations where an animal needs to react quickly, for example when a mouse sees a cat. The mouse feels stressed. Stress results in arousal and arousal makes the animal ready to respond in situations that threaten survival. A stress response is an **innate**, defensive, and adaptive reaction that promotes survival.

There are other situations where stressors require a less immediate response, such as when you know you have to get an assignment done by the following day and feel psychologically stressed (or distressed) as a result. This stress response is important because it makes you feel physiologically aroused, and this should increase your motivation and concentration. However, there are times when the stress response has the opposite effect, as we shall see.

The Role of the Autonomic Nervous System

In order to understand stress as a bodily response, we first need to understand the physiology of arousal (the response to stress), which basically involves the **autonomic nervous system** (ANS). Your nervous system is divided into two main sub-systems:

- The central nervous system (CNS): this consists of the brain and the spinal cord.
- The peripheral nervous system (PNS): this consists of all the other nerve cells in the body.

The PNS is further subdivided into:

- The somatic nervous system, which is concerned with voluntary movements of skeletal muscles (those attached to our bones).
- The autonomic nervous system, which is concerned with involuntary movements of non-skeletal muscles (e.g. those of the heart).

The stress response is important for survival. A mouse that does not feel stress when facing an enemy is not likely to survive because it does not become mobilised to respond.

The ANS is a largely *automatic* or self-regulating system, in other words it responds with little or no conscious thought on your part. The ANS is concerned with many vital functions such as breathing and digestion. If you had to think about these functions they might be forgotten, and then you would die! Therefore, certain physiological systems are automatically controlled.

Sympathetic and parasympathetic systems

The ANS has two general functions: to activate internal organs, or to save energy. These two functions are represented by what are called "branches" of the ANS:

- The **sympathetic branch** activates internal organs in situations needing energy and arousal, such as for "fight or flight".
- The **parasympathetic branch** is involved when the body is trying to conserve and store resources. It monitors the relaxed state, and promotes digestion and **metabolism**.

The sympathetic and parasympathetic nervous systems often operate in opposition (antagonistically) to each other so that, for example, when you are aroused the functions of digestion are suppressed. However, there are some exceptions. For example, the sympathetic nervous system is very active in states of fear, and yet parasympathetic activity can cause people who are fearful to have an involuntary discharge of their bladder or bowels. Another example is sex in the male. Parasympathetic activity is required to obtain an erection, whereas sympathetic activity is needed for ejaculation.

The level of activity in any of the internal organs depends on the relative levels of activity within the sympathetic and parasympathetic nervous systems. For example, heart rate will tend to be high if there is more sympathetic than parasympathetic nervous system activity, whereas it will be low if parasympathetic activity is greater.

Sweating is part of the parasympathetic nervous system's response to high body temperature. The evaporation of sweat from the skin helps to cool the body down.

Activities of the autonomic nervous system

Sympathetic branch	Parasympathetic branch
Increased heart rate	Decreased heart rate
Reduced activity within the stomach	Increased activity within the stomach
Saliva production is inhibited (mouth feels dry)	Saliva production increased to aid digestion
Pupil dilation or expansion	Pupil contraction
Relaxation of the bronchi of the lungs	Constriction of the bronchi of the lungs
Glucose is released	Glucose is stored

Endocrine system

The ANS achieves its effects via the **endocrine system** which consists of a number of ductless glands, including the following: the pituitary gland, the thyroid gland, the parathyroid gland, the adrenal gland, the pancreas, and the gonads. Most importantly, the endocrine glands secrete **hormones**, which are chemical substances released into the bloodstream. They are so important that they have sometimes been described as "the messengers of life". It is these hormones that control ANS activity.

Hormones can have dramatic effects on our behaviour and emotions, especially stress, which is an emotion. Hormones are produced in large quantities but

Nervous system	Endocrine system
• Consists of nerve cells	• Consists of ductless glands
• Acts by transmitting nerve impulses	• Acts by release of hormones
• Acts rapidly	• Acts slowly
• Direct control	• Indirect control
• Specific localised effects of neurotransmitters	• Hormones spread around the body
• Short-lived effects	• Hormones remain in the blood for some time

Where else have you read about the effects of hormones in this book?

disappear very quickly—if this wasn't the case we would go on feeling their effects for a long time, which wouldn't be helpful. However, they take some time to produce their effects because they are carried around the body relatively slowly by the bloodstream as compared with the central nervous system. However, if you consider just how quickly you are overtaken by feelings of fear when you see something scary, then you will realise that the hormones and ANS are only *relatively* slow. They work much more slowly than the central nervous system but have a more widespread effect.

Westen (1996, p.85) contrasted the effects of the nervous system and endocrine system:

> *The difference between the communication that takes place through the two systems is analogous to the difference between word of mouth [nervous system] and mass media [endocrine system] (which can communicate information to hundreds of millions of people at once).*

Homeostasis

The body's internal environment generally remains almost constant in spite of large changes in the external environment. This "steady state" or **homeostasis** (which literally means "same state") is the result of ANS activity and is a fundamental part of the stress response. When an individual is placed under stress, the body strives to return to its normal, steady state as soon as possible. The normal body state is controlled by the parasympathetic branch storing and conserving energy. The sympathetic branch produces arousal which is necessary to deal with emergencies. After such arousal the body needs to be automatically returned to its "baseline" state. One of the most obvious examples of homeostasis is body temperature, which in humans is normally very close to 98.6° F or 37° C. This is the case in spite of the fact that the external temperature in the United Kingdom can vary by as much as about 54° F or 30° C between winter and summer. The body continues to maintain a steady state regardless of external fluctuations. How does it do this?

Carlson (1994) outlined the regulatory mechanisms that govern homeostasis:

1. A *system variable*: this is the characteristic (e.g. temperature) that needs to be regulated.
2. A *set point*: the ideal or most appropriate value of the system variable.
3. A *detector*: the actual or current value of the system variable needs to be assessed.
4. A *correctional mechanism*: this serves to reduce or eliminate the discrepancy between the actual value and the ideal value.

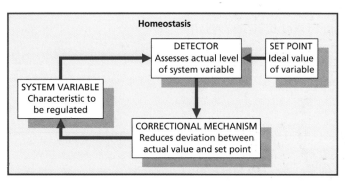

All these regulatory mechanisms are present in central heating systems, which are designed to regulate temperature. The thermostat is set to the chosen temperature, and it detects deviations between the actual and chosen temperatures. When the temperature falls too low, the boiler of the central heating system is activated to restore the chosen temperature. The body's homeostatic mechanism follows similar principles.

In terms of body temperature, when it goes too high certain mechanisms are put into action such as sweating, and vasodilation (blood vessels expanded) to increase heat loss which makes a person "go red". When the body temperature goes too low, other mechanisms are triggered to conserve heat loss and generate more heat, such as vasoconstriction and shivering.

Hypothalamic-pituitary-adrenal axis

At this point you may be wondering what happened to our focus on stress. The stress response originates in the hypothalamus, which forms the first link in a chain that also includes the pituitary and the adrenal glands, which are jointly responsible for arousing the ANS in response to a stressor. This is referred to as the "hypothalamic-pituitary-adrenal axis".

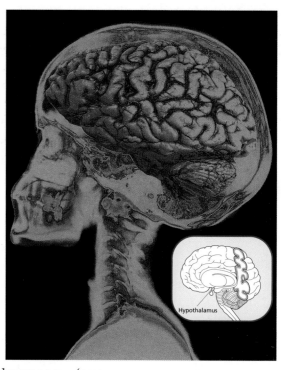

The hypothalamus triggers off the stress response. It is located at the base of the brain.

The hypothalamus and the pituitary gland

The glands of the endocrine system are distributed throughout the body. However, most of the endocrine system is controlled by the **hypothalamus**, which is a small structure at the base of the brain. The hypothalamus produces hormones (e.g. corticotrophin-releasing factor or CRF) which stimulate the anterior **pituitary gland** to secrete its hormones.

In view of its importance, the pituitary gland is often referred to as the "master gland" of the body. The anterior pituitary gland releases several hormones. In terms of the stress response, the one we are interested in is **adrenocorticotrophic hormone** (ACTH), which stimulates the adrenal glands.

Adrenal glands

There are two **adrenal glands**, which are located just above the kidneys. When the adrenal glands are stimulated by ACTH from the anterior pituitary gland, they secrete various steroids, such as corticosteroids and glucosteroids.

The corticosteroids released by the adrenal medulla include **adrenaline** and **noradrenaline** (Americans called these epinephrine and norepinephrine respectively). These hormones are produced as a response to a stressor and, in turn, they produce a stress response—arousal of the sympathetic nervous system and

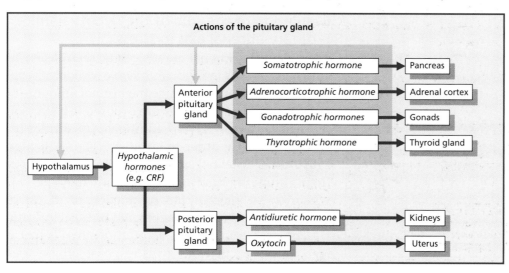

Steroids

Doctors prescribe steroids for some medical conditions, e.g. arthritis. Some athletes take steroids illegally to build muscle size and power. What are the advantages and disadvantages of each of these situations? What safeguards would you propose to try to make use of steroids safer (consider the immune system)?

reduced activity in the parasympathetic system. This includes: increased blood flow to the muscles, increased heart and respiration rate, reduced activity in the digestive system, and increased release of clotting factors into the bloodstream to reduce blood loss in the event of injury. These physiological responses are produced to cope with the stressor.

Glucocorticoids are so called because they have great effects on **glucose** metabolism. They help to break down protein and convert it to glucose, they help to make fats available for energy (all parasympathetic activity), and they increase the rate of blood flow (sympathetic activity). As a result, the individual is ready for "fight or flight". **Cortisol** is a glucocorticoid that is important for coping with long-term stress because it maintains a steady supply of fuel as opposed to the burst of energy needed for "fight or flight" responses. Cortisol is sometimes called the "stress hormone" because excess amounts can be found in the urine of individuals experiencing stress. It is used as a measure of stress.

Glucocorticoids also serve to suppress the **immune system**. The immune system has the task of protecting the body against intruders such as viruses and bacteria. When immune responses are low, we are more likely to become ill. When the adrenal cortex and ANS are activated, immune responses are suppressed.

The effects of the hypothalamic-pituitary-adrenal axis

What does this all mean for stress? The three systems: the hypothalamus, pituitary, and adrenal glands are jointly responsible for arousing the ANS. At times of stress it is the sympathetic hormones that will be released. The hypothalamus triggers the anterior pituitary via the hormone CRF, the anterior pituitary produces ACTH which stimulates the adrenal cortex, and the adrenal cortex produces adrenaline and noradrenaline which arouses the body. The adrenal cortex also produces cortisol which manages energy levels to cope with prolonged stress, and further hormones suppress the body's immune response.

The response of the sympathetic nervous system and the endocrine system to stress can be very useful in the short term because it equips the individual for fight or flight. However, there can be negative long-term consequences. Adrenaline and noradrenaline increase the output of the heart, which causes an increase in blood pressure. If this occurs over long periods of time, it can lead to cardiovascular (heart) disease as we shall see.

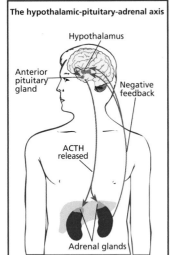

The hypothalamic-pituitary-adrenal axis

Hypothalamus

Anterior pituitary gland

Negative feedback

ACTH released

Adrenal glands

The measurement of stress

One way to measure stress is to use a lie detector. A lie detector, or more properly a "polygraph", is a machine used to tell if an individual is telling the truth. The machine measures a person's heart rate, blood pressure, breathing rate, and galvanic skin response (GSR). GSR tells us the extent to which your skin can conduct an electrical current because, when you sweat, the conductivity of your skin increases. These are all indicators of arousal of the sympathetic branch of the ANS. When a person is lying, their stress levels are elevated and so is their sympathetic arousal.

It would be nice if we could detect the difference between truth and lies so easily. However, people become sympathetically aroused for many reasons, such as fear of being falsely accused or being in a strange place. The polygraph is an excellent detector of nervousness but not of truthfulness. According to Forman and McCauley (1986) about half of all innocent people "fail" a lie detector test. In addition, many criminals are good liars and do not become aroused.

There are other physiological methods of measuring stress, including checking the size of the adrenal gland, which becomes enlarged under prolonged stress, and checking levels of cortisol in the urine.

Evaluation of the role of the hypothalamic-pituitary-adrenal axis in stress

The role of the adrenal glands can be seen clearly in adrenalectomised individuals (people without adrenal glands) who cannot produce the normal amounts of glucocorticoids. When they are exposed to a stressor, they have to be given additional quantities of glucocorticoid in order to survive (Tyrell & Baxter, 1981). Other potential support for this account comes from a study by Brady (see Key Study on page 124) where stress affected the production of digestive hormones in monkeys and ultimately resulted in death.

The problem with this account of stress is that it ignores the fact that the stress response often varies somewhat depending on the type of stressor. For example, Mason (1975) compared the reactions of individuals to stressors that varied in the degree of how much fear, anger, or uncertainty they created. The various stressors produced different patterns of adrenaline and noradrenaline secretion in different individuals.

Another limitation of this physiological account is that it assumes that people respond in a *passive* way to stressors. In fact, people typically react to stressors in an active way. According to Mason (1975) there is an active process of psychological appraisal (judgement) when people confront a stressor, and this process helps to determine the physiological response of the body. For example, Symington et al. (1955) compared the

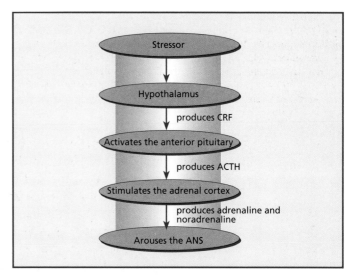

physiological responses of two groups of dying patients, consisting of those who remained conscious and those who were in a coma. There were many more signs of physiological stress in the patients who remained conscious, presumably because they engaged in stressful psychological appraisal of their state.

The General Adaptation Syndrome

Most of our emotional reactions have evolved because they are adaptive and functional in some way. However, it has often been argued that stress has a range of very negative effects such as making an individual unwell. Why, then, do we continue to have a stress reaction if it has harmful effects? This would suggest that the stress response is maladaptive rather than adaptive. According to Hans Selye (1936, 1950), stress is adaptive in the short term because it enables us to cope with or adapt to environmental demands. *Prolonged* stress, however, is very damaging.

Selye (see Key Study on page 125) first studied rats and, later, hospital patients with various injuries and illnesses. He noticed that they all seemed to show a similar pattern of bodily response. Selye called this pattern the **General Adaptation Syndrome** (GAS). He argued that it consisted of three stages:

1. *Alarm reaction stage*: this is the activation of the hypothalmic-pituitary-adrenal system as described earlier, which results in a stress response.
2. *Resistance stage*: the physiological efforts to deal with the stress, started in the alarm reaction stage, are at full capacity. This is the stage of adaptation (the "General Adaptation Syndrome"), the body is adapting or fitting in with the demands of the environment. However, as this stage proceeds, the parasympathetic nervous system (which is involved in energy-storing processes) must call for more careful use of the body's resources in order to cope. The system is being taxed to its limits.
3. *Exhaustion stage*: eventually the physiological systems used in the previous two stages become ineffective, and the initial ANS symptoms of arousal reappear (increased heart rate, sweating and so on). In extreme cases, the damaged adrenal cortex leads to failure of the parasympathetic system (metabolism and storage of energy) and collapse of the body's immune system. Stress-related diseases (e.g. high blood pressure, asthma, heart disease) become more likely.

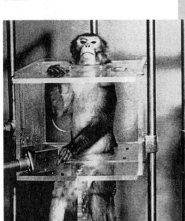

The executive monkey (left) and his yoked control (right). Both animals received shocks at regular intervals but only the executive had control, and only the executive developed the ulcers.

The role of stress in the development of ulcers

A classic study by Joseph Brady (1958) linked high levels of stress to increased hormone production and the development of ulcers. In an early study he placed monkeys in "restraining chairs" and conditioned them to press a lever. They were given shocks every 20 seconds unless the lever was pressed in the same time period. This investigation came to an 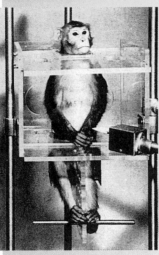 abrupt halt when many of the monkeys suddenly died. Post-mortem examination showed that the monkeys had raised gastro-intestinal hormone levels and that ulcers were the cause of death. The ulcers were not due to the restraint because other monkeys had been kept in restraining chairs for up to six months with no deaths occurring. The question was, were the ulcers due to the electric shocks or to the stress?

To test this Brady and his colleagues used yoked controls. One monkey, called the "executive", was responsible for controlling the lever while a second monkey received the shocks but had no control over the lever. Therefore only the "executive" monkey received the psychological stress of having to press the lever but both monkeys received the shocks.

After 23 days of a six hours on, six hours off schedule the executive monkey died due to a perforated ulcer. Initially Brady thought that stress might be related to the reinforcement schedule. He tried various routines, such as 18 hours on and 6 hours off, or 30 minutes on, 30 minutes off. However, no monkeys died from ulcers. He then tested the stomachs of executive monkeys on a 6 hour on, 6 hour off schedule, and found that stomach acidity was greatest during the rest period.

Brady concluded that it was clearly stress, not the shocks, that created the ulcers, and that the greatest danger occurred when the sympathetic arousal stopped and the stomach was flooded with digestive hormones, a parasympathetic rebound.

Discussion points

1. To what extent do you think it is reasonable to generalise from research on monkeys to human behaviour?

2. What ethical objections could be raised in connection with this study?

KEY STUDY EVALUATION — Brady

This study became very well known and for a long time confirmed a common belief that too much stress at work led to ulcers. The findings were supported in a study by Weiner et al. (1957) using army recruits. Prior to basic training, the soldiers were tested and classed as oversecretors or undersecretors of digestive enzymes. After four months of stressful training, 14% of the oversecretors had developed ulcers whereas none of the undersecretors had. This suggests not only that the same principles do apply to humans but also that individual differences may be important because not all of the oversecretors developed ulcers.

One criticism made of Brady's study in general was that the monkeys were not randomly selected, the "executive" was chosen because it was faster at learning an avoidance response. This may of course have parallels with the human world.

A more serious problem was raised in research by Marshall et al. (1985). They found strong evidence of another cause for stomach ulcers, a bacterium called *Helicobacter pylori*. It might be that stress has some influence on the development of ulcers but the danger was that people assumed this was the *only* cause. Marshall was so convinced that the bacterium was at fault that he deliberately gave himself the infection— and developed ulcers.

Evaluation of the General Adaptation Syndrome

Selye's contribution was to alert medicine to the importance of stress in disease. In terms of criticisms, the General Adaptation Syndrome incorporates the hypothalamic-pituitary-adrenal system, and therefore all the same criticisms apply here as outlined earlier, namely that GAS suggests a single, passive response to stressors whereas there is evidence that stress responses are different according to the individual, situation, and stressor, and also that individuals' responses are active rather than passive.

Selye has also been criticised for using non-human animals to support his research on human responses to stress. This may explain why his model

Selye and the General Adaptation Syndrome

Hans Selye conducted much research into stress from the 1930s until he died in 1982. In fact it was Selye who first popularised the term "stress" to describe the "forces" that impinge on an animal. Until this "invention" stress had not been used as a psychological concept.

In 1936 Selye published his first article on the effects of stress, reporting the results of an experiment with rats. He found that if he exposed the rats to "acute nocuous agents" a typical syndrome appeared. The nocuous agents included cold, surgical injury, excessive exercise, severing the spinal cord, or sub-lethal doses of various drugs! The symptoms exhibited could not be due to the stimuli themselves because the same symptoms appeared in response to all of them. Therefore the symptoms must be due to the more general state of what he described as "stress".

Stage 1: Alarm reaction. This developed 6–48 hours after the initial injury and included loss of muscular tone, drop in body temperature, and decrease in size of the spleen and liver.

Stage 2: Resistance. This second stage was initially marked by an increase in the size of the adrenal glands and a decrease in some pituitary activity, such as the production of growth hormone. If the treatment was continued at a lower level (for example, small doses of drugs or slight injuries) then the body returned to a near normal state.

Stage 3: Exhaustion. Within one to three months the animals lost their resistance and succumbed, returning to a state similar to their initial response.

Selye referred to this model as the "General Adaptation Syndrome" because it represented the body's attempt to cope in an **adaptive** fashion with stress. After the initial "alarm reaction" (stage 1) the organism does adapt and return to normal functioning. It is only after prolonged stress that exhaustion results.

In later research Selye (1950) confirmed these findings using data collected from hospital patients who were suffering various injuries and illnesses.

Discussion points

1. Why do you think the work of Selye has been so influential to the study of stress?

2. What are the weaknesses of his work in terms, for example, of the methodology or the ethics?

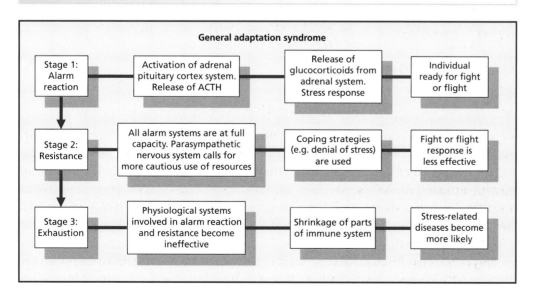

overemphasises physiological factors at the expense of psychological factors, such as the role of emotional and cognitive factors in stress—non-human animals are less affected by emotional and cognitive factors.

Selye did recognise some of the weaknesses of the model, and spent his life clarifying the way people cope with stress. He did recognise the importance of individual differences and the active nature of the stress response, as is illustrated here by one of his stories of an alcoholic's two sons (Selye, 1980, p.143):

One was a teetotaler and the other was a drunk. When asked to explain their drinking habits, both replied, "With a father like that, what do you expect?" This illustrates perhaps the most important moral we can draw from stress research: that it is not what we face but how we face it that matters ... We do have limited control over ourselves. It is the exercise of this control, or the lack of it, that can decide whether we are made or broken by the stress of life.

Stress and Physical Illness

The research by Selye pointed to the importance of stress as a factor in physical illness. Stress has subsequently been linked with a range of physical illnesses including headaches, infectious illness (e.g. influenza), cardiovascular disease, diabetes, asthma, and rheumatoid arthritis (Curtis, 2000). There is a considerable body of research evidence that supports this. For example, Cohen, Tyrrell, and Smith (1991) carried out a study in which the participants were given nasal drops containing cold viruses. The researchers determined stress levels by recording the number of life changes an individual had recently experienced and also the extent to which they "felt out of control". Both of these factors are associated with increased stress (as we will see in Section 11). Those participants who had the highest level of stress were almost *twice* as likely to develop colds as those with the lowest level of stress. This suggests a strong link between stress and illness.

Stress and ulcers

There is also evidence that stress may be a causal factor in stomach ulcers, as first described by Brady (1958) whose research is presented in the Key Study on page 124. Stress often increases the secretion of hydrochloric acid which causes ulcers. Stress also weakens the defences of the gastrointestinal tract against this acid. As a result, gastric ulcers can develop (Pinel, 1997).

Stress and hypertension

Perhaps the best known link is between stress and cardiovascular (heart) disease. **Hypertension** occurs when a person has experienced raised blood pressure consistently for several weeks or more. It is a major risk factor for coronary heart disease (CHD). Hypertension is caused by a variety of factors such as obesity, eating too much salt, drinking too much coffee (caffeine) or alcohol, lack of exercise, inherited predispositions, and finally psychosocial factors such as stress, anger, and hostility. Cobb and Rose (1973) produced evidence of a link between stress and hypertension in a study of men who worked as air traffic controllers and airmen. The researchers analysed annual medical records and found that hypertension rates were several times higher in the air traffic controllers, and also that those controllers working in airports with greater traffic density had higher levels of hypertension.

Stress and coronary heart disease

Studies of CHD itself have also implicated stress, most notably a study by Friedman and Rosenman (1959, see Key Study on page 141) which found that individuals who cope least well with stress (**Type A**) are much more likely to experience CHD than other personality types.

How does stress cause illness?

As we have seen, there is good evidence that stress can increase the chances of someone becoming ill. There are two major ways in which stress can cause illness:

1. Directly, by reducing the body's ability to fight illness.
2. Indirectly, by leading the stressed individual to adopt an unhealthy lifestyle (e.g. increased smoking and drinking).

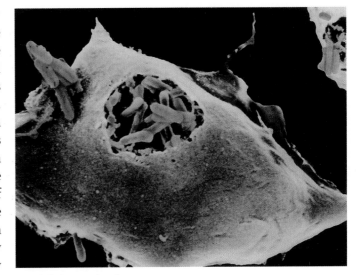

Like some monster in a movie, cells of the immune system kill "invaders" by engulfing them. In the photograph a macrophage cell is engulfing *M. Tuberculosis* bacteria.

Direct effects of stress on the immune system

There is increasing evidence that stress can cause illness by impairing the workings of the immune system. This system acts like an army, identifying and killing any intruders to the body. It consists of cells distributed throughout the body that fight disease. How does the immune system work? The cells within the immune system are known as white blood cells (**leucocytes**). These cells identify and destroy foreign bodies (called **antigens**) such as viruses. The presence of antigens leads to the production of **antibodies**. If you have ever had measles then your body will have produced antibodies as a result of the initial infection and these will help the leucocytes fight off any subsequent measles infection. Some vaccinations draw on this natural system of defence. You are injected with a mild dose of a disease so that your body can produce antibodies. At the time the body can fight off the small invasion of the virus, and later can cope with a larger, potentially dangerous invasion because the "troops" are ready.

There are several kinds of white blood cells or leucocytes within the immune system, including T cells, B cells, and **natural killer cells**. T cells destroy invaders, and T-helper cells increase immunological activity. Natural killer cells are involved in the fight against both viruses and tumours.

The reason AIDS has such a disastrous effect is because HIV attacks T-helper cells and this cripples the immune system.

Psychoneuroimmunology

The field of research that investigates the link between stress and other psychological states is called **psychoneuroimmunology** (PNI). One of the first studies to demonstrate the immunosuppressive effects (something that suppresses the immune system) of stress was conducted by Riley (1981) using mice. Stress was created by placing the mice on a turntable rotating at 45 rpm (at the speed of an old Beatles single!). Riley measured the mice's lymphocyte count over a five-hour period and found a marked decrease. In other words their immune response was suppressed, presumably by the stress of sitting on the revolving disc. In a later study Riley studied the link between stress and tumour growth by implanting cancer cells in mice. One group had 10 minutes of rotation per hour for three days (high-stress condition), another group had no stress. Riley found that tumour growth stopped in the no-stress group, presumably because their intact immune systems were able to control it, whereas the "stressed" mice developed large tumours, presumably because of their low levels of lymphocytes.

This research has been supported by studies with humans. For example, Schliefer et al. (1983) looked at the functioning of the immune system in the husbands of women who died from breast cancer. The husbands' immune system functioned less well after their wives had died than before, showing the impact of bereavement on the immune system. Further evidence of the immunosuppressive effects of stress is given by Kiecolt-Glaser et al. (1984), described in the Key Study below.

The endocrine system and immunosuppression

It is possible that the link between stress and illness is due to the effects of **endorphins**. These hormones are the body's natural painkillers. They are biochemical substances that are like opium and are released at times of pain or anxiety. In addition to decreasing sensations of pain they also suppress activity in the immune system, in particular the natural killer cells. So when a person is under stress their endorphins are ready to help cope with any pain, but at the same time the endorphins reduce the body's immune response.

The effects of stress on the immune system

Kiecolt-Glaser et al. (1984) studied human responses to stress by using a naturally occurring situation—examinations. The researchers took blood samples from 75 first-year medical students (49 males and 26 females), all of whom were volunteers. The samples were taken one month before their final examinations (the baseline sample) and again on the first day of their final examinations, after the students had completed two of the examinations. This was the "stress sample", taken when the students' stress levels should be at their highest.

Kiecolt-Glaser et al. found that natural killer cell activity declined between the two samples, confirming other research findings that stress is associated with a reduced immune response.

KEY STUDY EVALUATION — Kiecolt-Glaser et al.

There are many strengths to this study. First of all, it was a **natural experiment** which means that there can be fewer ethical objections but, at the same time, it does mean it was not a true experiment. At best we can say that stress and immune response are negatively correlated (as one increases the other decreases), we cannot say that one *caused* the other.

One advantage of this study, again related to the choice of **independent variable** (exam stress), is that it was a long-term form of stress. In previous studies with human participants, stress had been artificially induced, for example by restricting sleep for several days (Palmblad et al. 1979). This is likely to produce a different kind of stress to that experienced naturally.

The volunteers were also assessed using behavioural measures. On both occasions they were given questionnaires to assess psychiatric symptoms, loneliness, and life events. This was because there are theories which suggest that all three are associated with increased levels of stress. Kiecolt-Glaser et al. found that immune responses were *especially* weak in those students who reported feeling most lonely, as well as those who were experiencing other stressful life events and psychiatric symptoms such as depression or anxiety.

This means that there were two key findings from this study. One was that stress was associated with a lowered immune response in humans. The second was that there were a number of different sources of stress and factors that moderate it, an issue that we will explore in Sections 11 and 12.

Discussion points

1. This was a natural experiment. What are the advantages and disadvantages of such research?

2. How well do you feel these results would generalise to all humans?

In addition, many components of the immune system are governed by the endocrine system. T-cells mature in the thymus (an endocrine gland), and leukocytes are produced in the bone marrow and then migrate to the thymus. When endocrine activity is reduced, as in the GAS cycle, then immune system activity must be affected.

> The β-endorphins produced by the human body are natural opiates that can trigger the same feeling of euphoria as drugs such as opium. Prolonged and extreme exercise produces this effect in a safer way.

Finally, we have previously noted that adrenal glands produce glucocorticoids at times of stress, which also serve to suppress the immune system. It seems everything is acting against the immune system!

Evaluation. There is convincing evidence that stress can directly produce changes in the immune system, and there is also good evidence that stress can directly increase the probability that individuals develop various physical illnesses. However, this evidence is not conclusive. As Bachen, Cohen, and Marsland (1997) concluded, "It is not yet clear that either the nature or magnitude of immunological change found in PNI research bears any relevance to increased disease susceptibility."

One reason for this caution is that the functioning of the immune system in most stressed individuals is actually within the normal range. If it is not unduly increased, how could this have such major effects such as increased chances of CHD?

Another reason for caution is that the immune system is very complex, and so the quality of an individual's immune system is hard to assess. Recent research by Evans, Clow, and Hucklebridge (1997) into PNI has found the assumption that stress suppresses the immune system is oversimplified. Evans et al. have suggested that individual measures of the state of the immune system during stress may vary with the type of stress, its duration, and even its timing.

Indirect effects of stress on the immune system: Lifestyle

Stress can cause illness in an indirect way via changes to lifestyle. In technical terms, stressed individuals may be more likely to expose themselves to **pathogens**, which are agents causing physical illness. People who are stressed tended to smoke more, drink more alcohol, take less exercise, and sleep less than people who are not stressed (Cohen & Williamson, 1991). For example, adolescents who experience high levels of stress are more likely to start smoking than those whose lives are less stressful (Wills, 1985). Adults are more likely to resume smoking after having given up when they experience a high level of stress in their lives (Carey et al., 1993).

So far as alcohol is concerned, there is support for the alternative view—that it *reduces* stress (Ogden, 1996). Tension reduction theory proposes that tension in the form of anxiety, fear, or depression leads to an increase in alcohol consumption in order to reduce the level of tension.

Evidence that illness depends on lifestyle as well as on stress was reported by Brown (1991). The effects of stress in the form of negative life events were compared in students who were high in physical fitness and those low in physical fitness. Stress almost

Stress can lead to an unhealthy lifestyle.

Stress may cause illness indirectly through aspects of a person's lifestyle, such as alcohol consumption. Alcohol consumption is a risk factor in cardiovascular disease but, on the other hand, some people argue that drinking helps reduce stress.

trebled the number of visits to the health clinic made by unfit students, but had little effect on visits made by those who were physically fit.

Finally, Curtis (2000) notes that indirect effects are likely through changes in health practices that increase risks for illness. For example, engaging in risky behaviours (e.g. substance abuse) may lead indirectly to disease or illness using similar pathways.

SECTION 11
Sources of Stress

An alternative way to consider stress is to examine the factors that cause stress—potential stressors. The study by Kiecolt-Glaser et al. (see Key Study on page 128) indicated that individuals are often exposed to more than one stressor at any time. In this section we are going to consider some of the most important ones: life events and daily hassles; and work-related stressors, which include environmental stressors such as overcrowding, temperature, and noise.

In addition to having many sources of stress, we should also consider that there are many different responses to stress. At the beginning of the last section we considered Selye's definition of stress: "the nonspecific response of the body to any demand". However, there are problems with this definition because it suggests that there is only one kind of stress response, whereas in fact there are many responses to stress—such as anxiety, depression, anger, and even happiness (Selye called this last form of response "eustress"). The nature of the stress response depends on a variety of other factors—what we might loosely term "the situation". Selye's definition does not consider adequately the different sources of stress and responses to it.

Cox (1978) proposed a **transactional model** which described stress in terms of an interaction between the individual and his or her environment. Cox proposed that stress is experienced when the perceived demands of the environment are greater than the individual's perceived ability to cope. The use of the term "transaction" refers to the *interaction* between the individual and the environment.

Cox's transactional model can explain why learners find driving stressful whereas experienced drivers don't. The learner has limited ability to meet the demands of handling a car in traffic, which means that the demands of the environment are *greater* than their perceived ability to cope. For experienced drivers the perceived demands of the environment are *less* than their perceived ability to cope.

Life Events

Two medical doctors, Holmes and Rahe (1967), were the first to record the effects of life events. They noticed in their patients that certain **life events** seemed to be associated with stress and poor health. In particular, these life events could be characterised as those that involved change from a steady state, such as getting divorced or moving house. Even positive events, such as getting married, seemed to be associated with stress. They suggested that the changes associated with major life events absorb "psychic energy", leaving less available for other matters such as physical defence against illness. In order to demonstrate this correlation between life events, stress, and illness, Holmes and Rahe first needed some method of measuring life events. This led them to develop the Social Readjustment Rating Scale (SRRS) that is described in the Key Study on the next page.

The final scale consisted of 43 items or events. Some of these are shown in the table below. Respondents were asked to indicate which of the life events had happened to them over the last six months. Each life event has a value—given in life change units (LCUs). By adding up the value of the events ticked, it was possible to calculate a life event score (the total of the LCUs).

Change can be stressful, even the usually pleasant ones associated with going on holiday.

LIFE EVENTS		
Rank	**Life Event**	**Stress Value**
1	Death of a spouse	100
2	Divorce	73
3	Marital separation	65
4	Jail term	63
5	Death of a close family member	63
6	Personal injury or illness	50
7	Marriage	53
8	Fired at work	47
9	Marital reconciliation	43
10	Retirement	45
13	Sex difficulties	39
23	Son or daughter leaving	29
38	Change in sleeping habits	16
40	Change in eating habits	15
41	Vacation	13
42	Christmas	12
43	Minor violations of the law	11

Adapted from Holmes, T., & Rahe, R. (1967). The social readjustment rating scale. *Journal of Psychosomatic Research, 11*, 213–218.

Development of the Social Readjustment Rating Scale

Early work on life events was carried out by two medical doctors, Thomas Holmes and Richard Rahe (1967). They observed that patients tended to have experienced several life events in the months before the onset of illness. In order to test their hypothesis they developed the Social Readjustment Rating Scale, by examining 5000 patient records and making a list of 43 life events that seemed to precede illness. Next, they asked nearly 400 participants to rate each item in terms of the amount of stress it produced. They assigned an arbitrary value of 500 to marriage as a reference point. Specifically they asked participants to think of each event and to answer the question "Is this event indicative of more or less readjustment than marriage? Would the readjustment take longer or shorter to accomplish?"

At the end, they averaged everyone's results and divided by 10 to get a measure of the individual events in terms of life change units (LCUs). An LCU represented the degree of stress caused by an event. Next, Holmes and Rahe used their questionnaire with various sub-groups to see if the ratings were consistent. For example, they compared male and female scores, single and married, black and white, younger and older respondents. There was strong agreement between different groups which suggested that it was a valid measure for all types of people.

Using the SRRS involves asking participants to indicate which out of 43 life events have happened to them over a period of time (usually six or twelve months). A life event score is then calculated by adding up the LCUs for each event ticked. Why are holidays treated as stressful life events? According to Holmes and Rahe (1967), any change (whether desirable or undesirable) can be stressful.

KEY STUDY EVALUATION — Holmes and Rahe

There are various problems with evidence obtained from the use of the Social Readjustment Rating Scale. First, it is often not clear whether life events have caused some stress-related illness, or whether it was stress that caused the life events. For example, stress may cause a change in eating habits rather than a change in eating habits causing stress.

Second, the impact of most life events varies from person to person. For example, marital separation may be less stressful for someone who has already established an intimate relationship with someone else. Some alternative psychological measures take account of the context in which people experience life events. For example, this is true of the Life Events and Difficulties Schedule (LEDS; see Harris, 1997). It is also important to take subjective interpretation into account, as it is not the events themselves but their meaning that is important. Cohen (1983) developed a "perceived stress scale" to do this.

Third, the assumption that desirable life events can cause stress-related illnesses is not generally supported (Martin, 1989), and in addition the scale tends to muddle together different kinds of life events, most particularly those over which you have some control and those you do not. It is these latter events that may be most stressful.

The importance of this scale is not in its usefulness but in its status as a breakthrough. It triggered off a wealth of research and efforts to develop a more effective tool, such as the Hassles and Uplifts Scale devised by DeLongis et al. (see page 134).

The evidence from numerous studies using the Social Readjustment Rating Scale is that people who have experienced events totalling more than 300 life change units over a period of one year are more at risk for a wide range of physical and mental illnesses. These illnesses include heart attacks, diabetes, TB, asthma, anxiety, and depression (Martin, 1989). However, the correlations between life change units and susceptibility to any particular illness tend to be rather low, indicating a weak association between life events and illness.

Discussion points

1. What are the main reasons why some life events are much more stressful than others?

2. What criticisms can you make of the approach adopted by Holmes and Rahe?

Using the SRRS

Holmes and Rahe developed the SRRS in order to test their hypothesis that stress as created by life events was a cause of physical illness. One of the first attempts to do this was a study by Rahe, Mahan, and Arthur (1970) using a large sample of naval personnel: 2500 men who were the crew of three US navy cruisers. Just before a tour of duty, participants were asked to fill in a questionnaire relating to significant changes in their life over the past six months. This meant that a LCU (life change unit) value could be calculated for each of the naval personnel. During the six months tour of duty, a health record was kept for each participant by the ship's physician. Rahe et al. found a significant positive correlation of 0.118 between LCUs and illness. LCUs are positively correlated with illness. A correlation of 0.118 may sound like a very small and therefore insignificant figure (perfect correlation is 1.00 and no correlation is 0.00) but with a sample size of 2500 it is significant.

Further support has come from other studies. Rahe and Arthur (1977) found an increase of various psychological illnesses, athletic injuries, physical illness, and even traffic accidents, when LCUs were raised.

It is notable that all this supportive work was by Rahe. We might consider the influence of experimenter effects.

Evaluation of the SRRS evidence

There are several drawbacks to these studies. First the research is correlational, which means that we cannot know whether stress (or life change) actually caused the illness. It may be that stress caused a life event, such as divorce, rather than vice versa. It may also be the case that there are other intervening variables involved. For example, it may be that certain individuals do find life events stressful because they are vulnerable personalities and the reason they become ill may also be due to their personality rather than the events *per se*. Individual differences, such as your coping skills, past experiences, and physical strength, all moderate the extent to which a potentially stressful event will affect you. The issue of individual differences will be explored later in this section.

It may also be the case that different events affect people differently, and this may explain the weak correlations found. For example, retirement might be a dramatic change for some people but not for others. The SRRS tends to muddle together many different kinds of experience which will not affect everyone in the same way.

A further issue is that the data on LCUs were collected retrospectively and this may result in unreliable data, although most life events are not the kind of thing one would forget. However, it may be hard to recall exactly when such events did happen. Sometimes a major incident seems to have happened only a few months ago whereas in fact it was longer ago than that. The concept of "life events" should also be questioned; perhaps it is other factors that lead to stress rather than major "events", as we shall see next when we consider daily hassles.

Daily hassles

Anita DeLongis and her co-workers (1982) were critics of the life event approach, because of the various problems just outlined. Most importantly DeLongis et al. felt that the life events research studies had found at best a very weak correlation between life events and illness. An alternative would be to focus on the ongoing stresses and strains of daily living, what we generally call "hassles". In reality, according to DeLongis et al., it is these more than anything that determine the extent to which a person feels stressed. Therefore this would lead us to expect a stronger correlation between hassles and physical illness than was found for life events.

Can you think of some examples of "hassles"? Some ideas are given in the activity on page 135.

Delongis et al. (1982) investigated the relationship between hassles and physical health, as well as uplifts and physical health (see Key Study on the next page). They did find a correlation which was slightly better than that found for life events and health, but the scale suffered from rather similar problems to the SRRS. For example, the same hassle can be experienced in a different way on two occasions, and individual differences affect the extent to which a hassle is stressful or not.

In general this makes these "scale" approaches to stress rather unworkable. It is not possible to identify a global set of events, large or small, which can provide a clear link with subsequent stress. It may be more profitable to focus on particular "hassles" such as overcrowding, noise, and so on.

Hassles and uplifts

Most people experience major life events very infrequently. Therefore a better measure of stress might look at the stresses and strains of daily life. These are called "hassles". Delongis et al. (1982) compared the two measures: a life events scale and their own hassles scale, to see which was a better predictor of later health problems. They also considered the effects of "uplifts". Uplifts are events that make you feel good. How do these affect health?

Participants were asked to complete four questionnaires once a month for a period of a year:

- Hassles scale (117 hassles, such as: concerns about weight, rising prices, home maintenance, losing things, crime, and physical appearance).
- Uplifts scale (135 uplifts, such as: recreation, relations with friends, good weather, job promotion).
- Life events questionnaire (24 major events).
- A health status questionnaire consisting of questions on overall health status, bodily symptoms, and energy levels.

There were 100 participants from around the San Francisco area, aged between 45 and 64. They were predominantly well educated and had high income. The findings were that both the frequency and intensity of hassles were significantly correlated with overall health status and bodily symptoms. Daily uplifts had little effect on health. They also found no relationship between life events and health during the study, although there was a relationship for life events recorded for the 2½ years before the study.

Discussion points

1. How might the sample of respondents have biased the results obtained in this study?
2. Why might daily hassles be a better measure of stress than life events?

KEY STUDY EVALUATION — DeLongis et al.

This approach managed to avoid the problem of the relevance of major life events but it still overlooked many chronic "ongoing" sources of stress, such as poor housing, low incomes, strains of family life, unsatisfying work and so on. Health is probably affected by all three: hassles, chronic situations, and life changes.

One problem with the scales used in this study was that the same hassle can be experienced in different ways by different people or by the same person on different occasions. The same factors that are a hassle to one person may actually be an uplift to another, or the same factor might mean different things to the same person on different occasions. For example, a traffic jam may sometimes give you time to relax, whereas at other times it seems highly stressful. For this reason DeLongis, Folkman, and Lazarus (1988) later produced a single "Hassles and Uplifts Scale" where respondents could indicate the strength of a factor either as a hassle or an uplift. In other words, when asked to indicate how they felt about "sex" they could rate it as 0 1 2 3 as a hassle or 0 1 2 3 as an uplift.

A further problem concerns the original sample which was of people aged over 45, this sample bias may have affected the results. Khan and Patel (1996) found that older people tended to have less severe, and fewer, hassles than younger people.

Work-related Stress

Both the pressures of work and the work environment itself (overcrowding, noise, temperature) are sources of stress. Such stresses may lead to aggression or just increase general arousal and therefore increase any stress already felt. Stress is not just experienced by those who are in paid employment, but similar experiences are shared by, for example, volunteer workers and homemakers.

Overcrowding

In work environments, overcrowding may be a factor that increases feelings of stress. A classic study using rats showed to what extent the stress associated with overcrowding can have disastrous effects on behaviour. Calhoun (1962) established a population of rats in an enclosure. They had plenty of food, no predators, and little disease yet within two years they reached a steady population size of 150 adults. Why was there this limitation on their population? Why didn't the population just continue growing? Calhoun proposed that the answer was stress. Stress from social interactions disrupted maternal behaviour leading to a high infant mortality rate and resulting in population control. To confirm this, Calhoun designed several experiments again with rats. He observed various pathological behaviours such as hypersexual males who constantly sought sexually receptive females and also attacked and ate baby rats. Many females died giving birth, failed to build nests for their young, or to feed them, or to protect them from danger. In one experiment 95% of the young died before reaching maturity. There were also increases in aggression and physical illness. In this experiment stress acted as an important governing factor in maintaining an optimum population size.

It is always dangerous to generalise from non-human animal behaviour to humans because much more of human behaviour is governed by cognitive activity, however the study does suggest that overcrowding may result in stress (and stress leads to aggressive and abnormal behaviours). Clearly it is not possible to conduct experimental research on overcrowding with humans but situations where overcrowding exists can be observed. In another classic study, Freedman et al. (1975) correlated the incidence of various pathological conditions with urban living. He found high positive correlations between admissions to mental hospitals and urban density, as well as tuberculosis, and juvenile delinquency. In other words, the higher the urban density the more likely such problems were to appear.

■ Activity: You could conduct your own research into the effects of stress and illness using your own daily hassle index. Some examples are given below from an index that was designed specifically for college students. Illness can be assessed by, for example, checking absenteeism or asking people to keep a diary for a short period.

Hassles scale

Assess yourself by indicating how often each item irritates you, by entering a number between 1 and 10 in the box, where 10 = frequently, 5 = sometimes, and 0 = almost never.

Example items:

☐ Parking problems around campus

☐ Careless bike riders

☐ Library too noisy

☐ Too little time

☐ Too little money

☐ Boring teacher

☐ Not enough close friends

☐ Room temperatures

☐ Conflicts with family

☐ Too little sleep

☐ Writing essays

☐ Fixing hair in the morning

Adapted from Schafer, W. (1992), *Stress management for wellness* (2nd edn.). New York: Harcourt Brace Jovanovich.

Of course, as we know, a significant correlation does not mean that overcrowding *caused* the social pathologies. It may be that other factors act as intervening variables, such as low income which might cause both overcrowding and stress. In addition, there are cultures and situations where high density is not experienced as a stressor—such as at football matches or, possibly, for people living in Hong Kong.

Temperature and pollution

Temperature may also be a critical component of stress at work, in some work environments. Baron and Ransberger (1978) showed that incidences of violence could be related to high air temperatures. They used collected data on incidents of group violence in the US as well as the corresponding weather reports. They found that when the temperature was moderately hot, around 84° C, violence was highest; when temperatures got any hotter, aggression declined. This indicates that temperature can act as a stressor leading to the response of aggression.

Pollution is a particular issue with relation to smoking. Non-smokers find it very unpleasant to work in a smoky environment and this has lead to problems for smokers, who have to go somewhere else to smoke.

For some people overcrowding is very stressful but the same people may not feel stressed when they go to a football match.

You may think you can work just as well with background noise, but psychological research suggests that there is some psychic cost and it may contribute to your stress levels.

Noise

Many people would claim that they can concentrate quite well no matter what the noise levels are. In fact, research has found that this is true to some extent but Glass, Singer, and Friedman (1969) questioned whether people may just *appear* to cope with noise. There is still some psychic cost and this leaves the individual with fewer resources available to cope with stress. To investigate this hypothesis they arranged for 60 undergraduates to complete a number of cognitive tasks, such as word searches, under one of four conditions: loud or soft noise which was played at random (unpredictable) or fixed (predictable intervals). There was also a no-noise condition. During the task, physiological arousal was measured using the galvanic skin response (GSR, a measure of autonomic arousal or stress). After the task participants were asked to complete four puzzles. Two of them were insoluble. Frustration (stress) was measured in terms of the length of time that participants persisted at these tasks.

Participants did adapt to the noise. In the predictable noise condition, participants made less errors, and had lower GSR and higher task persistence than those in the random noise condition. Those in the no-noise condition made even fewer errors. This suggests that unpredictable noise has the greatest effect but even random noise creates some stress. Glass et al. suggested that this is because we can "tune out" constant stimuli while still attending at a preconscious level, but unpredictable stimuli require continued attention, and this reduces our ability to cope with stress. Therefore noise is, in itself, a stressor.

Predictability and controllability

There are two important features of the effects of noise: predictability and also controllability. In a further study Glass et al. (1969) arranged for participants to listen to random noise while performing the same tasks as before. There were two conditions: one where the participant was given a button to press so she could control the noise (the participants were all females), and a second condition where there was not an option to control the noise. Participants in the button condition were significantly more persistent on the insoluble task than those given no control over the noise. Presumably the greater sense of control increased the individual's ability to cope which thus reduced anxiety.

In Cohen et al.'s (1991) research on stress and the common cold those participants who felt their lives were unpredictable and uncontrollable were twice as likely to develop colds as those suffering low stress.

A replication of Glass et al.'s research provided rather neat support for the effects of controllability. In this replication, Gardner (1978) found no negative effects for unpredictability. Then he realised that he had asked his participants to sign a consent agreement saying that they understood their rights as a participants. He wondered if this had given them a sense of control that had not been present in the original study. He tested this by giving the consent forms to only half the participants, and found that the half without consent forms did experience stress whereas the other half did not.

In the last section we looked at the classic study of stress in "executive monkeys" (see Key Study on page 124). This indicated how the stress related to making decisions might be linked to physical illness, notably the formation of gastric ulcers. The monkey who lacked control (the "yoked" control) experienced no ill effects. This is in contrast with the findings from Glass et al. just described and Langer and Rodin (see Key Study on the next page). In these studies *lack* of control was associated with higher stress. The same finding emerged in a study by Marmot et al. (1997) of employees in the civil service, which found that those workers on the lowest employment grades were four times more likely to die of a heart attack than those on the most senior grades. They were also more likely to suffer from cancers, strokes, and gastrointestinal disorders. It was suggested that the difference between senior and lower positions was progressively less control. Low control was linked to higher stress.

Taken together we have explanations for why both managers and the work force might experience stress—either too much or too little responsibility or stress!

What comments might you make on the ethics of Gardner's study?

In these studies responsibility was taken to be equivalent to control. Do you think that responsibility is the same as control?

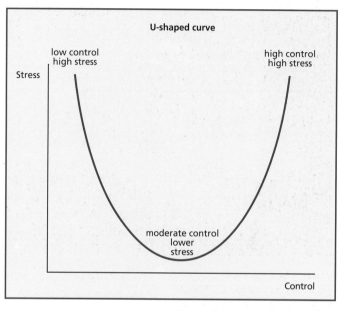

Research suggests that lack of control may lead to stress (e.g. Glass et al.) but also that high control may create stress (Brady). This is a curvilinear relationship as shown in the graph.

Studies of workplace stress

In work situations the usual causes of stress are such things as uncertainty about whether you may lose your job shortly, organisational change, interpersonal conflicts, sexual harassment, punitive management, lack of control, underutilisation of skills, responsibility for others, difficult tasks, shift work, lack of support, and a dangerous, unpleasant, or uncomfortable work environment. In fact the list is virtually endless!

The effects of work-related stress include absenteeism, high job turnover, alcohol and drug abuse, and poor performance in terms of quantity and quality. A good employer wishes to reduce work stress because the costs are high in terms of poor productivity.

Role conflict

The demands of the organisation, such as higher productivity or lower wage bills, may be in direct conflict with the needs of the workers, who may be highly resistant to the idea of working longer hours for smaller rewards. This creates **role conflict** and stress for the individual. If individuals do not accept organisational demands they may lose their jobs. If they do accept the demands this may conflict with other demands from their family, or they may fear for their health. Shirom (1989) found that there was a significant correlation between perceived role conflict and CHD. This relationship was only true for middle management (white-collar workers) rather than blue-collar workers (the "shop-floor"). Margolis and Kroes (1974) found that foremen were seven times more likely to develop gastric ulcers than shop-floor workers. This suggests more role conflict for those in greater control.

The health of residents in old people's homes

It is a disturbing fact that older people often experience a decline in their health when they begin living a home for the elderly. Ellen Langer and Judith Rodin (1976) questioned whether a key factor might be the loss of control they experience on becoming "inmates". To investigate this they set up a major study using residents in a nursing home. At the start of the study all the residents were similar in terms of psychological and physical health and had similar prior socioeconomic status. It was a modern, high-quality home consisting of two residential floors. The adults in the home were living on four floors; two floors were selected for the study:

- Floor one became the "responsibility induced" group. They were allowed to make certain decisions such as how to arrange their rooms, when they went to see movies, whether to receive visitors or not, and whether to have plants in their rooms.
- Floor two became the "traditional" group. They had their rooms arranged for them, had to see movies when they were scheduled, and had all other choices made for them.

When they nurses were asked to rate the participants, 71% of the traditional group were designated "more debilitated", and 93% of the responsibility induced group were seen as "improved". Other measures included self-rating and behavioural measures, such as how often they went to see a film. The responsibility induced group also rated themselves as more active and happier and this was still true a year and half later (Rodin & Langer, 1977). The responsibility induced group also saw more movies. This all suggests a significant effect from being given more personal control over their lives.

Furthermore mortality rates differed between the two groups. In the follow-up study only 15% of the responsibility group had died whereas twice as many of the other group had died. It is possible that higher death rates might be associated with less efficient immune systems.

Discussion points

1. Is it possible to generalise from this study to all human behaviour?

2. What ethical issues might concern us in relation to this study?

Shift work

Increasingly our society requires people to work irregular hours in order to maintain 24-hour services. It is estimated that approximately 20% of people employed in the United States work in shifts (US Congress, 1991). Having to adjust one's body clock to different sleep patterns results in considerable stress and has been associated with major industrial accidents. Czeisler, Moore-Ede, and Coleman (1982) found that shift work among manual workers in an industrial setting in Utah, USA correlated with raised accident rates, absenteeism, and chronic feelings of ill health. Major industrial disasters, such as Chernobyl, Bhopal, and Three-Mile Island, all happened between midnight and 4 a.m., and most lorry accidents occur between 4 a.m. and 7 a.m. Clearly shift work reduces work capacity because it acts as a stressor by disrupting bodily rhythms such as sleep.

Interpersonal relationships

Matteson and Ivancevich (1982) reported that the most common source of work stress was the inability to get on with other workers. Social support has an important moderating effect on the experience of stress (as we will see later) so it is not surprising that poor relationships are a source of stress. Karasek, Schwartz, and

Theorell (1982) studied workers in Sweden and found that job satisfaction was related to the amount of support they received from other workers.

Burnout

The concept of "**burnout**" became popular in the 1980s. It is the erosion of the human spirit that results from chronic exposure to high levels of work stress. The effects on work performance and personal health are enormous. It is a problem particularly for those who work in the human services professions, for example, nurses, teachers, social workers, and policemen. Maslach and Jackson (1982) measured burnout in terms of three psychosocial components:

1. *Emotional exhaustion*. Working with people, and particularly those who are in difficulty, is a strain on psychic resources.
2. *Depersonalisation*. Both worker and client experience **deindividuation**, a sense of losing individual identity. For example, a nurse who wears a uniform comes to feel he or she is just an automaton in the eyes of his or her patients, and equally may also start to regard those patients as objects.
3. *Perceived inadequacy*. The worker experiences low job satisfaction because they feel their efforts fail to produce the desired results.

It may be possible to help individuals who experience burnout through the provision of support groups and more varied work activities. In reality many such individuals take extended leave and never manage to return to full capacity. A key factor may be the extent to which someone has a good social support system and means of relaxing outside work.

Individual Differences

In the preceding discussion of factors that cause stress, a key consideration is the way that different individuals react. To state the obvious—everyone responds differently. Psychologists call this "**individual differences**". These may be innate temperamental differences, or the differences may be explained in terms of learning—through conditioning or by modelling one's behaviour on others. Or differences may be related to cultural styles that are also learned—different cultures teach different styles of coping. For example, the Japanese approach is to try to accept problems, as opposed the Western approach of taking control and trying to change a stressful problem (Wade & Tavris, 1993).

Personality: Types A, B, and C

There is a long history of "types" in psychology. The Greeks said there were melancholic types and phlegmatic types, and the reason they were melancholic or phlegmatic was because the individual's body produced too much of a particular "humour" or fluid. For example, melancholics had an

---

CASE STUDY: *Don't Let It Get You Down*

"Comfort always, cure rarely" is an old medical motto. And it may be nearer the truth than modern medicine would like to admit. Perhaps if patients were less depressed and more optimistic they might be more likely to recover from stressful operations.

In one study of 100 patients about to undergo bone marrow transplants for leukaemia it was found that 13 of the patients were severely depressed. Of these patients 12 had died within a year of the operation (92%) whereas only 61% of the not-depressed died within two years of the study.

Other research has looked at the effects of pessimism and found this to be the biggest single predictor of death from a heart attack. 122 men were evaluated for pessimism or optimism at the time they had a heart attack. Eight years later their state of mind was found to correlate with death more highly than any of the other standard risk factors such as damage to the heart, raised blood pressure, or high cholesterol levels. Of the 25 men who were most pessimistic, 21 had died whereas only 6 of the most optimistic 25 had died.

Peterson, Seligman, and Valliant (1988) studied optimists and pessimists. They suggested that pessimists tended to explain setbacks in their lives as the result of things within their personality that were unchangeable. In contrast, optimists tended to explain setbacks as the result of things arising from situations within their control, but which were not their own fault. Peterson et al. rated a number of Harvard undergraduates for pessimism and optimism on the basis of essays they wrote about their wartime experiences. After an interval of more than 20 years, the pessimists (aged 45) were more likely to be suffering from some chronic disease.

(Adapted from Goleman, 1991.)

You may think this person is not very good humoured. The use of the word "humour" comes from the Greeks who thought our moods and personalities were due to too much of certain bodily fluids called "humours".

Bearing in mind the characteristics of a Type A person, what types of careers would most suit such a personality type?

Cross-cultural issues: Do you think there are likely to be cultural differences in the prevalence of Type A and B individuals (i.e. between individualistic and collectivistic cultures)?

overproduction of black bile (melan = black, coln = bile) and this led to a sad, depressed individual.

In the 1950s two cardiologists, Meyer Friedman and Ray Rosenman introduced a new "typology" to psychology. They proposed that there were three personality types:

- Type As are competitive, ambitious, impatient, restless, and pressured.
- Type Bs lack these characteristics and are generally more relaxed.
- Type Cs are nice, industrious, conventional, sociable but tend to be repressed and react to stress or threat with a sense of helplessness.

Friedman and Rosenman (1959) argued that individuals with the Type A pattern are more stressed than Type B individuals, and so are more likely to suffer from coronary heart disease (CHD). To test their hypothesis they set up a long-term study of men, called the Western Collaborative Group Study, which is described in the Key Study on the page opposite. They did find strong evidence of the predicted association, although subsequent research has not always been as supportive. It may be that certain aspects of Type A behaviour, such as hostility, are most important.

Other research has looked at a possible link between Type C and cancer. Morris et al. (1981) proposed that the likelihood of developing cancer may be related to Type C behaviour because of the tendency for such individuals to deal with stressful events by repressing their emotions. To study this, Morris et al. interviewed 50 women seeking treatment for a breast lump. At the start of the study the women were being tested to see if the lump was malignant (cancerous) or benign (non-cancerous). The patients were assessed to determine their typical patterns of emotional behaviour using questionnaires and interviews. Morris et al. found that those women who were subsequently found to have a malignant lump had reported that they both experienced and expressed far less anger than those women who were diagnosed with a benign tumour. This supports the idea of a link between cancer and the suppression of anger. Emotional suppression is associated with increased stress, lowered effectiveness of the immune system, and illness.

Supporting evidence was given in a study by Thomas and Duszynski (1974) who followed 1000 medical students over a period of 15 years. They found that those who developed cancers also reported less family closeness. This may be due to stress, because people with poor social support systems suffer greater stress.

Hardiness

Kobasa (1979) argued that people differ considerably in their ability to cope with stressors. She used the term **hardiness** to describe a cluster of traits possessed by those people best able to cope with stress. According to Kobasa, "hardy" individuals have the following characteristics:

- *Commitment*. Hardy individuals are more involved in what they do and have a direction in life. They find meaning in their work and personal relationships.
- *Challenge*. Hardy individuals view potentially stressful situations as a challenge and an opportunity, rather than a problem or a threat.
- *Control*. Hardy individuals have a stronger sense of personal control. They feel they are able to influence events in their lives.

Type A behaviour and coronary heart disease

The Western Collaborative Group Study was set up in the 1960s to test Friedman and Rosenman's hypothesis that Type A individuals were more likely to develop heart disease than Type B. The Type A behaviour pattern was initially assessed by means of the Structured Interview. This assessment procedure makes use of two main kinds of information: (1) the answers given to the questions asked during the interview, and (2) the individual's behaviour, including aspects of his or her way of speaking (e.g. loudness and speed of talking). The individual's tendencies towards impatience and hostility are assessed by the interviewer deliberately interrupting the person being interviewed from time to time. The Type A behaviour pattern has also been assessed by various self-report questionnaires (e.g. the Jenkins Activity Survey).

On the basis of these measures the participants were classed as A1 (Type A), A2 (not fully Type A), X (equal amounts of A and B), and B, (fully Type B). Nearly 3200 healthy men aged between 39 and 59 living around San Francisco were assessed in 1960. Eight and a half years later (Friedman & Rosenman, 1974) 257 of the men in the original sample had developed coronary heart disease (CHD). The findings were striking—70% of those with CHD had been assessed as Type A, nearly twice as many as the Type Bs. This remained so, even when account was taken of various other factors (e.g. blood pressure, smoking, obesity) which are known to be associated with heart disease.

One of the limitations of the Western Collaborative Group Study was that it was not clear which aspect of the Type A behaviour pattern was most closely associated with heart disease. This issue was addressed by Matthews et al. (1977). They re-analysed the data from the Western Collaborative Group Study, and found that coronary heart disease was most associated with the hostility component of Type A.

Why is Type A (or its hostility component) associated with heart disease? As Ganster et al. (1991, p.145) pointed out, it has often been assumed that "chronic elevations of the sympathetic nervous system [in Type As] lead to deterioration of the cardiovascular system." Ganster et al. put their participants into stressful situations and recorded various physiological measures, including blood pressure and heart rate. Only the hostility component of Type A was associated with high levels of physiological reactivity. These findings, when combined with those of Matthews et al. (1977), suggest that high levels of hostility produce increased activity within the sympathetic nervous system, and this plays a role in the development of coronary heart disease.

Discussion points

1. Identify the methodological strengths and weaknesses of the Western Collaborative Group Study.

2. Do you think that the study may have affected the lives of the men taking part in the study in any way? How might that be an ethical issue?

KEY STUDY EVALUATION — Friedman and Rosenman

These findings were confirmed in another large-scale longitudinal study which involved both men and women, the Framingham Heart Study (Haynes et al., 1980) However, some researchers have failed to find any relationship between Type A and coronary heart disease. This has led a number of psychologists to doubt the importance of the Type A behaviour pattern as a factor in causing heart disease. However, Miller et al. (1991) reviewed the literature, and found that many of the negative findings were obtained in studies using self-report measures of Type A behaviour. Studies using the Structured Interview with initially healthy populations reported a mean correlation of +0.33 between Type A behaviour and coronary heart disease, supporting the initial finding of a moderate relationship between the two variables.

One problem for any study is that as soon as an individual knows they are at risk of CHD they may engage in behaviours which modify that risk, such as giving up smoking or taking more exercise. This may create lower long-term correlations between Type A and CHD.

The evidence has been applied successfully, for example Friedman, Tordoff, and Ramirez (1986) reported on the Recurrent Coronary Prevention Project which aimed to modify Type A behaviour and so reduce CHD in participants who had experienced a heart attack. At a five-year follow-up, those participants who had taken part in a behaviour modification did have fewer second heart attacks than those who received counselling or no treatment.

Kobasa's view was supported by a large-scale study she undertook (Kobasa, Maddi, & Puccetti, 1982) with highly stressed men who worked as managers for a large company. Those individuals who had high scores on hardiness, and who also exercised a lot, had the least illness. In another study (Kobasa et al., 1985) male executives in stressful jobs were interviewed and followed up a year later. Three factors—hardiness, exercise, and social support—were found to be important factors in their health, with hardiness playing the biggest role.

However, Funk (1992) criticised the model on the grounds that hardiness is quite difficult to assess. The research has also been criticised because it has relied on white, middle-class males as the main participants in the studies. Finally, the data are correlational and the conclusions have presumed that hardiness is the causal factor in health, whereas it could be that people who are ill find it harder to be psychologically hardy. On the positive side, the concept of hardiness has been used as a means of coping with stress (as we will see later).

Gender

There is reason to believe that there are gender differences in the way stressors affect individuals. Stoney, David, and Matthews (1987) argued that men respond more strenuously to stressors than women do and, in a later study, Stone et al. (1990)

After a major disaster many people suffer for many years with post traumatic stress disorder. During the First World War this was termed "shell shock" but has only fairly recently been given serious recognition.

CASE STUDY: *Post Traumatic Stress Disorder (PTSD)*

PTSD is a disabling reaction to stress following a traumatic event. When we say "traumatic" we mean exceptionally stressful events that threaten survival. The response is likely to be delayed, and appears some time after the event. Initial reactions may be those of shock. The reactions are long-lasting and typically include a number of the following features:

- *Reliving the event*. The person relives the event recurrently in flashbacks and has frequent nightmares about it. Any stimuli that trigger memories of the traumatic event are likely to cause intense emotional upset.

- *Emotional numbness* and avoidance of things that serve as a reminder. What often happens is that the individual tries to avoid trauma-related stimuli or thoughts, and there is fluctuation between re-experiencing the traumatic event and a numbing of response to stimuli associated with the event.

- *General anxiety* that was not previously present, including over-alertness, difficulties with concentration, impairments of memory, irritability, and outbursts of anger.

- *Survivor guilt*. Guilty feelings about surviving.

The term PTSD is relatively new but the symptoms have long been recognised. In the First World War it was called shell shock or combat fatigue. It is now recognised by health workers as a serious condition which can affect someone's ability to lead a normal life. Lack of control may be one of the key factors, because such traumas cause disorder in our orderly world. In the United States, about 1% of the population are diagnosed as suffering from PTSD. In a study in Detroit (discussed by Davison & Neale, 1996), 39% of adults had experienced a traumatic event, and 24% of them had developed PTSD.

found that women showed lower increases in blood pressure when performing stressful tasks. Many of the studies on the effects of stress on CHD have focused on men because many more men die from it than women, although for both sexes it is the leading cause of death. Why are women less prone to CHD? The answer may give us some insight into how to protect men from the disease.

One possibility is that women's hormones may afford some protection. Hastrup, Light, and Obrist (1980) tested womens' cardiovascular (heart) reactions and found that the women had lowered stress responses at the time in their menstrual cycle when their oestrogen levels were highest. This would suggest that the hormone oestrogen may have helped them to cope.

A second possibility is that women engage in fewer unhealthy behaviours than men. In the past women were much less likely to smoke or drink excessively and this may explain their lower CHD rates. In recent years, however, women are smoking and drinking more and their CHD rates have indeed risen, whereas men are smoking and drinking less. This would lead us to expect a narrowing of the gap in CHD mortality rates between the sexes, which Carroll (1992) confirmed was happening.

Finally, the importance of social support in reducing stress may explain gender differences. Women are more likely to have confidantes and friends than men, and women report making use of social support networks more than men (Carroll, 1992).

SECTION 12   CRITICAL ISSUE
Stress Management

Stress research has important applications in that it can advise us on how to manage our own, and others' stress reactions. This is an increasingly important application at a time when everyone appears to feel over-stressed.

There is a large variety of approaches to reducing stress levels. One way to classify these is in terms of whether they are physiological or psychological methods. Physiological methods include the following:

1. *Biofeedback.* A technique to learn how to control involuntary muscles, or voluntary muscles that are not normally controlled, such as blood pressure and heart rate. The aim is to reduce ANS activity and thus the bodily sensations associated with stress. In turn this will reduce the consequent effects of stress in terms of illness.
2. *Anti-anxiety drugs.* The body produces its own natural "drugs": hormones and neurotransmitters (substances that transmit information between nerves and cells). Manufactured drugs such as Valium can be used to mimic or intervene in the natural body processes but not always without some cost, such as in terms of addiction to the drugs or drowsiness as a side effect.

Psychological methods include:

1. *Cognitive therapies.* This form of **psychotherapy** aims to change the way that people think about their problem and thus alter the effects of the problem itself. Two examples are stress inoculation treatment and increasing hardiness.
2. *Increasing control.* The more in control a person is, the less stress they feel.
3. *Social support* from friends and family.

Social support is one of the psychological approaches to reducing stress levels.

Lazarus and Folkman (1984) made another distinction between problem-focused and emotion-focused strategies of stress management. Stress can be managed by tackling the problem itself (problem-focused) but often this is not possible and so a more realistic approach is to reduce the stress response (emotion-focused). Physiological methods of coping with stress tend to be emotion-focused because they deal with reducing the associated anxiety. Psychological methods sometimes aim to reduce the way the individual views the problem (problem-focused) and thus reduce the stress.

There is another distinction to be made between "coping" with stress and "managing" it. Most of us try to get on and cope as best we can, but the concept of "management" suggests the use of techniques to overcome chronic problems, or tackle stress before it occurs.

Biofeedback

Biofeedback is often used to reduce stress. In essence, **biofeedback** is "a technique for transforming some aspect of physiological behaviour into electrical signals which are made accessible to … awareness (usually vision or audition)" (Gatchel, 1997, p.198). An individual is attached to a machine that produces feedback about some physiological activity (thus, bio-feedback). For example, the machine would produce an auditory or visual signal to indicate whether an individual's heart rate is too high or about right. Today, humans can even learn to control their brain-waves, using electroencephalogram (EEG) biofeedback. The individual is also trained in techniques that have been found to reduce physiological aspects of stress. For example, there is relaxation training, part of which involves breathing in a regular and calm way. This means that the physiological activity is brought under control.

People learn to use biofeedback techniques to control normally involuntary bodily functions such as heart rate. The technique may involve a machine that monitors relevant bodily functions and produces visual or auditory signals. Through relaxation, the individual learns to alter the rate of these signals and thus control the involuntary functions.

The key feature is that these physiological activities are ones that we are not normally able to control. They either involve involuntary muscles (not under voluntary control), or voluntary muscles that are not usually controlled at a conscious level. The muscles involved with the ANS are automated specifically because they control behaviours that need to function without our conscious involvement. This makes it seem unlikely that we would be able to exert voluntary control over processes such as blood pressure.

In fact biofeedback probably does not involve learning *direct* control of, for example, heart rate and blood pressure. Control is exerted *indirectly*. For example, breathing deeply, using methods of relaxation, or simply moving around can produce changes in various physiological measures. And indeed biofeedback has been found to produce short- and long-term reductions in heart rate, blood pressure, skin temperature, and brain-wave rhythms.

Biofeedback training involves three stages:

1. Developing an awareness of the particular physiological response (e.g. heart rate).
2. Learning ways of controlling that physiological response in quiet conditions. This can include providing rewards for successful control in addition to feedback.
3. Transferring that control into the conditions of everyday life.

Supporting evidence for biofeedback

Can people actually learn to control involuntary muscles? Neal Miller and his colleagues conducted extensive research in the 1960s and 1970s to demonstrate that ordinary people can indeed learn to control their involuntary physiological systems. In one of the early experiments Miller and DiCara (1967, see Key Study on the next page) demonstrated that rats were able to learn how to control their cardiac muscles using operant conditioning techniques. The problem is that subsequent research has not been able to replicate this particular finding.

Other research support comes from work done by Dworkin and Dworkin (1988) with teenagers who were suffering from curvature of the spine (scoliosis). The teenagers successfully used biofeedback techniques to learn how to control the muscles of their spine and thus alter their posture and overcome the disorder. Budzynski et al. (1973) found that regular biofeedback sessions helped people suffering from chronic muscle-contraction headaches. They had less tension in their muscles and fewer headaches than a control group even three months later. This form of feedback has been used to successfully treat migraine headaches and Reynaud's disease (a vasoconstrictive disorder resulting in constricted blood flow to the fingers or toes) (Curtis, 2000). Some doctors even claim to use biofeedback techniques successfully with asthma and high blood pressure, although there is considerable controversy about the success rates (Wade & Tavris, 1993).

People who practise yoga have been reported to be able to slow their heartbeat down sufficiently for them to survive in a sealed booth long after most people would have suffocated to death. They use relaxation to control their bodily systems.

CASE STUDY: *Biofeedback is Back*

Imagine having hands so sensitive to cold that each winter they would swell and split open. Just grabbing a carton of milk out of the refrigerator makes them whiten and throb with pain. Then imagine learning to raise the temperature in your hands to the extent that you could put them into a bucket of ice without discomfort. This is a dramatic example of what biofeedback training can accomplish for certain medical problems such as Reynaud's disease, a circulatory disorder that can cause its victims extreme discomfort and debilitation, and sometimes even requires limb amputation.

Biofeedback training as a tool for relaxation and stress reduction enjoyed a brief surge of popularity following its inception in the late 1960s, but then largely slipped out of the public view during the 1970s and 1980s. Now biofeedback is making a quiet comeback, this time in mainstream medicine. Several decades of clinical experience (and hundreds of published studies) support the use of biofeedback training in many common medical problems, such as incontinence, anxiety, hypertension, migraine, circulatory problems, irritable bowel syndrome, pain control, and bed wetting.

How biofeedback works

Every time you scratch an itch, grab a snack when you're hungry, or use the bathroom when you feel the urge, you are responding to biofeedback cues from your body about your physiologic state. With

biofeedback training, however, you are cued by sensors attached to your body. These sensors measure "invisible" parameters like your heart rate, the temperature of your extremities, the muscle tension in specific muscle groups. This information is conveyed by visual displays or sounds. Using imagery and mental exercises, you learn to control these functions, using the feedback provided by the sensors as a gauge of success. With practice, you can learn to "tune in" without instrumentation, and control these functions at will during ordinary life.

For example, in a training session to "warm up" your hands and feet, you might imagine basking in the sun on a beach while listening to a script like "I feel warm … my hands are growing warm and heavy … " Both the image and the script would be tailored to you personally to evoke a vivid and relaxing mental image. After your training session, you'd be sent home with this script on audiotape and small thermometers to use for your biofeedback.

The major advantages of biofeedback are that it is non-invasive, has virtually no side effects, and is effective over the long term. The major disadvantage is that it requires effort, commitment, and involvement on the part of patients.

(Adapted from Lisa H. Underhill, 1999, http://bewell.healthgate.com/healthy/mind/1999/biofeedback/index)

Reducing heart rate with biofeedback

Pavlov's studies of **classical conditioning** showed how animals learn to associate a reflex response with a new stimulus. Animals are born with reflex responses to certain stimuli, for example you blink if a puff of air is blown into your eye or you salivate when you see food (salivation is called an unconditioned response and food is the unconditioned stimulus). Pavlov realised that if you rung a bell at the same time as you presented food this forged an association between bell, food, and salivation so that a new stimulus–response link was learned (bell becomes the conditioned stimulus which also now produces the reflex response of salivation).

Thus classical conditioning shows how a bodily response can be learned. Miller and DiCara (1967) set out to show that such bodily responses can also be learned through **operant conditioning**. This form of learning involves the stamping in or out of responses through reinforcement. An animal "operates" in the environment. Some of the behaviours happen to produce rewards (and become "stamped in"), such as obtaining food or pleasure. Other behaviours produce punishments (and are "stamped out"). Gradually animals learn repertoires of useful behaviours.

It should be possible to learn bodily responses through operant conditioning, if the responses are rewarded. Miller and DiCara tested this by completely paralysing 24 rats using curare, and artificially respirating them. Half of the rats were rewarded whenever their heart rates slowed down ("slow" group), and the other half were rewarded whenever their heart rates speeded up ("fast" group). The rewards were given by electrically stimulating a part of the brain that produces a sensation of pleasure. At first the rats received a small reward for a random instance when their heart rate changed. Thus the heart rate changes were **reinforced**. Gradually a larger and larger change was required to receive a reward. This process is called **shaping**.

The rats in the "fast" group increased their heart rates from 422 beats per minute (bpm) to a final 510 bpm, whereas in the "slow" group heart rates dropped from 400 to 316 bpm. The difference between the two groups was highly significant and was found in all but two of the experimental rats.

As the rats were paralysed they could not be using any form of voluntary control. Therefore this must be a demonstration of the operant conditioning of involuntary muscles.

KEY STUDY EVALUATION — Miller and DiCara

The major problem with this research is that it used non-human animals and we cannot assume that the same principles operate in humans. Behaviourists would argue that human behaviour consists of the same building blocks: stimulus–response links. However, we also know that human behaviour is greatly influenced by cognitive control whereas this is less true of non-human animals. A second problem with this study is that attempts to replicate it have never been as successful (Dworkin & Miller, 1986).

Discussion points

1. How could you apply these principles to a real-life situation?

2. In what way is the above procedure a form of biofeedback?

How does biofeedback work?

As we have seen in Miller and DiCara's (1967) study above, learning involuntary control may happen by means of operant conditioning. The ANS responds to rewards and reinforcement, so that those autonomic responses that are reinforced occur more frequently. However, Miller and DiCara's research has not been replicated which casts doubt on this explanation that involuntary muscles are controlled through operant conditioning.

Another possibility is that biofeedback results in a restoration of homeostasis because it involves relaxation. Stress may disrupt the normal functioning of the body and mean that it is difficult to maintain homeostasis. Without this natural system of regulation various physiological activities are out of control—high blood pressure, intestinal distress, and pain can develop. Relaxation (biofeedback) may help the body return to its normal state of balance or homeostasis.

Evaluation of biofeedback

Biofeedback has produced significant long-term reductions in stress in everyday life, even though it is likely that people have no *direct* feedback about their current physiological state. However, caution is needed when considering the evidence. For example, it is hard to *interpret* the beneficial effects of biofeedback. Relaxation training is often given along with the biofeedback, making it hard to tell whether it is the biofeedback or the relaxation training that is more effective. Biofeedback may lead to benefits by producing a sense of control rather than through purely physiological mechanisms. Gatchel (1997, p.199) commented that, "There have been claims for the therapeutic efficacy of biofeedback which have been grossly exaggerated and even wrong."

However, we should consider the effects of individual differences. Biofeedback may be more successful with some people more than others, such as with children rather than adults. Attanasio et al. (1985) studied a biofeedback programme that reduced muscle-contraction headaches and found that children benefited more than adults, possibly because the children were more enthusiastic and less sceptical. This more positive attitude would make them more willing to try hard to succeed.

Anti-anxiety Drugs

Another way of reducing people's level of stress is by giving them anti-anxiety drugs. This is directly related to our understanding of the body's responses to stress, which we considered in Section 10. The body produces chemicals (hormones) that create anxiety. These can be countered using other chemical substances (i.e. drugs) that reduce anxiety. There are several different types of drugs that work via different mechanisms.

Barbiturates

At one time, **barbiturates** were the most used class of anti-anxiety drug. They are depressants of the central nervous system, and long-acting barbiturates are effective in reducing anxiety. However, they have various side effects. These include problems of concentration, lack of coordination, and slurred speech. In addition, the barbiturates tend to be addictive. Anxious patients who stop taking barbiturates report numerous symptoms such as delirium, irritability, and increased sweating. The problems with the barbiturates led to their replacement by the benzodiazepines in the 1960s.

Benzodiazepines

The most used anti-anxiety drugs today are the **benzodiazepines** such as Valium and Librium. These work in the following way: At the junctions between nerves (**synapses**) substances called **neurotransmitters** are released. The task of these substances is to send signals to other nerves and the body generally. There are many neurotransmitters and each is produced in specific areas of the body and has a range of special functions. For example, noradrenaline, which is a hormone produced by the adrenal glands (see page 121), is also a neurotransmitter produced by cells at the base of the brain. It is thought to affect memory and mood.

The neurotransmitter of most interest to us here is **GABA** (gamma-amino-butyric-acid). It is produced at synapses all over the body but is especially

The famous escapologist Harry Houdini used biofeedback in some of his feats. For example, he managed to escape when he was securely shackled, with his clothes and body having been searched thoroughly to ensure he was not hiding any keys. How did he do it? He held a key suspended in his throat, and regurgitated it when no-one was looking. The natural reaction to having an object stuck in your throat is to gag. However, Houdini had spent hours practising until he was able to control his gag reflex.

Ethical issues: To what extent can patients give fully informed consent to taking medication?

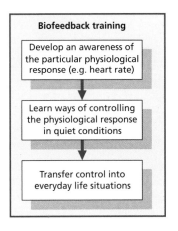

Biofeedback training

Develop an awareness of the particular physiological response (e.g. heart rate)

↓

Learn ways of controlling the physiological response in quiet conditions

↓

Transfer control into everyday life situations

manufactured by neurons in the brain. At times of anxiety GABA is produced as the body's natural form of anxiety relief. GABA acts as a neuromodulator—affecting the production of other neurotransmitters, notably reducing **serotonin** levels. *Decreases* in serotonin are related to increased arousal and aggressiveness; *increases* of serotonin are linked with decreased arousal and sleep.

Drugs can intervene in natural processes by controlling the action of neurotransmitters. The benzodiazepines increase the activity of the neurotransmitter GABA, which then reduces serotonin activity, which then in turn reduces arousal. In this way the benzodiazepines are very effective at reducing anxiety, and it is for this reason that they are used by hundreds of millions of people around the world.

Side effects of benzodiazepines

In spite of the effectiveness of the benzodiazepines, they have several unwanted side effects. They often have sedative effects, and can make people feel drowsy. In addition, the benzodiazepines can cause cognitive and memory impairments, they sometimes lead to feelings of depression, and they can interact unpredictably with alcohol (Ashton, 1997). All of these effects are linked to low levels of serotonin. As a result, individuals taking benzodiazepines are more likely to be involved in accidents. Finally, many people become dependent on benzodiazepines, and find it hard to stop taking them. Sudden removal of benzodiazepines can lead to a return of the initial symptoms of intense stress and anxiety.

More recent developments

A more recent anti-anxiety drug, **buspirone**, offers some advantages over benzodiazepines. It is a serotonin agonist, meaning that it helps or "facilitates" the effects of the neurotransmitter serotonin. It does not have the sedative effects of benzodiazepines, and there are no marked withdrawal symptoms. However, buspirone produces other side effects such as headaches and depression (Goa & Ward, 1986).

Evaluation of anti-anxiety drugs

Anti-anxiety drugs can be very effective at reducing intense feelings of stress. However, they do not address the problems that are causing the stress, i.e. they are emotion-focused rather than problem-focused; they help *cope* with stress but not to manage it.

Drugs can also have unfortunate side effects. The recommendation is that the benzodiazepines should generally be limited to short-term use of no more than four weeks (Ashton, 1997). It is also recommended that they should only be given to individuals with severe anxiety symptoms, and the drugs should be given in the minimal effective doses. Individuals who have become dependent on benzodiazepines should have their dosage reduced gradually. The good news is that about 70% of dependent users of benzodiazepines, who are motivated to give them up, manage to do this for periods of several years or more (Ashton, 1997).

Stress can be treated with anti-anxiety drugs such as Valium that reduce the effects of stress but not the problems that cause it. Such drugs often have undesirable side effects.

Cognitive Therapies

Psychologists and psychiatrists have developed a huge assortment of psychological treatments for abnormal behaviours and some of these are designed especially for stress disorders. **Cognitive therapies** are especially appropriate for dealing with stress. Their aim, in general, is replace negative and irrational thoughts (e.g. "I am totally incompetent") with positive and rational ones (e.g. "I can achieve many things if I try hard enough"). The assumptions behind the cognitive approach are that it is not the problem that is the core issue, but it is the way one thinks about the problem that is **maladaptive**. If one can be trained to restructure one's thinking and self-beliefs, the problem may simply disappear.

Stress inoculation training

Meichenbaum (1977, 1985) argued that we should use cognitive therapy *before* a person becomes very anxious or depressed rather than afterwards. This led Meichenbaum to develop stress *inoculation* training, a form of coping and management. There are three main phases in **stress inoculation training**:

1. *Assessment*: the therapist discusses the nature of the problem with the individual, and solicits the individual's perception of how to eliminate it.
2. *Stress reduction techniques*: the individual learns various techniques for reducing stress, such as relaxation and self-instruction. The essence of self-instruction is that the individual practises coping self-statements such as "If I keep calm, I can handle this situation" or "stop worrying, because it's pointless" (see box below for more examples of coping self-statements).
3. *Application and follow-through*: the individual imagines using the stress reduction techniques learned in the second phase in difficult situations, and/or engages in role play of such situations with the therapist. Finally, the techniques are used in real-life situations.

Empirical support

Meichenbaum (1977) compared his stress inoculation technique to other forms of treatment. For example, he considered the relative benefits of stress inoculation therapy as compared with a form of behaviour therapy known as desensitisation, where patients are gradually introduced to the object of their fear while being taught simultaneously how to relax. In order to compare the two forms of therapy, Meichenbaum treated individuals suffering from both snake phobia and rat phobia. Each patient received treatment for only one phobia, using one of the two methods. Meichenbaum found that both forms of treatment were effective in reducing or eliminating the phobia that was treated. However, stress inoculation also greatly reduced the non-treated phobia, whereas desensitisation did not. The implication is that self-instruction easily generalises to new situations, which makes it more useful than very specific forms of treatment.

Examples of coping self-statements used in Meichenbaum's stress inoculation training

Preparing for a stressful situation:
  What is it you have to do?
  You can develop a plan to deal with it.
  Just think about what you can do. That's better than getting anxious.
  Maybe what you think is anxiety is in fact eagerness to confront it.

Confronting and handling a stressful situation:
  Just "psych" yourself up—you can meet this challenge.
  One step at a time, you can handle the situation.
  This tenseness can be an ally, a cue to cope.
  Relax; you're in control. Take a slow deep breath. Ah, good.

Coping with the feeling of being overwhelmed:
  When fear comes, just pause.
  Keep the focus on the present; what is it you have to do?
  You should expect your fear to rise.
  It's not the worst thing that can happen.

Reinforcing self-statements:
  It wasn't as bad as you expected.
  Wait until you tell your therapist about this.
  You made more out of the fear than it was worth.
  You did it!

Evaluation of stress inoculation training

Stress inoculation has proved to be fairly effective in reducing the stress that people experience in moderately stressful situations. However, it is of less value when treating individuals who are highly stressed or exposed to very stressful situations. Individuals differ in how easy they find it to use coping self-statements in stressful situations.

Why do you think stress inoculation training is less valuable in highly stressful situations? How might this problem be addressed?

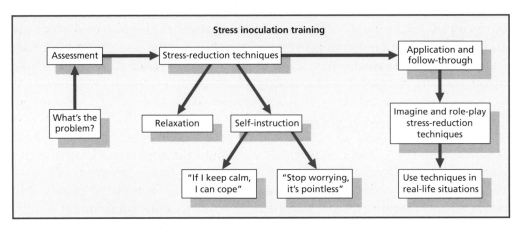

Hardiness training

One way to describe individual differences in stress responses is in terms of **hardiness** (see page 140); some people cope better because they are more "hardy". Kobasa (1986) suggested that this concept of hardiness could form the basis of a form of stress management programme. If we increase our hardiness, then we will decrease our sense of stress—this is hardiness training. Her programme consists of three techniques:

1. *Focusing*. People are often only vaguely aware of their stress, especially because they are used to tolerating small signs of stress, such as muscle tightness. Therefore you should focus on physical signs of stress and be aware when further attention is needed.
2. *Reconstructing stress situations*. Think about recent stressful situations and make two short lists: one of the ways it might have turned out better and the other of the ways it might have turned out worse. Doing this means that you become aware that things could actually have been worse and allows you to feel more positive.
3. *Compensating through self-improvement*. If you are affected by a stressor that cannot be changed or avoided then it may be helpful to take on another challenge that can be mastered. This reassures you that you can cope.

Evaluation of hardiness training

Sarafino (1990) reports that people who have followed the kind of programme just outlined do score higher on a test of hardiness, report feeling less stressed, and have lower blood pressure than before.

Increased Sense of Control

Personal control is an important element of hardiness, and we have also seen that a sense of control reduces the extent to which a situation may be experienced as stressful (Glass et al., 1969). This would lead us to expect that increasing one's sense

Avoidance-oriented strategy

of control would be an important method of coping with and managing stress. Langer and Rodin's (1976) study of elderly residents in a nursing home (see Key Study on page 138) demonstrates how control can lead to significant improvements in health and happiness.

It may be that the intervening factor is the immune system, as some studies have demonstrated that control does effect the immune system. Breier et al. (1987) placed participants in two stress situations. In one of the situations the participants could control the noise level by pressing a button. Blood samples were obtained after each session and it was found that, in the uncontrolled stress situation, participants had higher levels of adrenaline than in the controlled trial. In another study, this time using rats, Laudenslager et al. (1983) showed direct effects on the immune system. The rats were placed in three groups, one received controllable shocks, the second group were a yoked control (they received the same shocks as the first rat to whom they were "yoked", but they had no direct control over the shocks), and a third group received no shocks. All the rats were injected with cancer cells. Laudenslager et al. found that 65% of the controlled shock group rejected the cancer cells, as compared with only 27% of the yoked control, and 55% of the no-shock group. This suggests that control is important to the functioning of the immune system. In Brady's experiment (see Key Study on page 124) the monkey with control was the one to suffer most, but the conditions were different as the "executive" monkey was not fighting off infection but coping with prolonged stress.

Do you think that giving electric shocks is a good way to induce stress experimentally?

Social Support

It has often been claimed that social support can help to provide protection against stress. For example, Kiecolt-Glaser et al. (1984, see Key Study on page 128) found that students who had more social support suffered less reduction of their immune responses prior to university examinations.

Before discussing further evidence, however, we need to consider definitions of social support. Schaefer et al. (1981) argued that the term social support has two rather different meanings:

1. *Social network*: the number of people who are available to provide support.
2. *Perceived support*: the strength of social support that can be provided by these individuals.

According to Schaefer et al., the effects of these types of social support on health and well-being are very different. Perceived support (basically the quality of social support) is positively related to health and well-being, whereas social network (basically the quantity of social support) is unrelated to well-being. Social network can even be negatively related to well-being, because it is very time-consuming and demanding to maintain a large social network. In reality, however, the extent of a person's social network and their perceived sense of support are positively correlated.

Studies of social networks and perceived support

The importance of perceived social support was shown by Brown and Harris (1978). They found that 61% of severely depressed women had experienced a very stressful life event in the previous nine months, compared with only 25% of non-depressed women. However, many women managed to cope with

■ Activity: Cohen et al. (1997) have continued their research on colds. They asked participants to list how many of 12 intimate social roles they engaged in, for example as a parent, spouse, child, or close friend. Those who reported fewer than three roles were four times more likely to catch a cold when exposed to the virus under experimental conditions, than those with six or more social roles.

You might try a similar study by asking people to list their social roles and also answer a questionnaire about recent illness (illness can be assessed in terms of, for example, time off work).

severe life events without becoming depressed. Of those women who experienced a serious life event, 37% of those without an intimate friend became depressed, against only 10% of those who did have a very close friend.

The effects of both social networks and perceived support on physical well-being were examined by Nuckolls, Cassel, and Kaplan (1972) in a study on pregnant women. They made use of a general measure of "psychosocial assets" including measures of social network and perceived support. Women exposed to many stressful life events were much more likely to have medical complications during pregnancy if they had low psychosocial assets.

Tache, Selye, and Day (1979) found that cancer was more common among adults who were divorced, widowed, or separated, than among those who were married. The most likely explanation is that those who were not married were more stressed because of a lack of social support. However, it is hard to establish causal relationships from such data. Perhaps those who were divorced or separated were more vulnerable to stress than those who were married, and this stress vulnerability played a role in the collapse of their marriages.

Individual Differences

Individuals show consistent differences in the coping strategies they use to handle stressful situations. Endler and Parker (1990) devised the Multidimensional Coping Inventory to assess three major coping strategies:

- *Task-oriented strategy*: this involves obtaining information about the stressful situation and about alternative courses of action and their probable outcome. It also involves deciding priorities and acting so as to deal directly with the stressful situation.
- *Emotion-oriented strategy*: this can involve efforts to maintain hope and to control one's emotions. It can also involve venting feelings of anger and frustration, or deciding that nothing can be done to change things.
- *Avoidance-oriented strategy*: this involves denying or minimising the seriousness of the situation. It also involves conscious suppression of stressful thoughts and their replacement by self-protective thoughts.

■ Activity: Try to classify each of the stress management techniques in this section in terms of whether they are a task-, emotion-, and/or avoidance-oriented strategy.

How well does this classification scheme work?

■ Activity: Find out from other people which kind of stress management strategy they prefer to use. You might try to devise a suitable questionnaire to collect these data. Are there differences in people who, say, prefer a task-oriented strategy to an emotion-focused one? Do people who experience a lot of stress prefer one strategy more than another, in comparison with people who experience very little stress? Do people vary their strategies depending on the situation? What kinds of strategies are best for which situations?

Individuals who are high in the personality dimension of trait anxiety, and thus experience much stress and anxiety, tend to use the emotion-oriented and avoidance-oriented strategies rather than the task-oriented strategy (Endler & Parker, 1990). The situation is very different in those with the Type A behaviour pattern. They have a strong tendency to use the task-oriented strategy, even when it is not appropriate (Eysenck, 1994).

Which kind of coping strategy is most effective in reducing stress? There is no simple answer, because the effectiveness of any coping strategy depends on the nature of the stressful situation. In general terms, task-oriented coping tends to be most effective when the individual has the resources to sort out the stressful situation. On the other hand, emotion-oriented coping is preferable when the individual cannot resolve the situation (Eysenck, 1994). So individual differences are important but so are the parameters surrounding the stress situation.

> You have reached the end of the chapter on physiological psychology. Physiological psychology is an approach or perspective in psychology. The material in this chapter has exemplified the way that physiological psychologists explain behaviour. They look at behaviour in terms of the way the bodily systems work (for example, nerves and hormones, parts of the brain and bodily organs). This is often regarded as a "reductionist" approach because it reduces complex behaviour and experiences to simpler processes and explanations.

CHAPTER SUMMARY

❖ Stress is a nonspecific response to any demand. It is an innate and defensive response to situations that threaten survival.

Stress as a bodily response

❖ The autonomic nervous system (ANS) is concerned with involuntary movements and vital bodily functions, and is automatic. The sympathetic branch activates internal organs for fight or flight. The parasympathetic branch conserves energy and promotes metabolism. These two branches often operate antagonistically and maintain homeostasis. The ANS achieves its effects via the endocrine system which produces hormones. In situations of stress the sympathetic branch of the ANS is aroused and then homeostatic mechanisms seek to return the body to its steady, parasympathetic state.

❖ The hypothalamic-pituitary-adrenal axis governs the stress response. The hypothalamus directs ANS activity by releasing corticotrophin-releasing factor (CRF) that stimulates the anterior pituitary (the "master gland") which triggers the release of hormones in the endocrine system, a group of ductless glands. The pituitary hormone ACTH simulates the adrenal cortex, which in turn produces adrenaline and noradrenaline. Both of these are released as a response to stress and they then create sympathetic arousal—raised heart rate, sweating, and so on. The adrenal cortex also releases hormones (glucocorticoids such as cortisol) that activate parasympathetic activity and that suppress the immune system. This physiological account does not explain how people respond differently to different stressors.

❖ Selye described the General Adaptation Syndrome (GAS), a model of how the stress response adapts physiological systems to a stressor. Eventually, however, resources become depleted and illness ensues. The three stages of the model are: alarm reaction, resistance, and exhaustion. Selye's model alerted medicine to the importance of stress in illness but failed to adequately account for situational and individual differences.

❖ Psychological research has demonstrated a link between stress and a range of physical illnesses, such as colds, gastric ulcers, and cardiovascular disease. The field of psychoneuroimmunology (PNI) investigates how stress may cause illness *directly* by affecting the workings of the immune system, in particular the activity of lymphocytes, killer cells, and endorphins. This approach has been criticised for being oversimplified. Alternatively, stress may cause illness *indirectly* in terms of lifestyles that expose individuals to pathogens.

❖ There are many different sources of stress and different responses to stress. Cox's transactional model expresses stress in terms of an imbalance between the perceived demands of the environment and the individual's perceived ability to cope.

Sources of stress

❖ Life events may be a source of stress because they involve change which absorbs psychic energy. The SRRS (Social Readjustment Rating Scale) has been used to measure life change units (LCUs) and demonstrate a small but significant correlation between LCUs and physical illness. However, we do not know that life events *caused* the illness nor can we be certain that all events affect people in the same way. An alternative is to look at daily hassles—the ongoing stressors of daily life.

❖ Work stress can come from environmental factors or pressures of work. Overcrowding creates stress in both animals and humans, although other factors may moderate these effects. In some situations of overcrowding people do not become aggressive. Heat, pollution, and noise may also make people become aggressive, although it may be possible to cope with predictable noise without experiencing stress because one can "tune" it out. Unpredictable noise requires vigilance and reduces our psychic energy, so enhancing feelings of stress.

❖ Controllability is also an important factor in the effects of stressors. Work stress may also arise from a host of job-related sources such as too much or too little control, role conflict, shift work, and interpersonal relationships at work. The relationship between these various factors is complex. Burnout is an extreme effect of work-related stress.

❖ Individual differences must be taken into account when considering the effects of stressors. Type A individuals cope less well with stress and are more likely to suffer from coronary heart disease. Type C individuals may be more prone to cancer because they respond to stress by repressing their emotions. Individuals who are more "hardy" are better able to cope with stress, although it could be that people who are ill find it more difficult to be psychologically hardy. Women may be better able to cope with stress than men, possibly as a result of their hormones or possibly because of their more healthy lifestyles.

Critical issue—
Stress management

❖ Ways of reducing stress can be classified as physiological or psychological, problem-focused or emotion-focused. There is also a difference between coping with stress and managing it!

❖ Biofeedback has been used to reduce stress by giving individuals feedback about the action of involuntary muscles or voluntary muscles that are not usually under conscious control. It works in the short term, but it is less clear that biofeedback can produce long-term reductions in stress in everyday life. Operant conditioning may be one plausible explanation. Alternatively, it may work indirectly through relaxation which impacts on involuntary physiological functions, or by restoring homeostasis.

❖ Anti-anxiety drugs are also used to reduce stress. Barbiturates were the earliest anti-anxiety drug, which generally depress the central nervous system. There are problems with associated side effects. Benzodiazepines increase the activity of the neurotransmitter GABA, which inhibits activation throughout the nervous system by reducing e.g. serotonin levels. However, these drugs also have undesirable side effects, and their sudden removal can lead to intense anxiety. A newer drug, buspirone, does not have the sedative effects of the other drugs, but it can produce headaches and depression. Anti-anxiety drugs reduce stress, but they do not address the problems causing stress. They should be used for short periods of time in low doses.

❖ Cognitive therapies aim to treat the way an individual thinks about the problem and thus alter their ability to cope. One example of this approach is stress inoculation training, a scheme to manage stress before it becomes a problem. Participants are taught to use coping self-statements which may generalise to other situations. Another cognitive approach to stress management is hardiness training. Individuals are taught to become more "hardy" by focusing on the stress response, seeing the positive side of any stress situation, and taking on other challenges where one can experience success.

❖ Enhancing one's sense of control is another way of decreasing stress. Control has been shown to have direct effects on the immune system. Perceived social support is a further way of coping with stress.

❖ Individual differences are an important consideration with respect to managing stress. Different individuals will find different strategies to be successful. The Multidimensional Coping Inventory offers a means of assessing which strategies will suit which individuals.

FURTHER READING

There are further accounts of stress, stressors, and stress responses in N.R. Carlson (1994) *Physiology of behaviour (5th Edn.)* (Boston: Allyn & Bacon). There are brief discussions of the topics covered in this chapter in S. Green (1994) *Principles of biopsychology* (Hove, UK: Psychology Press). E.P. Sarafino (1990) *Health psychology* (New York: John Wiley & Sons) discusses many aspects of stress and stress management as does A. Curtis (2000) *Health psychology* (London: Routledge).

Revision Questions

The examination questions aim to *sample* the material in this whole chapter. For advice on how to answer such questions, refer to Chapter 1, Section 3. You will always have a choice of two questions in the AQA AS-level exam and 30 minutes in which to answer the question you choose:

Question 1
a. Describe the main features of Selye's General Adaptation Syndrome.   (6 marks)
b. Describe *one* research study into the effects on physical illness.   (6 marks)
c. Give *two* criticisms of this study.   (3 marks + 3 marks)
d. "Psychological research doesn't always appear to have any usefulness but this is not true of research into stress." To what extent can psychological research provide useful forms of stress management technique?   (12 marks)

Question 2
a. Outline the effects of stress on the body.   (6 marks)
b. Describe *one* research study into life changes as a source of stress.   (6 marks)
c. Describe *one* research study into workplace stressors.   (6 marks)
d. "Stress is the result of the body responding at a physiological level to nonspecific demands from the environment." Evaluate the extent to which stress can be explained in terms of being a physiological response.   (12 marks)

Individual differences is an approach or perspective in psychology. The material in this chapter will exemplify the approach insofar as abnormal behaviour is one of the ways that individuals vary.

The study of "individual differences" is literally the study of the ways that individuals differ in terms of their psychological characteristics. Individuals differ *physically* in terms of, for example, height and hair colour. They differ psychologically in terms of intelligence, aggressiveness, willingness to conform, masculinity and femininity, and just about every behaviour you can think of.

An important individual difference can be found in the degree to which a person is mentally healthy. This is specifically referred to as the study of abnormal or atypical psychology.

5

Individual Differences
Abnormality

The palm tree on the left differs from the norm.

This chapter explores one topic in the study of individual differences—abnormality. What is **abnormality**?

Clinicians who want to provide treatment for patients with mental disorders need to distinguish between normal and abnormal behaviour. In order to do this they need some way of defining abnormality. Mental disorder has been likened to physical illness. Having a cold is an abnormal and undesirable state. To what extent are mental disorders the same? This is one question we will try to answer in this chapter.

Clinicians also seek to explain *why* some people have mental disorders. Is an eating disorder "caught" in the same way that you catch a cold? If not, then how do we explain why some people suffer from such disorders and other people don't? We will explore the question of mental abnormality and its potential undesirability in this chapter.

Most of our definitions of abnormality and our explanations for mental disorders are based on Western beliefs. In recent years, however, there has been a growing recognition that it is very important to take account of cultural and sub-cultural differences. This chapter examines all of these issues and finally looks at them in the context of one group of mental disorders—eating disorders.

- *Section 13: Defining psychological abnormality*. This section explores the question "What is abnormality?" by looking at various possible definitions. We will also consider the limitations of these definitions, including the problem of cultural relativism.
- *Section 14: Biological and psychological models of abnormality*. It may be possible to explain mental disorders in the same way that we explain physical illnesses—in terms of biological or physical causes. This is called the medical model. Or we might use psychological explanations, such as those based on learning theory (the behavioural model), or on Freud's views (a psycho-dynamic model), or using a cognitive approach. We will also consider the implications of these models for treatment.
- Section *15: Critical issue—Eating disorders: anorexia nervosa and bulimia nervosa*. We can use the models of abnormality to try to understand what causes eating disorders. Two conditions will be described and considered: anorexia nervosa and bulimia nervosa.

SECTION 13
Defining Psychological Abnormality

What is Abnormality?

The term "abnormal" is defined as "deviating from what is normal or usual". What, then, is meant by the term "normal"? Conforming to a standard of some sort. But how do we establish the standard? There are several approaches that will be considered here.

- First, a standard can be defined in statistical terms—what most people are doing.
- Second, the standard can be defined in social terms—what is considered socially acceptable and, therefore, what is socially deviant.
- Third, we might use the standard of "adequate functioning"—being able to cope with day-to-day living.
- Finally, there is the concept of ideal mental health—a state of contentment that we all strive to achieve.

Statistical Infrequency

The statistical approach is based, not surprisingly, on the idea that certain behaviours are statistically rare in the population. Consider, for example, trait anxiety (the tendency to experience high levels of anxiety) as assessed by Spielberger's State-Trait Anxiety Inventory. The mean score for trait anxiety is about 40 and only 2% of the population will obtain a score higher than 55. Thus, those who score 55 or more can be regarded as abnormal, in the sense that their scores deviate from those of the great majority of the population. We can express this concept of deviation from the majority in terms of the **normal distribution**, which is discussed in the box below.

Statistical deviation from a normal distribution

If you measure any aspect of human behaviour, such as height or intelligence or aggressiveness, you should find that people with varying degrees of the behaviour are normally distributed around the mean. For example, there are a lot of people who are "averagely" tall or aggressive, whereas there are very few who are very small or highly aggressive. The shape of this distribution is shown in the figure on the right. The majority of individuals are clustered round the mean, which is why the curve is highest at this point. The further away you go from the mean, the fewer individuals there are. There are as many people above and below the mean. In other words, (theoretically) there are as many non-aggressive as there are very aggressive people, and as many people who are taller than average as there are people who are shorter than average. Furthermore, we can specify the percentage of people who are within one or two **standard deviations** of the mean (this concept is explained further in Chapter 7 Section 21). Basically, a standard deviation is a measure of "average" distance from the mean. A very unusual behaviour will be more than 2 standard deviations from the mean, that is it will be found in less than 5% of the population. With reference to the normal curve in the figure, you can see that only very few people are in the "tail" regions.

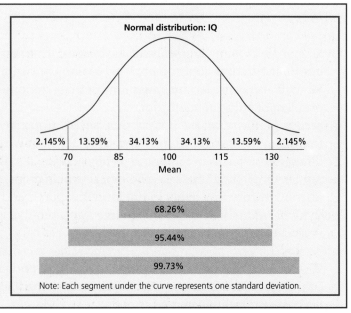

Normal distribution: IQ

2.145% 13.59% 34.13% 34.13% 13.59% 2.145%
70   85   100   115   130
                Mean

68.26%
95.44%
99.73%

Note: Each segment under the curve represents one standard deviation.

Limitations of the statistical approach

There are problems with this approach. In terms of a trait such as anxiety, we would expect to find a normal distribution of that trait within any population. Most people cluster around the mean score with just a few individuals scoring very high or very low. An "abnormally" high score on trait anxiety would suggest that treatment might be helpful. A low score on trait anxiety (scores of 25 or less) would also be statistically abnormal. However, a low susceptibility to anxiety hardly indicates clinical abnormality. In fact it might be quite desirable.

This leads us to conclude that the concept of statistical abnormality communicates an important meaning but it does not permit us to identify what behaviours require treatment. It overlooks the important issue of *desirability*. Some statistically abnormal behaviours are undesirable, such as high trait anxiety, whereas other statistically abnormal behaviours are actually quite desirable such as low anxiety or, for example, genius. When treating mental disorder we need a definition that will identify those behaviours that are statistically rare but also are regarded as undesirable and damaging to the individual.

A further problem with the statistical approach is deciding by how much a behaviour must deviate from the norm before it will be considered abnormal. For example, if a person is three centimetres below the mean in height, is this abnormal? Statistical definitions rely on an arbitrary cut-off point, which might be in terms of standard deviations. We could use this as an arbitrary cut-off for anxiety. However, this means that we have based our definition on the measurement of anxiety in one population but then used this with many different groups of people. Our cut-off point might not apply to another cultural group where anxiety is rather differently distributed.

In what ways are you abnormal?

This leads us to a third problem with statistical definitions. They are related to a standard that is set by a particular population. The same standard or norms may not apply to people in different age groups or different cultures. In terms of anxiety, what is normal for adults is not normal for children. Children have more irrational fears than adults, such as fears of the dark, and we accept this as normal *for their age*. Also, what is seen as normal behaviour in Britain may not be normal behaviour in, for example, India. People in other societies have quite different standards of behaviour but when such a person comes to live in this country, or even sometimes when they are living in their home country, they are judged by our standards or norms. Nevertheless, on the positive side, the statistical approach is less affected by value judgements than some of the other approaches we will look at.

Spitting at policemen is considered unacceptable, a deviation from social norms.

Deviation from Social Norms

An important part of what is missing from the statistical approach to abnormality is any consideration of the impact of an individual's behaviour on others. This has led some psychologists to emphasise the notion of social deviance: people who behave in a socially deviant and apparently incomprehensible way should be regarded as abnormal.

This approach also allows us to account for desirability of a behaviour. Social norms identify behaviours that are desirable for both the individual

Abnormal behaviour...?

and for society as a whole. Deviance from social norms is abnormal and undesirable. Many people who are labelled as clinically abnormal do behave in a socially deviant way. Consider, for instance, anti-social personality disorder which describes individuals who lack a conscience and therefore behave aggressively towards others because they feel no guilt. Consider, also, the case histories described below and on the next page. Both Simon and Sarah exhibit behaviours that deviate from what is socially acceptable.

Limitations of the social deviance approach

There are a large number of problems with this approach. We will consider a few here. First, the concept of social deviancy is related to moral standards. This is a standard or norm that is subjectively defined by a society, and one that varies over time as a consequence of prevailing social attitudes. For example, until fairly recently in Britain it was not acceptable to have a child out of wedlock. Single women who became pregnant were seen as social deviants and some were locked up in psychiatric institutions as a result. Early in the 20th century, in Russia, individuals who disagreed with the communist government were called dissidents. Their attitudes were seen as symptoms of mental derangement and they were locked up in mental hospitals. Using social deviancy as a means of establishing a standard allows serious abuses of human rights to occur. Szasz (1960) suggested that the concept of mental illness is a myth, used by the state as a means of control. It is certainly open to such abuse.

A second problem is that social deviance is defined by the context in which a behaviour occurs. If you see someone wearing very few clothes this would be acceptable on a beach but not in the High Street. Cultural context is also important. For example, the Kwakiutl Indians engage in a special ceremony in which they burn valuable blankets in order to cast shame on their rivals. If someone in our society deliberately set fire to his or her most valuable possessions, they would be regarded as very odd or mentally ill (Gleitman, 1986). Even

Moral codes

The subjective judgements we make when deciding whether or not a particular form of behaviour is normal are derived from the moral codes or standards that we have observed in the behaviour of significant others. We never become entirely independent in our moral thinking. Even as adults our thinking about morality often refers to a collective understanding of the right way to behave in a given situation. Someone who demonstrates a deviation from this may be perceived as either "mad" or "bad".

CASE STUDY: *Simon, An Acute Schizophrenic*

Simon lived at home with his parents. Over some months his parents had become increasingly concerned about his behaviour. He had grown reclusive, spending a lot of time in his room, and he had lost contact with his friends. His parents feared he might be taking drugs. They decided to call the doctor when they found that he had scratched the words "good" and "evil" on his arms, along with other unusual symbols. The GP was also concerned and contacted a psychiatrist who visited Simon at home. Simon at first pretended to be out. After some negotiation, he agreed to let the psychiatrist in. Initially, Simon was very suspicious and denied that there was a problem. Eventually, he told the psychiatrist that he was very worried about all the evil in the world, and had discovered that he could tell whether people were good or evil just by looking at them. He described receiving messages from the radio and TV.

The psychiatrist was concerned when Simon said that he left the house at night to look for evil people, believing it was his duty to fight them.

The psychiatrist found that Simon's bedroom was painted black and the curtains were taped shut. The walls were covered with crucifixes and mystical symbols, and Simon slept with a large knife near his bed in case he was confronted by evil people at night.

Simon was asked if he was willing to be admitted to a local hospital. He refused, saying he did not need help. The psychiatrist was sufficiently concerned about the possible risks to Simon or others that he arranged for Simon to be admitted under the Mental Health Act. For the first few weeks in hospital, Simon continued to claim that he was not ill and did not need treatment. Drug therapy resulted in significant improvements and he eventually returned home, continuing with his medication.

(Adapted from J.D. Stirling & J.S.E. Hellewell, 1999, *Psychopathology*. London: Routledge.)

within societies there are sub-cultural differences in relation to, for example, different religious groups which have different norms, such as Mormons who believe it is acceptable to have several wives.

It is also important to recognise that social deviancy is not necessarily a bad thing. There are several different reasons why someone is socially deviant. Some people are socially deviant because they have chosen a non-conformist lifestyle. Others are socially deviant because their behaviour is motivated by high principles, such as those "deviants" in Nazi Germany who spoke out against the atrocities that were being committed.

The fact that social deviance should be rejected as the sole criterion of abnormality does not mean that it is entirely irrelevant. After all, people derive much of their pleasure in life from their interactions with other people. As a result, most people find it important for a contented existence to avoid behaving in socially deviant ways that bemuse or upset others.

...Not when rescuing a cat!

Failure to Function Adequately

The concept of a "contented existence" leads us to the next possible way of defining abnormality—a failure to function adequately. Most persons who seek psychiatric help are suffering from a sense of psychological distress or discomfort (Sue et al., 1994). For example a person who is chronically depressed may have difficulty sleeping and take time off work, as well as being aware of feelings of anguish and misery. They cannot motivate themselves to do anything. Eventually their failure to cope with day-to-day life leads them to seek psychiatric help. We could say that this recognition of not functioning adequately could act as a standard of abnormality.

In most societies we have expectations about how people should live their lives and how they should contribute to the social groups around them. When an individual is unable to meet these obligations then both we and they usually feel they are not functioning adequately.

Rosenhan and Seligman (1989) suggested that the concept of distress and failure to function can be extended to encompass a number of behaviours. These are described in the Key Study on the next page.

CASE STUDY: *Sarah: A Case of Agoraphobia*

Sarah, a woman in her mid-thirties, was shopping for bargains in a crowded department store during the January sales. Without warning and without knowing why, she suddenly felt anxious and dizzy. She worried that she was about to faint or have a heart attack. She dropped her shopping and rushed straight home. As she neared home, she noticed that her feelings of panic lessened.

A few days later she decided to go shopping again. On entering the store, she felt herself becoming increasingly anxious After a few minutes she had become so anxious that a shopkeeper asked her if she was alright and took her to a first aid room. Once there her feelings of panic became worse and she grew particularly embarrassed at all the attention she was attracting.

After this she avoided going to the large store again. She even started to worry when going into smaller shops because she thought she might have another panic attack, and this worry turned into intense anxiety.

Eventually she stopped shopping altogether, asking her husband to do it for her.

Over the next few months, Sarah found that she had panic attacks in more and more places. The typical pattern was that she became progressively anxious the further away from her house she got. She tried to avoid the places where she might have a panic attack but, as the months passed, she found that this restricted her activities. Some days she found it impossible to leave the house at all. She felt that her marriage was becoming strained and that her husband resented her dependence on him.

Clearly Sarah's behaviour was abnormal, in many of the ways described in the text. It was statistically infrequent and socially deviant. It interfered with her ability to function adequately, both from her own point of view and of her husband. She did not have many of the signs of mental healthiness.

(Adapted from J.D. Stirling & J.S.E. Hellewell, 1999, *Psychopathology*. London: Routledge.)

Seven features of abnormality

Rosenhan and Seligman (1989) suggest that the most suitable approach to defining mental abnormality may be to identify a set of abnormal *characteristics*. Each of these on its own may not be sufficient to cause a problem but, when several are present, then they are symptomatic of abnormality. The fewer of the seven features of abnormality displayed by individuals in their everyday lives, the more they can be regarded as normal. This approach enables us to think in terms of degrees of normality and abnormality, rather than simply making judgements about whether a behaviour or a person is abnormal or not.

KEY STUDY EVALUATION — Rosenhan and Seligman

One of the greatest problems with the seven features of abnormality proposed by Rosenhan and Seligman is that most of them involve making subjective judgements. Behaviour that causes severe discomfort to one observer may have no effect on another observer, and behaviour that violates one person's moral standards may be consistent with another person's moral standards, as we have noted earlier.

Another problem with some of the proposed features of abnormality (e.g. irrationality and incomprehensibility, unpredictability and loss of control, vividness and unconventionality) is that they also apply to people who are nonconformists or who simply have their own idiosyncratic style. This issue was addressed in the introduction to the third revised version of the *Diagnostic and Statistical Manual of Mental Disorders* (DSM-III-R), published in 1987 (p.xxii):

> Neither deviant behaviour, e.g. political, religious, or sexual, nor conflicts that are primarily between the individual and society are mental disorders unless the deviance or condition is a symptom of a dysfunction (i.e. impairment of function) in the person.

This does support the concept of "dysfunction" that is subjective but in a way that allows us to view the experience of mental disorder from the point of view of the person experiencing it.

- *Suffering*. Most abnormal individuals report that they are suffering, and so the presence of suffering is a key feature of abnormality. However, it is not adequate on its own because, for example, nearly all normal individuals grieve and suffer when a loved one dies. In addition, some abnormal individuals (e.g. psychopaths or those with anti-social personality disorder) treat other people very badly but do not seem to suffer themselves.

- *Maladaptiveness*. Maladaptive behaviour is behaviour that prevents an individual from achieving major life goals such as enjoying good relationships with other people or working effectively. Most abnormal behaviour is maladaptive in this sense. However, maladaptive behaviour can occur because of an absence of relevant knowledge or skills as well as because of abnormality.

- *Vividness and unconventionality of behaviour*. Vivid and unconventional behaviour is behaviour that is relatively unusual. The ways in which abnormal individuals behave in various situations differ substantially from the ways in which we would expect most people to behave in those situations. However, the same is true of non-conformists.

- *Unpredictability and loss of control*. Most people behave in a fairly predictable and controlled way. In contrast, the behaviour of abnormal individuals is often very variable and uncontrolled, and is inappropriate. However, most people can sometimes behave in unpredictable and uncontrolled ways.

- *Irrationality and incomprehensibility*. A common feature of abnormal behaviour is that it is not clear why anyone would choose to behave in that way. In other words, the behaviour is irrational and incomprehensible. However, behaviour can seem incomprehensible simply because we do not know the reasons for it. For example, a migraine may cause someone to behave in ways that are incomprehensible to other people.

- *Observer discomfort*. Our social behaviour is governed by a number of unspoken rules of behaviour. These include maintaining reasonable eye contact with other people and not standing too close to other people. Those who see these rules being broken often experience some discomfort. Observer discomfort may reflect cultural differences in behaviour and style rather than abnormality. For example, Arabs like to stand very close to other people, and this can be disturbing to Europeans.

- *Violation of moral and ideal standards*. Behaviour may be judged to be abnormal when it violates moral standards, even when many or most people fail to maintain those standards. For example, religious leaders have sometimes claimed that masturbation is wicked and abnormal, in spite of the fact that it is widespread.

■ Activity: The seven features of abnormality

Imagine a continuum from extremely abnormal behaviour at one end to normality at the other. At what point does our behaviour become unacceptable? Bearing in mind Rosenhan and Seligman's definitions, consider the experiences described on the right. For each one describe what would be acceptable behaviour and what would be regarded as abnormal. For example, what kind of expression of grief would go beyond the bounds of normality?

Suffering: Grief at the loss of a loved one.

Maladaptiveness: Disregard for one's own safety, e.g. taking part in extreme sports.

Vividness and unconventionality: Tattooing or body piercing.

Unpredictability and loss of control: Losing one's temper.

Irrationality and incomprehensibility: Remaining friendly towards someone who is hostile.

Observer discomfort: Laughing at inappropriate times, e.g. when someone is describing a sad event.

Violation of moral and ideal standards: Removing one's clothes to sunbathe on the beach.

- Are the criteria we use influenced by our cultural and personal backgrounds?
- Try to think of other examples for each standard.

Limitations of the "failure to function" approach

The main problem with this way of defining abnormality is that not all people who experience mental disorder are aware of their failure to function. For example, schizophrenics often deny that they have a problem (see the case study of Simon on page 160). In such cases the problem *is* distressing to others, and therefore others may be able to judge that the individual is not functioning adequately and so seek help on their behalf, as was the case with Simon.

On the positive side, it is relatively easy to assess the consequences of dysfunctional behaviour, such as using absenteeism from work or number of rows with one's spouse, as measures of the level of functioning. However, value judgements are still required as to what degree of impairment is abnormal and therefore worrying. In the end this approach is fairly tied to the social deviancy approach because it involves decisions about what is or is not acceptable.

The "failure to function adequately" model does have the advantage that it recognises the subjective experience of the individual. However, inevitably, such judgements are made by others and are influenced by social and cultural beliefs and biases.

Deviation From Ideal Mental Health

If we take the view that abnormality is related to the lack of a "contented existence" then we might seek a definition in terms of ideal mental health. This is the view put forward by **humanistic psychologists**, such as Carl Rogers and Abraham Maslow. They both felt that **self-actualisation** was a key standard and goal for human endeavour. Self-actualisation is self-fulfilment and the realisation of one's potential.

Rogers (1959) was the founder of **client-centred therapy**, or counselling. He believed that maladjustment or abnormal development occurred because a child received conditional love from his or her parents. This results in a conflict between the self and ideal self, and means the individual is likely to try to be someone else in order to receive the love they want. Healthy psychological development occurs through receiving unconditional positive regard from significant others, which leads to high **self-esteem** and self-acceptance. It frees the individual from seeking social approval and enables him or her to seek self-actualisation, and fulfil their potential.

Maslow (1954) was interested in the factors that drive or motivate individuals. He claimed that we seek first to have our basic needs satisfied, for example those

Maslow characterised Abraham Lincoln as a famous individual who demonstrated "self-actualisation" —including characteristics such as self-acceptance, resistance to cultural influences, empathy and creativeness.

According to Rogers, young children should receive unconditional positive regard from their parents. Parents should not withhold love as a punishment, or make it conditional on specific behaviours or achievements.

for hunger and safety. Once we can easily satisfy these needs, people are then "driven" by "higher" motives such as for love and belonging, and for knowledge. The highest motive of all is to seek self-actualisation (see diagram below).

The humanistic view was therefore to define the ultimate goals of human behaviour, and thus the factors that were important to mental health. Normal people should strive for these goals. Abnormality will result from a failure to achieve them. Marie Jahoda (1958) proposed a list of characteristics which could be used to define ideal mental health (see the Key Study on the next page). These include self-acceptance, potential for growth, autonomy, accurate perception of reality, and positive interpersonal relations.

Limitations of the ideal mental health approach

One advantage of this approach is that it focuses on positive characteristics—on health rather than illness. However, the criteria used to establish health, such as "self-actualisation", are hard to define. They are abstract ideals and, in addition, they are related to our particular culture. Not all societies feel that these are the ultimate aims for psychological health. Societies that are

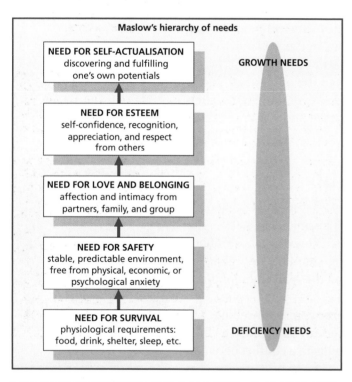

Maslow's hierarchy of needs

NEED FOR SELF-ACTUALISATION
discovering and fulfilling one's own potentials

GROWTH NEEDS

NEED FOR ESTEEM
self-confidence, recognition, appreciation, and respect from others

NEED FOR LOVE AND BELONGING
affection and intimacy from partners, family, and group

NEED FOR SAFETY
stable, predictable environment, free from physical, economic, or psychological anxiety

NEED FOR SURVIVAL
physiological requirements: food, drink, shelter, sleep, etc.

DEFICIENCY NEEDS

■ Activity: Write a brief description of how you see yourself (call this "A"). Then write a brief description of the person you would like to be (call this "B"). How different are A and B? Remember that our "ideal selves" are often different from our perceived selves.

Assertiveness is regarded as normal and desirable behaviour in our culture whereas in Thailand it would be judged to be naughty.

The characteristics of mental health

We define physical health in terms of the presence of healthy behaviours, such as a normal body temperature and normal skin colour. Why not do the same for mental illness? We can consider abnormality as the absence of normality. In fact Marie Jahoda (1958) argued that the concepts of abnormality and normality were useless because they rely on the identification of a reference population. She suggested that it was preferable to identify the criteria for positive mental health and then look at the frequency of their distribution in any population.

Jahoda wrote a report for the Joint Commission on Mental Illness and Health. She drew on the views of others and tried to identify common concepts that were used when describing mental health. In her report she proposed that there were six categories that clinicians typically related to mental health:

1. *Self-attitudes*. High self-esteem and a strong sense of identity are related to mental health.

2. *Personal growth*. The extent of an individual's growth, development, or self-actualisation is important. These criteria are not concerned with one's self-perception but more with what a person does over a period of time.

3. *Integration*. This is a "synthesising psychological function", the extent to which the above two concepts are integrated. It can be assessed in terms of the individual's ability to cope with stressful situations.

4. *Autonomy*. The degree to which an individual is independent of social influences and able to regulate his or herself.

5. *Perception of reality*. Many clinicians identify the link with reality as a prime factor in mental healthiness. This includes being free from "need-distortion" (an individual's need to distort their perception of reality) and demonstrating empathy and social sensitivity.

6. *Environmental mastery*. The extent to which an individual is successful and well adapted. This includes the ability to love, adequacy at work and play, adequacy in interpersonal relations, efficiency in meeting situational requirements, capacity for adaptation and adjustment, and efficient problem-solving!

Discussion points

1. Which of the above categories might be affected by cultural biases? In what way?

2. How might you criticise the "environmental mastery" category?

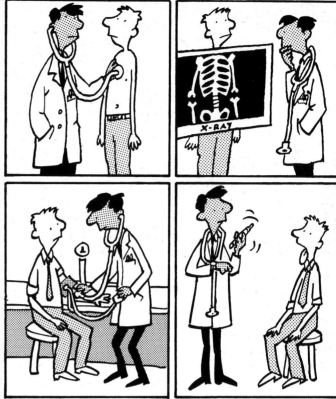

Results of medical tests provide more precise information than is available to psychiatrists and clinical psychologists.

KEY STUDY EVALUATION — Jahoda

This approach has the benefit of being positive. It seeks to identify the characteristics that people need to be mentally healthy rather than identifying the problems (i.e. "ill health"). As such it could be translated into useful therapeutic aims—goals to set during treatment.

However, it may not provide useful criteria for identifying what constitutes abnormality. When we use signs of physical health to identify physical ill health, we rely on fairly objective measurements, such as blood pressure. The same is not true when we are using psychological concepts. A psychological scale that measures a person's self-esteem can never be an objective measurement.

A further problem is that any set of values is inevitably culture-bound; related to a specific historic period and the views of a particular society. Nobles (1976) wrote about the extended concept of self in African people. He claimed that they have a sense of "we" instead of the Western "me". This means that they value co-operation whereas Westerners value independence and autonomy, as reflected in Jahoda's list of mentally healthy behaviours.

---

collectivistic strive for the greater good of the community rather than focusing on individual achievement. Such societies would not see self-centred goals as the ultimate in human behaviour.

A second problem with the use of these vague criteria is the difficulty in measuring them. The concept of "health" works reasonably well with respect to physical conditions because the signs of health (such as a normal temperature and a normal skin colour) are easy to measure. But how can we rate positive interpersonal relations or self-acceptance? Finally, we should consider the fact that these "healthy behaviours" are ideals. Very few people ever achieve them and therefore many of us would be classed as abnormal.

Cultural Relativism

A central limitation to all the definitions of abnormality we have examined is the extent to which they are culturally specific. The concept of **cultural relativism** means that value judgements are *relative* to individual cultural contexts and we cannot make absolute statements about what is normal or abnormal in human behaviour.

As we have seen, notions of abnormality vary from one culture to another, and within the same culture at different periods in history. For example, the way in which homosexuality is regarded has altered over successive editions of DSM (the Diagnostic and Statistical Manual of Mental Disorders, see box below), the system used to classify mental illness in America. In DSM-II, which was published in 1968, homosexuality was classified as a sexual deviation. In DSM-III, published in 1980, homosexuality was no longer categorised as a mental disorder. However, there was a new category of "ego-dystonic homosexuality", which was to be used only for homosexuals who wished to become heterosexual. In DSM-III-R, the category of ego-dystonic homosexuality had disappeared. However, there was a category of "sexual disorder not otherwise specified", with "persistent and marked distress about one's sexual orientation" being included. This remains the case in **DSM-IV**. On a lay person's level, many people continue to view homosexuality as an aberrant mental state.

The importance of the cultural context can be seen if we return to the seven features of abnormality proposed by Rosenhan and Seligman. Many of the features (e.g. vividness and unconventional behaviour, irrationality and incomprehensibility, observer discomfort) refer to behaviour that is defined by the social norms or expectations of the culture. As the social norms or expectations vary across cultures, it follows that abnormality has a somewhat different meaning from one culture to another. For example, in some societies hallucinations are considered normal in certain situations, whereas in the Western world they are seen as a manifestation of a mental disorder (Sue et al. 1994).

On the other hand, some of the features identified by Rosenhan and Seligman are universal indicators of undesirable behaviour—both for the individual concerned and those around them. Failure to eat,

Cross-cultural issues: DSM aims to provide an objective means of assessing mental disorders. To what extent might it apply only to our culture?

Homosexuality ceased to be categorised as a mental disorder in the 1980 edition of DSM.

Labels and symptoms

Imagine that you are in a situation where you have been wrongly diagnosed as suffering from a mental disorder such as schizophrenia. How would you react to such a situation? Would you be incredulous? Furious? Tearful? Shocked and withdrawn? How could all those emotions be interpreted by those people whose job it is to assess your mental condition?

CASE STUDY: *The DSM Classification of Mental Disorder*

Another way to define abnormality is by constructing a classification system that enables clinicians to diagnose mental disorders. The DSM classification is used largely in the US and is now in its fourth revision—DSM-IV. It consists of five axes which permit the description of a person's disorder in five dimensions.

Axis 1 lists the major types of illness. A clinician identifies clusters of symptoms that lead to a primary diagnosis in certain groups, such as: childhood disorder, delirium or dementia, substance-abuse, schizophrenia, mood disorder, anxiety disorder, sexual- or gender-identity disorder.

Axis 2 distinguishes mental handicap from personality disorders, both of which are lifelong conditions.

Axis 3 permits the identification of medical or physical symptoms, such as an overactive thyroid gland, which might have an effect on the diagnosis, or even account for the symptoms.

Axis 4 codes psychosocial problems so that account can be taken of the extent and severity of stressors in a person's life.

Axis 5 is a global assessment of the individual's ability to function, a scale from 0–100 that enables the clinician to express the extent to which the individual can cope at home, at work, and in leisure activities.

chronic depression, fear of going outdoors, and anti-social behaviour would be seen as undesirable behaviours in any culture. Furthermore all societies would want to offer some form of help for the individual. This suggests that there *are* some universal indicators of abnormality.

Conclusions

Concepts differ very much in their precision. "Abnormality" is an imprecise concept, which is as hard to define as the concept "games". Thus, abnormal behaviour can take different forms, and can involve different features. Moreover, there is no single feature that can always be relied on to distinguish between normal and abnormal behaviour. What is needed is to identify the main features that are *more likely* to be found in abnormal than in normal individuals. The seven features proposed by Rosenhan and Seligman (1989) may offer a combined and realistic approach. The more of these features possessed by an individual, the greater the likelihood that he or she will be categorised as abnormal.

SECTION 14
Biological and Psychological Models of Abnormality

A different way to approach the question "what is abnormality", is to consider explanations of *why* it happens. Several models of abnormality have been put forward over the years. These models have been very influential, because the form of treatment for any given mental disorder is based in part on our understanding of the causes of that disorder.

The dominant model, at least until fairly recently, was the medical model. According to the medical model, mental disorders are regarded as illnesses. Most **psychiatrists** accept the medical model, whereas most clinical psychologists reject it in favour of psychological models. There are several psychologically based models of abnormality, but we will focus on the three most important ones here: the behavioural, psychodynamic, and cognitive models.

Why are there several different models of abnormality? Mental disorders are caused by numerous factors, and each of the models emphasises some of these factors at the expense of others. Some models are appropriate for some disorders but not others, for example the psychodynamic approach is helpful for disorders where

What do you think is the difference between a psychological model and a medical one?

Ethical issues: Behavioural approaches to the treatment of mental disorders have been successful but they assume that the patient and therapist share the same goals for behaviour. In what way might such treatments be seen as "social manipulation"?

the individual has some insight into their condition, and the behavioural model is good for treating disorders with distinct behavioural symptoms such as phobias.

Another reason for the variety of models is that each individual psychologist or psychiatrist has his or her own life philosophy, and different models are more in keeping with their general views. An optimistic person might find that the humanistic approach was more in line with their view of human nature, whereas a person who looks for hidden meanings would prefer the psychodynamic approach.

It is probable that each of the models is partially correct, and that a full understanding of the origins of mental disorders requires us to combine information from all of them.

The Medical Model

The essence of the medical model is that "abnormal behaviours result from physical problems and should be treated medically". In other words, mental disorders resemble physical diseases, in that they are both illnesses with a physical cause. As a result, this model suggests that we should approach mental disorders from the perspective of medicine.

There are four kinds of medical explanation that can be used to explain the cause of abnormality.

Infection

Germs or micro-organisms such as bacteria or viruses are known to produce disease states. Many common physical illnesses are caused in this way, such as measles and influenza. Some mental illnesses have also been linked to known micro-organisms as in the case of general paresis (see Key Study on the page opposite). Micro-organisms have also been suggested as a cause of schizophrenia, for example Barr et al. (1990) found that there was increased incidence of schizophrenia in children whose mothers had flu when they were pregnant, thereby suggesting that the cause of the disorder might be a disease.

One way to investigate the genetic cause of mental disorders is to look at genetically related individuals. If relatives of a person with a mental disorder are found also to suffer from it, then this suggests a genetic basis for mental disorders.

Genetic factors

Individuals may inherit predispositions to certain illnesses. These predispositions are carried on **genes** which pass from one generation to the next. One way to demonstrate the inheritance of mental disorder is by looking at patterns of such illnesses within families or within twin pairs. If a disorder is caused genetically then we would expect individuals who are closely related to be more likely to have it, especially when they have been reared apart (and therefore there are no shared environmental influences). There is considerable evidence of this sort, for example Kendler, Masterson, and Davis (1985) found that relatives of schizophrenics were 18 times more likely to be diagnosed with schizophrenia than we would normally expect.

General paresis

Records from the 16th century describe individuals with a particular kind of mental illness which involved delusions of grandeur, progressive forgetfulness, dullness, and mental deterioration. What set this group of people apart from the general range of madmen was the fact that, later in life, they would become paralysed and then die. These symptoms were recorded by various people over the centuries and little was made of it until one medical student formally described the symptoms of the disorder. He argued that deterioration, paralysis, and death were a distinct *syndrome*, to be called "general paresis" (Rosenhan & Seligman, 1989).

This formal identification of a cluster symptoms marked a fundamental step in finding a treatment for the disorder. Medical diagnosis relies on having a set of symptoms which, if they co-occur, indicate the presence of a disorder. For example, what is measles? We diagnose the disorder when we can observe sufficient of the following symptoms: runny nose, reddened eyes, followed by appearance of spots that turn into a rash, high temperature, and dry cough. The practice of medicine relies on the identification of a set of symptoms that can be labelled as an illness. Only once the illness can be diagnosed, can one experiment with suitable treatments.

Some people thought that general paresis was caused by the syphilis bacterium, but this was not easy to prove as many of those who had the illness denied having ever had syphilis, a sexually transmitted disease. However, late in the 19th century it was recognised that people who were known to have had syphilis never got the disease again, even if they were exposed to it. So the German neurologist Richard von Krafft-Ebing performed a critical experiment. He argued that if general paresis was caused by the syphilis bacterium then it should not be possible to re-infect someone with general paresis with syphilis, because they would have immunity. He selected nine paretics who denied ever having syphilis and injected them with material from syphilitic sores! None of them developed the sores themselves. In other words they were immune to the disease and therefore must have had syphilis before. Once the cause was known a cure could be found, which happened in 1909, and that was the end of general paresis.

> ### KEY STUDY EVALUATION — von Krafft-Ebing
>
> It is doubtful that von Krafft-Ebing's research would have been permitted today. Some researchers have the solution of using themselves as the experimental participant, but clearly this is not always possible. A researcher certainly needs to be quite confident about his or her hypothesis in order to test it in this way. But the consequences are enormous. Imagine if we found that schizophrenia or anorexia nervosa were actually caused by a micro-organism. That would effectively be the end of such disorders, in the same way that we are today seeing the end of childhood illnesses such as scarlet fever.
>
> In reality this is unlikely to ever be the case with most mental disorders because they do not form such distinct syndromes nor do they have one cause. But this is the aim of the medical approach—if we can diagnose a syndrome then we might find a cure. The one relies on the other.

Discussion points

1. What comments would you make on the ethics of von Krafft-Ebing's work, given that general paresis was a disease that killed many people?
2. What can we learn from this research about medical diagnosis?

Another way to study **genetic** influences is to actually identify particular genes and demonstrate that they are more likely to be present in individuals with a disorder than in individuals without the disorder. **Gene-mapping** studies have found specific genes which may be implicated in particular disorders. For example, Sherrington et al. (1988) have found evidence of a link between schizophrenia and a gene located on chromosome 5, although subsequent research has been unable to confirm this.

How might research on gene-mapping be used when counselling prospective parents?

Biochemistry

A third possible cause of abnormality lies in the patient's **biochemistry**. For example, several theorists have argued that one of the factors involved in schizophrenia is an excessive amount of dopamine, a chemical substance in the brain. However, research has only identified *correlations* between the disorder and the raised biochemical levels. Therefore we cannot be certain whether such excesses are *causes* or whether they are *effects* of a disorder. A disordered state may raise levels of anxiety, causing levels of certain hormones to rise, as we saw in the section on bodily responses to stress (Chapter 4, Section 10). In such cases the psychological state is causing the biochemical abnormality, rather than vice versa.

Neuroanatomy

A fourth possible cause lies in **neuroanatomy**, that is, the structure of the nervous system. For example, amnesia usually occurs because the part of the brain in which long-term memories are stored is damaged. In the case of schizophrenics there is evidence from post-mortem studies that their brains are different from those of normal individuals. Again, however, we cannot be certain whether schizophrenia caused the neuroanatomical changes or whether the differences were the cause of the mental disorder.

Implications of the medical model for treatment

The medical model has clear implications for treatment. If mental illnesses are basically illnesses of the body, then treatment should involve direct manipulation of bodily processes. For example, if a mental disorder (e.g. schizophrenia) involves biochemical abnormalities, then drugs can be used to correct these abnormalities. Drugs have been used with some success to treat various disorders such as schizophrenia, anxiety, and depression (see Chapter 4, Section 12). However, it should be noted that the success of drug therapy in treating a mental disorder does not prove that the disorder was caused by biological factors. Drugs may also be used in conjunction with other therapies, such as **counselling**, so that anxiety or depression can be reduced, thus allowing the individual to be able to reflect more clearly on the sources of their problem.

The main drawback with drug therapy is the side effects, such as drowsiness, as well as the problems of psychological and physical addiction. A further consideration is the fact that drugs do not cure any disorder but usually offer fairly temporary relief.

Other forms of treatment based on the medical model include fairly drastic methods such as **electroconvulsive shock therapy** (ECT) and brain surgery. ECT is not the barbaric treatment it once was. Patients are given sedatives before treatment and then brief shocks are applied to the person's non-dominant hemisphere. The treatment has been found to be successful for patients suffering from chronic depression, and long-term side effects are unusual (Stirling & Hellewell, 1999). Brain surgery (**psychosurgery**) is used in extremely rare conditions, where no other treatment seems appropriate. Sections of the brain are removed or lesions are made separating regions of the brain. The technique was first pioneered by Antonio Egas Moniz (1937), who performed prefrontal lobotomies, in which fibres running from the frontal lobes to other parts of the brain were cut. Lobotomies typically make patients calmer.

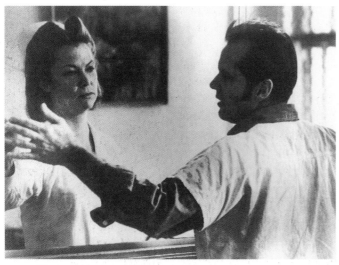

In the film ***One Flew Over the Cuckoo's Nest***, Jack Nicholson played Randle Patrick McMurphy, who inspired and awakened his fellow patients, whilst falling out with the authorities. Eventually, the character is lobotomised, and becomes calmer and easier to handle, but loses all his intellectual spark and energy.

However, the side effects include apathy, diminished intellectual powers, impaired judgement, and even coma and death. In view of the dangers of lobotomies, it is ironic that Moniz was shot in the spine by one of his own lobotomised patients.

Evaluation of the medical model

The medical model has had an enormous influence on the terms used to refer to mental disorders and their treatment. As Maher (1966, p.22) pointed out, deviant behaviour

> is termed pathological *and is classified on the basis of symptoms, classification being called* diagnosis. *Processes designed to change behaviour are called* therapies, *and are [sometimes] applied to patients in mental* hospitals. *If the deviant behaviour ceases, the patient is described as* cured.

The medical model approach is clearly successful in the case of some psychological conditions. For example the condition of phenylketonuria (PKU), which is a cause of mental retardation, can be simply and effectively treated by physical means. This is a condition where an individual is born with an inability to metabolise (process) the amino acid phenylalanine. As a result, the concentration of phenylalanine increases, and there is permanent brain damage. In addition, there are usually seizures and behaviour problems. PKU is preventable if it is detected early enough. Infants are given a special diet low in phenylalanine and this has proved very successful in preventing the development of PKU.

But how useful is the medical model approach to most mental disorders? On the positive side, it has the merit of being based on well-established sciences such as medicine and biochemistry. Some forms of mental disorder (e.g. schizophrenia) can be understood from the perspective of the medical model, and numerous mental disorders are caused *in part* by **genetic** factors. Drug therapies based on the medical model have often proved effective, at least in the sense of reducing the symptoms of those suffering from mental disorder. They are also popular because they require little effort on the part of the patient.

On the negative side, there is generally only a loose analogy between physical and mental illness. It is easier to establish the causes of most physical illnesses than mental ones, and symptoms of mental disorders are often more subjective than those of physical illnesses. The medical model seems to apply much better to some mental disorders than others. For example, it tells us rather little about the origins of phobias.

One important difficulty is knowing whether any biological difference between individuals with a mental disorder and those without such disorder is a by-product of the disorder, rather than being a direct cause.

Another criticism is that the focus within the medical model is too much on symptoms, and not enough on the patient's experiences and internal processes. The role of psychological and social factors (e.g. life events and personal difficulties) in explaining mental disorders is ignored. This is especially important because many of the symptoms of mental disorders are given in psychological and social terms (such as anxiety and isolation) and therefore the application of medical principles is inappropriate.

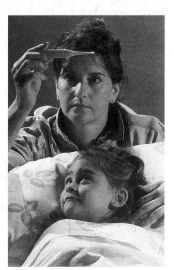

It may not be appropriate to think that mental illnesses are the same as physical ones.

One of the biggest critics of the medical approach, Thomas Szasz, suggested that mental illnesses were more appropriately described as "problems in living" rather than as disease states:

> *It is customary to define psychiatry as a medical specialty concerned with the study, diagnosis, and treatment of mental illnesses. This is a worthless and misleading definition. Mental illness is a myth. Psychiatrists are not concerned with mental illnesses and their treatment. In actual practice they deal with personal, social and ethical problems in living.*

> *I have argued that, today, the notion of a person "having a mental illness" is scientifically crippling. It provides professional assent to a popular rationalization, namely that problems of living ... expressed in terms of so-called psychiatric symptoms are basically similar to bodily diseases ... We must recast and redefine the problem of "mental illness" so that it may be encompassed in a morally explicit science of man. (1960, p.269)*

Ethical implications of the medical model

The notion that individuals with mental disorders are suffering from an illness could be regarded as ethically desirable, because it suggests that they are not responsible for their condition. However, when someone is labelled as suffering from a mental illness, this may cause other people to be frightened or wary of that person, and that is clearly ethically undesirable. In addition, it may be undesirable to encourage individuals with mental disorders to hand over complete responsibility for their recovery to experts trained in treating "mental illness".

Assumptions of the medical model

- All mental disorders have a physical cause (micro-organisms, genetics, biochemistry, or neuroanatomy).
- Mental illnesses can be described in terms of clusters of symptoms.
- Symptoms can be identified, leading to the diagnosis of an illness.
- Diagnosis leads to appropriate physical treatments.

The notion that genetic factors often play a significant role in the development of mental disorders raises some ethical issues. The relatives of an individual diagnosed as suffering from such a disorder may well become very anxious, and this could greatly increase their chances of developing the disorder.

Many of the forms of treatment based on the medical model raise important ethical issues. Drugs can have serious side effects and lead to drug dependence. More direct interventions such as electroconvulsive shock therapy and brain surgery can make the lives of patients worse rather than better.

Finally, there are ethical issues raised by the relative neglect of psychological factors within the medical model. For example, therapy may take much longer than necessary if the therapist ignores such factors when providing treatment.

The Psychodynamic Model

The term "psychodynamic" refers to a group of explanations that try to account for the *dynamics* of behaviour, or the forces that motivate it. Sigmund Freud's psychoanalytic theory is the best-known example, and he has probably been the most influential person in clinical psychology. His view was that mental illness did not have a physical origin. Instead he suggested that it arises out of unresolved, unconscious conflicts which form in early childhood.

To understand this we need to look briefly at Freud's theory of personality development, a recap of what was already covered in Chapter 1, Section 2. Freud argued that the mind is divided into three parts. First, there is the id. This consists mainly of unconscious sexual and aggressive instincts. The motivating force is called the libido, an innate drive for sexual (or physical) satisfaction. Second, there is the

Sigmund Freud, 1856–1939.

ego, which is the rational and conscious part of the mind. Third, there is the superego or conscience. The three parts of the mind are often in conflict with each other. Conflicts occur most often between the id and the superego, because the id wants immediate gratification, whereas the superego takes account of moral standards.

The psychodynamic model put forward by Freud was based on his theory of **psychosexual development**. The child passes through a series of stages (oral, anal, phallic, latency, and genital). Major conflicts or excessive gratification at any of these stages can mean that the child spends an unusually long time at that stage of development (this process is known as fixation). If an adult experiences great personal problems, he or she will tend to show regression (going backwards through the stages of psychosexual development) to the stage at which he or she had previously been fixated.

Conflicts cause anxiety, and the ego defends itself against anxiety by using several defence mechanisms to prevent traumatic thoughts and feelings reaching consciousness. The major defence mechanism is **repression**, which forces memories of conflicts and traumas out of consciousness and into the unconscious mind. Other defence mechanisms include displacement and projection. Displacement occurs when aggressive or other impulses are transferred away from a threatening person to someone non-threatening, as when someone who has been bullied by their boss kicks the cat. **Projection** occurs when someone who possesses an undesirable characteristic attributes it to other people. For example, someone who is very hostile may claim that other people are hostile to him or her.

Freud suggested that conflicts between parents and children during one stage of development could lead to fixation at that stage.

According to Freud, mental disorders can arise when an individual has unresolved conflicts and traumas from childhood. Defence mechanisms may be used to reduce the anxiety caused by such unresolved conflicts, but they act more as sticking plaster than as a way of sorting out an individual's problems.

> **Defence mechanisms**
>
> Another example of a defence mechanism is reaction formation, e.g. in an adult who has developed a fear of close, intimate relationships due to a disappointment or hurt experienced during childhood. As a consequence, when this adult meets someone to whom they feel a strong attraction, they may consciously experience the opposite emotion of dislike, or even hatred.

Implications of the psychodynamic model for treatment

The implications for treatment are that a prime goal of therapy is to enable patients to gain access to their repressed ideas and conflicts, and to encourage them to face up to whatever emerges from the unconscious. Freud used the term "insight" to refer to the processes involved. He assumed that insight would permit the repressed memories to be integrated into the ego or conscious self, after which the patient would be better able to cope with life.

In the beginning, Freud used hypnosis as a means of accessing repressed memories (see the case study overleaf of Anna O) but later felt that this was an unreliable method. The other two methods were dreams, as the "royal road" to the unconscious, and **free association**, a technique where the client is encouraged to say the first thing that comes into his or her mind.

Try free association yourself. Start with a thought and see what else comes into your head. Were the subsequent thoughts "revealing"?

Psychoanalysis depends heavily on the therapist's interpretation of what the client says. How, for example, does the therapist know that a girl dreaming about riding a horse is actually thinking about having sex rather than simply about horse-riding? Freud argued that the acid test was the client's reaction to the therapist's proposed interpretation. If the client accepts the accuracy of the interpretation, then it is probably correct. If the client vehemently rejects the therapist's interpretation of a dream, that may simply be resistance by the client's conscious mind to an unacceptable but entirely accurate interpretation.

There is a problem here. The therapist wins both ways because he or she either uses the client's acceptance or denial of the reasonableness of a dream interpretation as supporting evidence that the interpretation is correct! Freud argued that we can regard psychoanalysis as similar to solving a jigsaw puzzle. It may be hard to decide whether a given interpretation is correct, or to decide where to place a particular piece of the puzzle. However, the interpretations of dozens of a client's free associations and dreams should form a coherent picture, just as the pieces of a jigsaw puzzle can only be arranged in one way.

Treatment based on the psychodynamic model is generally very time-consuming, because of the patient's reluctance to face up to his or her past. In the words of Freud (1917, p.289):

The patient attempts to escape by every possible means. First he says nothing comes into his head, then that so much comes into his head that he can't grasp any of it … At last he admits that he really cannot say anything, he is ashamed to … So it goes on, with untold variations.

CASE STUDY: *Anna O*

Freud's theory was largely based on the observations he made during consultations with patients. He suggested that his work was similar to that of an archaeologist, who digs away layers of earth before uncovering what he or she was seeking. In a similar way, the psychiatrist seeks to dig down to the unconscious and discover the key to the individual's personality dynamic.

"Anna O. was a girl of twenty-one, of a high degree of intelligence. Her illness first appeared while she was caring for her father, whom she tenderly loved, during the severe illness which led to his death. The patient had a severe paralysis of both right extremities, disturbance of eye-movements, an intense nausea when she attempted to take nourishment, and at one time for several weeks a loss of the power to drink, in spite of tormenting thirst. She occasionally became confused or delirious and mumbled several words to herself. If these same words were later repeated to her, when she was in a hypnotic state, she engaged in deeply sad, often poetically beautiful, day dreams, we might call them, which commonly took as their starting point the situation of a girl beside the sick-bed of her father. The patient jokingly called this treatment 'chimney sweeping'.

Dr. Breuer [Freud's colleague] soon hit upon the fact that through such cleansing of the soul more could be accomplished than a temporary removal of the constantly recurring mental 'clouds'.

During one session, the patient recalled an occasion when she was with her governess, and how that lady's little dog, that she abhorred, had drunk out of a glass. Out of respect for the conventions the patient had remained silent, but now under hypnosis she gave energetic expression to her restrained anger, and then drank a large quantity of water without trouble, and woke from hypnosis with the glass at her lips. The symptom thereupon vanished permanently.

Permit me to dwell for a moment on this experience. No one had ever cured an hysterical symptom by such means before, or had come so near understanding its cause. This would be a pregnant discovery if the expectation could be confirmed that still other, perhaps the majority of symptoms, originated in this way and could be removed by the same method.

Such was indeed the case, almost all the symptoms originated in exactly this way, as we were to discover. The patient's illness originated at the time when she was caring for her sick father, and her symptoms could only be regarded as memory symbols of his sickness and death. While she was seated by her father's sick bed, she was careful to betray nothing of her anxiety and her painful depression to the patient. When, later, she reproduced the same scene before the physician, the emotion which she had suppressed on the occurrence of the scene burst out with especial strength, as though it had been pent up all along.

In her normal state she was entirely ignorant of the pathogenic scenes and of their connection with her symptoms. She had forgotten those scenes. When the patient was hypnotized, it was possible, after considerable difficulty, to recall those scenes to her memory, and by this means of recall the symptoms were removed."

(Adapted from Sigmund Freud, 1910, The origin and development of psychoanalysis. *American Journal of Psychology, 21*, 181–218.)

Freud asked his patients to lie on a couch during psychoanalysis. This is a photograph of his couch in his London house which is now a museum.

Evaluation of the psychodynamic model

The psychodynamic model proposed by Freud was the first systematic model of abnormality that focused specifically on psychological factors as the cause of mental disorder and on psychological forms of treatment. Before Freud, all explanations of mental illness were in terms of physical causes or ideas such as possession by evil spirits. Psychoanalysis paved the way for later psychological models. Another advantage of the psychodynamic model is that it identified traumatic childhood experiences as a factor in the development of adult disorders, an assumption for which there is good evidence (Barlow & Durand, 1995).

A great weakness of the psychoanalytic model as put forward by Freud was the relative lack of interest in the current problems his patients were facing. Even if childhood experiences stored in the unconscious play a part in the development of mental disorders, that does not mean that adult experiences can safely be ignored. Current psychodynamic therapy has evolved out of Freud's approach, but it has more of an emphasis on current problems as well as on childhood experiences.

Another weakness of Freud's approach was that he tended to focus too much on sexual factors as the cause of mental disorders, while de-emphasising the importance of interpersonal and social factors in causing and maintaining mental disorders. These factors are generally regarded as important by most psychodynamic therapists nowadays. Most modern

> **Positive aspects of the Freudian approach**
>
> Freud's work is often criticised, and it is true that it is difficult to verify the workings of the subconscious mind through scientific investigations. However, post-Freudian study of the importance of subjective feelings and experience has been a major undertaking in both psychology and other dissociated fields such as creative writing, literary theory, and art history. Freud's ideas about the importance of the subconscious mind have been one of the most profound influences on human thought of the 20th century, leading to in-depth questioning of human motives and intentions. It is hard for us to think about the world without employing Freudian concepts.

psychodynamic therapists believe that sexual problems are a *result* of poor relationships with others rather than a cause of disorder.

The psychodynamic model is not based on a solid foundation of scientific research. Freud's theoretical views emerged mainly from his interactions with patients in the therapeutic situation. However, this was a weak form of evidence that was probably contaminated by Freud's biases and preconceptions.

In sum, the psychodynamic approach is limited because it tends to ignore genetic factors involved in the development of mental disorders. In its original form, the patient's current concerns and interpersonal relationships were de-emphasised, and there was undue focus on childhood experiences and sexual problems. In practice, the psychodynamic model has been applied mainly to patients suffering from anxiety disorders or depression rather than from severe disorders such as schizophrenia.

Ethical implications of the psychodynamic model

One of the implications of the psychodynamic model is that individuals are not really responsible for their own mental disorders. This is so because these disorders depend on unconscious processes over which individuals have no control. However, the notion that adult mental disorders have their basis in childhood experiences suggests that parents or other caregivers are at least partially to blame. This can easily cause them distress, if they are led to believe that they are responsible for their child's disorder.

> **Assumptions of the psychodynamic model**
> - Much of our behaviour is driven by unconscious motives.
> - Childhood is a critical period in development.
> - Mental disorders arise from unresolved, unconscious conflicts originating in childhood.
> - Resolution occurs through accessing and coming to terms with repressed ideas and conflicts.

Very serious ethical issues are raised by numerous recent cases of **false memory syndrome**. In these cases, patients undergoing psychotherapy have made allegations about childhood physical or sexual abuse that have sometimes turned out to have no basis in fact. It is often very hard to know whether such allegations are true or not. We have not space here to fully consider this matter, which is still hotly debated.

Freud argued that males and females have their own biologically determined sexual natures, and anxiety disorders or depression can develop when the natural course of their sexual development is thwarted. This approach is dubious, in that it ignores the importance of cultural differences in sexual attitudes and behaviour. It is also very sexist in its emphasis that behavioural differences between men and women stem from biology rather than from social and cultural factors.

The Behavioural Model

The behavioural model of abnormality was developed out of the behaviourist approach to psychology put forward mainly by John Watson and B.F. Skinner. According to this model, individuals with mental disorders possess **maladaptive** forms of behaviour, which have been learned. Most of the learning takes the form of classical conditioning or operant conditioning (see Chapter 1 Section 2). A reminder of these processes is shown in the box at the top of the next page.

Classical conditioning

Classical conditioning is a form of learning that was first demonstrated by Pavlov. In essence, a neutral stimulus is paired repeatedly with a second stimulus. After a while, the natural response to the second stimulus comes to be made in response to the neutral stimulus when it is presented on its own. The fear response can be conditioned to neutral stimuli in this way. This was demonstrated in a classic study by Watson and Rayner involving an infant called "Little Albert" (see Key Study on the next page). It has been claimed that mental illnesses, such as specific phobias or extreme fears of certain stimuli (e.g. snakes), develop through classical conditioning.

Operant conditioning

Operant conditioning involves learning a new response as a result of the fact that, in the past, the same response has resulted in a reward or reinforcement. The reinforcement increases the likelihood that the behaviour will be repeated. If a behaviour results in unpleasant consequences or punishment, then it is less likely that it will be repeated. For example, Lewinsohn (1974) argued that depression occurs as a result of a low level of reinforcement. When people receive less reinforcement, they produce fewer responses. As a result, they receive even less reinforcement, and this causes them to experience depression.

Social learning theory

Bandura (1986) further developed conditioning theory by arguing that observational learning or modelling is important. This is a form of learning in which individuals learn by imitating the behaviour of someone else. Observational learning is especially likely to influence behaviour when the other person's behaviour is rewarded or reinforced. This is called vicarious reinforcement because you are experiencing the reward by watching someone else receive it. Observational learning or modelling may be relevant to several mental disorders. For instance, Mineka et al. (1984) found that monkeys could develop snake phobia simply by watching another monkey experience fear in the presence of a snake. One might assume that the same principles apply to humans.

Implications of the behavioural model for treatment

As we have seen, it is assumed within the behavioural model that mental disorders arise as a result of maladaptive forms of learning based on conditioning or observational learning. It follows, fairly logically, that an appropriate form of treatment involves further conditioning or observational learning designed to eliminate the maladaptive forms of behaviour that have been learned. In other words, if a behaviour was learned in the first place, then it can be unlearned—using the same processes of conditioning and observational learning.

Classical conditioning can be seen in **aversion therapy**. Patients learn to associate things they previously enjoyed with unpleasant responses, and thus the undesirable behaviour is discouraged. For example, alcoholics consume large amounts of alcohol. If they are given a drug that makes them vomit as soon as they drink anything alcoholic, they quickly come to feel nauseous as soon as they smell the alcohol and they certainly avoid it, at least while taking the drug. The treatment requires the co-operation of the patient and there are some doubts about the long-term effectiveness of aversion therapy.

Systematic desensitisation is a less controversial method which is also based on classical conditioning. It is a form of **counterconditioning**, and involves the attempt

---

Classical conditioning

- Unconditioned stimulus (US) e.g. food → causes → reflex response e.g. salivation.
- Neutral stimulus (NS) e.g. bell → causes → no response.
- NS and US are paired in time (they occur at the same time).
- NS (e.g. bell) is now a conditioned stimulus (CS) → which produces → a conditioned response (CR) [a new stimulus–response link is learned, the bell causes salivation].

Operant conditioning

- A behaviour that has a positive effect is more likely to be repeated.
- Positive and negative reinforcement (escape from aversive stimulus) are agreeable.
- Punishment is disagreeable.

Watson and Rayner taught a boy "Little Albert" to fear white fluffy objects by striking a metal bar (unconditioned stimulus) every time he touched the previously unfeared object (neutral stimulus). Thus they demonstrated that fears could be learned through classical conditioning.

KEY STUDY EVALUATION — Watson and Rayner

Not all research has found it possible to condition people to fear neutral stimuli by pairing them with unpleasant ones in the laboratory (Davison & Neale, 1996), and research into phobias has not found that all phobics have had prior traumatic experiences. For example, Menzies and Clarke (1993) carried out a study on child participants suffering from water phobia. Only 2% of them reported a direct conditioning experience involving water. DiNardo et al. (1988) found that about 50% of dog phobics had become very anxious during an encounter with a dog, which seems to support conditioning theory. However, they also found that about 50% of normal controls without dog phobia had also had an anxious encounter with a dog! Thus, these findings suggest that dog phobia does *not* depend on having had a frightening encounter with a dog.

Clearly there are ethical concerns in relation to this study, especially as Albert was never re-conditioned. Watson and Rayner acknowledged these ethical issues from the outset. They said they conducted the research with hesitation, but decided that it was justifiable because children do experience fearful situations in day-to-day life and therefore they were not exposing Albert to anything out of the usual. They also did intend that he should be re-conditioned.

The classical conditioning of fear

According to the behaviourists, specific phobias may develop through classical conditioning. If a neutral stimulus (e.g. furry rabbit) is presented at the same time as a frightening (unconditioned) stimulus (e.g. very loud noise), then the two become paired so that eventually the neutral stimulus produces the same fear response as the frightening stimulus. This is what John B. Watson and Rosalie Rayner (1920) aimed to demonstrate in what has become a classic experiment in psychology. They wished to show that emotions could be classically conditioned in the same way as any response is conditioned.

Their participant was an 11-month-old boy called "Little Albert", an orphan living in a hospital. The nurses described him as a healthy boy, both emotionally and physically. At the start of the experiment Watson and Rayner established that such items as a white rat, a rabbit, and white cotton wool provoked no fear response. They were the neutral stimuli. The next phase of the experiment was to induce a fear response. Fear is an unconditioned response because no learning is required—fear is an innate reflex. Watson and Rayner put a steel bar 4 feet in length behind Albert and struck it with a hammer. Albert was startled and it made him cry.

Next, they gave him a white rat to play with and, as he reached out to touch it, they struck the bar to make him frightened. They repeated this three times, and did the same a week later. After this, when they showed the rat to Albert he began to cry, rolled over and started to crawl away so fast that the researchers had to rush to catch him before he fell off the table.

Watson and Rayner found that, now, the sight of any object that was white and furry, such as a white fur coat and a Father Christmas beard, provoked a fear response. This is called **generalisation**, Albert had learned to generalise his fear of the white rat to other similar objects. They intended to "recondition" Albert to eliminate these fearful reactions but he was taken away from the hospital before this could happen.

This explanation of the origin of phobias was extended by Mowrer (1947) into a two-process theory. The first stage involves classical conditioning (e.g. linking the white rat and the loud noise). Then the second stage involves operant conditioning, because avoidance of the phobic stimulus reduces fear and is thus reinforcing.

Discussion points

1. Try to use classical conditioning to explain some other abnormal behaviour.

2. How could this experiment have been made more ethically acceptable?

John Watson, 1878–1958.

CASE STUDY: *John Watson*

At the time the "Little Albert" study was conducted, Watson was a major figure in behaviourism and psychology. In 1913 he published a key paper arguing that psychology had to throw out introspection as a research method, and dismiss vague concepts such as "the mind" in order to become a respectable science. Psychologists, he suggested, should instead focus on observable, directly measurable behaviours. In short, he was largely responsible for founding the behaviourist movement, drawing on the ideas of Pavlov.

At the time he was the Professor of Psychology at Johns Hopkins University, Baltimore, USA, where he conducted research into animal behaviour until 1918 when he turned his attention to conditioning infants. However in 1920 he was involved in a rather sensational divorce as a result of his affair with his research assistant Rosalie Rayner, whom he subsequently married. This led him to resign from his job and he went into the advertising business. He continued to have an interest in psychology, publishing a book on infant and child care, but for the most part devoted himself entirely to business where he applied the principles of behaviourism to the world of advertising. In fact he probably was the first applied psychologist and had an extremely successful second career.

to replace the fear response to phobic stimuli (such as a spider) with a new response that is incompatible with the fear. This new response is usually muscle relaxation. Clients are initially given special training in deep relaxation until they can rapidly achieve muscle relaxation when instructed to do so.

What happens next is that the client and the therapist together construct what is known as an "anxiety hierarchy", in which the client's feared situations are ordered from the least to the most anxiety-provoking. Thus, for example, a spider phobic might regard one small, stationary spider five metres away as only modestly threatening, but a large, rapidly moving spider one metre away as highly threatening. The client reaches a state of deep relaxation, and is then asked to imagine (or is confronted by) the least threatening situation in the anxiety hierarchy. The client repeatedly imagines (or is confronted by) this situation until it fails to evoke any anxiety at all, indicating that the counterconditioning has been successful. This process is repeated while working through all of the situations in the anxiety hierarchy until the most anxiety-provoking situation of all is reached.

Reinforcement increases the likelihood that the behaviour will be repeated...

Operant conditioning can be seen in a form of therapy called **token economy**. This is used with institutionalised patients, who are given tokens (e.g. coloured counters) for behaving in appropriate ways. The tokens act as a reward or reinforcement and tokens can later be used to obtain various privileges (e.g. playing snooker, or cigarettes). Ayllon and Azrin (1968) carried out a classic study. Female patients who had been hospitalised for an average of 16 years were rewarded with plastic tokens for actions such as making their beds or combing their hair. The tokens were exchanged for pleasant activities such as seeing a film or having an additional visit to the canteen. This token economy was very successful. The number of chores the patients performed each day increased from about 5 to over 40 when this was rewarded with tokens. The main problem with token economies is that the beneficial effects they produce are often greatly reduced when good behaviour is no longer followed by the rewards that the patients have grown used to receiving.

This 18cm poisonous spider is perhaps more terrifying than the type that would be used in modelling therapy!

Modelling can also be used in order to treat phobias. A patient watches the therapist experiencing the phobic situation and then imitates the same behaviour. Bandura, Blanchard, and Ritter (1969) found that the therapy was most effective when working with a live example of the feared object (such as a real snake) rather than a symbolic representation. Modelling has been successfully used to help people cope better in social situations and situations they found fearful, such as going to the dentist. They watch other people coping well in such situations and then imitate their behaviour.

If an individual has a fear of dogs, systematic desensitisation could be used to overcome this. The client might have learned their fear in the following way:

- Child is bitten by dog. Unpleasant bite (US) → fear (UR).
- Dog (NS) paired with US, becomes CS → fear (now CR).

This can be overcome by associating the dog with a new response—relaxation.

- Dog (CS) → fear (CR).
- Dog paired with new US (relaxation) → pleasant feelings (CR).

Evaluation of the behavioural model

The starting point for any of these treatments is to identify those aspects of behaviour that are maladaptive and require changing. After that, conditioning or observational learning techniques are used to reduce or eliminate those maladaptive responses. In contrast to the other psychological approaches, the focus is very much on the patient's behavioural symptoms rather than on the underlying cause of his or her disorder, which is a key criticism of this approach. For example, a Freudian might say that the symptoms may have been cured but the cause still remains in the client's unconscious mind, only to resurface in a different way.

On the other hand behavioural therapies have been very successful with certain kinds of disorder, such as phobias. They are more applicable to disorders with easily identifiable behavioural symptoms. The behavioural model exaggerates the importance of environmental factors in causing disorders, and minimises the role played by genetic factors. As a result, it is of little value in explaining disorders such as schizophrenia which is likely to have a genetic basis. The behavioural model also minimises the role played by internal processes (e.g. thinking and feeling).

Those who favour the behavioural model are correct in assuming that the experiences people have in life, including the forms of conditioning to which they have been exposed, play a part in the development of mental disorders. However, conditioning is generally less important in humans than in the animal species studied in the laboratory by behaviourists.

In general terms, the behavioural model is oversimplified and rather narrow in scope. On the basis of the available evidence, it seems that only a small fraction of mental disorders depend to any great extent on the individual patient's conditioning history.

Ethical implications of the behavioural model

The behavioural model has some advantages from the ethical perspective. First, it is assumed that mental disorders result from maladaptive learning and thus should not be regarded as "illnesses". Second, the focus on each individual's particular experiences and conditioning history means that the behavioural model is sensitive to cultural and social factors. Third, the behavioural approach tends to be non-judgemental, in the sense that treatment is recommended only when an individual's behaviour causes severe problems to that person or to other people. Fourth, it is assumed within the behavioural model that abnormal behaviour is determined mainly by environmental factors. As a result, individuals who develop mental disorders should not be held responsible for those disorders.

There are ethical problems with some of the forms of treatment based on the behavioural model. Aversion therapy involves giving very unpleasant stimuli (e.g. electric shocks and nausea-inducing drugs) to patients in order to stop some undesirable form of behaviour, such as drinking in alcoholics. There has been much controversy about the morality of causing high levels of pain and discomfort. Most forms of treatment focus mainly on changing behaviour, and it could be argued that it is dehumanising to neglect the patient's internal experiences and feelings. Therapies derived from the behavioural model can be seen as manipulative.

Assumptions of the behavioural model

- All behaviour is learned, and maladaptive behaviour is no different.
- This learning can be understood in terms of the principles of conditioning and modelling.
- What was learned can be unlearned, using the same principles.
- The same laws apply to human and non-human animal behaviour.

The Cognitive Model

The central notion in the cognitive model is that individuals who suffer from mental disorders have distorted and irrational thinking—in contrast to having maladaptive *behaviour*, as in the behavioural model. Warren and Zgourides (1991) pointed out that many of these thoughts have a "must" quality about them. Examples are as follows: "I *must* perform well and/or win the approval of others, or else it's awful", "You *must* treat me fairly and considerately and not unduly frustrate me, or it's awful", "My life conditions *must* give me the things I want easily and with little frustration … or else life is unbearable." These distorted thoughts and beliefs influence feelings and behaviour, and can play an important role in the development of mental disorders.

Some of the key ideas underlying the cognitive model were expressed by Kovacs and Beck (1978), who argued that psychological problems

> *may result from commonplace processes such as faulty learning, making incorrect inferences on the basis of inadequate or incorrect information, not distinguishing adequately between imagination and reality.*

This points to the link between behaviourist and cognitive approaches. The latter also consider faulty learning to be important but the end result is disordered thinking, which most distinctly is not part of the behavioural model because behaviourists do not use internal processes in their explanations (in fact some even deny the existence of such things).

Implications of the cognitive model for treatment

The implication is that abnormal behaviour can be dealt with by altering the faulty thinking that has caused it. Active steps should be taken to replace the patient's irrational and distorted thoughts and beliefs with ones that are rational and undistorted. The common features of cognitive therapy were identified by Beck and Weishaar (1989, p.308):

> *Cognitive therapy consists of highly specific learning experiences designed to teach patients (1) to monitor their negative, automatic thoughts (cognitions); (2) to recognise the connections between cognition, affect, and behaviour; (3) to examine the evidence for and against distorted automatic thoughts; (4) to substitute more reality-oriented interpretations for these biased cognitions; and (5) to learn to identify and alter the beliefs that predispose them to distort their experiences.*

The term **cognitive restructuring** is used to refer to the techniques used to make the patient's thoughts more positive and rational. The therapist may question or challenge a patient's beliefs. Alternatively, he or she may persuade patients to test their beliefs in real-world settings to demonstrate how irrational those beliefs are. For example, socially anxious patients who believe that their work colleagues dislike them may be persuaded to ask them out for a drink to put this belief to the test.

Meichenbaum's **stress inoculation training** (see page 149) is also an example of a cognitive therapy. Meichenbaum (1977) argued that an important aspect in many mental disorders is the patient's internal dialogue. Many patients say very

How might you devise a programme of cognitive restructuring for someone with anorexia nervosa?

negative and unhelpful things to themselves when problems are encountered, and this helps to maintain the disorder.

Probably the most influential cognitive therapist is Aaron Beck. He has developed forms of cognitive therapy for anxiety, but is better known for his work on depression. Beck (1976) argued that therapy for depression should involve uncovering and challenging the negative and unrealistic beliefs of depressed clients. Of great importance is the **cognitive triad**. This consists of negative thoughts that depressed individuals have about themselves, about the world, and about the future (these three things form the triad). Depressed clients typically regard themselves as helpless, worthless, and inadequate. They interpret events in the world in an unrealistically negative and defeatist way, and they see the world as posing obstacles that cannot be handled. The final part of the cognitive triad involves depressed individuals seeing the future as totally hopeless, because their worthlessness will prevent any improvement occurring in their situation.

According to Beck et al. (1979), the first stage of cognitive therapy involves the therapist and the client agreeing on the nature of the problem and on the goals for therapy. This stage is called collaborative empiricism. The client's negative thoughts are then tested out by the therapist challenging them or by the client engaging in certain forms of behaviour between therapy sessions. Finally, it is hoped that the client will come to accept that many of his or her negative thoughts are irrational and unrealistic. For example, a depressed client who argues that people are always avoiding him or her can be asked to keep a diary of specific occasions on which this happens. It is very likely that it happens much less often than the patient imagines.

Think of an occasion when you felt helpless or worthless. Could you try to re-interpret the occasion in a more positive way?

Evaluation of the cognitive model

The cognitive model of abnormality has become very influential in recent years. There is no doubt that distorted and irrational beliefs are very common among patients with mental disorders. Such beliefs seem to be of central importance in anxiety disorders and depression (Beck & Clark, 1988), but their importance has not been shown for most other disorders. It is also generally not clear whether distorted beliefs help to cause the disorder, or whether they are merely a by-product of the disorder.

The cognitive approach grew out of a dissatisfaction with the behavioural model and its focus on external factors only. The cognitive model emphasised internal, mental influences and the power of the individual to shape their own thinking. In recent years, there have been increasing signs of an integration between the behavioural and cognitive models. According to this cognitive-behavioural model, mental disorders involve maladaptive behaviour as well as distorted thoughts and beliefs.

On the negative side, the cognitive approach to abnormality is rather limited. Genetic factors are ignored, and little attention is paid to the role of social and interpersonal factors or of individuals' life experiences in producing mental disorders.

Aaron Beck's cognitive triad.

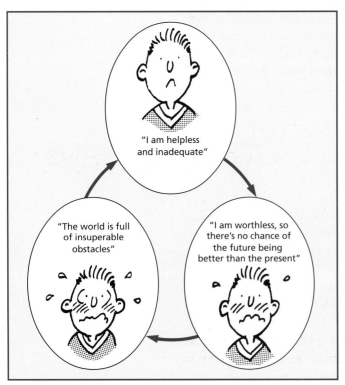

"I am helpless and inadequate"

"The world is full of insuperable obstacles"

"I am worthless, so there's no chance of the future being better than the present"

Ethical implications of the cognitive model

According to the cognitive model, individuals with mental disorders have distorted thoughts and beliefs, and so the disorders are mainly their own fault. That notion raises a number of ethical issues. First, patients may find it stressful to accept responsibility for their mental disorder. Second, it may be unfair to "blame" individuals for their mental disorder, because others around them may be mainly responsible. It is suggested that the root of maladaptive experiences may be childhood experiences. Third, the negative thoughts and beliefs of those with mental disorders are often entirely rational, and reflect accurately the unfortunate circumstances in which a person is living. Attempts to put the blame on to the patient may inhibit efforts to produce desirable changes.

> **Assumptions of the cognitive model**
> - Maladaptive behaviour is caused by faulty and irrational cognitions.
> - It is the way you think about a problem, rather than the problem itself, which causes mental disorder.
> - Individuals can overcome mental disorders by learning to use more appropriate cognitions.
> - Aim to be positive and rational.

The Multi-dimensional Approach

At the beginning of this section, we noted that some models are appropriate for some disorders but not others, that each model is partially correct, and that a full understanding of the origins of mental disorders requires us to combine information from all the models. This is called a multi-dimensional approach. One way to express this is in terms of the **diathesis–stress model**. According to this model, the occurrence of psychological disorders depends on two factors:

1. Diathesis: a genetic vulnerability or predisposition to disease or disorder.
2. Stress: some severe or disturbing environmental event.

The key notion in the diathesis–stress model is that both diathesis, or genetic vulnerability, *and* stress are necessary for a psychological disorder to occur.

This would explain why, when one identical twin develops a disorder, their twin does not always go on to develop the disorder—because an environmental trigger is required. The diathesis–stress model also explains why one individual might have a disorder but a sibling, who has shared the same childhood experiences, does not develop the disorder—because they are genetically different, so only one had the genetic vulnerability.

SECTION 15   CRITICAL ISSUE
Eating Disorders: Anorexia Nervosa and Bulimia Nervosa

There are several eating disorders. The most common (and the ones discussed in detail here) are anorexia nervosa and bulimia nervosa. However, there are other, considerably rarer eating disorders, such as the following:

- Rumination disorder: a disorder in which partially digested food is regurgitated and then swallowed for a second time.
- Pica: a disorder in which non-food substances such as sand, leaves, or string are eaten.

As we will see, there has been a large increase in the number of people suffering from eating disorders over the past 20 years or so. The increase has been so great that Barlow and Durand (1995) described it as an epidemic.

Characteristics of the Disorders

Anorexia nervosa

One of the two main eating disorders identified by DSM-IV is **anorexia nervosa**. According to DSM-IV, there are four criteria for anorexia nervosa:

- *Weight*. The individual has a body weight that is less than 85% of that expected.
- *Anxiety*. There is an intense fear of becoming fat in spite of being considerably underweight.
- *Body-image distortion*. The individual's thinking about his or her body weight is distorted, either by exaggerating its importance or by minimising the dangers of being considerably underweight.
- *Amenorrhoea*, the absence of menstruation. In females, the absence of three or more consecutive menstrual cycles is an indication of anorexia.

Over 90% of patients with anorexia nervosa are female, and the age of onset is typically during adolescence. There has been an increase in the frequency of anorexia nervosa in Western societies in recent decades (Cooper, 1994). This probably reflects the growing media emphasis on the attractiveness of slimness in young women. More strikingly, anorexia nervosa used to be very rare among Black people in the United States, but has recently shown signs of a marked increase (Hsu, 1990). Within Western cultures, it is more common in middle-class than working-class individuals. It is potentially a very serious disorder. The near-starvation that anorexics impose on themselves can produce physiological changes, causing about 5% of sufferers to die.

Cross-cultural issues: Why do you think eating disorders occur more in some cultures than others?

CASE STUDY: *An Eating Disorder*

At the age of 12, JC had weighed 115 pounds and had been teased by friends and family for being "podgy". At first JC had started to restrict her food intake by eating less at meal times, becoming selective about what she ate, and cutting out snacks between meals. Initially, JC's progressive weight loss was supported by her family and friends. However, as she began to lose pounds she would set herself new targets, ignoring feelings of hunger by focusing on each new target. In her first year of dieting JC's weight dropped from 115 pounds to 88 pounds. Her initial goal had been to lose 10 pounds. JC's periods stopped shortly after she started her regime, her appearance changed dramatically, and in the second year of her regime her weight loss was considered to be out of control. Her personality had also changed, and she was not the active, spontaneous, and cheerful girl she had been before dieting. Her girlfriends were less enthusiastic about coming over to her house, because JC would be stubborn and argumentative, designing strict programmes of activities for them to carry out.

JC's family had asked their GP for help. He had been alarmed at JC's appearance and designed a high calorific diet for her. However, JC believed that there was something inside her that would not let her gain weight. She would pretend to eat, often listing food she claimed to have eaten which had in fact been flushed down the toilet, or would not swallow food she put in her mouth. JC admitted that when she felt down over the past two years she would still feel driven to lose weight, and as a result would go on walks, run errands, or spend long periods of time keeping her room immaculate.   (Adapted from Leon, 1984.)

Bulimia nervosa

The other main eating disorder discussed in DSM-IV is **bulimia nervosa**. According to DSM-IV, bulimia nervosa is defined by the following five criteria:

- *Binge*. There are numerous episodes of binge eating, in which much more food is eaten within a two-hour period than most people would consume in that time, and the eater experiences a lack of control over his or her eating behaviour.
- *Purge*. There is frequent inappropriate compensatory behaviour to prevent weight from being gained. Examples include self-induced vomiting, excessive exercise, going without meals, and misuse of laxatives.
- *Frequency*. Binge eating and inappropriate compensatory behaviour occur at a rate of twice a week, or more, over a three-month period.
- *Body image*. The individual's self-evaluation depends excessively on his or her shape and weight.

- *Distinct condition.* Binge eating and compensatory behaviour do not occur only during episodes of anorexia nervosa.

There has been a dramatic increase in the number of patients suffering from bulimia nervosa since the late 1970s. Garner and Fairburn (1988) reported some relevant figures from an eating disorder centre in Canada. The number of patients treated for bulimia nervosa increased from 15 in 1979 to over 140 in 1986. As with anorexia nervosa, bulimia nervosa is mostly confined to women, with under 5% of cases presenting for treatment being men. Most patients with bulimia nervosa are in their 20s, and so are somewhat older than sufferers from anorexia. Bulimia nervosa resembles anorexia nervosa in that both disorders are far more common in Western societies than elsewhere in the world, and they occur more often in middle-class than working-class families.

What could be the reasons for the increased incidence of eating disorders in recent years?

The self-induced vomiting found in most bulimics can produce a variety of medical effects. For example, it can damage the teeth by eroding dental enamel. It can also change the levels of sodium and potassium in bodily fluids, and these changes can be life-threatening.

Anorexia and bulimia

There is some overlap between bulimia nervosa and anorexia nervosa, with many bulimic patients also having a history of anorexia. However, there are also important distinctions, such as the tendency for anorexics to strive for perfection whereas bulimics are trying to satisfy a constant craving. The case histories below and on the next page give insight into both conditions. Bulimia nervosa is far more common in Western society than anorexia nervosa. Another key difference is that nearly all patients with bulimia nervosa are within about 10% of their normal weight, whereas anorexic patients by definition are at least 15% below their normal weight.

Case studies are often used as a way of understanding unusual behaviours. What are the advantages and limitations of using this method of research?

CASE STUDIES: *Anorexics*

Hilde Bruch (1971) developed a theory of anorexia based on her experience in treating such patients. The cases below are adapted from her records:

Case 1

A 12-year-old girl from a prominent upper-class family was seen when her mother consulted the psychiatrist about an older sister who was obese. The mother felt that she wanted to punish this daughter for being overweight, but spoke in glowing terms about her younger daughter who in every way was an ideal child. Her teachers would refer to her as the "best balanced" girl in the school, and relied on her helpfulness and kindness when another child was having difficulty making friends.

Later, when the anorexia developed, it became apparent to what extent the anxious and punitive behaviours of the mother had affected the way the younger daughter felt and thought about herself. She had become convinced that being fat was most shameful. As she began to put on weight in puberty, she felt horrified and that, if she was to retain respect, she would have to maintain her thinness. This led her to go on a starvation regime. At the same time she also began to realise that she didn't have to be an ideal daughter and do what others expected of her, but she could be the master of her own fate.

Case 2

A mother sought psychoanalytic treatment because she had become depressed. Her daughter was her one great satisfaction in life. The girl

(aged 14) had always been a happy child who had no problems. She had had a governess, but the mother fed the daughter herself, making a special effort to provide good food and tastefully present it.

Shortly after the mother had consulted the psychiatrist the daughter became anorexic, having started to get plump. When she visited the psychiatrist her version of childhood was the exact opposite of her mother's account. She remembered it as a time of constant misery and that she could never have what she wanted but always had to have exactly what her mother wanted. She knew her mother had talked about what she should be eating with their doctor, and this made her feel that every bite that went into her mouth was watched. The concern about her fatness was reinforced by her father's excessive attention to appearance. Theirs was a wealthy home and there were always lavish arrays of food. Her father showed his superiority by eating very little and making snide remarks about people who ate too much.

When the girl became plump at puberty she tried to outdo her father's haughty control. She felt she owed it to him to remain slim and aristocratic. Her life was dominated by trying to satisfy her father. She did well at school but was haunted by the fear of being found out to be stupid. She described her life as "I never deserved what they gave me" and that she was "worthless". Keeping her weight as low as possible was her only way of proving herself to be "deserving" and having "dignity".

(Adapted from H. Bruch, 1971, Family transactions in eating disorders. *Comprehensive Psychiatry, 12*(3), 38–248.)

CASE STUDY: *The Life of a Bulimic*

Julie's life is food. In her dingy bedsit there is scarcely space to move around among the empty drinks cans, crisp packets, piles of clothes, and ornaments. Her fridge is stuffed to overflowing with different kinds of chocolates. Eating occupies many hours of her day but you wouldn't think it to look at her. She is a tiny thing, and when she pushes her sleeves up she reveals wrists no larger than sparrow's legs. For the best part of 20 years she has been trapped in an eating and vomiting cycle. At her lowest weight of four stone she found work as a dancer in a freak show.

Breakfast starts her day. "Half a box of cereal, two pints of milk, half a large sliced and buttered loaf which I eat with a packet of bacon or ham, about three eggs and sausages. I eat the other half of the sliced loaf with butter and marmalade. I drink cooking oil with all my meals to wash the food down. After I've finished that I have a brief pause, then I need some chocolate. I eat until I can't breathe."

Then she trips out to the bathroom to collect a square plastic washing-up bowl, and begins the process of bringing up all that food. When she has finished the bowl is full. Then there is a fleeting release from the self-loathing and the yearning for food which has nothing to do with hunger.

She had a boyfriend, another bulimic, who recently died. "I need someone to love but it's too difficult with ordinary men." She loved her father until, at the age of 10, he developed schizophrenia. "From then on it was as if he hated me." It was soon after that that she started bingeing. She made herself sick and then tried to tell her mum, who could only cope by pretending it wasn't happening. Julie attempted suicide three times before the age of 19 and was then placed in a mental hospital and drip-fed. She says she now wouldn't go back even to save her life, and recognises that she will probably die soon.

On Sundays she visits her mum who lives close by but otherwise she goes out very little. When we met she was planning a birthday treat for herself. "I get a birthday cake, little fairy cakes and biscuits and lemonade—all the things I had as a child for parties—and then I binge by myself."

(Adapted from Angela Neustatter in the *Daily Telegraph*, 7 March 1998.)

In the eating disorder bulimia nervosa, sufferers consume much more food over a short period than most people would and compensate by making themselves vomit or by taking laxatives.

What causes anorexia nervosa and bulimia nervosa? In the last section we looked at the various models of abnormality. We can now apply these models to the specific problems of anorexia and bulimia. We will look at the two eating disorders simultaneously because many of the explanations apply equally to both conditions.

The Biological Approach

Infection

It is possible that physical illness may act as a precipitating factor in eating disorders. Park, Lawrie, and Freeman (1995) studied four females suffering from anorexia nervosa, all of whom had had glandular fever or a similar disease shortly before the onset of the eating disorder. Park et al. (1995) argued, rather speculatively, that the physical disease may have influenced the functioning of the **hypothalamus**, and this caused homeostatic imbalances (**homeostasis** is described on page 120).

Genetic factors

There is increasing evidence that genetic factors play a part in the development of eating disorders. For example, relatives of patients with eating disorders are about four or five times more likely than other members of society to suffer from an eating disorder (e.g. Strober & Humphrey, 1987).

Twin studies

Another line of evidence for genetic factors comes from twin studies. **Monozygotic (MZ) twins** share exactly the same genes whereas **dizygotic** (DZ) or non-identical twins have the same genetic relatedness as any siblings (about 50%). If an eating disorder is inherited then we would expect to find more cases of MZ twins both having the disorder than DZ twins. Both kinds of twins will usually share a similar environment—they both shared the same womb and they are both sharing similar experiences as they grow up. So the only differences between MZ and DZ twins are in terms of their degree of genetic similarity.

In twin studies, researchers look at **concordance rates**, the extent to which a certain trait in both twins is in "concord" or agreement. Holland, Sicotte, and Treasure (1988) studied anorexia in MZ and DZ twins. The concordance rate for monozygotic or identical twins was 56% compared to 5% for dizygotic twins (see Key Study below). Kendler et al. (1991) carried out a similar study on bulimia in 2163 female twins. They reported a concordance rate of 23% for monozygotic twins compared to 9% for dizygotic twins. These studies provide strong support for the genetic hypothesis.

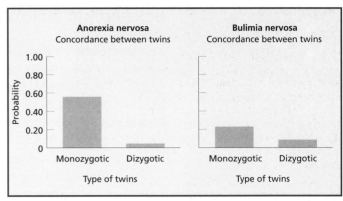

Holland et al. (1988) and Kendler et al. (1991) studied anorexia and bulimia in twins.

Evaluation: Genetic factors

On the face of it, these findings suggest that genetic factors play a part in the development of eating disorders, especially anorexia nervosa. However the fact that not *all* MZ twins had the disorder means that other factors are important as well as the inherited genes. If it was solely due to your inherited genes we would expect 100% concordance rates in MZ twins. It may be that genes *predispose* individuals to develop the disorder, creating a **genetic vulnerability**, as suggested by the diathesis–stress model.

Another argument against the genetic explanation taken on its own refers to the recent dramatic increase in the number of people suffering from eating disorders. This cannot be explained in genetic terms alone, because it is utterly improbable that there have been major genetic changes over the past 20–30 years.

Genetic vulnerability in anorexics

Previous research has suggested that mental disorders may have a genetic basis. Holland et al. (1988) conducted a study involving 34 pairs of twins and one set of triplets who were selected because one member of the pair (or triplet) had anorexia nervosa. The diagnosis was based on standard criteria and genetic relatedness was established by blood group analysis or by use of a physical resemblance questionnaire.

Holland et al. found an extraordinarily high concordance for the monozygotic (MZ) twins in comparison with the dizygotic (DZ) twins. In 30 female twin pairs, 16 were MZ and 14 were DZ:

- 56% (9 out of 16) of the monozygotic were concordant for anorexia nervosa.
- 7% (1 out of 14) of the dizygotic pairs were concordant.

Furthermore, in three of the cases where a twin did not have anorexia, the twin was found to have had other psychiatric illnesses, and two had minor eating disorders. This suggests a genetic vulnerability for psychiatric illness that, in adverse circumstances (environmental triggers) results in anorexia.

KEY STUDY EVALUATION — Holland et al.

This study was a so-called "natural" experiment because the independent variable (genetic relatedness) was not directly manipulated by the experimenter. This means that we cannot claim that genetics was the cause of anorexia but it is strongly implicated (cause can only be demonstrated when the IV has been directly manipulated). However, there is always a problem, in twin research, of being certain about the genetic relatedness of twins. Identical twins don't always look exactly alike and non-identical twins may look quite similar. In this study blood tests were used to confirm some of the diagnosis.

It is possible that we can explain the greater similarity between MZ twins in terms of environmental rather than genetic influences. It may be that the family environment experienced by the MZ twins is more similar than that experienced by the twins within DZ twin pairs (Loehlin & Nichols, 1976). The fact that MZ twins look and behave more alike may cause people to treat them more similarly, whereas DZ twins create quite different interpersonal relationships which may be quite significant in a family setting.

It could also be that one twin imitates the other twin who developed the disorder first. This is unlikely though because some of the twins developed the disorder when living in separate countries and concealing it from each other. This would also not account for the difference between MZ and DZ twins.

Discussion points

1. An interesting finding was that none of the four male anorexics had a twin with anorexia nervosa. How would you explain this?
2. What explanations can account for the differences between MZ and DZ twins?

One suggestion is that eating large amounts of starchy food may increase seratonin levels and improve mood in individuals suffering from an eating disorder.

Biochemical factors

Serotonin may be involved in some cases of eating disorder. We have come across serotonin before. It is a **neurotransmitter** that is implicated in a number of behaviours such as arousal, aggressiveness, and sleep. Fava et al. (1989) reported links between anorexic behaviour and changes in the levels of serotonin and also noradrenaline (also related to arousal and stress). Eating large amounts of starchy foods containing carbohydrates can increase serotonin levels in the brain, and this may improve mood in individuals who have low serotonin levels.

In addition, antidepressants (especially SSRIs—selective serotonin reuptake indicators) have been used successfully on people with eating disorders. This supports the possibility of an underlying neurotransmitter dysfunction.

Finally, it has also been suggested that the link between anorexia and amenorrhea is because of an underlying problem with the endocrine system, which is responsible for producing hormones such as those that govern the menstrual cycle.

Evaluation: Biochemical factors

The problem with the starchy food explanation is that patients with bulimia nervosa do not seem to focus specifically on foods containing carbohydrates when they binge (Barlow & Durand, 1995). It may of course be that biochemical imbalances *result* from the disorder rather than causing it. In other words endocrine imbalance would be an effect rather than a cause of eating disorders. This is probably more likely, as menstruation is known to be affected by periods of emotional upset or privation (Russell, 1972).

Barlow and Durand (1995, p.319) concluded, "The consensus is that some neurobiological and endocrinological abnormalities do exist in eating disorders, but they are a *result* of semi-starvation or a binge-purge cycle, rather than a cause."

Neuroanatomy

Another suggestion is that individuals with eating disorders may have brain abnormalities. For example, the parts of the hypothalamus that control eating, sexual activity, and menstruation may function abnormally in anorexics. There is certainly convincing evidence that the hypothalamus plays a central role in hunger regulation. The lateral hypothalamus (LH) and ventromedial hypothalamus (VMH) act together to maintain weight homeostasis (bodily balance). The LH produces feelings of hunger and the VMH suppresses hunger. When weight is low, the LH is activated. When weight goes over a set point the VMH is triggered. It is possible that anorexics have disturbed hypothalamic functioning (Garfinkel & Garner, 1982).

Evaluation: Neuroanatomy

However, again, altered hypothalamic activity may well not be a cause of anorexia nervosa. It is more likely to occur as a result of the weight loss or the anorexic's emotional distress. In addition, post-mortems have not revealed any lesions in this area of the brain.

Identical twins offer the opportunity of conducting a natural experiment. They are the same genetically so any differences in their behaviour should be due to the environment. However they usually share the same environment as well.

The Psychodynamic Approach

There have been various psychodynamic approaches to anorexia nervosa.

Sexual development

The fact that the disorder generally emerges in adolescent girls has suggested to some psychodynamic theorists that anorexia is related to the onset of sexual development and sexual fears, such as increasing sexual desires or a fear of becoming pregnant, even a fear of "oral impregnation" (becoming pregnant orally). If eating is linked to getting pregnant, then semi-starvation will prevent pregnancy. Not eating also results in amenorrhoea which again prevents pregnancy because ovulation stops.

A somewhat different psychodynamic account, still focused on sexual development, is based on the notion that anorexia nervosa occurs in females who have an unconscious desire to remain pre-pubescent. Their weight loss prevents them from developing the body shape associated with adult females, and thus allows them to preserve the illusion that they are still children.

There is some evidence that at least some people with eating disorders were sexually abused as children. This may lead them to reject and destroy their own bodies, and would support a link between eating disorders and sexual development.

Family systems theory

Minuchin, Rosenman, and Baker (1978) developed the notion that the family may play a key role in the development of anorexia nervosa. The family of an anorexic is characterised by **enmeshment**, meaning that none of the members of the family has a clear identity because everything is done together. Such families impose great constraints on children, because they are not allowed to become independent. According to psychodynamic theory, adolescence is the fifth phase of psychosexual development, and is a time of developing independence. Blos (1967) suggested that adolescence was like a second period of individuation. The first took place when the infant became a self-reliant toddler. A child growing up in an enmeshed family may be denied this "reindividuation" and rebel against its constraints by refusing to eat.

Minuchin et al. (1978) also argued that enmeshed families find it hard to resolve conflicts. In psychodynamic theory, this would create anxieties which are dealt with by ego-defences. Parents may cope with their anxieties by the need to attend to the symptoms of their anorexic child, so the "ill" child plays an important role in the family dynamic.

There is some evidence for high levels of parental conflict within the families of anorexics (e.g. Kalucy, Crisp, & Harding, 1977) and Hsu (1990) reported that families with an anorexic child tend to be ambitious, to deny or ignore conflicts, and to blame other people for their problems. Family conflicts have also been identified in families with a child who shows signs of bulimia as well as anorexia. Such families have more negative and fewer positive interactions than families with a normal adolescent (Humphrey, Apple, & Kirschenbaum, 1986).

Evaluation of family systems theory

There are several problems with this explanation. First, these parental conflicts may be more a result of having an anorexic child than a cause of anorexia. Second, these conflicts have occurred in families throughout history and therefore this explanation

Psychodynamic theories can explain why adolescent girls are most likely to suffer from eating disorders, but can they account for cultural differences?

cannot account for the recent increase in eating disorders. Similarly, it doesn't explain why many more girls suffer from eating disorders than boys or why the disorder occurs during adolescence.

Struggle for autonomy

Some of the drawbacks to family systems theory are overcome in the model proposed by the psychoanalyst Hilda Bruch (1971, see case studies on page 185). She analysed 64 anorexic patients (55 females and 9 males) and proposed that individuals with anorexia nervosa are engaged in a struggle for their own sense of identity and autonomy, and are in conflict with their parents, especially their mother. She concluded that a prime characteristic of the mothers was that they did not provide appropriate responses to child-initiated expressions of need. For example, children were offered food at the "correct time" or when the mother felt hungry not when the child said she was hungry. In addition, the mothers often used food as a means of providing comfort. If the child said she was unhappy, food was offered as a compensation. So food became not only the currency of affection but also was a battle-ground for dominance.

Evaluation of Bruch's approach

The problem with this, as with many psychoanalytic explanations, is that the evidence lacks objectivity. It is an interpretation of the facts from only one particular perspective.

The Behavioural Approach

Conditioning theory

We can explain anorexia nervosa using the principles of **classical conditioning**. According to Leitenberg, Agras, and Thomson (1968), anorexics may have learned to associate eating with anxiety, because eating too much makes people overweight and unattractive. Therefore they seek to lose weight to reduce their anxiety. Weight loss is associated with relief from an unpleasant or aversive stimulus.

The second part of the process can be explained in terms of operant conditioning. Food avoidance can be rewarding or reinforcing, because it is a good way of gaining attention. It can also be rewarding or reinforcing in that those who are slim are more likely to be admired by other people.

A behaviourist approach can also be applied to bulimia nervosa. According to Rosen and Leitenberg (1985), bingeing causes anxiety, and the subsequent vomiting or other compensatory behaviour reduces that anxiety. This reduction in anxiety is reinforcing and helps to maintain the cycle of bingeing followed by vomiting.

Evaluation of conditioning theory

The behaviourist approach helps to provide some of the reasons why anorexics and bulimics maintain their disorders. There has been some success in using behavioural therapies as a means of treating bulimia (Hallstein, 1965), for example rewarding clients when

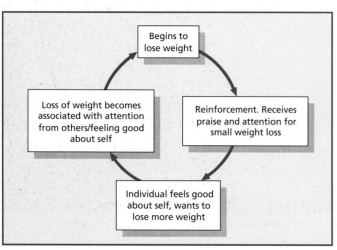

Begins to lose weight

Loss of weight becomes associated with attention from others/feeling good about self

Reinforcement. Receives praise and attention for small weight loss

Individual feels good about self, wants to lose more weight

they attain and maintain certain target body weights. This would suggest that rewards may be part of the cycle. However, conditioning alone does not account for individual differences in vulnerability to eating disorders.

Could conditioning theory be used to explain cultural differences?

Modelling

One of the most striking facts about eating disorders is that they are considerably more common in Western than in non-Western societies (Cooper, 1994). Indeed, eating disorders may well be more strongly specific to certain cultures than any other psychological disorders. This can be explained in terms of the role models available to young women. In our society we see women rewarded for looking slim in terms of the attention and admiration they receive. This is vicarious reinforcement. Social learning theory also predicts that we are most likely to imitate people we admire and identify with.

The fact that slimness is seen as attractive is illustrated by the finding that more than half of Miss America contestants are 15% or more below their expected body weight (Barlow & Durand, 1995). Being underweight by that amount is one of the criteria for anorexia nervosa! Further evidence to support the importance of Western role models in the development of eating disorders was reported by Nasser (1986), who compared Egyptian women studying in Cairo and in London. None of the

Fashions in body shapes have changed dramatically over recent decades; from the flat-chested "flapper" of the 1920s (left), through the curvaceous "hour-glass" figure of Marilyn Monroe (centre) to the currently popular "waif-like" shape epitomised by the model Kate Moss (right).

women studying in Cairo developed an eating disorder, in contrast to 12% of those studying in London. Lee, Hsu, and Wing (1992) noted that bulimia was almost non-existent among the Chinese in Hong Kong and suggest that this can largely be explained in terms of socio-cultural differences (see the Key Study below).

Why is it that adolescent girls are most likely to suffer from eating disorders? The cultural pressures are greatest on adolescent girls for two reasons. One reason is that most of them have reached the stage at which they want to appear attractive to boys. The other reason is that most of the weight girls gain after puberty is in the form of fat tissue, which makes it harder for them to match the ideal shape.

Evaluation of the role of models

Social learning theory can explain many features of the disorders, such as the increased prevalence in recent years and in Western society. It can also explain age

How might you explain the fact that 1 in 100 girls in private schools suffer with eating disorders compared to 1 in 300 in state schools?

Eating disorders among the Chinese

Lee et al. (1992) report that anorexia nervosa remains very rare among the Chinese populations of Singapore, Malaysia, and Hong Kong. Bulimia is even rarer although this picture is now changing in Hong Kong, where Lee et al.'s study took place. They suggest that one reason for this may be that clinicians in Hong Kong are still unfamiliar with the characteristics of the disease and are therefore not making the diagnosis when it is appropriate.

Another reason may be that obesity is relatively rare among the Chinese and therefore dieting is uncommon. Chinese girls are usually slim, even underweight, and therefore do not share the Western "fear of fatness". The Chinese traditionally have even valued fatness, and the greeting "Oh, you have put on weight" is taken as a compliment. Obesity is not seen as a sign of weak control or moral impairment, as it is in the West. The Chinese regard thinness as a sign of ill-health rather than the Western view that it is a sign of self-discipline and economic well-being.

Chinese attitudes towards food are also different. The diet of the Chinese is generally low in fat and high in fibre, whereas Westerners prepare a lot of fattening foods and then suffer guilt and shame about eating them. This means that in Western culture there is a predisposition to feel guilty about eating whereas the Chinese have no need to practise restraint with regard to eating.

Lee et al. suggest a further difference between the two cultures in terms of role conflict. Western women experience role conflicts between home and career, and their inner and outer selves. This may result in low self-esteem and ambivalence towards oneself, whereas Chinese women live in a society where their success is more related to "traditional" values such as success within the family rather than a good personal appearance or career accomplishment.

The media attention given to bulimia in the Western world may provide individuals with the idea that self-induced vomiting is an effective method of weight control, and provide them with specific information about how to do it. The lack of publicity for such methods in Hong Kong may explain why the method is not favoured. In addition there is a traditional belief among the Chinese that wasting food by vomiting will lead to bad luck and severe punishment by the gods.

Lee et al. conclude that the rarity of bulimia nervosa in Hong Kong is related mainly to the absence of the relevant sociocultural factors.

Discussion points

1. What cultural differences are identified in this research paper?

2. What explanations can you suggest for these cultural differences?

KEY STUDY EVALUATION — Lee et al.

Lee et al. provide an interesting account of their view of the differences between Chinese and Western cultures. Many of these factors may discourage the prevalence of the disorder but they will not prevent it, and many of them are social factors that are bound to change as the Chinese culture becomes more influenced by Western ways.

Like many psychological explanations there is no proof for the assertions made here, but they are offered because they appear to fit the facts well. Alternative possibilities could include genetic differences in predisposition to the disease between ethnic groups. Genetic differences could also explain the fact that the Chinese do tend to be slimmer than Westerners.

and gender effects, as well as why eating disorders are increasing in men (as a result of changing stereotypes).

However, cultural factors cannot be the only reason for the occurrence of eating disorders. The great majority of young women who are exposed to cultural pressures towards slimness do not develop eating disorders. It is only young women who are already vulnerable who are likely to be greatly affected by such pressures.

The Cognitive Approach

Distortion of body image

As has already been mentioned, sufferers from eating disorders typically have distorted views about body shape and weight. These are known as *cognitive biases*. In order to assess anorexics' perception of their own body size, they can be exposed to an image-distorting technique designed to provide information about their perception of their whole body. Garfinkel and Garner (1982) found that anorexic patients typically over-estimate their body size. It has also been shown that this overestimation is greater than that found in controls.

Bulimic patients also have distorted beliefs. In spite of the fact that they are typically not overweight, patients with bulimia usually show a substantial discrepancy between their estimation of their actual body size and their desired body size (Cooper & Taylor, 1988). This discrepancy arises both because they

Why do you think there were fewer anorexics in Victorian Britain than now?

Tennis star Andre Agassi said "Image is everything." This may seem like an exaggeration, but body image is a powerful factor in how people feel about themselves. If one suffers from body image disturbance, it often leads to a host of difficulties, ranging from low self-esteem to bulimia nervosa or anorexia nervosa.

Even when sufferers from anorexia nervosa are significantly underweight, they continue to fear becoming fat.

You have reached the end of the chapter on individual differences. Individual differences is an approach or perspective in psychology. The material in this chapter has exemplified this approach in so far as abnormal behaviour is one of the ways that individuals vary. Individual differences can be explained in terms of biological (physiological), behaviourist (learning theory), psychoanalytic, and cognitive explanations. All of these explanations have also appeared elsewhere in this book and are important "tools" for explaining behaviour.

overestimate their actual body size more than other people, and because their desired body size is smaller than that of most people.

Distorted beliefs about body size are found even among those not suffering from an eating disorder. Fallon and Rozin (1985) asked males and females to indicate their ideal body size and the body size that would be most attractive to the opposite sex. Females rated their ideal body weight as significantly *lower* than the weight males thought most attractive, whereas males rated their ideal body weight as *higher* than the weight women found most attractive. These differences place extra pressure on females to be slim.

Evaluation of the cognitive approach

We know that most patients with anorexia nervosa and bulimia nervosa have strong cognitive biases that, for example, lead them to overestimate their own body size. What is unclear is whether these cognitive biases exist *before* the onset of eating disorders and thus may play a part in their development. The alternative is that these cognitive biases only develop *after* the onset of eating disorders, in which case they cannot be a causal factor.

CHAPTER SUMMARY

Defining psychological abnormality

❖ According to the statistical approach, abnormality is that which is statistically rare in the population. The normal distribution is one way to describe a statistical distribution. The statistical approach is limited because it takes no account of whether deviations from the average are desirable or undesirable. It also does not indicate how much statistical deviation is undesirable nor does it account for cultural or sub-cultural differences. It is, however, less affected by value judgements than some other approaches.

❖ Social groups have norms of what is considered to be socially acceptable behaviour. Deviance away from these norms is abnormal and undesirable. Clinical abnormality should not be equated with social deviance, in part because what is socially deviant varies across cultures (historical changes and ethnic or religious differences). Social deviance also depends on social context. In some situations, such as dissidence in Nazi Germany, it is desirable to be socially deviant. The concept of social deviance is not irrelevant but it can permit serious abuse of human rights.

❖ Many mental disorders result in an inability to function adequately in terms of day-to-day life and social interactions. An absence of distress and the ability to function are standards of normal behaviour. This approach has the benefit of taking the individual's experience into account but not all persons with mental disorders are aware of their own distress or dysfunction. If we permit others to make judgements on their behalf, these judgements may be biased by cultural beliefs, although there are objective measures that can be used, such as absenteeism. Rosenhan and Seligman have extended the "failure to function" model to cover seven sufficient, but not necessary features, associated with abnormality. However, these again rely on making subjective judgements.

❖ It may be helpful to define abnormality in terms of ideal mental health, a more positive approach. Humanistic psychologists consider the factors that may be important for normal development, such as unconditional positive regard. They also see self-actualisation as an ultimate goal. However, these are all abstract and culturally relative ideals, not shared by collectivistic societies. It is more difficult to measure signs of psychological health than it is to assess signs of physical health.

❖ Cultural relativism is a recurring problem in all the approaches described. The definitions inevitably refer to some subjective, culturally determined set of values. However there are also cultural universals—behaviours such as anti-social behaviour or chronic depression are universally viewed as abnormal and undesirable. The resolution may lie in using a combined approach that focuses on which features are more likely to be associated with abnormality.

❖ There are five major models of abnormality, each of which provides explanations of the origins of mental disorders, and each of which has implications for treatment. These models are not mutually exclusive, and all of them have contributed to our understanding of the causes of mental disorders.

Biological and psychological models of abnormality

❖ According to the medical model, the causes of mental disorders resemble those of physical illnesses. Clusters of symptoms can be identified and a diagnosis made, followed by suitable treatment. There is some evidence that infection, genetics, biochemistry, and/or neuroanatomy may account for mental disorders. If the causes are physical then the treatments should be physical as well, and the medical model recommends direct manipulation of the body processes, such as using drugs, ECT, and psychosurgery. This model is less appropriate for disorders with psychological symptoms, and is of little relevance to some disorders (e.g. eating disorders). Drug therapies have undesirable side effects, although they are an effective and popular form of treatment.

❖ According to the psychodynamic model, the roots of mental disorder are to be found in unresolved conflicts and traumas from childhood. Treatment is based on various techniques designed to permit the patient to retrieve and understand repressed memories, such as using dreams and free association. This model may focus to much on the past at the cost of understanding current problems, and too much on sexual problems rather than interpersonal and social issues. Ethical concerns include the problem of false memory syndrome and the sexist nature of the theory. The approach is best for conditions where patients have insight, such as anxiety disorder.

❖ According to the behavioural model, mental disorders are caused by learning maladaptive behaviour via conditioning or observational learning. Anything that is learned can be unlearned using the same techniques. There are successful therapies based on classical conditioning (aversion therapy and systematic desensitisation), operant conditioning (token economy), and modelling, although these are not suitable for all mental disorders. The approach is most suited to explaining (and treating) those disorders that emphasise external behaviours, such as phobias. The behavioural model is oversimplified and more appropriate to non-human animal behaviour. Ethically, there are advantages such as the lack of blame attached to a person with a mental disorder, but the treatments can be painful and manipulative.

❖ According to the cognitive model, distorted and irrational beliefs are crucially involved in most mental disorders. Examples of treatments arising from this model include cognitive restructuring and stress inoculation training. Perhaps the best known is Beck's cognitive treatment for depression based on his concept of the cognitive triad. Limitations of the cognitive model include the problem of whether distorted thinking is a cause or an effect, and the circularity of the explanations. The model suggests that individuals are to blame for their problems. The cognitive–behavioural model is a recent and popular development, combining both approaches.

❖ The diathesis–stress model offers a multi-dimensional approach: genetic vulnerability (diathesis) and an environmental trigger (stress).

Critical issue— Eating disorders: Anorexia nervosa and bulimia nervosa

❖ Anorexia nervosa is typified by low body weight, anxiety, unrealistic body-image, and amenorrhoea. It is a disorder found mostly in young women in Western and middle-class culture, and has increased in the last 20 years.

❖ Bulimia nervosa involves bingeing and purging more than twice a week. Sufferers may have been anorexic. The condition is also increasing in Western society as well as elsewhere.

❖ The biological approach considers the possibility of infection, which is an unlikely cause of eating disorders. Twin studies provide good evidence of a genetic vulnerability, although environmental factors are also implicated. Biochemical factors are suggested by changed hormone levels, endocrine dysfunction, and the success of drug therapy. However it is not clear whether such factors are causes or effects of eating disorders. It is also possible that there are neuroanatomical abnormalities, such as in the hypothalamus, but this again may be an effect rather than a cause.

❖ There have been a variety of psychodynamic explanations. One possibility is that eating disorders act as a means of avoiding sexual maturity. Minuchin's family systems theory suggests that anorexia develops as a result of enmeshed family dynamics. Bruch's view was that anorexia is related to mother–daughter conflicts over dominance and autonomy. Psychodynamic explanations tend to lack objective support and cannot explain recent increases in the incidence of these disorders.

❖ The behavioural approach outlines anorexia as the result of conditioning, both classical (eating associated with anxiety) and operant (rewards for being slim). The success of behaviour modification therapy supports these explanations. One of the best accounts of eating disorders is based on social learning theory; sufferers imitate cultural role models. This explains features of the disorder such as its cultural specificity and the rise in incidence in recent years but cannot explain why all women do not develop eating disorders.

❖ Cognitive explanations focus on the distorted body image held by both anorexics and bulimics, but these cognitions may be an effect rather than a cause of the disorder.

FURTHER READING

The various models of abnormality are discussed fully in P.C. Kendall and C. Hammen (1998) *Abnormal psychology (2nd Edn.)* (Boston: Houghton Mifflin). The evidence on causal factors in mental disorders is discussed in D.H. Barlow and V.M. Durand (1995) *Abnormal psychology: An integrative approach* (New York: Brooks/Cole). The other topics in this chapter are covered in an accessible way in R.P. Halgin and S.K. Whitbourne (1997) *Abnormal psychology: The human experience of psychological disorders* (Madison, WI: Brown & Benchmark). Another textbook with good coverage of most mental disorders is the well established G.C. Davison and J.M. Neale (1996) *Abnormal psychology (revised 6th Edn.)* (New York: Wiley).

Revision Questions

The examination questions aim to *sample* the material in this whole chapter. For advice on how to answer such questions, refer to Chapter 1, Section 3. You will always have a choice of two questions in the AQA AS-level exam and 30 minutes in which to answer the question you choose:

Question 1
a. Describe *two* characteristics of anorexia nervosa.   (3 marks + 3 marks)
b. Describe *one* study of anorexia nervosa.   (6 marks)
c. Give *two* criticisms of this study.   (3 marks + 3 marks)
d. "Individuals who are described as abnormal are not that different from
    the rest of us." To what extent is it possible to distinguish between normal
    and abnormal individuals?   (12 marks)

Question 2
a. What are the main characteristics of anorexia nervosa?   (6 marks)
b. Describe the medical model of abnormality.   (6 marks)
c. Describe *one* psychological model of abnormality.   (6 marks)
d. "It is naive to believe that there are no cultural universals in abnormality but, at the
    same time, what is normal in one society is not always regarded as normal in another
    society." Discuss the question of cultural relativism in relation to attempts to
    define abnormality.   (12 marks)

Social psychology is an approach or perspective in psychology. The material in this chapter illustrates the way that social psychologists explain behaviour.

"Social" refers to any situation involving two or more members of the same species. Social psychologists are interested in the way people affect each other. They look at, for example, interpersonal relationships, group behaviour, leadership, conformity, obedience to those in authority, and the influence of the media. Social psychology differs from sociology in that it places greater emphasis on the individual as a separate entity; sociologists are interested in the structure and functioning of groups, whereas social psychologists look at how these processes influence the individual members of a social group.

6

Social Psychology
Social Influence

A scarlet envelope drops through your letter box. It is an invitation to Tom's 18th birthday party. You don't know him well but you do know that he and his friends have extravagant and elegant parties. On the night of the party you arrive wearing something very smart—only to find that everyone else is in jeans. How do you feel?

As you are walking down the street, you hear a voice:
"WOULD EVERYONE LIE DOWN IMMEDIATELY." What do you do?

Group membership: even non-conformists may conform to some norms.

This chapter explores one topic in social psychology—social influence. What we say, and what we do are very much influenced by other people. When you are out of step with the behaviour of other people it makes you feel very uncomfortable. We all have a strong sense of wanting to be like (and be liked by) other people, and to do what we are told. These issues all relate to **social influence**, which "involves the exercise of social power by a person or group to change the attitudes or behaviour of others in a particular direction" (Franzoi, 1996).

This chapter of the book examines two of the most common kinds of social influence: **conformity** and **obedience**, as well as one critical issue which is related to studies of social influence.

- *Section 16: Conformity and minority influence.* Individuals show conformity when they behave in ways that are expected by other members of a group. Conforming to the **norms** of the group is majority influence but there are also cases when a minority can influence the behaviour of a group. This section looks at research studies into why people yield to both majority and minority influence.
- *Section 17: Obedience to authority.* Individuals show obedience to authority when they unthinkingly follow the orders of authority figures. This section considers research studies into obedience to authority and explanations of the psychological processes involved in obedience: the reasons why people obey *and* how people might resist being obedient.
- *Section 18: Critical issue—Ethical issues in psychological research.* Any research must take into account what is deemed to be acceptable in terms of human behaviour. This section considers the use of deception, informed consent, and protection from harm, in the context of social influence research.

SECTION 16
Conformity and Minority Influence

Even the most independent of individuals can feel the need to conform under social pressure from peers.

Conformity can be defined as yielding to group pressures, something that nearly all of us do at least some of the time. Suppose, for example, that you and some of your friends go to see a film. You didn't think the film was much good, but all of your friends thought it was brilliant. You might be tempted to conform by pretending to agree with their verdict on the film rather than being the odd one out. As we will see, conformity to group pressures occurs much more often than most people imagine.

Is Conformity Undesirable?

As you read about the research on conformity, you may think that conformity to group pressures is undesirable. There are certainly cases in which that is true. For example, consider the case of Rodney King. He was a black man who was assaulted by four Los Angeles police officers. The assault was videotaped by a local resident, and shown in court to the jurors. In spite of the fact that this videotape seemed to show that Rodney King was a victim of police brutality, the police officers were acquitted. Afterwards, one of the jurors, Virginia Loya, admitted that she had changed her vote from guilty to not guilty because of pressures to conform to the views of the other jury members. She did this while remaining unconvinced of their views: "The tape was the big evidence to me. They [fellow jurors] couldn't see. To me, they were people who were blind and couldn't get their glasses clean." In spite of examples like the Rodney King case, it is not clear that conformity is always undesirable. Collins (1970, p.21) pointed out:

> *It would be a mistake to oversimplify the question and ask whether conformity is good or bad. A person who refused to accept anyone's word of advice on any topic whatsoever ... would probably make just as big a botch of his [sic] life ... as a person who always conformed and never formed a judgement on the basis of his own individual sources of information.*

On the other hand, there are probably many more cases where conformity is desirable and even necessary behaviour. People live together and abide by social rules in order to facilitate their interactions. You only have to think of traffic on the road to realise that conformity is necessary. Furthermore, we know that other people possess useful knowledge about the world, and it is often sensible to take account of what they say. In addition, we want to be liked by other people, and to fit into society.

Group decisions can lead people to deny the evidence in front of their eyes. This picture shows Rodney King, victim of a videotaped beating by Los Angeles police officers in 1992. The police officers involved were acquitted.

Why Do People Conform?

In a very early psychology experiment, Jenness (1932) asked students to estimate the number of beans in a bottle and then arranged for them to discuss their guesses with a group. Later, when they were asked to give their estimates again, he found that their individual judgements had converged towards the group estimate. Why? In situations where we do not know the answer to a question, we inevitably are influenced by the opinions of others. This is called **informational social influence** and is demonstrated in a classic study by Sherif (1935, see Key Study below).

Asch (1955) questioned the results of Sherif's study. In the latter study the participants probably conformed because the stimulus was *ambiguous*. When people are uncertain it is likely that they will look to others to find out what to do. Asch wondered, "What would happen if there was no uncertainty? Would people be less likely to conform?" In another classic study Asch (1956, see Key Study on the next page) demonstrated that individuals would still conform to group opinion even if the stimulus was not ambiguous and the answer they gave was clearly wrong. In this case, participants are not following informational social influence because they do not need guidance on the "information". It is more likely that they are responding to **normative social influence**, responding to group norms because they want to be liked and a part of the group.

> **CASE STUDY: *A Murder With 38 Witnesses***
>
> In Chapter 1 Section 1 we considered the case of Kitty Genovese, who was returning home at 3 a.m. after a night at work. If you recall, she lived in a suburb of New York city. She parked her car and started to walk to her apartment when a man came out of the shadows and attacked her. She screamed "Oh my god, he stabbed me! Please help me!" Many lights came on and one man shouted out of his window. The attacker fled but no-one came to help Kitty. She struggled to get to her home but the man returned and attacked her again. She screamed "I am dying." Again lights went on, again he fled, and again no one appeared. For the third time, the man reappeared, by which time Kitty had got to the doorway of her own apartment. This time he stabbed her to death.
>
> Why did none of the witnesses answer her pleas for help? The reason suggested in Chapter 1 was that the *number* of bystanders present meant that no-one did anything. This can be explained in terms of conformity and informational social influence. The witnesses were all bystanders—watching and waiting. The fact that each individual did nothing sent a message to each other individual: "it's OK don't do anything". The behaviour of the majority was to do nothing and so everyone conformed to this norm.
>
> (From A.M. Rosenthal, 1964, *Thirty-eight witnesses*. New York: McGraw Hill.)

What is the difference between informational and normative social influence?

A moving point of light

The first major study of conformity was carried out by Muzafer Sherif (1935). He made use of what is known as the **autokinetic effect**. If we look at a stationary spot of light in a darkened room, then very small movements of the eyes make the light seem to move. In Sherif's key condition, the participants were first of all tested one at a time, and then in small groups of three. They were asked to say how much the light seemed to move, and in what direction. Each participant rapidly developed his or her own personal norm. This norm was stable, but it varied considerably between individuals. When three individuals with very different personal norms were then put together into a group, they tended to make judgements that were very close to each other. The fact that a group norm rapidly replaced the personal norms of the members of the group indicates the existence of social influence.

Sherif (1935) also used a condition in which individuals started the experiment in groups of three, and then were tested on their own. Once again, a group norm tended to develop within the group. When the members of the group were then tested on their own, their judgements concerning the movement of the light continued to reflect the influence of the group.

> **KEY STUDY EVALUATION — Sherif**
>
> There are three major limitations with Sherif's (1935) research. First, he used a very artificial situation, and it is not clear how relevant his findings are for most everyday situations. Second, there was no "correct" answer in his situation. It is not very surprising that individuals rely on the judgements of others when they have no clear way of deciding what judgements to make. Third, conformity effects can be assessed more directly by arranging for all but one of the participants in an experiment to give the same judgement, and then seeing what effect this has on the remaining participant. This was done by Jacobs and Campbell (1961) using the autokinetic effect, and they found strong evidence of conformity.

Discussion points

1. What factors might have influenced the likelihood that participants conformed in this study?
2. The participants in this study were in groups of three. How do you think increasing the size of the group might have affected the results?

Conformity in unambiguous situations

Solomon Asch (1951, 1956) investigated the question of whether people would conform even in highly *unambiguous* situations (Sherif's study had looked at an ambiguous situation, where conformity might be more likely).

Asch set up a situation in which seven people all sat looking at a display. They were given the task of saying out loud which one of the three lines A, B, or C was the same length as a given stimulus line, with the experimenter working his way around the group members in turn (see illustration below). All but one of the participants were confederates of the experimenter. Most of the time the confederates gave the right answer but on some "critical" trials they were instructed to unanimously give the wrong answer. The one genuine participant was the last (or the last but one) to offer his opinion on each trial. The performance of participants exposed to such group pressure was compared to performance in a control condition in which there were no confederates. Asch's (1951, 1956) findings were dramatic. On the crucial trials on which the confederates all gave the same wrong answer, the genuine participants also gave the wrong answer on approximately 37% of these trials. This should be compared against an error rate of only 0.7% in the control condition. Thus, the correct answers were obvious, and it might have been expected that nearly all the participants would have given them.

Asch (1956) manipulated a number of aspects of the situation in order to understand more fully the factors underlying conformity behaviour. For example, he found that the conformity effect increased as the number of confederates went up from one to three, but there was no increase between three and sixteen confederates. However, other researchers have often found that there is a small increase in conformity as the number of confederates goes up above three (see van Avermaet, 1996, for a review).

Another important factor was whether the genuine participant had a supporter in the form of a confederate who gave the correct answer on all trials, and who gave his answers before the genuine participant. Asch (1956) found that the presence of such a supporter produced a dramatic drop in conformity to the majority. In the case of having a supporter only 5% of the true participants now conformed to the majority.

Asch's (1951) research on conformity has had an enormous influence. He found that, surprisingly, there are large conformity effects in an unambiguous situation in which the correct answer is obvious. He showed convincingly that group pressures to conform are much stronger than had been thought previously.

Discussion points

1. Asch carried out his research in the United States. Why might the findings be different in other cultures?

2. What does this study tell us about non-conformity?

Identify the different findings that Asch produced in his research.

Ethical issues: Asch's participants weren't told the true nature of the study. Was this ethical?

Asch showed lines like this to his participants. Line X is clearly not the same as line A, yet when everyone in a group of confederates agreed that they were the same, the true participant agreed 37% of the time. This is called normative social influence—you behave like everyone else because you want to be liked by them and feel part of the group.

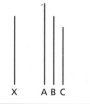

X   A B C

Informational and normative social influence

Deutsch and Gerard (1955) were the first to identify these two explanations for conformity.

- *Informational influence* occurs when an individual conforms because of the superior knowledge or judgement of others, as in Sherif's (1935) study. Informational influence tends to lead to a change in private opinion.
- *Normative influence* occurs when an individual conforms because he or she wants to be liked by the other members of the group, and also wants to avoid being rejected. This played an important part in Asch's (1956) research, and may have played some part in Sherif's (1935) study. Normative influence is not likely to change private opinion. It affects public opinions.

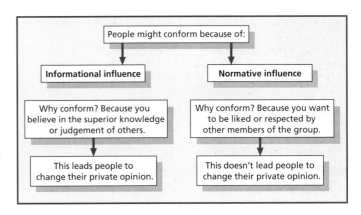

Three more reasons for conformity

As we have seen, conformity can be related to the extent to which an individual changes their private and/or public opinion. Kelman (1958) has used this distinction to outline three different kinds of conformity:

Do some individuals and groups have more influence over you than others? If so, why do you think this might be the case?

1. **Compliance** involves conforming with the majority in spite of not really agreeing with them. As the conformity is only superficial, compliance stops when there are no group pressures to conform. In a sense this is not "true conformity" because it is transient. Informational influence is a kind of compliance.
2. **Identification** occurs when someone conforms to the demands of a given role in society, as seen in the behaviour of a nurse or a traffic warden. The conformity generally extends over several aspects of behaviour. For example, stewards and stewardesses on planes try to be cheerful, polite, and helpful to the passengers at all times regardless of how they may actually be feeling. They behave in this way because they are conforming to what is expected of them. Zimbardo's prison study (see Key Study on the next page) is another example of this kind of conformity. The individual identifies with a role and this leads to conformity to a norm. There may still be no change to personal opinion.
3. **Internalisation** occurs when someone conforms because they are really in agreement with the views of those who are seeking to influence them. For example, the parents of a small girl may believe it is very important for her to spend a lot of time with other children. If friends of theirs start sending their daughters to the Brownies, they will probably conform to the suggestion that they might also send their daughter. Conformity based on internalisation is like pushing on an open door, in the sense that the individual is being persuaded to do something he or she really wants to do. As a result, conformity behaviour based on internalisation continues even when there is no external pressure to conform. In this case personal opinion does change because the new norms are internalised.

Which of these are examples of "true conformity"?

The Stanford prison experiment

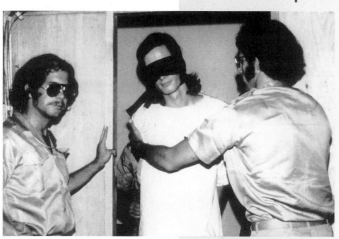

Zimbardo tried to minimise the after-effects of participation in his Stanford prison experiment by asking the participants to sign an informed consent form before the experiment began. Even so, some of the mock guards became very aggressive during the experiment, and four of the mock prisoners had to be released early.

In the 1960s, there were numerous reports of problems in American prisons. Many of these reports referred to brutal attacks by prison guards on the prisoners in their care. Why did this brutality occur? One possibility is that those who choose to put themselves into a position of power by becoming prison guards tend to have aggressive or sadistic personalities. Another possibility is that the behaviour of prison guards is due mainly to the social environment of prisons, including the rigid power structure that is found in them. These are considered to be dispositional and situational explanations respectively.

Philip Zimbardo (1973) studied this issue in what is often referred to as the "Stanford prison experiment" because it was conducted in the basement of the psychology department at Stanford University. Emotionally stable individuals agreed to act as "guards" and "prisoners" in a mock prison. Zimbardo was interested in seeing whether the hostility found in many real prisons would also be found in his mock prison. If hostility were found in spite of not using sadistic guards, this would suggest that it is the power structure of prisons that creates hostility.

In the Stanford prison experiment, the aim was to make the participants' experience as realistic as possible. Upon arrival at the "Stanford County Prison", the prisoners were stripped naked, skin-searched, deloused, and issued with a uniform, bedding, and basic supplies. The prisoners were only allowed to eat at specified times. They needed the permission of a guard to do almost anything, including writing letters and going to the toilet. In all, there were 16 rules which the guards were asked to enforce.

What went on in the mock prison was so unpleasant and dangerous that the entire experiment had to be stopped after six days instead of the intended fourteen. Violence and rebellion broke out within two days of the start. The prisoners ripped off their clothing, and shouted and cursed at the guards. In return, the guards put down this rebellion violently using fire extinguishers. They also played the prisoners off against one another, and harassed them almost constantly. One of the prisoners showed such severe symptoms of emotional disturbance (disorganised thinking, uncontrollable crying, and screaming) that he had to be released after only one day. On the fourth day, two more prisoners showed symptoms of severe disturbance and were released.

There were some interesting changes in the behaviour of the guards and prisoners over time. The prisoners became more and more subdued and submissive, often slouching and keeping their eyes fixed on the ground. At the same time, the use of force, harassment, and aggression by the guards increased steadily from day to day. The guards began to enjoy the power to control other people, and the passive reaction of the prisoners encouraged them to exert more and more power.

What can we learn from the Stanford prison experiment? According to Zimbardo, the experiment showed the great importance of the power structure within prisons. Real prison guards may be somewhat more sadistic than other people. However, the prison environment seems to be the main factor leading to brutal behaviour by guards.

In terms of conformity, both "guards" and "prisoners" conformed to their roles in situations where one might have

KEY STUDY EVALUATION — Zimbardo

Many critics have argued that it was not ethically acceptable to expose people to such degradation and hostility, even with their informed consent. Was it reasonable for Zimbardo to stand by while the guards forced prisoners to clean toilets with their bare hands, hosed them with fire extinguishers, and made them do push-ups with a guard standing on their back? Savin (1973) argued that the mock prison was a "hell". In reply, Zimbardo pointed out that he had tried to reduce any negative effects on the participants by holding day-long debriefing sessions, in which the moral conflicts posed by the study were discussed. He also pointed out that most of the participants reported that they had learned valuable things about themselves. It is true that the study was of value. However, it is not clear that this begins to justify the level of degradation and physical assault that happened.

Were the participants "just" role-playing? In other words, rather than conforming to real roles, were they just acting certain parts? Banuazizi and Mohavedi (1973) argued that people have such strong stereotypes of how prison guards and prisoners behave in real prisons, that they simply engaged in role-playing based on these stereotypes. It is true that most people have stereotypes about prison guards and prisoners. However, it is unlikely that the participants were merely "acting out" stereotypically defined roles. If Banuazizi and Mohavedi were correct, why didn't the participants behave in a stereotypical way from the outset? In addition, the physical abuse and harassment shown by the prison guards seem to have gone a long way beyond what would have been expected from mere play-acting. Although acting is most likely in the presence of an audience, Zimbardo (1973) actually found that harassment of prisoners was greater when individual guards were alone with solitary prisoners or out of range of the experiment's recording equipment.

thought that someone would say "Hang on, I'm only acting." One prisoner even asked to be paroled instead of simply saying that he wished to quit the study. This study shows that conformity exerts a very strong social influence.

Discussion points

1. Are you surprised by the findings from the Stanford prison experiment?
2. How can the concept of "**demand characteristics**" be used to explain the behaviour of the participants in this study?

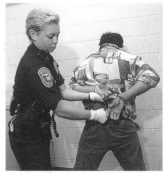

Wearing a uniform may lead individuals to conform to an expected role, as they did in Zimbardo's prison study.

According to Kelman, then, conformity serves one of three purposes: group acceptance (compliance), group membership (identification), or acceptance of group norms (internalisation).

Minority Influence

In many of the conformity studies described so far it was a minority group who were conforming to the majority. Moscovici (1976, 1980) argued along different lines. He claimed that Asch and others had put too much emphasis on the notion that the majority in a group has a large influence on the minority. In his opinion, it is also possible for a minority to influence the majority. In fact Asch agreed with Moscovici. He too felt that minority influence did occur, and that it was potentially a more valuable issue to study—to focus on why some people might follow minority opinion and resist group pressure (reported by Spencer & Perrin, 1998).

Moscovici drew a distinction between compliance and conversion. As we have seen, compliance is involved when a majority influences a minority, and usually

> ■ Activity: Conforming to group norms
>
> You can test informational social influence by asking participants an ambiguous question or one with no clear answer, such as "How many beans are there in this jar?" or "What percentage of people believed in the millennium bug?" Ask them to respond on a sheet of paper where you have recorded the answers of other (supposed) participants.
>
> How will you know whether a participant has conformed or not? Prepare two sets of answers, one consisting of low estimates, the other of high estimates. Give one group of participants the low estimates and the other group the high estimates. Compare the responses of your two groups of participants.
>
> To improve the design of this study, it would be better to ask participants more than one question. The other questions might have more unambiguous answers. This would prevent participants guessing the purpose of your experiment.

Norms are a set of rules established by the behaviour of a group of people. Conforming to group norms is a part of group membership. At a football game, different people are conforming to different norms—the home team has prescribed behaviours (clothes, songs, slogans), and so has the away team (such as unwritten "rules" for how to behave at an away match). The players, the referees, and the police all have their own norms. Some norms are externally enforced—a player who turns up wearing the wrong colour socks wouldn't be allowed to play but equally a supporter who wasn't wearing the team scarf might be ostracised by his or her comrades.

What is the difference between compliance and conversion?

results in public agreement with the majority but not private agreement. **Conversion** is how a minority can influence a majority. It involves convincing the majority that the minority's views are correct, and often produces more private agreement than public agreement with the minority. In other words, individuals might still appear to go along with the majority (for the sake of their safety!) but privately their opinions have changed. As minority opinion becomes more widespread, individuals feel safer about expressing what is their true opinion. Individuals often comply with the majority whereas they are converted by the minority.

An important real-life example of a minority influencing a majority was the suffragette movement in the early years of the 20th century. A relatively small group of suffragettes argued strongly for the initially unpopular view that women should be allowed to vote. The hard work of the suffragettes, combined with the justice of their case, finally led the majority to accept their point of view.

How does the study of minority influence explain why some individuals do influence the majority?

Moscovici conducted his own research (Moscovici, Lage, & Naffrenchoux, 1969, see Key Study opposite) and was able to demonstrate that individuals will indeed conform to a minority on an Asch-like task. The rates were lower than in Asch's experiment but there was a significant amount of conformity.

Explaining the minority effect

Moscovici (1985) argued that conversion is most likely to occur under certain conditions:

1. *Consistency*. The minority must be consistent in their opinion.
2. *Flexibility*. The minority must not appear to be rigid and dogmatic.
3. *Commitment*. A committed *minority* will lead people to rethink their position. This is conversion not compliance. Majority influence involves the reverse: compliance but not conversion.
4. *Relevance*. The minority will be more successful if their views are in line with social trends.

In fact minority influence is probably of more importance than majority influence in terms of social change. Can you think of an example where a minority of one changed the course of human history?

Majority and Minority Influence

Might it be possible to explain both majority and minority influence with the same theory? The research examined so far contains a contradiction. For example, Asch found that once there were more than three people behaving in a certain way, conformity was likely; yet an individual with a partner, i.e. a minority of two, can resist a majority. In order words, the number of other people behaving in a particular ways leads to conformity but can also lead to anti-conformity. This suggests that conformity cannot be explained simply in terms of number of people present.

Latané and Wolf (1981) proposed **social impact theory** which offers a more complex explanation and can account for both majority and minority influence (as well as being a general explanation for social behaviour, such as for bystander behaviour). According to this theory, an individual's behaviour in any situation can be predicted in terms of three factors:

It is hard to believe that women being allowed to vote was once a minority opinion. The direct action of the suffragette movement in the early part of the 20th century eventually secured the right for women to vote.

- *Strength*. This is determined by, for example, numbers of people present, or the consistency of the message. Hearing the opinion of a group of friends, who may not all be in close agreement, would be similar in strength to one person, such as a politician, forcefully delivering a message every night on television.

Calling a blue slide green

Moscovici et al.'s (1969) view was that psychologists paid too much attention to majority influences and overlooked minority influences. In the history of humankind, minority influence has been a much stronger force for change than majority influence, just think of revolutionary groups and leaders who have changed the course of history.

Moscovici demonstrated minority influence in an experiment that involved groups of six participants. Each group was presented with blue slides varying in intensity, and each individual had to name aloud a simple colour. Two confederates of the experimenter said "green" either on every trial or on two-thirds of the trials. The percentage of "green" responses given by the majority was 8% when the minority responded in a consistent way, but was only 1% when the minority responded inconsistently.

Why is it important for the members of the minority to be consistent in their opinions? A plausible answer is to be found in Kelley's (1967) **attribution theory**. According to that theory, we try to decide whether other people's behaviour is due to internal causes (e.g. their genuine beliefs) or to external causes (e.g. social pressures). If someone's behaviour differs from that of other people in the same situation, and they consistently behave in that way, then we are likely to infer that it is due to internal causes. Thus, if members of the minority are consistent in their opinions, they are likely to convince the other group members that these opinions are sincere, and so they will be taken seriously.

Nemeth, Swedlund, and Kanki (1974) found that consistency is necessary in order for a minority to influence the majority, but that it is not always sufficient. They essentially replicated the study by Moscovici et al. (1969), but the participants were allowed to respond with all of the colours they saw in the slides rather than only a single colour. There were three conditions of interest:

1. The two confederates of the experimenter said "green" on half of the trials and "green-blue" on the other half in a random way.
2. As (1), except that the confederates said "green" to the brighter slides and "green-blue" to the dimmer slides, or vice versa.
3. The two confederates said "green" on every trial.

Nemeth et al. (1974) found that nearly 21% of the responses of the majority were influenced in condition 2, but that the minority had no influence at all in conditions 1 and 3. The minority had no effect in condition 1 because it did not respond in a consistent way. The minority in condition 3 did respond in a consistent way, but its refusal to use more complex descriptions of the stimuli (e.g. "blue-green") made its behaviour seem rigid and unrealistic.

Discussion points

1. To what extent can we generalise about human behaviour from these studies?
2. How do the results of this study compare with the studies that looked at majority influence?

Leaders exert minority influence and their views may have much greater influence than the norms created by majority opinion.

- *Status and knowledge.* People will be equally influenced by a lot of amateurs or one independent expert. The same would apply to individuals who have greater status—you need fewer of them to make the same impact.
- *Immediacy.* The closer you are (physically or psychologically) to the influencer, the more effect their message will have. An example of the effects of physical closeness would be hearing a message face-to-face, this would have greater influence that hearing a message on the radio. An example of psychological

> ■ Activity: The true test of a theory is that it can account for the facts. Can social impact theory do this? Try to use it to explain one of the studies in this chapter, for example the variations of Asch's research.

closeness would be hearing a message from a close friend, this would have a stronger effect than hearing the same message from an acquaintance.

The effect of social influence in any situation is a combination of all three factors and, for each factor, a question of degree. The greater the strength, status, and immediacy, the greater the social influence. In some situations this would lead to majority influence (for example, where strength in terms of number is high, and status and immediacy may be low). In other situations a minority influence would occur (for example, where strength in numbers is low but the person saying the message has high status and consistency).

Evaluation of social impact theory

The attractiveness of this theory is that it can account for many different kinds of social behaviour. It can account for bystander behaviour, such as in the case of Kitty Genovese when people were not willing to help. The theory can also explain majority and minority influence, as in Asch's studies where there was conformity to the majority, but also dissension from the majority when a co-dissenter was present (minority influence). The theory offers a way of explaining both majority and minority influence using the same terms of social impact.

Important Influences on Conformity

Tarde, a famous sociologist, said "Social man is a somnambulist". In other words social behaviour is like sleep walking. What do you think he meant by this?

We can further explain conformity behaviour in terms of individual differences. Different people conform differently because of situational factors (such as culture) or dispositional factors (such as personality).

Cultural factors

One of the possible limitations of Asch's work on conformity is the cultural background of the participants. The study was carried out in the United States. It has often been assumed that Americans are more conformist than other people so the results may not generalise to other, less conformist cultures. The study was also culturally biased in terms of the historical period during which it took place—the late 1940s and early 1950s. It is possible that people were more willing to conform in the days before it became fashionable to "do your own thing". Thus, it could be argued that the levels of conformity found by Asch reflected the particular culture prevailing in a particular place (United States) and historical time.

Historical differences
Perrin and Spencer (1980) tried to repeat Asch's study in England in the late 1970s. They found very little evidence of conformity, leading them to conclude that the Asch effect was "a child of its time". However, the low level of conformity in Perrin and Spencer's study may have occurred because they used engineering students who had been given training in the importance of accurate measurement and therefore

Are we more likely to assume that this man is sleeping rough because of situational factors (he's been taken ill, forgotten his house keys) or dispositional factors (he can't keep a job, he's drunk and rowdy in accommodation, for example)?

had more confidence in their own opinions. Smith and Bond (1993) carried out an analysis of a number of studies that had used Asch's task in the United States. They concluded (1993, p.124) that: "Levels of conformity in general had steadily declined since Asch's studies in the early 1950s."

Perrin and Spencer (1980) carried out two more studies on cultural factors in conformity. In one study, the participants were young men on probation. Mixed in with these true participants were some confederates of the experimenter who were primed to give the wrong answers. The level of conformity shown was about the same as in the Asch studies. In the other study, the participants and the confederates were both young unemployed men with Afro-Caribbean backgrounds. Once again, conformity levels were comparable to those reported by Asch (1951).

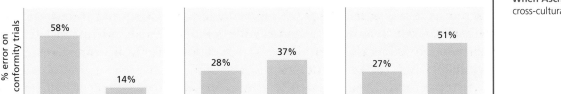

Studies in other countries

There have been over 20 other cross-cultural studies of conformity using Asch's experimental design. The findings from these studies were summarised by Smith and Bond (1993). Asch (1951) found that students gave the wrong answer on 37% of the conformity trials. The average figure in Smith and Bond's **meta-analysis** was about 30% for the other studies carried out in several parts of the world. The highest figure was 58% wrong answers for Indian teachers in Fiji, and the lowest figure (apart from Perrin & Spencer, 1980) was 14% among Belgian students.

Individualism and collectivism

In general terms, it is possible to distinguish between **individualistic** and **collectivistic** cultures. Individualist societies, such as the United Kingdom and the United States, emphasise the desirability of individuals being responsible for their own well-being and having a sense of personal identity. In contrast, collectivist cultures (e.g. China) emphasise the priority of group needs over individual ones, and value the feeling of group identity. One would expect individuals to be less conformist in individualistic societies, a hypothesis that was supported by Smith and Bond (1993). They conducted a further meta-analysis on 133 Asch-type studies drawn from 17 countries and found that conformity was indeed higher in collectivistic cultures than in individualistic cultures.

Deindividuation

There are some situations where conformity is more likely to occur, as we have seen, such as among a group of strangers. **Deindividuation** is another factor that may affect levels of conformity. The term refers to the loss of a sense of personal identity that can occur when we are, for example, in a crowd or

Why might engineering students be less likely to conform in these kinds of studies than other students?

When Asch's study was replicated, cross-cultural differences emerged.

Why do you think students were less likely to conform (28%) than non-students (37%)?

What are some of the limitations of cross-cultural studies?

wearing a mask. Zimbardo (1973, see Key Study on page 204) demonstrated an extremely high level of conformity among experimental participants who were conforming to the roles of being a prisoner or a prison guard. A key factor in their tendency to conform to stereotypical roles was the fact that they were deindividuated. All participants wore uniforms; guards had reflective sunglasses to increase their sense of deindividuation, and prisoners wore stockings on their heads.

In another study, Zimbardo (1969) conducted a Milgram-type obedience experiment (Milgram's experiment is described in the Key Study on page 213). Female participants were told to give electric shocks to other women. Deindividuation was produced in half of the participants by having them wear laboratory coats and hoods that covered their faces. In addition, the experimenter addressed them as a group rather than as individuals. The main finding was that the intensity of electric shocks given by the deindividuated participants was twice as great as that of participants who wore their own clothes and were treated as individuals. Why was this? Presumably the deindividuated participants felt more able to simply follow the experimenter's instructions, to conform to the stereotypical role of obeying a person in authority.

If you feel deindividuated, do you think this would make you more or less likely to conform to group norms? Or to follow orders?

Johnson and Downing (1979) were not convinced that it was really deindividuation that was responsible for the findings of Zimbardo. They pointed out that the clothing worn by the deindividuated participants resembled that worn by the Ku Klux Klan (a secret organisation in the United States which carried out many violent acts against American black people). In their own study Jones and Downing found that deindividuated individuals who were dressed as nurses actually gave fewer electric shocks than did those who wore their own clothes. But this still means that the participants in Zimbardo's study were *conforming* to a role—that of a prison guard. Participants in the Johnson and Downing study were also conforming to a role—that of a nurse who would be less likely to act aggressively.

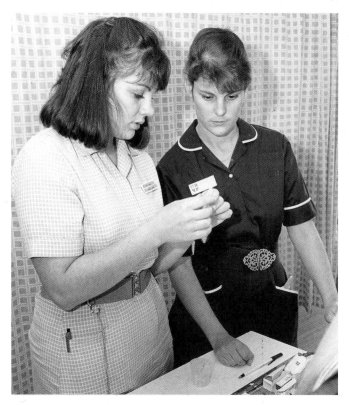

Uniforms, such as those worn by nurses, increase an individual's sense of anonymity and make it more likely that they will conform to the role associated with the uniform. In a study where individuals wore Ku Klux Klan-type outfits participants behaved more aggressively than when individuals were wearing nurses' uniforms—but both sets of people were conforming to the role suggested by the uniform.

So this again supports the view that uniforms and deindividuation create greater conformity.

Personality

Some people are more conformist than others, due either to their biology or their experience. Participants who were students made errors on 28% of conformity trials, whereas non-students made errors on 37% of trials. Why was there this difference? Students may learn to be more independent in their thinking than non-students, or their higher level of intelligence may make them more confident in their opinions.

Desire for personal control may be important as well. Burger and Cooper (1979) asked participants to rate a set of cartoons in terms of their funniness in the presence of a confederate who was expressing his own opinion. Participants who had previously measured high in terms of their desire for personal control were less influenced by the confederate. Some studies have found gender differences, with women being more conformist than men (Eagly & Carli, 1981) although Eagly (1978) has suggested that this may be because women are more oriented towards interpersonal goals and therefore *appear* to be more conformist in experimental situations.

Finally, research by Adorno et al. (1950) produced evidence that some individuals become more conformist as a result of the kind of parenting they receive. This research is described on page 221.

Non-conformity—reactance

Some people express their sense of personal control by displaying **reactance**, reacting against attempts to restrict personal choice. Venkatesan (1966) demonstrated this in a study where a group of students were asked to select their favourite suit. In fact all the suits were identical. The true participant made their choice last and tended to conform to majority opinion (remember that the situation was one of ambiguity) *except* when everyone strongly favoured the same suit. Then the participant tended to go for a different choice. It was suggested that in such a situation the participant would have felt strong pressure to conform and reacted by asserting their independence.

Driving down the wrong side of the road is an example of non-conformity (as well as downright foolishness). Can you think of other examples where conformity is desirable?

Consider how you might use social impact theory to explain Venkatesan's study.

CASE STUDY: *Groupthink*

Conformity to group opinion has many important applications, such as in juries and in the management committees of large organisations. The way individuals behave in these groups is likely to matter a lot. Janis (1972) coined the term "groupthink" to describe how the thinking of people in these situations is often disastrously affected by conformity.

Janis was describing the "Bay of Pigs" disaster to his teenage daughter and she challenged him, as a psychologist, to explain why such experts could make such poor decisions. (The Bay of Pigs invasion took place in 1961. President Kennedy and a group of government advisers made a series of bad decisions which resulted in this extremely unsuccessful invasion of the Bay of Pigs in Cuba—disastrous because 1000 men from the invasion force were only released after a ransom payment of fifty-three million dollars-worth of food and medicine, and also because ultimately the invasion resulted in the Cuban missile crisis and a threat of nuclear war.) Janis suggested that there are a number of group

factors that tend to increase conformity and result in bad decision-making:

- Group factors. People in groups do not want to be ostracised, they want to be liked and therefore tend to do things to be accepted as one of the group.

- Decisional stress. A group feels under pressure to reach a decision. To reduce this sense of pressure they try to reach the decision quickly and with little argument.

- Isolation. Groups often work in isolation which means there are no challenges to the way they are thinking.

- Institutional factors. Often people who are appointed to higher positions are those who tend to conform, following the principle that a good soldier makes a good commander.

SECTION 17
Obedience to Authority

In nearly all societies, certain people are given power and authority over others. In our society, for example, parents, teachers, and managers are invested with varying degrees of authority. Most of the time, this does not cause any problems. If the doctor tells us to take some tablets three times a day, we accept that he or she is the expert. If the school crossing attendant says "Cross now" it would be foolish not to obey—except if you could see a car approaching. The desirability of obeying authority is related to the reasonableness of their commands.

Unquestioning obedience to authority may have catastrophic consequences. The picture shows survivors of the Auschwitz concentration camp at the end of the war in 1945, following a decade of persecution, imprisonment, and genocide.

Obedience to Unjust Commands

An issue that has been of interest to psychologists for many years is to work out how far most people are willing to go in their obedience to authority. What happens if you are asked by a person in authority to do something that you think is wrong? The lesson of history seems to be that many people are willing to do terrible things when ordered to do so. For example, Adolf Eichmann was found guilty of having played a major role in ordering the deaths of millions of Jews during the Second World War. He denied any moral responsibility, and said he had simply been doing his job.

The best-known research on this issue was carried out by Stanley Milgram (1974), and is discussed at length in the Key Studies on pages 213 and 215. The main criticisms of his research concern the lack of experimental and ecological validity, and the contravention of ethical codes. We will consider these criticisms now.

Validity of Obedience Research

"Validity" refers to the extent to which something is true or valid. An experiment may produce a significant finding and "prove" the researcher's initial expectation, but this does not mean that the finding is "true" or "real".

How does obedience differ from conformity?

Both obedience and conformity involve social pressure. In obedience the pressure comes from behaving as you are instructed to do, whereas in conformity the pressure comes from group norms. A further distinction can be made in terms of the effects on private opinion. Obedience is more likely to involve public behaviour only.

Research on obedience to authority differs in at least three ways from research on conformity. First, the participants are ordered to behave in certain ways rather being fairly free to decide what to do. Second, the participant is of lower status than the person issuing the orders, whereas in studies of conformity the participant is usually of equal status to the group members trying to influence him or her. Third, participants' behaviour in obedience studies is determined by social power, whereas in conformity studies it is influenced mostly by the need for acceptance.

Differences between obedience and conformity

OBEDIENCE	CONFORMITY
Occurs within a hierarchy. Actor feels the person above has the right to prescribe behaviour. Links one status to another. Emphasis is on power.	Regulates the behaviour among those of equal status. Emphasis is on acceptance.
Behaviour adopted differs from behaviour of authority figure.	Behaviour adopted is similar to that of peers.
Prescription for action is explicit.	Requirement of going along with the group is often implicit.
Participants embrace obedience as an explanation for their behaviour.	Participants deny conformity as an explanation for their behaviour.

Electric shocks and learning

Stanley Milgram (1974) advertised in a local paper for men to take part in an experiment concerning memory and learning, to be conducted at the prestigious Yale University in America. Forty men, aged between 20 and 50 volunteered. They were paid $4.50 simply for turning up; payment did not depend on staying in the study.

When participants arrived they were told that there would be two participants, a "learner" and a "teacher". The experimenter drew lots to see which participant would take which part. At this point you should know that the design of this experiment was "**single blind**". The participant was not told the true details of the research. The truth was that the other participant was in fact a confederate of the experimenter, and the "experimenter" was also a confederate. The true participant always ended up being given the role of the "teacher".

The "teacher" was told to give electric shocks to the "learner" every time the wrong answer was given, and the shock intensity was increased each time. In fact, the apparatus was arranged so that the learner never actually received any shocks, but the teacher did not realise this. At 180 volts, the learner yelled "I can't stand the pain", and by 270 volts the response had become an agonised scream. The maximum intensity of shock was 450 volts. If the teacher was unwilling to give the shocks, the experimenter urged him to continue, saying such things as "It is absolutely essential that you should continue."

Do you think you would have been willing to give the maximum (and potentially deadly) 450-volt shock in this study? Milgram (1974) asked 14 psychology students to predict what participants would do. They estimated that no more than 3% of the participants would go up to 450 volts. In fact, about 65% of Milgram's participants gave the maximum shock.

One of the most striking cases of total obedience was that of Pasqual Gino, a 43-year-old water inspector. Towards the end of the experiment, he found himself thinking, "Good God, he's dead. Well, here we go, we'll finish him. And I just continued all the way through to 450 volts." Other participants found the experience very distressing. They were seen to "sweat, tremble, stutter, bite their lips, groan and dig their finger-nails into their flesh".

Milgram reported that three participants even had "full-blown uncontrollable seizures".

At the end of the experiment all participants were debriefed by being told the actual nature of the study. They were introduced to the "learner" and assured that he had experienced no actual shocks. They were told that their behaviour was entirely normal and, when interviewed later by questionnaire, 74% said they had learned something of personal importance. Only one person expressed regret about having taken part.

Discussion points

1. Milgram's study is invariably described as an "experiment". Why might this be more correctly described as a "controlled observational study"?

2. In what ways was the initial sample a biased one?

The photographs show the electric shock machine used in Milgram's classic experiment where 65% of the participants gave a potentially lethal shock to the "learner', shown in the bottom photograph. The learner was actually a confederate of the experimenter, a 47-year-old accountant called "Mr Wallace". The photographs show the experimenter (in the overall) and the true participant, the "teacher".

There are several ways we can look at validity. One is **experimental validity**, a measure of the extent to which the experimental design actually did the job it set out to do. If the experimental set-up was not believable then the participants probably would not behave as they would normally do in such situations. This is sometimes also called *internal* validity because it concerns what goes on inside the experiment.

The other form of validity is **ecological validity**, the extent to which the results of a study can be applied to other situations and other individuals. This is also referred to as *external* validity because it concerns issues outside the study. We will consider each of these in relation to obedience research.

What is the difference between internal and external validity?

Experimental validity

To what extent did Milgram's participants actually believe that they were giving electric shocks to the "learner"? Orne and Holland (1968), in a paper entitled "On the ecological validity of laboratory deception", claimed that Milgram's experiment lacked **experimental realism** because the participants couldn't have believed in the set-up. For example, surely they would have questioned why the experimenter wasn't giving the shocks himself; why employ someone else if there wasn't some kind of subterfuge going on? However, in a replication of Milgram's experiment by Rosenhan (1969), nearly 70% of participants reported that they believed the whole set-up.

Milgram's own response was that there is evidence that participants will believe and comply with almost anything. For example, in one study conducted by Turner and Solomon (1962), participants were willing to be *given* strong shocks and therefore must have believed the experimental task. Coolican (1996) agrees with Milgram on the basis of film evidence which shows that the participants in Milgram's (and Asch's) studies were taking the situation very seriously and appeared to be experiencing quite real distress.

What other reasons could there be for the fact that so many of Milgram's participants said they were glad to have taken part in the experiments? Might the fact that they were paid volunteers have had any effect on what they said they felt?

Orne and Holland also considered the question of **demand characteristics** in relation to experimental validity. Demand characteristics are those cues in an experiment that "invite" participants to behave in certain predictable ways. One demand characteristic of *any* experiment is that participants should obey the experimenter's instructions. Therefore obedience is a demand characteristic—it is the response to the cues given by the experimenter. This means that, in Milgram's experiment, the reason the participants obeyed so completely was not necessarily because they were very obedient, but perhaps more because they realised that this is how one should behave in an experiment. This would lead us to conclude that the Milgram finding lacks validity. It does not tell us about human obedience behaviour but tells us instead about how willing participants are to obey in experiments.

The Milgram experiment may also lack validity as a consequence of the fact that the participants behaved as they did because they had entered into a social contract with the experimenter. In exchange for payment ($4.50) participants would feel that they should obey the instructions. Therefore their behaviour did not demonstrate obedience in the real world but obedience only within a contractual relationship. They were told that they could leave and still be paid but, at the same time, the instructions "You must continue" must have made it quite difficult to leave. However, Gross (1999) argues that life is as much a social situation as the experiment is, therefore an experiment (being a social situation) is a reflection of life.

Do you feel that Milgram's experiment did or did not have experimental validity?

Variations on Milgram's first experiment

Milgram (1974) carried out several variations on his basic experiment. He found that there were two main ways in which obedience to authority could be reduced:

1. Increasing the obviousness of the learner's plight. This was studied by comparing obedience in four situations differing in the obviousness of the learner's plight (the percentage of participants who were totally obedient is shown in brackets):

- Remote feedback: the victim could not be heard or seen (66%).
- Voice feedback: the victim could be heard but not seen (62%).
- Proximity: the victim was only one metre away from the participant (40%).
- Touch-proximity: this was like the proximity condition, except that the participant had to force the learner's hand onto the shockplate (30%).

2. Reducing the authority or influence of the experimenter:

- Staging the experiment in a run-down office building rather than at Yale University (48%).
- Orders by telephone rather than having experimenter sitting close to the participant (20.5%). The effect of distance may help to explain why it is less stressful to kill people by dropping bombs from a plane than by shooting them at close range.
- The experimenter was an ordinary member of the public rather than a white-coated scientist (20%).
- Giving the participant a confederate who refused to give shocks (10%).

Discussion points

1. Do most people simply obey authority in a rather mindless way?
2. What are the main factors determining whether or not there is obedience to authority?

KEY STUDY EVALUATION — Milgram

These variations give us greater insight into the conditions under which people will obey unjust requests. They also show us something about independent behaviour because in many situations the majority of participants behaved independently.

There were ethical criticisms made of the original study by Milgram. One of Milgram's defences was that he could not anticipate how many participants would obey and therefore suffer the stress associated with knowing what they did. In these later variations Milgram could not use this defence.

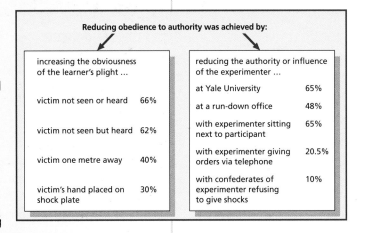

Reducing obedience to authority was achieved by:

increasing the obviousness of the learner's plight ...		reducing the authority or influence of the experimenter ...	
victim not seen or heard	66%	at Yale University	65%
		at a run-down office	48%
victim not seen but heard	62%	with experimenter sitting next to participant	65%
victim one metre away	40%	with experimenter giving orders via telephone	20.5%
victim's hand placed on shock plate	30%	with confederates of experimenter refusing to give shocks	10%

Why do you think that the setting in which the experiments took place made such a difference?

Ecological validity

Ecological validity concerns the extent to which we can generalise the findings of a study to other situations. Milgram conducted many variations of the original experiment and found many different levels of obedience (see Key Study above).

The main challenge to ecological validity in all of Milgram's research on obedience to authority is that it was carried out in laboratory situations. This would lead us to suggest that we might not be able to generalise the findings to the real world. One way to answer this criticism is to consider Gross's point made earlier, that experiments are like real-life social situations. Another way to answer the ecological validity criticism is by reference to the distinction made between experimental and **mundane realism** (Carlsmith, Ellsworth, & Aronson, 1976). Any research set-up that is like real life can be said to have mundane realism in so far as it appears real (mundane) rather than artificial to the participants. Some experiments lack mundane realism, but **experimental realism** can compensate for this when the way the experiment is conducted is so engaging that participants are fooled into thinking the set-up is real rather than artificial.

Milgram argued that his study had both mundane and experimental realism. It had mundane realism because the demands of an authority figure are the same whether the setting is artificial or occurring more naturally outside the laboratory. It had experimental realism because the experiment must have been highly engaging in order for the participants to behave in the way they did.

Ecological validity can also be demonstrated through attempts to replicate the research in more natural situations, for example Bickman's study (1974, see Key Study below) which produced some similar findings on obedience to Milgram. Perhaps the best-known replication is a real-life study by Hofling et al. (1966) in which 22 nurses were phoned up by someone who claimed to be "Dr Smith". He asked the nurses to check that a drug called Astroten was available. When the nurses did this, they saw on the bottle that the maximum dosage of this drug was supposed to be 10mg. When they reported back to Dr Smith, he told them to give 20mg of the drug to a patient.

There were two good reasons why the nurses should have refused to do as they were instructed. First, the dose was double the maximum safe dose. Second, the nurses did not know Dr Smith, and they were only supposed to take instructions from doctors they knew. However, the nurses' training had led them to obey instructions from doctors. There is a clear power structure in medical settings, with doctors in a more powerful position than nurses. As you probably guessed, the nurses were more influenced by the power structure than by the two hospital regulations they were meant to obey. All but one of the nurses did as Dr Smith instructed. When the nurses were asked what other nurses would have done in the circumstances, they all predicted that other nurses would *not* have obeyed the instructions. This provides evidence that the pressures to show obedience to authority are greater than most people imagine.

Many people suggest that Hofling's study had greater ecological validity than Milgram's, but in fact attempts to replicate Hofling's study (e.g. Rank & Jacobsen, 1977) have failed whereas there have been many replications of Milgram's studies.

KEY STUDY EVALUATION — Bickman

Field experiments may have increased ecological validity and mundane realism but the cost is decreased control. They also raise more ethical concerns because informed consent cannot be sought and it is difficult to debrief participants without alerting others to the experiment.

Bickman's study differs from Milgram's in one important way. The orders were not quite so unreasonable; therefore obedience was more understandable.

A field study of obedience

Leonard Bickman (1974) tested the ecological validity of Milgram's work by conducting an experiment in a more realistic setting. In this study three male experimenters gave orders to 153 randomly selected pedestrians in Brooklyn, New York. The experimenters were dressed in one of three ways: a sports coat and tie, a milkman's uniform, or a guard's uniform that made them look like a police officer. The experimenter gave one of three orders:

1. Pointing to a bag on the street, "Pick up this bag for me."

2. Nodding in the direction of a confederate "This fellow is overparked at the meter but doesn't have any change. Give him a dime."

3. Approaching a participant at a bus stop, "Don't you know you have to stand on the other side of the pole? This sign says 'No standing'."

Bickman found that participants were most likely to obey the experimenter dressed as a guard than the milkman or civilian. This supports one of the variations of Milgram's findings, that obedience can be related to the amount of perceived authority.

Discussion points

1. What ethical codes are infringed in this study?

2. In what way are these findings more or less "valid" than Milgram's?

And this is the criterion for ecological validity—that the finding should be replicable in other settings. Milgram's research has been replicated in other situations and other countries, as we will see.

Cross-cultural support for ecological validity

Milgram's (1974) studies were carried out in the United States. It is important to know whether similar findings would be obtained in other cultures as a confirmation of the validity of the original findings. The relevant cross-cultural evidence has been collected by Smith and Bond (1993), as shown in the graph on the right. Unfortunately, key aspects of the procedure varied from one culture to another, and so it is very difficult to interpret the cross-cultural differences in obedience. However, the percentages of participants who were willing to give the most severe shock were very high in several countries. The percentage figure was 80% or higher in studies carried out in Italy, Spain, Germany, Austria, and Holland. These findings suggest that there is substantial obedience to authority in numerous cultures.

An interesting series of studies was conducted by Meeus and Raaijmakers (1995) in Holland, which gave support to the extent of obedience in another culture, as well as providing further insight into obedience to authority. This study is described in the Key Study on the next page.

Ethical Issues Raised by Obedience Research

Milgram's work raises some important ethical issues—issues that also apply to many studies of obedience and conformity. In fact Milgram's study has become almost more famous for the ethical issues it raised than for its findings related to obedience.

Distress

Baumrind (1964) criticised Milgram for the severe distress he caused many if not all of his participants. Milgram's defence was that this effect was not anticipated nor was it deliberate. Prior to conducting the study he had surveyed opinion about how people would behave and had reason to expect very little obedience and therefore very little distress. However, this does not justify all the subsequent variations he conducted, which must have been equally stressful. Both Zimbardo (1973, see Key Study on page 204) and Gamson, Fireman, and Rytina (1982, see Key Study on page 222) stopped their studies because of the concern they felt for the participants.

Milgram also pointed out that the participants appeared to recover well afterwards, as evidenced in post-experiment interviews. Nearly 84% of the original participants said they were glad to have participated, and Milgram arranged for 40 of the participants to be interviewed by a psychiatrist who reported no signs of them having been harmed. The fact that very few complained afterwards could be explained in terms of denial, Freud's suggested ego-defence for dealing with anxiety. That is, in order for the participants to accept their own behaviour, they denied that there was anything to feel bad about.

Milgram's initial hypothesis was that German obedience during the Second World War was a facet of German culture. He was going to compare how Americans behaved with how Germans behaved but he found, to his astonishment, that Americans were extremely obedient—and therefore concluded that obedience was in human nature not just German nature.

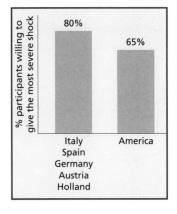

A study of obedience in Holland

Meeus and Raaijmakers (1995) conducted a study of obedience to authority which provides us with a number of useful insights. First of all, the study was conducted in Holland, so it tells us about obedience rates in another culture. Second, it was carried out in a real-life setting and therefore has greater ecological validity and mundane realism than Milgram's study.

KEY STUDY EVALUATION — Meeus and Raaijmakers

It was assumed in this study that the task facing the participants would be regarded as unreasonable and stressful, but some participants may not have felt this way. This would mean that the study lacked experimental realism. In which case the fact that the participants were so willing to obey would not be especially remarkable.

The dubious ethics of creating distress to participants remains in this study as much as in Milgram's research. Even though the participants were role-playing, the experimental manipulation was specifically designed to create stress.

Meeus and Raaijmakers told participants that the study was to see how job applicants would handle stress in an interview. The participant was given the role of being the interviewer. They believed that they were interviewing real applicants, but the interviewees were actually confederates of the experimenter. The participants were instructed to behave in such a way as to create stress during the interview for the interviewee. To do this they were given a set of negative statements, which ranged from mild to utterly humiliating, such as "This job is too difficult for you." The statements were designed to create an escalating sense of distress.

At the time of the study, unemployment rates were very high in Holland and therefore the interviewers (participants) would have felt bad about making an interview more difficult for the person trying to get a job. Thus we might not expect them to obey. The confederates were instructed to start off behaving confidently but to gradually appear more and more distressed as the interviewer's statements became more humiliating. The interviewee's performance deteriorated and they finally pleaded to the interviewer to stop interrupting, eventually refusing to answer any more questions. Nevertheless, 22 out of the total of 24 participants (interviewers) delivered all 15 "stress remarks". They clearly felt stressed themselves but nevertheless obeyed the experimenter's authority and continued with the task. They reportedly attempted to hide their stress from the victim and to act as if nothing was wrong.

This experiment again demonstrates the willingness of individuals to obey even when both their stress and that of the receiver is apparent. The explanation for the high level of obedience may lie in their attitude to social institutions and their distant relationship with fellow citizens.

Discussion points

1. To what extent can the same criticisms be applied to this study as were raised against Milgram's original experiment?
2. In what way does this study have greater validity than Milgram's study?

Deception

The participants were not told the true nature of Milgram's experiment; they were told that it was a memory experiment. Milgram (1992) has argued that the deception (or "illusion") was a necessary part of the experiment because, without it, the experiment would lack experimental realism. The value of the experimental findings (the ends) justifies the methods (means)—and ethics is a question of balancing ends and means. Brown (1986, p.6) says:

As far as the ethics of research on human [participants] is concerned, I think Milgram is absolutely in the clear and deserves to be praised for doing research of the highest human consequence while showing great concern for the welfare of his [participants]. The slight personal risk involved is justified by the importance of the topic.

In addition, Milgram claimed that the fact that participants did not find fault with his procedures is a sufficient judgement of his deception.

Lack of informed consent

Clearly where an experiment involves deception the participant is not in a position to provide informed consent. "**Informed consent**" refers to the participants giving their agreement to participate, on the basis of knowing what they have been asked to do. In Milgram's experiment they were not told that the study might cause conflict and distress, and so they were not in a position to give their informed consent. There are several ways to overcome the objections in relation to deception. One is to replace informed consent with **presumptive consent**, that is to obtain the views of other people about the acceptability of the experimental procedures. It is argued that if they felt it would be acceptable to take part, then we can *presume* that the actual participants would have felt this way if they had been asked. Milgram did obtain this form of consent from a group of psychiatrists as well as his students.

The second way to overcome objections about deception is to thoroughly debrief participants afterwards, offering them the opportunity to withdraw their data from the findings as a means of exercising some control over their participation. It is not on record whether Milgram did offer this to his participants but he did debrief them.

Ethical issues: To what extent can a patient with a mental disorder give their informed consent to participate in a treatment programme?

A third way is to use role-play, as Zimbardo did. Meeus and Raaijmakers (1995) claim that it is a viable alternative to the obedience experiment.

The right to withdraw

A further ethical consideration is the freedom of the participant to withdraw at any time. Coolican (1990) claims that this was not the case in Milgram's experiment. Ostensibly participants were able to withdraw at any time but in reality they were more or less ordered to continue. The experimenter had a script to follow. Each time the participant said he wanted to quit, the experimenter gave the next prompt or "prod":

- Prod 1: Please continue.
- Prod 2: The experiment requires that you continue.
- Prod 3: It is absolutely essential that you continue.
- Prod 4: You have no other choice, you must go on.

So participants were not really free to leave if that was what they wanted to do, although Milgram claims they were told at the beginning that they could leave and be paid regardless. Of central importance to current ethical guidelines is the emphasis that the rights and status of the participant are equal to those of the researcher (this is discussed in the next section). It has been argued that Milgram totally failed to do this, because his research was specifically designed to see how far the researcher could exploit his superior position to compel participants to behave in ways in which they did not want to behave.

Conclusion relating to ethical issues

Erikson (1968) summed up Milgram's findings thus: it is "to man himself, not to 'the devil' belongs the responsibility for, and the control of, his inhumane actions."

Aronson (1988) argued that there might have been no ethical objections if the findings had been less distasteful, and Milgram (1974) also suggested that the ethical concerns would have been reduced if the participants had disobeyed. This would mean that it is not the method that is unethical, but the distasteful findings lead one to want to find some way to discredit them.

Why Do People Obey?

Erikson's conclusion was that people obey because obedience is a feature of human nature. This is a dispositional explanation. Is it basic human *nature* to obey anyone who is perceived as "in authority"? Or is it only in some *situations* that people obey?

Gross (1999) uses the example of the Ik who are a society of hunter-gatherers now forced to live in a confined territory with few resources because of the changes that have occurred in their native Uganda. Their harsh living environment has forced them not to have many of the values that we Europeans hold. They are extremely selfish to the point of even depriving their own children of food. The conclusion is that, *in certain situations*, people are "forced" to behave in anti-social ways.

Situational explanations

Milgram (1974) identified three main features of the situation that were conducive to obedience.

1. A socially obedient environment. Our experience has taught us that authorities are generally trustworthy and legitimate. This creates a socially obedient environment.
2. Graduated commitment. The orders given by the experimenter moved gradually from the reasonable (small shocks) to the unreasonable (harmful shocks), and so it was hard for the participants to notice when they began to be asked to behave in an unreasonable way. This is similar to something called "the foot-in-the-door-technique" used by salespeople— they start with a minor request, such as "Can I ask you a few questions?" (getting their foot metaphorically in the door) and then gradually make larger requests. Before you know it, you have bought some item you could not afford!
3. The agentic state. The participants were put into an **agentic state**. This means acting as an agent for someone or becoming the "instrument" of an authority figure. When a person is in an agentic state they cease to act according to their consciences. The attitude of those in the agentic state is as follows: "I am not responsible, I act as I do because I was ordered to do it!" Milgram proposed that we have two states of consciousness: the agentic state and the **autonomous state**. In the latter state we are aware of the consequences of our actions and therefore voluntarily direct our behaviour.

Why do you think situational explanations may be more common in some cultures than others?

Dispositional explanations

Adorno et al. (1950) felt that personality was a better explanation of obedience. They proposed that some people had an **authoritarian personality**. Such people are most likely to be obedient (and most likely also to be prejudiced). An individual with an authoritarian personality has the following characteristics:

- Rigid beliefs in conventional values.
- General hostility towards other groups.
- Intolerance of ambiguity.
- Submissive attitudes towards authority figures.

Early experiences

Adorno et al. argued that childhood experiences play a key role in the development of the authoritarian personality. Harsh treatment causes the child to have much hostility towards his or her parents. This hostility remains unconscious, because the child is unwilling to admit to it. This causes motivated forgetting, or what Freud called repression. The child seems to idealise his or her parents, and in later life acts in a submissive way towards authority figures. However, there is still much hostility lying below the surface. This hostility is displaced on to non-threatening minority groups, and appears in the form of prejudice.

The F Scale

Adorno et al. devised a number of questionnaires relating to their theory. The most important questionnaire was the **F (Fascism) Scale**, which was designed to measure the attitudes of the authoritarian personality. A clearer idea of what the F-Scale measures can be seen by looking at a few items, shown in the box below. Adorno et al. gave the test to about 2000 people and found that those who scored high on the F-Scale also scored high on a scale that measured prejudice, thus confirming the validity of the scale. Milgram (1974) found that high scorers on the F-Scale gave stronger shocks than low scorers when ordered to do so by an authority figure.

Resisting Obedience and Conformity

We have seen that social pressures to conform or to obey authority can exert powerful effects on people's behaviour. However, some people manage to resist the pressures to conform or to obey and thus exhibit **independent behaviour**. In all the studies reviewed so far, there were always some people who didn't obey or conform. Why did they remain in an autonomous state while others were in an agentic state?

Situational factors

Remaining autonomous is easier to do in some circumstances, especially when one or more other people are seen to behave independently. For example, as we have seen, conformity in the Asch situation dropped from 37% to 5% when there was one confederate who gave the correct answer on all trials (an example of minority influence). And Milgram (1974) found that when two rebellious confederates acted as additional "teachers" this reduced the participant's levels of obedience from 65% to 10%. The fact that two other people resisted the pressures to obey authority made it easier for the true participant to show independent behaviour.

> **CASE STUDY:** *War Criminals*
>
> After the Second World War, the Allies tried many of the high-ranking Nazi officers at Nuremburg. Adolf Eichmann argued that he had only been obeying orders. He was not the "monster" that the newspapers described but simply an ordinary person caught up in an extraordinary situation. Eichmann was described as having no violent anti-Jewish feelings (Arendt, 1963). He was an autonomous individual who became agentic when he joined the SS and subscribed to the military code of obedience to those in authority.

As you can see, the concept of the authoritarian personality owes a lot to the psychoanalytic perspective.

At the same time as research in America found that authoritarian personalities tended to favour strongly the American way of life, authoritarians in Russia were equally committed to the Communist ideals. This photograph of the Russian leader Khrushchev shows him in a typically authoritarian mood.

> **Items from the F scale devised by Adorno et al.**
>
> Indicate whether you hold slight, moderate or strong support OR slight, moderate or strong opposition to the following:
>
> "Obedience and respect for authority are the most important virtues children should learn."
>
> "Most of our social problems would be solved if we could somehow get rid of the immoral, crooked, and feeble-minded people."
>
> "What the youth needs most is strict discipline, rugged determination, and the will to work for family and country."
>
> "Familiarity breeds contempt."
>
> "Sex crimes, such as rape and attacks on children, deserve more than mere imprisonment, such criminals ought to be publicly whipped."

The variations Milgram conducted (see Key Study on page 215) indicate a number of other situational factors that increase independent behaviour, and an interesting study by Gamson et al. (1982) demonstrated how conformity can lead to disobedience, and that rebellion is more likely in a group situation (see Key Study below).

Individual differences

There are large individual differences between participants in their responses to situations, such as those devised by Asch and by Milgram. As we will see, various attempts have been made to identify the personality and other characteristics of individuals whose behaviour is independent.

Crowne and Marlowe (1964) reported a number of studies in which conformity was assessed in high and low scorers on the Marlowe–Crowne Social Desirability

Resisting the command to obey

Gamson et al. (1982) devised a new procedure to study, like Milgram, encounters with unjust authority. They set up a fictitious public relations firm called MHRC (Manufacturer's Human Relations Consultants). Participants were employed to help the company collect opinions on moral standards. A group of nine participants met at a motel, and were paid $10 for two hours work. They were asked to engage in a discussion which would be video taped.

The situation was as follows: Mr C managed a service station for an oil company but his franchise had been revoked because, the company claimed, he had behaved immorally and this made him unfit to be their local representative (he was living with a young woman and they were not married). Mr C was suing the company for unfair dismissal. It also transpired that Mr C had spoken out on television against higher petrol prices.

KEY STUDY EVALUATION — Gamson et al.

Ethical issues should concern us in relation to this study. Many of the participants reported feelings of anxiety and stress. One said "I'm glad to have done it but I'm really shook and my blood pressure will be high for hours." Another called the experiment "the most stressful experience I've had in the past year". The researchers recognised their moral obligations and stopped the study before it was completed. They had planned to run a total of 80 groups but stopped after 33 because of the stress.

The participants were asked to discuss their attitudes towards Mr C's lifestyle. The co-ordinator switched off the cameras at various times and instructed individuals to argue as if they were offended by Mr C's behaviour. Then the co-ordinator switched the cameras back on. The groups soon realised what was happening. They were being manipulated to produce a tape of evidence supporting the oil company's position. In some of the groups, the participants threatened to confiscate the video tapes of the discussion, and to expose the oil company to the media. In all groups there was some rebellion, and all but four of the groups refused to sign the affidavit giving MHRC permission to use the video tape in a trial.

This study provides a marked contrast with Milgram because in 29 out of the 33 groups there was successful resistance to unjust authority. Why did rebellion occur instead of obedience? In the MHRC groups there were no confederates. One member in each group spontaneously rebelled and this minority opinion swayed most of the groups. It is possible that this change in behaviour reflects the fact that this study took place at a time when Americans had come to be more challenging of authority. It may also be that the person in charge (the MHRC co-ordinator) had less authority than the experimenter in Milgram's study. Finally, it may be because the MHRC study involved groups and groups behave differently from individuals because the possibility of collective action exists (i.e. everyone knows that they can group together to resist authority).

Discussion points

1. In the light of this study, how can we re-interpret Asch's research (see page 202)?

2. How would you explain the findings of this study?

Scale. There has been some controversy about exactly what this scale measures, but it seems in part to assess the need for social approval. As might be expected, those low in need for social approval were more likely to show independent behaviour by refusing to conform in the Asch situation. In other conformity studies (e.g. Stang, 1972) it has been found that individuals high in self-esteem are more likely to behave independently than those low in self-esteem.

When Milgram used female participants in his experiment he found that obedience rates were much the same. However, other studies have found some gender differences. For example, Kilham and Mann (1974) used the Milgram baseline experiment and found that Australian women were less obedient than men (10% as compared with 40%). On the other hand, Eagly and Carli (1981), as we previously mentioned, claimed that women are more likely to be influenced than men, but this may be because women are more oriented towards interpersonal goals and therefore *appear* to be more influenced.

Why is it that people high in self-esteem are more likely to resist orders to obey?

It is also likely that a tendency to prefer an autonomous state would be associated with greater desire for personal control as Burger and Cooper (1979) found (see page 211).

Evaluation of individual differences

There are two main reasons why some individuals might show more independent behaviour than most other people. First, they may have a high opinion of themselves and of the correctness of their own judgements. This would explain why those high in self-esteem, who believe themselves to be highly competent, who are intelligent, and who have leadership ability, show little conformity behaviour. Second, the "independent" types may be relatively unconcerned about the approval of others, and so have little motive for submitting to the judgements of other people. This would explain why those low in need for social approval and high in assertiveness may behave in an independent way.

CASE STUDY: *The My Lai Massacre*

The My Lai massacre has become known as one of the most controversial incidents in the Vietnam War. On 14 December 1969 almost 400 Vietnamese villagers were killed in under 4 hours. The following transcript is from a CBS News interview with a soldier who took part in the massacre.

Q. How many people did you round up?

A. Well, there was about forty, fifty people that we gathered in the center of the village. And we placed them in there, and it was like a little island, right there in the center of the village, I'd say … And …

Q. What kind of people—men, women, children?

A. Men, women, children.

Q. Babies?

A. Babies. And we huddled them up. We made them squat down and Lieutenant Calley came over and said, "You know what to do with them, don't you?" And I said yes. So I took it for granted that he just wanted us to watch them. And he left, and came back about ten or fifteen minutes later and said, "How come you ain't killed them yet?" And I told him that I didn't think you wanted us to kill them, that you just wanted us to guard them. He said, "No. I want them dead." So—

Q. He told this to all of you, or to you particularly?

A. Well, I was facing him. So, but the other three, four guys heard it and so he stepped back about ten, fifteen feet, and he started

shooting them. And he told me to start shooting. So I started shooting, I poured about four clips into the group.

Q. You fired four clips from your …

A. M-16.

Q. And that's about how many clips—I mean, how many—

A. I carried seventeen rounds to each clip.

Q. So you fired something like sixty-seven shots?

A. Right.

Q. And you killed how many? At that time?

A. Well, I fired them automatic, so you can't—You just spray the area on them and so you can't know how many you killed 'cause they were going fast. So I might have killed ten or fifteen of them.

Q. Men, women and children?

A. Men, women and children.

Q. And babies?

A. And babies.

William Calley stood trial for his involvement in this massacre. His defence was that he was only obeying orders. Before the massacre Calley showed no criminal tendencies and afterwards he returned to a life of quiet respectability. His behaviour was that of a "normal" person. Kelman and Lawrence (1972) conducted a survey after the trial and found that half of the respondents said that it was "normal, even desirable" to obey legitimate authority.

CASE STUDY: *Stanley Milgram's Other Research*

Milgram's name is synonymous with obedience research, however he did conduct a number of other studies and was always seeking to test new ideas. Tavris (1974) called him "a man with thousand ideas". He wrote songs, including a musical, and devised light-shows and machines.

In relation to conformity, he tried the following with a group of students (Tavris, 1974). He asked them to go up to someone on an underground train and say "Can I have your seat?" They all recoiled in horror at the idea. Why were they so frightened? Milgram tried the task himself, assuming that it would be easy, but when he tried to say the actual words to a stranger on the underground he froze. He found he was overwhelmed by paralysing inhibition, and suggested that this shows how social rules exert extremely strong pressure.

Two final points need to be made. First, it is the case that the personality and other characteristics of those who show independent behaviour often differ surprisingly *little* from those who conform. Second, research into independent behaviour is important, because it serves to remind us that conformity behaviour and obedience to authority depend on two factors: (1) the individual; and (2) the social situation. It also depends on the behaviour that is being requested—conforming to traffic rules or obeying a traffic warden is one thing, whereas conforming to anti-social behaviour or obeying an unjust request is quite another.

The Surprising Nature of Milgram's Findings

Why was this study so important? Milgram's research on obedience to authority is of great importance, because of the light it sheds on human behaviour and because of the surprising findings he obtained. However, it seems to portray a very pessimistic view of human nature. According to Milgram (1974):

> *The capacity for man to abandon his humanity, indeed the inevitability that he does so, as he merges his unique personality into the larger institutional structures … is the fatal flaw nature has designed into us, and which in the long run gives our species only a modest chance for survival.*

Milgram (1974) seems to have been unduly pessimistic in his conclusions. Most of the obedient participants indicated in their behaviour that they were experiencing a strong conflict between the demands of the experimenter and the dictates of their consciences. They appeared very tense and nervous, they perspired, they bit their lips, and they clenched and unclenched their fists. Such behaviour does not suggest that they were in simply an agentic state.

Milgram and others have suggested that there are links between his findings and the horrors of Nazi Germany. However, it is important not to exaggerate the similarities. In the first place, the values underlying Milgram's studies were the positive ones of understanding more about human learning and memory, whereas the values in Nazi Germany were morally vile. Second, most of the participants in Milgram's studies needed to be watched closely in order to ensure their obedience, whereas this was not necessary in Nazi Germany. Third, as we have seen, most of Milgram's participants were in a state of great conflict and agitation. In contrast, those who carried out the atrocities in Nazi Germany typically seemed unconcerned about moral issues.

Attribution

Why was the actual behaviour of the participants in Milgram's studies so different from what most people would have expected? Part of the answer is probably to be found in the **fundamental attribution error**, which is the tendency to underestimate the role of situational factors in determining behaviour, and to overestimate the role of personality and other personal characteristics. When asked to decide how many people would show total obedience in Milgram's situation, we tend to think along the following lines: "Only a psychopath would give massive electric shocks to another person. There aren't many psychopaths about, and so only a tiny percentage of people would be totally obedient." This line of reasoning focuses exclusively on the individual participant's characteristics. In line with the fundamental attribution error, it ignores the relevant situational factors (e.g. the scientific expertise and status of the experimenter; the insistence of the experimenter that the participant continue to give electric shocks).

> ■ Activity: On the basis of the psychological evidence, what advice would you give to the management committee of a children's home for difficult children? They want to know how to increase obedience and reduce group conformity. List three things for obedience and three things for conformity, citing the relevant evidence to support your argument.

SECTION 18 CRITICAL ISSUE
Ethical Issues in Psychological Research

The questions of ethics is critical to psychological research. Not least because a professional group of people is one that "polices" itself and therefore these ethical standards are a key feature of the professionalism of psychology. In this section we will consider some important ethical issues in detail and relate these to the social influence research we have been examining. At the end we will consider how psychologists deal with these issues using ethical guidelines.

Ethics in Psychology

Ethics are a set of moral principles used to guide human behaviour. There are no absolutes in ethics but any society or group of people develop ethics as a means of determining what is considered right and wrong for that group. The term "ethics" tends to be used when considering moral behaviour among professionals, such as doctors or lawyers. The term "morals" is used to refer to everyday standards of right and wrong, such as honesty and kindness. Ethics are determined by a balance between ends and means, or a **cost–benefit analysis**. Certain things may be less acceptable than others, but if the ultimate end is for the good of humankind, then we may feel that an undesirable behaviour (such as causing stress to an animal) is acceptable.

Scientists often confront important ethical questions in the course of their work. For example, was it morally defensible for physicists to develop the atomic bomb during the 1940s? Can research on human embryos be justified? Should scientists participate in the development of chemical weapons that could potentially kill millions of people? All these questions about the ethics of scientific research are hard to answer, because there are good arguments for and against each programme of research.

Ethical issues: Which do you think are more important, the interests of the individual or the interests of society as a whole?

There are probably more major ethical issues associated with research in psychology than in any other scientific discipline. There are various reasons for this. First, all psychological experiments involve the study of living creatures (whether human or the members of some other species), and the rights of these participants to be treated in a caring and respectful way can be infringed by an unprincipled or careless experimenter.

Second, the findings of psychological research may reveal what seem to be unpleasant or unacceptable facts about human nature, or about certain groups within society. No matter how morally upright the experimenter may be, there is always the danger that extreme political organisations will use research findings to further their political aims.

Third, these political aims may include social control. There is the danger that the techniques discovered in psychological research might be exploited by dictators or others seeking to exert unjustifiable influence on society or to inflame people's prejudices.

The key ethical issues to consider are: the use of deception, informed consent, and the protection of participants from harm. These issues are especially relevant to research into social influence because of the potential for harm to participants and the potential uses of the findings.

The Use of Deception

Honesty is a key moral and ethical principle. It is a fundamental expectation to be given full information when you agree to take part in psychological research. However, deception is sometimes necessary. A well-known example of research involving deception is the work of Asch (1956, see Key Study on page 202). The aim of the experiment was to see whether the genuine participants would conform to group pressure, which happened on about one-third of the trials. If the participants had been told the experiment was designed to study conformity to group pressure, and that all the other participants were confederates of the experimenter, then this important study would have been pointless.

Deception is certainly widespread. Menges (1973) considered about 1000 experimental studies that had been carried out in the United States. Full information about what was going to happen was provided in only 3% of cases.

One possible reaction is to argue that there should never be any deception in psychological experiments, even if that means that some lines of research have to stop. However, this ignores the fact that many forms of deception are entirely harmless. For example, some memory researchers are interested in incidental learning (see Chapter 2), which involves people's ability to remember information they were not asked to remember. This can only be done by deceiving the participants as to the true purpose of the experiment until the memory test is presented.

When is deception justified? There is no simple answer. Various relevant factors need to be taken into consideration. First, the less potentially damaging the consequences of the deception, the more likely it is to be acceptable. Second, it is easier to justify the use of deception in studies that are important in scientific terms than in those that are trivial. Third, deception is more justifiable when there are no alternative, deception-free ways of studying an issue.

Handling the deception issue

One way of avoiding the ethical problems associated with deception is the use of **role-playing experiments**. The participants are asked to play the role of participants in a deception experiment, but they are told beforehand about the experimental manipulations. This approach eliminates the ethical problems of deception studies, but it is not clear that it is a satisfactory way of studying behaviour. As Freedman (1969) pointed out, what we are likely to obtain from role-playing studies are "people's guesses as to how they would behave if they were in a particular situation". Zimbardo's experiment (1973, see Key Study on page 204) involved role playing and also involved considerable distress to participants. The study by Meeus and Raaijmakers (1995, see Key Study on page 218) also involved role playing. Deception was largely avoided but there were other problems in both studies, namely distress.

Debriefing

How could a role-playing experiment be used in this teacher's meeting without deceiving the participants?

Debriefing is an important part of using deception, a means of compensating for the dishonesty of deception. At the end of the research study, participants should be told the actual nature and purpose of the research. They are then asked to ensure that they do not tell any future participants.

Debriefing can also be used to reduce any distress that may have been caused by the experiment. However, the fact that participants are debriefed does not justify carrying out any unethical procedures. According to Aronson (1988) participants should leave the research situation in "a frame of mind that is at least as sound as it was when they entered". This might not be the case even after debriefing. You might consider Milgram's research in this context.

Informed Consent

It is considered the right of participants, wherever possible, to provide voluntary informed consent. This means several things: being informed about what will be required, being informed about the purpose of the research, being informed of your rights (e.g. the right to confidentiality, the right to leave the research at any time), and finally, giving your consent. There are many situations where this is not possible:

- When children or participants who have impairments that limit understanding and/or communication are involved. In this case, the informed consent of an adult is sought, although some critics might feel that this is not sufficient.
- When deception is a necessary part of the research design, as in Asch's or Milgram's experiment.
- In field experiments when participants are not even aware that they are taking part in a piece of psychological research. A classic study by Piliavin et al. (1969) involved a confederate pretending to collapse on an underground train with the aim of finding out how many people would offer help. None of the participants gave their consent. Bickman's (1974) study of obedience (see Key Study on page 216) was also a field experiment.
- Retrospective case studies, where data in the public domain are used as psychological evidence (such as the case of Kitty Genovese on page 201, or HM on page 37).
- There is even the question as to whether truly informed consent is ever possible. How easy is it for a non-psychologist to understand the aims of psychological research and fully comprehend what is expected of him or her? Prior to participation, would the "teachers" in Milgram's experiment have anticipated how they would feel when administering shocks? The evidence

How does a field experiment differ from a laboratory experiment?

> ### CASE STUDY: *Subjects or Participants?*
>
> Until recently members of the public who took part in psychology experiments were called "subjects". This reflected the view that they were only passively involved in the research process (they did what the researcher told them) and it emphasised the power of the researcher (as the person in authority). The subject in a psychological experiment was in a rather vulnerable and exploitable position. Kelman (1972, p.993) pointed out, "most ethical problems arising in social research can be traced to the subject's power deficiency." It follows that steps need to be taken to ensure that the participant is not placed in a powerless and vulnerable position. This is the task of an ethical code.
>
> As a consequence of this insight it has become the practice to refer to such individuals as participants rather than subjects. Perhaps this process is analogous to the historical shift from having a political regime with "rulers and subjects" to the more modern conception of "leaders and followers". Both participants and followers have an active role to play and it would be foolish to think otherwise. The change in terminology allows for a more humane respect for individuals who participate in psychology experiments.

of Milgram's pre-experiment surveys suggests that people would not have anticipated their own behaviour, let alone how they would feel.

Other ways to obtain consent

One possibility is to ascertain acceptability by asking the opinions of members of the population from which the participants in the research are to be drawn. This is what Milgram did, and it is called seeking **presumptive consent**.

An alternative approach is to gain **prior general consent**. This is what Gamson et al. (1982) did. In their study (which is described on page 222) they gained participants' consent using the following ruse: they advertised for participants and when interested individuals telephoned, the potential participants were asked whether they were willing to take part in any or all of the following kinds of research:

1. Research on brand recognition of commercial products.
2. Research on product safety.
3. Research in which you will be misled about the purpose until afterwards.
4. Research involving group standards.

Could the approach adopted by Gamson et al. be adapted to handle the deception issue in most kinds of research?

Most people said yes to all four and then were told that only the last kind of research was in progress. However, they had agreed to the third kind of research and thus consented to be deceived, probably without really being aware of it. So the experimenters felt ethically vindicated and they also had participants who were not primed to be suspicious about the purpose of the research.

■ Activity: You might try out Gamson et al.'s technique with various people. Pretend that you are about to conduct an experiment and ask the potential participant whether they are willing to take part in any of the following kinds of research. Show them the list from Gamson et al.'s study. Afterwards, debrief them by telling them the true purpose of your research and ask what they felt about the deception and the use of prior general consent.

The right to withhold data

Another means of offering informed consent is to do it retrospectively. After the research, during debriefing, the participant should be offered the opportunity to withhold their data. In essence this gives them the same power as if they had refused to take part in the first place. If they withhold their data it is as if they had been informed at the start and not consented to take part.

Protection From Harm

"Harm" can mean a number of different things. It encompasses both physical and psychological damage. The key test of whether or not a participant has been harmed is to ask whether the risk of harm was greater than in ordinary life.

Physical harm

If you recall, Watson and Rayner claimed that their experiment with Little Albert was ethical because the psychological harm inflicted was no greater than what he might experience in real life. Is this acceptable?

We might include excessive anxiety as physical harm because the results can be physically evident. For example, if you consider the description of some of Milgram's participants it is clear that they experienced physical as well as psychological harm—some of them had full-blown seizures, whereas many perspired and bit their lips. We also know from Chapter 4 that stress (a psychological state) has a physical basis.

Psychological harm

Psychological harm is much more difficult to quantify, but there is no doubt that many studies infringe what might be called psychological "safety". Loss of self-esteem, for instance, would constitute psychological harm. It has been suggested that Milgram's participants would have felt disappointed with their own apparent willingness to obey unjust authority, which may have led to decreased self-esteem, a form of psychological harm

We can also consider the issues of **confidentiality** and the **right to privacy** as forms of protecting participants from psychological harm. The latter is a matter of concern when conducting observational research. It would not be appropriate, for example, to observe a person's behaviour in their bedroom without their permission but it would be acceptable to observe people in a public place, such as a park, where public scrutiny is expected.

Finally, you might consider the study by Berkun et al. (1962) described in the Key Study below, which shows how attitudes to psychological research have

CASE STUDY: *Zimbardo's Defence*

Zimbardo pointed out that all of his participants had signed a formal informed consent form, which indicated that there would be an invasion of privacy, loss of some civil rights, and harassment. He also noted that day-long debriefing sessions were held with the participants, so that they could understand the moral conflicts being studied. However, Zimbardo failed to protect his participants from physical and mental harm. It was entirely predictable that the mock guards would attack the mock prisoners, because that is exactly what had happened in a pilot study that Zimbardo carried out before the main study.

Confidentiality and anonymity

Anonymity is an important part of confidentiality. The discussion of case notes at a public lecture or in a published article or book must not involve identifying the client. A breach of this aspect of confidentiality could result in the client or client's relatives taking legal action against the therapist concerned. In situations like these, and of course with the permission of those involved, clients are usually identified by pseudonyms or initials only.

Army stress experiments

Society's views on ethically acceptable and unacceptable treatment of human participants in research have changed considerably in recent decades. Research carried out by Berkun et al. (1962) did not cause an outcry at the time, but would certainly be regarded as totally unacceptable nowadays. In one of their experiments, the participants were flying in a military plane when one of the engines failed. They were told to fill in an "emergency procedure" form for insurance purposes before the plane ditched in the sea. As you may have guessed, there was nothing actually wrong with the plane—the situation was set up on purpose by the experimenters to observe the effects of fear on behaviour.

Berkun et al. carried out another study in which soldiers were on their own out in the field, and could only communicate with base by using a radio transmitter. Some of the soldiers were exposed to explosions sounding like artillery shells, others were told that there had been an accident causing dangerous radioactive fall-out in the area, and still others were enveloped in smoke so that they thought a forest fire had broken out. When they tried to contact base, they discovered that their radio transmitters would not work.

Berkun et al. found from blood and urine samples that all three groups of soldiers differed biochemically from control soldiers who were not exposed to stress. They assessed the effects of stress on performance by seeing how rapidly the soldiers repaired the radio. Surprisingly, only soldiers exposed to the artillery shells showed worse performance on this task than the control soldiers.

KEY STUDY EVALUATION — Berkun et al.

Some might argue that as these studies were carried out in an environment where individuals expect some loss of personal control this makes them ethically more acceptable. The BPS code (see pages 230–231) does advise that risks should be similar to those that individuals experience in their everyday lives.

Discussion points

1. Why would research such as that of Berkun et al. be regarded as ethically unacceptable nowadays?

2. Why do you think that views about the kinds of research that are ethically unacceptable have changed over the years?

When setting up observational research it is important to consider whether the participants would normally expect to be observed by strangers in the situation. For example, making observations of the people in this picture would be acceptable, but observing them in a changing room would not.

changed. People used to be more accepting of the ways that experimental participants were treated, whereas this kind of physical and psychological harm would not be acceptable now.

Ethical Guidelines

The need for ethical control leads to the establishment of a set of rules or guidelines which can be used to judge the acceptableness of behaviour. During the Second World War the Nazis conducted many horrific experiments with their concentration camp prisoners, such as placing them in freezing water to see how long it took for them to die. At the end of the war, the perpetrators were tried in Nuremburg and one of the outcomes was that it became apparent that a code of ethics was needed as a reference point for what is acceptable in scientific research. The 10-point "Nuremburg code" was drawn up which introduced important concepts, such as that of informed consent.

This code has been adapted by professional bodies all over the world. Within psychology there are such organisations in every country, each with their own code of conduct, such as the British Psychological Society (BPS), the American Psychological Association (APA), and the German Psychology Association (Deutschen Gesellschaft für Psychologie, DGP).

Ethical committees

One way of trying to ensure that psychological research is ethically acceptable is by setting up **ethical committees**. Most institutions (e.g. universities, research units) in which research is carried out now have their own ethical committee, which considers all research proposals from the perspective of the rights and dignity of the participants. The existence of such committees helps to correct the power imbalance between experimenter and participant. However, if all the members of an ethical committee are researchers in psychology, they may be disinclined to turn down proposals from professional colleagues. For this and other reasons, it is desirable for every ethical committee to include some non-psychologists and at least one non-expert member of the public.

In the United States, every complaint against psychologists is investigated by the American Psychological Association's Committee on Scientific and Professional Ethics. If the complaint is found to be justified, then the psychologist concerned is either suspended or expelled from the Association.

The BPS code of conduct

The BPS code of conduct concerns (a) research and (b) practice. The former is enshrined in two documents *Ethical principles for conducting research with human participants* (1993) and *Guidelines for the use of animals in research* (1965); the latter is represented in the *Guidelines for the professional practice of clinical psychology* (1983).

We are only concerned in this book with the BPS ethical principles for human participants, which are summarised in the box on the page opposite. They should be followed by all researchers in the United Kingdom, including students carrying out research as part of their course.

Ethical Guidelines for Research With Human Participants

(based on standards put forward by the British Psychological Society)

1. Introduction

Ethical guidelines are necessary to clarify the conditions under which psychological research is acceptable.

2. General

The essential principle is that the investigation should be considered from the standpoint of all participants; foreseeable threats to their psychological well-being, health, values, or dignity should be eliminated. It should be borne in mind that the best judge of whether an investigation will cause offence may be members of the population from which the participants in the research are to be drawn.

3. Consent

Participants should be informed of the objectives of the investigation and all other aspects of the research that might reasonably be expected to influence their willingness to participate—only such information allows informed consent to be given. Special care needs to be taken when research is conducted with children or with participants who have impairments that limit understanding and/or communication such that they are unable to give their real consent. This situation requires special safeguarding procedures.

4. Deception

Intentional deception of the participant over the purpose and general nature of the investigation should be avoided wherever possible. Participants should never be deliberately misled without extremely strong scientific or medical justification.

5. Debriefing

In the studies where the participants are aware that they have taken part in an investigation, when the data have been collected, the investigator should provide the participants with any necessary information to complete their understanding of the nature of the research in order to monitor any unforeseen negative effects or misconceptions.

6. Withdrawal from the investigation

At the onset of the investigation investigators should make plain to participants their right to withdraw from the research at any time, irrespective of whether or not payment or other inducement has been offered. In the light of experience of the investigation or as a result of debriefing, the participant has the right to withdraw retrospectively any consent given, and to require that their own data be destroyed.

7. Confidentiality

Subject to the requirements of legislation, information obtained about a participant during an investigation is confidential unless otherwise agreed in advance. Investigators who are put under pressure to disclose confidential information should draw this point to the attention of those exerting such pressure.

8. Protection of participants

Investigators have a primary responsibility to protect participants from physical and mental harm during the investigation. Normally the risk of harm must be no greater than in ordinary life, i.e. participants should not be exposed to risks greater than or additional to those encountered in their normal lifestyles.

Where research may involve behaviour or experiences that participants may regard as personal and private, the participants must be protected from stress by all appropriate measures, including the assurance that answers to personal questions need not be given. In research involving children, great caution should be exercised when discussing the results with parents, teachers, or those in *loco parentis*, as evaluative statements may carry unintended weight.

9. Observational research

Studies based on observation must respect the privacy and psychological well-being of the individuals studied. Unless those being observed give their consent to being observed, observational research is only acceptable in situations where those observed would expect to be observed by strangers.

10. Giving advice

During research, an investigator may obtain evidence of psychological or physical problems of which a participant is apparently unaware. In such cases the investigator has a responsibility to inform the participant if the investigator believes that by not doing so the participant's future well-being may be endangered.

This flow chart shows ethical decisions to be taken by researchers designing a psychological study.

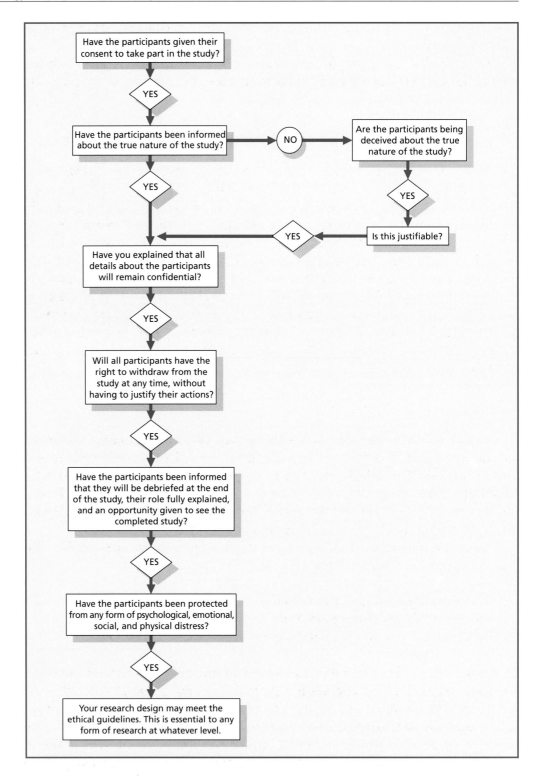

Limitations of ethical guidelines

In reality most professional guidelines have only some force. A person who infringes the code is not committing a crime, although they may well be barred from the professional organisation. There are other drawbacks. The establishment of a set of ethical guidelines enshrines its principles and may close off discussions regarding more appropriate solutions to a particular ethical dilemma. The code makes it seem as if there are ethical "truths", whereas the fact that such guidelines are constantly reviewed, and that they vary from one country to another (see later), indicates that

Without ethical guidelines, how difficult would it be to express misgivings about questionable research methods?

there are no universal ethical truths (Gale, 1995). This is partly because of changing social attitudes.

Ethical codes may also take personal responsibility away from the individual researcher, and may invite individuals to find loopholes and "play the system" (Homan, 1991).

The cost–benefit analysis

Diener and Crandall (1978) suggested the following drawbacks to the cost–benefit approach that underlies much psychological research. The cost–benefit approach involves weighing up the potential findings of the research (benefits) against the potential harm (costs). First of all it is difficult, if not impossible, to predict both costs and benefits prior to conducting a study. Second, even after the study it is hard to quantify them, partly because it can depend on who is making the judgements. A participant may judge the costs differently from the researcher, and benefits may be judged differently in years to come. Finally, cost–benefit analyses tend to ignore the substantive rights of individuals in favour of practical, utilitarian considerations.

Baumrind (1975) has made the point that cost–benefit analyses inevitably lead to moral dilemmas, yet the function of ethical guidelines is precisely to avoid such dilemmas.

Cross-cultural comparisons

Kimmel (1996) compared the ethical codes produced by 11 different countries. An ethical code in psychology was first published in the United States in 1953. Several other countries (Australia, France, Germany, and the Netherlands) followed in the 1960s. The United Kingdom had its first ethical code in psychology in 1978, followed by Slovenia (1982), Canada (1986), and Scandinavia (1989). Finally, Spain and Switzerland produced ethical codes in the early 1990s.

There are important similarities among the ethical codes produced by the various countries. Most focus on three basic principles:

1. Protection of individuals from physical harm.
2. Protection of individuals from psychological harm.
3. Confidentiality of the data obtained from individual participants.

It is argued in nearly all of the ethical codes that informed consent and avoidance of deception are important in ensuring that the first two principles are achieved.

There are some differences in the ethical codes adopted by different countries. The French ethical code emphasises the fundamental rights of individuals, but has little to say about the ways in which research should be conducted, or on the importance of informed consent. The British ethical code differs from many others in that it is mainly concerned with research rather than the ethical issues posed by the professional activities of clinical psychologists. The ethical code in the Netherlands contains many very general statements, and so is hard to use in practice. One example is as follows: "The psychologist shall not employ methods that are in any way detrimental to the client's dignity or that penetrate into the client's private life deeper than is necessary for the objectives set." Another example is: "The psychologist shall do everything within his power to ensure that the client is entirely free to decide in a responsible manner whether to enter into the professional relationship."

You have reached the end of the chapter on social psychology. Social psychology is an approach or perspective in psychology. The material in this chapter has exemplified the way that social psychologists explain behaviour. They look at behaviour in terms of the ways in which other people affect our behaviour. Nowhere is this clearer than in social influence research. Ancient astrologers believed that people's actions were affected by an airy fluid that flowed down from the heavenly bodies. This fluid force-field was called *"influentia"*. The concept of influences comes from this—they are both invisible and very powerful, as we have seen.

There is a valuable feature of the American and Canadian ethical codes that is absent from the other nine. These two codes made use of an empirical approach, in which professional psychologists were asked to indicate how they personally resolved ethical issues. As a result, the American and Canadian codes contain case examples and applications of key research principles. These concrete examples make it easier for psychologists to follow ethical principles in the ways intended.

CHAPTER SUMMARY

Conformity and minority influence

❖ Conformity is usually but not always a desirable social influence.

❖ The two main explanations for conformity are that we conform to gain information (informational social influence) and to be liked (normative social influence). Only informational influence is likely to change private opinion. Conformity can also be described in terms of compliance (group acceptance), identification (group membership), and internalisation (acceptance of group norms and change of private opinion).

❖ Individuals often comply with the majority whereas they are converted by the minority. The likely conditions for minority influence are: consistency, flexibility, commitment, and relevance of minority arguments.

❖ Social impact theory can be used to explain both majority and minority influence. The theory proposes that social influence can be related to: strength, number and status, and immediacy.

❖ We can further explain conformity in terms of the factors that influence it. People differ in the extent of their conformity as a consequence of situational or dispositional factors. Examples of situational factors are culture (historical and ethnicity) and deindividuation. Examples of dispositional (personality) factors include the need for personal control and gender effects. Non-conformity can be explained in terms of reactance.

Obedience to authority

❖ Obedience to authority is usually a desirable social influence, except when the command is unjust. Obedience is generally a positive response to social instruction. But when the request is unjust, as with Nazis, then we are concerned. Milgram's experiment concerned obedience to unjust authority.

❖ Obedience and conformity differ in terms of the source of the social pressure, and the extent to which private opinion is changed.

❖ The classic study of obedience was conducted by Milgram, demonstrating that people are far more obedient than we would imagine. Milgram conducted many variations of the original experiment. The main criticisms of his research concern the lack of experimental and ecological validity, and the contravention of ethical codes.

❖ Experimental validity concerns the extent to which a participant believes in the experimental manipulation and therefore the extent to which the participant's behaviour can tell us anything about real behaviour. The role of demand characteristics and social contracts are important considerations.

❖ Ecological validity is the extent to which the results of a study can be applied to other situations and other individuals. Laboratory experiments are seen as artificial and unreal (lacking mundane realism). However, if such experiments have experimental realism this may make them ecologically valid (if participants regard the experimental situation as real, then it is not artificial). Further support for ecological validity comes from research in American and in other cultural settings that has replicated Milgram's study and found similar results; this shows that the findings can be applied to other situations and other people.

❖ The ethical issues raised by Milgram's research include: distress, deception, and lack of informed consent and the right to withdraw from the experiment. Milgram responded to the ethical objections with the following: the distress could be excused on the grounds that it was not anticipated nor did there appear to be any long-term harm. Deception can be excused as a trade-off between means and ends. Informed consent was replaced by presumptive consent, and helped through subsequent debriefing. The right to withdraw was in fact available. Both Milgram and Aronson argued that people made ethical objections because of the actual (distasteful) findings, not because of the methods used.

❖ There are dispositional and situational explanations for obedience (as there were for conformity). Situational explanations include: being in a socially obedient environment, making graduated commitments, and being in an agentic state (a state caused by external events). The authoritarian personality is an example of a dispositional explanation for obedience. Individuals with authoritarian personalities have repressed their hostility towards controlling parents and remain submissive to authority.

❖ A more positive focus for research is to consider the factors surrounding independent behaviour. This again can be explained in terms of situational or dispositional factors. Situational factors include the presence of other dissenters, and the possibility of collective action as in Gamson's study.

Dispositional factors include need for social approval, self-esteem, gender, and personal control.

❖ The unexpected nature of Milgram's findings should give us pause for thought. Our surprise may be explained in terms of the fundamental attribution error. It was the situation, rather than personality factors, which can explain the behaviour of the participants.

Critical issue—
Ethical issues in
psychological research

❖ The term ethics is used when considering moral behaviour among professionals. There are three key ethical issues: deception, informed consent, and protection from harm. These apply especially to research in social psychology.

❖ Deception is not desirable but sometimes necessary. It is not always harmful, such as in research involving incidental learning. Objections can be overcome by conducting role-playing experiments and carrying out adequate debriefing.

❖ Participants should be given the opportunity to provide informed consent. However, it is not always possible, as is the case with research that involves children or deception, in field experiments, or retrospective case studies. Informed consent may be an unrealistic ideal in any study. Informed consent can be obtained using presumptive consent or prior general consent, as well as the right to withhold data as a kind of retrospective informed consent.

❖ Participants should be protected from both physical and psychological harm, this includes the right to confidentiality and the right to privacy. Psychologists can assume that anything that occurs during "ordinary life" would not constitute "harm".

❖ An ethical code or set of guidelines is developed by separate professional bodies as a means of judging what behaviour is or is not acceptable to that professional group. In this country the British Psychology Society (BPS) regularly produces updated versions of ethical guidelines for psychologists.

❖ Ethical guidelines have limitations in terms of their enforcement and the image they portray of being objective and universal. They remove personal responsibility from the researcher.

❖ Cost–benefit analyses may not be workable because such evaluations are hard to quantify before or after a study. There are many cross-cultural similarities in ethical guidelines but also some differences. Case studies may be a useful way of demonstrating how to resolve ethical issues.

FURTHER READING

Most of the topics discussed in this chapter are dealt with in various chapters in M. Hewstone, W. Stroebe, and G.M. Stephenson (Eds.) (1996) *Introduction to social psychology* (Oxford, UK: Blackwell). Two other books providing good coverage of social influence are as follows: N. Hayes (1994) *Principles of social psychology* (Hove, UK: Psychology Press), and S.L. Franzoi (1996) *Social psychology* (Chicago: Brown & Benchmark). Ethical issues are discussed in M.W. Eysenck (1994) *Perspectives on psychology* (Hove, UK: Psychology Press). Anyone who is considering carrying out any kind of study on human participants is strongly urged to consult the following before proceeding: British Psychological Society (1993) Ethical principles for conducting research with human participants. *The Psychologist, 6,* 33–35.

Revision Questions

The examination questions aim to *sample* the material in this whole chapter. For advice on how to answer such questions, refer to Chapter 1, Section 3. You will always have a choice of two questions in the AQA AS-level exam and 30 minutes in which to answer the question you choose:

Question 1

a. Distinguish between minority and majority influence.   (3 marks + 3 marks)

b. Describe *one* study that demonstrates conformity to majority influence.   (6 marks)

c. Give *two* explanations for why people conform to majority influence.   (6 marks)

d. "Milgram's experiments have been criticised for their lack of ecological validity and ethical infringements but the same comments could be applied to other studies of obedience." To what extent do studies of obedience infringe ethical guidelines?   (12 marks)

Question 2

a. Explain what is meant by experimental and ecological validity.   (3 marks + 3 marks)

b. Describe *two* studies that demonstrate obedience to authority.   (6 marks + 6 marks)

c. "When one thinks of conformity, one thinks of conforming to a majority yet there is evidence that even one individual can create a conformity effect." To what extent can conformity be explained in terms of minority rather than majority influence?   (12 marks)

Research Methods

Everyone has opinions about human behaviour. For example, your dad might say:

"Children today have no respect for their elders. It's because they see everyone behaving like that on Eastenders and they just imitate it."

"I know why he did it! His mother treated him badly when he was young and so he now wants to punish all women."

In a sense we are all "armchair psychologists". However, actual psychologists rely on research evidence as a way to support their opinions. This is what differentiates psychology from "anecdote". Psychologists don't just present theories about why people behave as they do, but they also seek to support or challenge these theories with **research**. Research can be defined as any attempt to study a problem systematically. It includes experiments, interviews, and case studies. Throughout this book we have relied on such evidence as a means of analysing theories. In this chapter of the book we will consider the different methods used to conduct research, as well as other important features of the research process.

What methods might be used to measure the effect of violent TV on viewers?

- *Section 19: Quantitative and qualitative research methods.* Some research methods aim to quantify behaviour (count frequencies) whereas other methods focus more on experience (called qualitative research). In this section we consider the relative advantages and weaknesses of both kinds of quantitative and qualitative methods, as well as their usage and the ethical issues raised by each method.
- *Section 20: Research design and implementation.* In order to conduct meaningful research psychologists have developed standard procedures that aim to avoid bias. In this section we consider some of these procedures, such as specifying aims and hypotheses, designing research, improving and measuring reliability and validity, and selecting participants.
- *Section 21: Data analysis.* A key aspect of the research process is the final interpretation of the results. Statistical methods, such as using the mean or looking at graphical representation, enable us to interpret research findings and draw conclusions.

SECTION 19
Quantitative and Qualitative Research Methods

The Scientific Approach

In common with other **sciences**, psychology is concerned with theories and with data. All sciences share one fundamental feature: they aim to discover facts about the world by using systematic and objective methods of investigation. The research process starts with casual observations about one feature of the world, for example, that people imitate the violence they see on television. These observations collectively form a **theory** (a general explanation or account of certain findings or data). Theories invariably produce a number of further expectations (for example, if people imitate aggression on television, they are also likely to imitate other things such as helpful behaviour). These expectations can be stated as a **research hypothesis**. A hypothesis is a formal and unambiguous statement about what you believe to be true. It is stated with the purpose of attempting to prove or disprove it. And that is what scientists conduct research to do—prove or disprove their hypotheses. If it is disproved, then the theory has to be adjusted, and a new hypothesis produced, and tested, and so on. This process is shown in the diagram below.

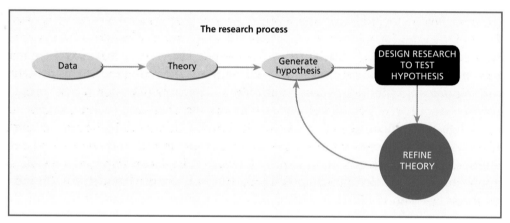

The research process

Data → Theory → Generate hypothesis → DESIGN RESEARCH TO TEST HYPOTHESIS → REFINE THEORY

Psychologists spend a lot of their time collecting data in order to test various hypotheses. Most people assume that this data collection involves experiments carried out under laboratory conditions, and it is true that literally millions of laboratory experiments have been carried out in psychology. However, psychologists make use of many different methods of investigation, each of which can provide useful information about human behaviour.

The Experimental Method

The method of investigation used most often by psychologists is the experimental method. It is by no means the only scientific method but it is perhaps the most scientific because it is claimed to be highly objective and systematic.

Dependent and independent variables

In order to understand what is involved in the experimental method, we will consider a concrete example. Suppose that a psychologist wants to know if loud,

As you read through the various methods of investigation, it is natural to wonder which methods are the best. In some ways, it may be useful to compare the methods used by psychologists to the clubs used by the golf professional. The driver is not a better or worse club than the putter, it is simply used for a different purpose. In a similar way, each method of investigation used by psychologists is very useful for testing some hypotheses, but may be of little or no use for testing other hypotheses.

continuous noise will have a disruptive effect on the performance of a memory task. This would lead the psychologist to formulate a hypothesis: "loud, continuous noise reduces performance of a memory task".

In order to test this hypothesis, the experimenter would probably compare the performance of one group of people who are exposed to a lot of noise with the performance of other people who hear less noise.

This hypothesis refers to two **variables**: the amount of noise and the performance of the people doing the task. Both of these things will vary during the course of the test. One of the variables is directly manipulated by the experimenter. This is called the **independent variable** (IV). In our example, the independent variable would be the level of noise. The other variable is the one that is affected by the independent variable, and it is called the **dependent variable** (DV). In our example, it would be an assessment of how well each individual does on the named task. The dependent variable is some aspect of behaviour that is going to be measured or assessed. It is called *dependent* because it depends on something the experimenter controls. We assess the dependent variable because then we can decide whether or not the independent variable did cause a change in behaviour.

A variable is something that varies! How long you sleep each night is a variable whereas the number of days in a week is a fixed quantity.

> The experimental process can be summarised thus:
> - Experimenter acts on IV
> - Changes in IV lead to changes in DV
> - Changes in DV measured by experimenter

Experimental control

We come now to the most important principle of the experimental method: control. The independent variable is manipulated, the dependent variable is free to vary, but all other variables must be *controlled*, i.e. kept constant. This permits us to assume that the only variable that is causing any subsequent change in the dependent variable *must* be the independent variable. In terms of our example, we might expose one group of participants to very intense noise, and a second group to no noise. What would we need to do to ensure that any difference in the performance of the two groups was due to the noise rather than any other factor? We would control all other aspects of the situation (variables) by, for example, always using the same room for the experiment, keeping the temperature the same, and having the same lighting.

Confounding variables

The variables that are controlled are called **confounding variables**. These are variables that may get in the way of the link between the independent and dependent variable. For example, suppose that the participants exposed to intense noise performed the task in poor lighting conditions, so that they could hardly see what they were doing, whereas those exposed to no noise enjoyed good lighting conditions. If the former group performed much worse than the latter group, we would not know whether this was due to the intense noise, the poor lighting, or some combination of the two. In this example, the variation in lighting is a confounding variable which needs to be controlled. The presence of any confounding variables has grave consequences, because it prevents us from being able to interpret our findings. Confounding variables must be controlled.

You might think that it would be easy to ensure that there were no confounding variables in an experiment. However, there are many well-known experiments containing confounding variables. Consider, for example, the study by Jenkins and Dallenbach (1924), described on page 52. They gave a learning task to a group of

Participants in a psychological experiment should be tested under constant controlled conditions (e.g. consistent lighting, temperature, and sound levels).

The type of experimenter could act as a confounding variable. Some participants may feel more comfortable than others in the study situation...

participants in the morning, and then tested their memory for the material later in the day. The same learning task was given to a second group of participants in the evening, and their memory was tested the following morning after a night's sleep.

What did Jenkins and Dallenbach find? Memory performance was much higher for the second group than for the first. They argued that this was due to there being less interference with memory when people are asleep than when they are awake. Can you see the flaw in this argument? The two groups learned the material at different times of day, and so time of day was a confounding variable. Hockey et al. (1972) discovered many years later that the time of day at which learning occurs is much more important than whether or not the participants sleep between learning and the memory test.

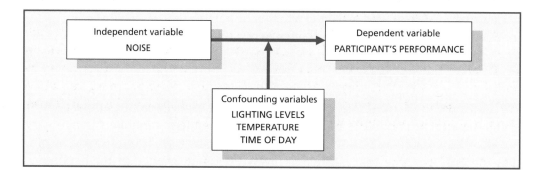

Participants and settings

Proper use of the experimental method requires careful consideration of the ways in which the participants are allocated to the various conditions. Suppose that the participants exposed to intense noise (Group 1) were on average much less intelligent than those exposed to no noise (Group 2). We would then be unable to tell whether poorer performance by group 1 was due to the intense noise or to their low intelligence. The main way of guarding against this possibility is by means of **randomisation**, in which the participants are allocated at random to the two conditions.

Numerous studies are carried out using students as participants. This raises the issue of whether students are representative of society as a whole. For example, it is possible that students would be less distracted than other people by intense noise because they are used to studying over long periods of time in conditions that can be noisy, such as halls of residence.

How else do you think students, as research participants, might differ from society in general?

Advantages of the experimental method

Causal relationships

What is generally regarded as the greatest advantage of the experimental method is that it allows us to establish cause and effect relationships. In the terms we have been using, the independent variable in an experiment is often regarded as a cause, and the dependent variable is the effect. We assume that, if y (e.g. poor performance) follows x (e.g. intense noise), then it is reasonable to infer that x caused y.

We can see why findings from studies based on the experimental method do not necessarily establish causality from the following imaginary example. An experiment on malaria is carried out in a hot country. Half of the participants sleep in bedrooms with the windows open, and the other half sleep in bedrooms with the windows closed. Those who are put in bedrooms with the windows open are found to be more likely to catch malaria. It would obviously be wrong to argue that having the window open caused malaria. Having the window open or closed is relevant to catching the disease, but it tells us nothing directly about the major causal factor in malaria (infected mosquitoes).

Can you think of another example of a situation in which a wrong causal inference could be made, i.e. y followed x, but x did not cause y?

Replication

The other major advantage of the experimental method concerns what is known as **replication**. If an experiment has been conducted in a carefully controlled way, it should be possible for other researchers to repeat or replicate the findings obtained from that experiment. There have been numerous failures to replicate using the experimental method, but the essential point is that the chances of replication are greater when the experimental method is used than when it is not because experiments are well controlled.

Replication is important in order to confirm an experimental result. If the result is "real", then it should be possible to obtain the same result when you repeat the experiment. If the result of one experiment was a fluke, then it is not likely to be repeatable. Therefore, it is highly desirable in research to be able to replicate a study using precisely the same techniques and conditions. If the conditions aren't the same, that may explain why the results are not the same.

Methodological issues: What are the main obstacles to replication in research using human participants?

Disadvantages of the experimental method

Artificiality

The artificiality of laboratory experimentation was emphasised by Heather (1976, pp.31–33):

> *Psychologists have attempted to squeeze the study of human life into a laboratory situation where it becomes unrecognisably different from its naturally occurring form … Experiments in psychology … are social situations involving strangers, and it might be suggested that the main kind of knowledge gleaned from years of experimentation with human [participants] is information about how strangers interact in the highly artificial and unusual setting of the psychological experiment.*

How much does it matter that laboratory experiments are artificial? As Coolican (1998) pointed out, "In scientific investigation, it is often *necessary* to create artificial circumstances in order to *isolate* a hypothesised effect." If we are interested in studying basic cognitive processes, such as those involved in perception or attention, then the artificiality of the laboratory is unlikely to affect the results. On the other hand, if we are interested in studying social behaviour,

If participants know they are being watched this may affect their behaviour. Zegoib et al. (1975) found that mothers behaved in a warmer and more patient way with their children when they knew they were being observed than when they did not.

then the issue of artificiality does matter. For example, Zegoib, Arnold, and Forehand (1975) found that mothers behaved in a warmer and more patient way with their children when they knew they were being observed than in situations when they did not.

Carlsmith et al. (1976) drew a distinction between **mundane realism** and **experimental realism**, as we have already discussed in Chapter 6. Mundane realism refers to experiments in which the situation is set up to resemble situations often found in everyday life. In contrast, experimental realism refers to experiments in which the situation may be rather artificial, but the experimental set-up is sufficiently interesting to produce full involvement from the participants. Milgram's (1974) research on obedience to authority is a good example of high experimental realism which therefore compensates for the possibly lower mundane realism (see Chapter 6). The key point is that experimental realism may be more important than mundane realism in producing findings that generalise to real-life situations.

If Milgram's experiment is an example of experimental realism, can you think of an example of mundane realism?

The effects of being observed

An important reason why laboratory experiments are more artificial than other research methods is because the participants in laboratory experiments are aware that their behaviour is being observed. As Silverman (1977) pointed out, "Virtually the only condition in which a [participant] in a psychological study will not behave as a [participant] is if he does not know he is in one." One consequence of being observed is that the participants try to work out the experimenter's hypothesis, and then act accordingly. In this connection, Orne (1962) emphasised the importance of **demand characteristics**, which are "the totality of cues which convey an experimental hypothesis to the [participants]." More simply stated, they are the features of an experiment that "invite" participants to behave in certain predictable ways. Orne found that the participants in one of his studies were willing to spend several hours adding numbers on random number sheets and then tearing up each completed sheet. Presumably the participants interpreted the experiment as a test of endurance, and this motivated them to keep going.

Psychology students often use other psychology students as the participants in their research. What problems are likely to arise, for example, in terms of evaluation apprehension and demand characteristics?

Another consequence of the participants in laboratory experiments knowing they are being observed is **evaluation apprehension**. Rosenberg (1965) defined this as "an active anxiety-toned concern that [the participant] will win a positive evaluation from the experimenter or at least that [the participant] will provide no grounds for a negative one."

Sigall, Aronson, and Van Hoose (1970) contrasted the effects of demand characteristics and evaluation apprehension on the task of copying telephone numbers. The experimenter told participants doing the task for the second time that he expected them to perform it at a rate that was actually slower than their previous performance. Adherence to the demand characteristics would have led to slow performance, whereas evaluation apprehension and the need to be capable would have produced fast times. The participants actually performed more quickly than they had done before, indicating the greater importance of evaluation apprehension.

This conclusion was strengthened by the findings from a second condition, in which the experimenter

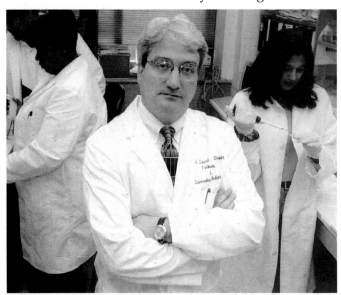

Participants in psychological experiments usually try to perform the task set by the experimenter as well as they can, in order to gain his or her approval.

not only said that he expected the participants to perform at a slower rate, but also told them that those who rush are probably obsessive-compulsive. The participants in this condition performed the task slowly, because they wanted to be evaluated positively.

Experiments and ethical issues

Ethical issues in psychological research are discussed in detail in Chapter 6, Section 18. What we will do here is to discuss a few ethical issues that are of special relevance to laboratory experiments. In an experiment, there is a danger that the participants will be willing to behave in a laboratory in ways they would not behave elsewhere. For example, Milgram (1974) found in his work on obedience to authority that 65% of his participants were prepared to give very intense electric shocks to someone else when the experiment took place in a laboratory at Yale University. In contrast, the figure was only 48% when the same study was carried out in a run-down office building. Thus, participants are often willing to do what they would not normally do in the setting of a prestigeful laboratory.

Another ethical issue that applies especially to laboratory experiments concerns the participant's **right to withdraw** from the experiment at any time. It is general practice to inform participants of this right at the start of the experiment. However, participants may feel reluctant to exercise this right if they think it will cause serious disruption to the experimenter's research.

> **Laboratory experiments**
>
> Advantages:
> - Establishes cause and effect relationships
> - Allows for replication
> - Good control of confounding variables
>
> Limitations:
> - Artificial
> - Participants know they are being observed (demand characteristics and evaluation apprehension)
> - Low in external validity
> - Ethical concerns, such as the right to withdraw

Field Experiments

Many people associate the idea of an "experiment" with laboratories, but some experiments are not conducted in laboratories. These are called **field experiments**, experiments carried out in natural settings such as in the street, in a school, or at work. Some of the advantages of the experimental method are shared by both laboratory and field experiments, whereas other advantages and limitations are specific to one type of experiment. Field experiments, like laboratory experiments, involve direct control of the independent variable by the experimenter and also direct allocation of participants to conditions. This means that causal relationships can be determined. Field experiments are also reasonably well controlled which means that they can be replicated.

As an example of a field experiment, let us consider a study by Shotland and Straw (1976). They arranged for a man and a woman to stage an argument and a fight fairly close to a number of bystanders. In one condition, the woman screamed, "I don't know you." In a second condition, she screamed, "I don't know why I ever married you!" When the bystanders thought the fight involved strangers, 65% of them intervened, against only 19% when they thought it involved a married couple. Thus, the experiment showed that people were less likely to lend a helping hand when it was a "lovers' quarrel" than when it was not. The bystanders were convinced that the fight was

When bystanders saw a staged fight in an experiment by Shotland and Straw (1976) they were more likely to help when they thought two strangers were involved than if they thought the couple were married.

genuine, as was shown by the fact that 30% of the women were so alarmed that they shut the doors of their rooms, turned off the lights, and locked their doors.

Laboratory vs. field experiments

The greatest advantage of laboratory experiments over field experiments is that it is generally easier to eliminate confounding variables in the laboratory than in the field. The experimenter is unlikely to be able to control every aspect of a natural situation.

Another clear advantage of laboratory experiments over field experiments is that it is much easier to obtain large amounts of very detailed information from participants in the laboratory. For example, it is hard to see how information about participants' physiological activity or speed of performing a range of complex cognitive tasks could be obtained in a field experiment carried out in a natural setting. There are two main reasons why field experiments are limited in this way. First, it is not generally possible to introduce bulky equipment into a natural setting. Second, the participants in a field experiment are likely to realise they are taking part in an experiment if attempts are made to obtain a lot of information from them, and then the study loses its "naturalness".

One of the advantages of field experiments over laboratory experiments is that the behaviour of the participants is often more *typical* of their normal behaviour and therefore less artificial. In other words, field experiments tend to have greater external validity.

The respective strengths and weaknesses of laboratory experiments and field experiments can be summed up with reference to the two different kinds of validity: **experimental (or internal) validity** and **ecological (or external) validity**. Internal validity refers to the validity of an experiment within the confines of the context in which it is carried out, whereas external validity refers to the validity of an experiment outside the research situation itself. Laboratory experiments tend to be high in internal validity but low in external validity, whereas field experiments are high in external validity but low in internal validity.

Field experiments and ethical issues

So far as field experiments are concerned, the main ethical issue relates to the principle of voluntary informed consent, which is regarded as central to ethical human research (see Chapter 6, Section 18). By their very nature, most field experiments do not lend themselves to obtaining informed consent from the participants. For example, the study by Shotland and Straw (1976) would have been rendered almost meaningless if the participants had been asked beforehand to give their consent to witnessing a staged quarrel! In addition, the participants in that study could reasonably have complained about being exposed to a violent quarrel.

Another ethical issue with field experiments is that it is not possible in most field experiments to tell the participants that they have the right to withdraw at any time without offering a reason. It is also difficult to offer **debriefing**.

Field experiments

Advantages:

- Establishes cause and effect relationships
- Allows for replication
- Behaviour of participants more typical than in a laboratory experiment, high external validity

Limitations:

- Ethical issues, such as a lack of voluntary informed consent
- Low in internal validity, poor control

Quasi-experiments

"True" experiments based on the experimental method provide the best way of being able to draw causal inferences with confidence. However, it is often the case that there are practical or ethical reasons why it is simply not possible to carry out a **true experiment**. In such circumstances, investigators often carry out what is known as a **quasi-experiment**. Quasi-experimental designs "resemble experiments but are weak on some of the characteristics" (Raulin & Graziano, 1994). There are two main ways in which quasi-experiments tend to fall short of being true experiments:

- *Direct manipulation.* The manipulation of the independent variable is often not under the control of the experimenter.
- *Random allocation.* It is usually not possible to allocate the participants randomly to groups.

There are numerous hypotheses in psychology that can only be studied by means of quasi-experiments rather than true experiments. For example, suppose that we are interested in studying the effects of divorce on young children. We could do this by comparing children whose parents had divorced with those whose parents were still married. There would, of course, be no possibility of allocating children at random to the divorced or non-divorced parent groups! Studies in which pre-existing groups are compared often qualify as quasi-experiments. Examples of such quasi-experiments would be comparing the learning performance of males and females (gender is the independent variable), or comparing the social behaviour of introverted and extraverted individuals (personality is the independent variable).

A true experiment involves manipulation of the IV by the experimenter. How is a quasi-experiment different?

Natural experiments

In the studies just described, use is made of pre-existing groups of people. We might also make use of a naturally occurring event for research purposes. Such **natural experiments** are a kind of quasi-experiment. Do such studies qualify as genuine experiments? The answer is "No". Use of the experimental method requires that the independent variable is *manipulated* by the experimenter, but clearly the experimenter cannot decide whether a given person is going to be male or female for the purposes of the study!

An example of a natural experiment is a study by Williams (1986) on the effects of television on aggressive behaviour in Canadian children aged between 6 and 11 years. Three communities were compared: one in which television had just been introduced, one in which there was only one television channel, and one in which there were several channels. The children in the first community showed a significant increase in verbal and physical aggression during the first two years after television was introduced, whereas those in the other two communities did not. This was not a true experiment, because the children were not allocated randomly to the three conditions or communities. The naturally occurring event was the availability of television.

Adams and Adams (1984) carried out a natural experiment following the eruption of the Mount St. Helens volcano in 1980. As the volcanic eruption had been predicted, they were able to assess the inhabitants of the nearby small town of Othello before and after it happened. There was a 50% increase in mental health appointments, a 198% increase in stress-aggravated illness, and a 235% increase in diagnoses of mental illness.

Adams and Adams (1984) designed a natural experiment around the eruption of the Mount St. Helens volcano in which they assessed the effects of stress on the population of a small town threatened by the eruption.

What might be the practical uses of results such as those from the Mount St. Helen's study?

Advantages of natural experiments

The main advantage is that the participants in natural experiments are often not aware that they are taking part in an experiment, even though they are likely to know that their behaviour is being observed. This means that they behave more naturally. Another advantage of natural experiments is that they allow us to study the effects on behaviour of independent variables that it would be unethical for the experimenter to manipulate. For example, in the Mount St. Helens study, Adams and Adams (1984) were interested in observing the effects of a major stressor on physical and mental illness. No ethical committee would have allowed them to expose their participants deliberately to stressors that might cause mental illness, but they were able to take advantage of a natural disaster to conduct a natural experiment.

Limitations of natural experiments

The greatest limitation occurs because the participants have not been assigned at random to conditions. As a result, observed differences in behaviour between groups may be due to differences in the types of participants in the groups rather than to the effects of the independent variable. Consider, for example, the study by Williams (1986) described earlier. The children in the community that had just been exposed to television *might* have been naturally more aggressive than the children in the other community.

It is usually possible to check whether the participants in the various conditions are comparable. For example, they can be compared with respect to variables such as age, sex, socioeconomic status, and so on. If the groups do differ significantly in some respects irrelevant to the independent variable, then this greatly complicates the task of interpreting the findings of a natural experiment.

The other major limitation of natural experiments involves the independent variable. In some natural experiments, it is hard to know exactly what aspects of the independent variable have caused any effects on behaviour. For example, there is no doubt that the eruption of Mount St. Helens was a major stressor. It caused stress in part because of the possibility that it might erupt again and produce more physical devastation. However, social factors were also probably involved. If people in Othello observed that one of their neighbours was highly anxious because of the eruption, this may have heightened their level of anxiety.

Natural experiments and ethical issues

It can be argued that there are fewer ethical issues with natural experiments than with many other kinds of research. The reason is that the experimenter is not responsible for the fact that the participants have been exposed to the independent variable. However, natural experiments can raise various ethical issues. First, there can be the question of voluntary informed consent, in view of the fact that

■ Activity: In groups of three, design a summary table to illustrate the ethical issues involved in laboratory, field, and natural experiments, with each group member taking one type of experiment then reporting back to the group.

QUASI-EXPERIMENTS

Advantages	Limitations
• Participants behave naturally	• IV not directly manipulated
• Investigates the effects of independent variables that it would be unethical to manipulate	• Participants not allocated at random to conditions
	• Difficult to identify what aspects of the independent variable have caused the effects on behaviour
	• Requires ethical sensitivity

the participants are often not aware that they are taking part in an experiment. Second, experimenters carrying out natural experiments need to be sensitive to the situation in which the participants find themselves. People who have been exposed to a natural disaster such as a volcanic eruption may resent it if experimenters start asking them detailed questions about their mental health or psychological well-being.

Studies Using Correlational Analysis

Suppose that we were interested in the hypothesis that watching violence on television leads to aggressive behaviour. One way of testing this hypothesis would be to obtain two kinds of information from a number of people: (1) the amount of violent television they watched, and (2) the extent to which they behaved aggressively in various situations. If the hypothesis is correct, then we would expect that those who have seen the most violence on television would tend to be the most aggressive. In technical terms, this study would be looking for a **correlation**, or association, between watching violent programmes and being aggressive. The closer the link between them, the greater would be the correlation or association.

The issue of whether or not there is a correlation between violence on television and aggressive behaviour is frequently debated in the media.

One of the best-known uses of the correlational approach is in the study of the role of **nature and nurture** in intelligence. What is done is to assess the intelligence of pairs of identical twins. As they are genetically identical we would expect their IQs to be quite similar (if nature has the greater influence). If one twin has a high IQ we would expect the other one to have a high IQ, and if one twin has a low IQ we would expect his/her twin to have a similarly low IQ. As predicted, the correlation between IQs is generally very high for identical twins. In this study the **co-variables** are the IQ of twin 1 and twin 2. These two numbers vary together.

The term "concordance" is used to describe high correlation between two things.

Limitations of correlational studies

Correlational designs are generally regarded as inferior to experimental designs, because it is hard (or impossible) to establish cause and effect. In our example, the existence of an association between the amount of television violence watched and aggressive behaviour would certainly be consistent with the hypothesis that watching violent programmes can *cause* aggressive behaviour. However, there are other possible interpretations of the data. It could equally be that aggressive individuals may choose to watch more violent programmes than those who are less aggressive, in other words the causality operates in the other direction. Another possible interpretation could be that there is a third variable which accounts for the association between the variables of interest, i.e. watching violent programmes and aggressive behaviour. For example, people in disadvantaged families may watch more television programmes of all kinds than those in non-disadvantaged families, and their deprived circumstances may also cause them to behave aggressively. If that were the case, then the

Correlation or causation?

number of violent television programmes watched might have no direct effect at all on aggressive behaviour.

Advantages of correlational studies

In spite of the interpretive problems posed by the findings of correlational studies, there are several reasons why psychologists continue to use this method. First, many hypotheses cannot be examined directly by means of experimental designs. For example, the hypothesis that smoking causes a number of physical diseases cannot be tested by forcing some people to smoke and forcing others not to smoke! All that can be done is to examine correlations or associations between the number of cigarettes smoked and the probability of suffering from various diseases. Such a study might start with the hypothesis that "smoking is related to ill health", and a correlational study would obtain data for each individual about, for example, the amount they smoke and the number of times they are absent from work through the year (as a measure of their ill health).

Second, it is often possible to obtain large amounts of data on a number of variables in a correlational study much more rapidly and efficiently than would be possible using experimental designs. Use of a questionnaire, for example, would permit a researcher to investigate the associations between aggressive behaviour and a wide range of activities (such as watching violent films in the cinema, reading violent books, being frustrated at work or at home).

Third, correlational research *can* produce definite information about causal relationships if there is *no* association between the two co-variables. For example, if it were found that there was no association at all between the amount of violent television a person watched and the extent that their behaviour might be classified as aggressive, this would provide fairly strong evidence that aggressive behaviour is *not* caused by watching violent programmes on television.

When would one have to use a correlational design?

Correlational studies and ethical issues

There is the possibility that the public at large will misinterpret the findings from correlational studies. For example, the finding that there was a correlation between the amount of television violence watched by children and their level of aggression led many influential people to argue that television violence was having a damaging effect. In other words, they mistakenly supposed that correlational evidence can demonstrate a causal relation. Television companies may have suffered from such over-interpretation of findings. This is especially important because correlational analyses are often used in socially sensitive research, that is research that raises political and/or social issues. For example,

---

CORRELATIONAL STUDIES

Advantages
- Allows study of hypotheses that cannot be examined directly
- More data on more variables can be collected more quickly than in an experimental set-up
- Problems of interpretation are reduced when no association is found

Limitations
- Interpretation of results is difficult
- Cause and effect cannot be established
- Direction of causality is uncertain
- Variables other than the one of interest may be operating

consider the correlational evidence suggesting that individual differences in intelligence depend in part on genetic factors. Some people have argued, mistakenly, that this implies that *race* differences in intelligence also depend on genetic factors. The key ethical issue here (and in many other correlational studies) is for the researcher to be fully aware of the social sensitivity of the findings that he or she has obtained, and the lack of causal evidence.

Naturalistic Observation

Naturalistic observation involves methods designed to examine behaviour without the experimenter interfering with it in any way. This approach was originally developed by the **ethologists** such as Lorenz (see Chapter 3). They studied non-human animals in their natural habitat rather than in the laboratory, and discovered much about the animals' behaviour. An example of the use of naturalistic observation in human research is the study by Anderson (1972). He observed children in a London park and noticed that it was rare indeed to see a child under the age of 3 who wandered further than 200 feet from his or her mother before returning, perhaps just to touch her knee or come close. This showed that attachment is like a piece of invisible string.

Intrusion

One of the key requirements of the method of naturalistic observation is to avoid *intrusion*. Dane (1994, p.1149) defined this as "anything that lessens the participants' perception of an event as natural." There are various ways in which intrusion can occur. For example, there will be intrusion if observations are made in an environment that the participants regard as a research setting. There will also be intrusion if the participants are aware that they are being observed. In many studies, the experimenter is in the same room as the participants, and so they are almost certain to realise they are being observed. When this is the case, the experimenter may try to become a familiar and predictable part of the situation before any observations are recorded.

Advantages of naturalistic observation

First, if the participants are unaware that they are being observed, then this method provides a way of observing people behaving naturally. When this happens, there are no problems from demand characteristics and evaluation apprehension.

Second, many studies based on naturalistic observation provide richer and fuller information than typical laboratory experiments. For example, participants' behaviour may be observed in a range of different social contexts rather than on their own in the laboratory.

Third, it is sometimes possible to use naturalistic observation when other methods cannot be used. For example, the participants may be unwilling to be interviewed or to complete a questionnaire. In the case of participants being observed at work, it may be impossible to obtain permission to disrupt their work in order to carry out an experiment.

Finally, there are some participants who do not cope well with other forms of research, such as children and non-human animals. Naturalistic observation is a more suitable method to use with these participants.

What advantages might be gained by observing children in a naturalistic environment rather than in a laboratory?

Try to fit in as a member of the group and remain detached as an observer.

Limitations of naturalistic observation

There are a number of limitations. These are some of the major ones: the experimenter has essentially no control over the situation. This can make it very hard or impossible to decide what caused the participants to behave as they did. The participants are often aware that they are being observed, with the result that their behaviour is not natural.

There can be problems of **reliability** with the observational measures taken, because of bias on the part of the observer or because the categories into which behaviour is coded are imprecise. Attempts to produce good reliability often involve the use of very precise but narrow categories, leading to much of the participants' behaviour simply being ignored. Reliability can be assessed by correlating the observational records of two different observers. This produces a measure of inter-rater or **inter-observer reliability**.

There are often problems of replication with studies of naturalistic observation. For example, the observed behaviour of children in one school may depend in part on the fact that most of the teachers are very lenient and fail to impose discipline. The findings might be very different at another school in which the teachers are more strict.

Naturalistic observations and ethical issues

Naturalistic observation poses ethical problems if the participants do not realise that their behaviour is being observed. This is called **undisclosed observation**. Examples include the use of one-way mirrors and participants being observed in public places. In those circumstances, they obviously cannot give their voluntary informed consent to be involved in the study. There can also be problems about **confidentiality**. Suppose, for example, that naturalistic observation takes place in a particular school, and the published results indicate that many of the children are badly behaved. Even if the name of the school is not mentioned in the report, many people reading it will probably be able to identify the school because they know that the researchers made detailed observations there.

Another issue was raised by Coolican (1994) in his discussion of the work of Whyte (1943). Whyte joined an Italian street gang in Chicago, and became a **participant observer**. The problem he encountered in interpreting his observations was that his presence in the gang influenced their behaviour. A member of the gang expressed this point as follows: "You've slowed me down plenty since you've been down here. Now, when I do something, I have to think what Bill Whyte would want

Sometimes it is not possible to write field notes as events are happening. What does memory research tell us about the usefulness and accuracy of notes written after the event?

NATURALISTIC OBSERVATION	
Advantages	**Limitations**
• People tend to behave naturally	• Experimenter has no control over the situation
• Information that is gathered is rich and full	• Participants can be aware of being watched and this can affect behaviour
• Can be used where other methods are not possible	• Problems of reliability due to bias or imprecise categorisation of behaviour
	• Problems of validity due to observers' or coders' assumptions
	• Replication is not usually possible

me to know about it and how I can explain it." This is an important ethical concern related to observations. The observer has actually changed the participants possibly without their prior consent.

Interviews and Questionnaire Surveys

Interviews and surveys come in many different forms. They vary in terms of the amount of structure and whether they are conducted face-to-face (interviews) or require written answers (questionnaire surveys). In what follows, we will first consider interviews, using Coolican's (1994) categorisation of different types of interview, and then present information about questionnaire surveys.

There are various types of interviews used for psychological experimentation, from non-directive interviews to fully structured designs that have a standard set of questions with restricted-choice answers.

Non-directive interviews

Non-directive interviews possess the least structure, with the person interviewed (the interviewee) being free to discuss almost anything he or she wants. The role of the interviewer in non-directive interviews is to guide the discussion and to encourage the interviewee to be more forthcoming. This type of interview is used very often in treatment of mental disorders, but has little relevance to research.

Informal interviews

Informal interviews resemble non-directive interviews, in that the interviewer listens patiently and focuses mainly on encouraging the interviewee to discuss issues in more depth or detail. However, informal interviews differ in that there are certain general topics that the interviewer wishes to explore. One of the best known examples involving informal interviews was a large-scale study of workers at the Hawthorne works of Western Electric (see the Key Study on page 272). The aim of this study was to explore industrial relations via a series of interviews. What emerged from informal interviews was that the relatively minor issues initially raised by the workers generally reflected deeper and more serious worries (Roethlisberger & Dickson, 1939).

Guided interviews

Informal but guided interviews possess a little more structure than informal interviews. Beforehand, the interviewer identifies the issues to be addressed. During the course of the interview, further decisions are made about how and when to raise these issues. Structured but open-ended interviews use a formal procedure in which all interviewees are asked precisely the same questions in the same order. Such a procedure prevents the interviewee from side-tracking the interview and taking control of it away from the interviewer. The interviews are open-ended, in the sense that the questions that are asked allow plenty of scope for various kinds of answers (e.g. "How do you see your career developing?").

Clinical interviews

The clinical interview or clinical method resembles the structured but open-ended interview. Clinical interviews are often used by clinical psychologists to assess patients with mental disorders. In essence, all of the interviewees or participants are asked the same questions, but the choice of follow-up questions depends on the answers that are given. Piaget (1970) made much use of the clinical method in his research with children. Piaget understood that children might perform poorly on a task because they did not understand fully what the experimenter wanted them to do. One way of trying to avoid this problem was by giving the experimenter the flexibility to ask questions in various ways.

Fully structured interviews

Finally, there is the fully structured interview. In this type of interview, a standard set of questions is asked in the same fixed order to all of the interviewees, and they are only allowed to choose their answers from a restricted set of possibilities (e.g. "Yes", "No", "Don't know"). As Coolican (1994, pp.121–122) points out, "this approach is hardly an interview worth the name at all. It is a face-to-face data-gathering technique, but could be conducted by telephone or by post."

Questionnaire surveys

Written questionnaires are a special form of interview, where respondents are asked to record their own answers. The advantage of this method is that large amounts of data can be collected at relatively little cost. However the method is clearly only suitable for certain kinds of participants—those who are literate and willing to spend time filling in a questionnaire, therefore the sample is often biased. Designing questionnaires requires considerable skill, as discussed in the box on page 262.

Have you ever been interviewed while out shopping? How would you classify the interview style?

Advantages of interviews

As might be expected, the precise advantages depend on the type of interview. Relatively unstructured interviews have the advantage that they are responsive to the personality, interests, and motivations of the interviewee. In principle, they can reveal more about the interviewee than more structured interviews. The unstructured interview tends to produce *qualitative* rather than quantitative data.

One of the advantages of fairly structured interviews is that it is easy to compare the responses of different interviewees, all of whom have been asked the same questions. Another advantage is good reliability, in that two different interviewers are likely to obtain similar responses from an interviewee when they ask exactly the same questions in the same order. A further advantage is that there is a reasonable probability of being able to replicate or repeat the findings from a study using structured interviews. Finally, structured interviews have the advantage that it is usually fairly easy to analyse the data obtained from them because the data collected tend to be more *quantitative* rather than qualitative.

Can you describe the difference between quantitative and qualitative data?

Limitations of interviews

So far as unstructured interviews are concerned, there is the problem that the kinds of information obtained from different interviewees vary in an unsystematic way. As a result, the data from unstructured interviews tend to be hard to analyse. A further limitation with unstructured interviews is that what the interviewee says is determined in a complex way by the interaction between him or her and the interviewer. In other words, the personality and other characteristics of the interviewer typically influence the course of the interview, and make it hard to work out which of the interviewee's contributions are and are not affected by the interviewer. This is called **interviewer bias**. Finally, the fact that the information obtained from interviewees in unstructured interviews is influenced by the interviewer means that the data obtained can be viewed as unreliable.

One of the main limitations with structured interviews is that what the interviewee says may be somewhat constrained and artificial because of the high level of structure built into the interview. Another limitation is that there is little or none of the flexibility associated with unstructured interviews.

Finally, we need to consider three limitations that are common to all types of interview. First, there is the issue of **social desirability bias**. Most people want to present a favourable impression of themselves to other people, and this may lead them to distort their answers to personal questions. For example, people are much more willing to admit that they are unhappy when filling in a questionnaire anonymously than when being interviewed (Eysenck, 1990). There are several methods used to try to overcome the social desirability bias. One is to use a **lie scale**. Some of the questions in the interview are intended to assess the extent to which the respondent is telling the truth or whether they are giving socially desirable answers. For example, a question about honesty might be included: "Do you always tell the truth?" An honest answer would be "No". If a respondent demonstrates a social desirability bias on a range of lie scale questions, then we might exclude their responses from our sample.

A second problem with interviews is that we can only extract information of which the interviewee is consciously aware. This is a significant limitation, because people are often unaware of the reasons why they behave in certain ways (Nisbett & Wilson, 1977). Third, there is the limitation that many interviewers lack some of the skills necessary to conduct interviews successfully. Good interviewers are able to make an interview

■ Activity: Divide the class into small groups and ask each group to prepare one kind of interview technique. They should present a short demonstration to the class. Which ones worked best? What problems arose? Which would be the best ways to collect data?

How would research results be affected by the possibility that people might decide to give the socially acceptable response to statements such as "Smacking children is an appropriate form of punishment"?

■ Activity: List all the research methods covered in this section and, for each of them, say how they might produce qualitative and quantitative data.

People adjust what they say to fit the circumstances.

Interviews and questionnaires

Advantages:

- Unstructured interviews can be more revealing
- Structured interviews permit comparison between interviewees and facilitate replication
- Questionnaires allow for collection of large amounts of data

Limitations:

- Interviewer bias
- Social desirability bias
- People don't always know what they think
- Good interviewing requires skill

People are more willing to answer embarrassing or personal questions on an anonymous written questionnaire than in a face-to-face interview.

seem natural, they are sensitive to non-verbal cues, and they have well-developed listening skills (Coolican, 1994).

Interviews and ethical issues

Interviews (especially clinical interviews) are often concerned with personal issues about which the interviewee is sensitive. This clearly raises the issue of confidentiality. There are various ways in which confidentiality can be broken. For example, Coolican (1994) discussed a study by Vidich and Bensman (1958) in which direct quotations from interviewees in Springdale in the United States were published. Made-up names were used, but the people of Springdale were able to identify the actual individuals on the basis of what they said.

Confidentiality can also be broken if a detailed written account or video recording of an interview falls into the wrong hands. Finally, of course, the interviewer himself or herself could disclose sensitive personal information about the interviewee to other people.

There is another ethical issue that is of particular importance with structured interviews. Interviewees may be aware that several other interviewees are being asked the same questions, and that their answers will be compared. As a result, some interviewees may feel that they must answer embarrassing questions in order not to spoil the research study.

Research Design and Implementation

In order to carry out a study successfully, care and attention must be devoted to each stage in its design and implementation. This section is concerned with these issues. We will focus on *experimental* designs, although many of the same issues also apply to producing good non-experimental designs. As we will see, several decisions need to be made when designing an experimental study.

■ Activity: Devising hypotheses

Devise suitable null and experimental hypotheses for the following:

- An investigator considers the effect of noise on students' ability to concentrate and complete a word-grid. One group only is subjected to the noise in the form of a distractor, i.e. a television programme.
- An investigator explores the view that there might be a link between the amount of television children watch and their behaviour at school.

Aims and Hypotheses

The first step that needs to be taken when designing an experimental (or non-experimental) study is to decide on the **aims** and **hypotheses** of the study. The aims are usually more general than the hypotheses, and they help to explain the reasons for the investigator deciding to test some specific hypothesis or hypotheses. In other words, the aims tell us *why* a given study is being carried out, whereas the hypotheses tell us *what* the study is designed to test.

The distinction between aims and hypotheses can be seen more clearly if we consider an example. Suppose that we decide to test the levels of processing theory put forward by Craik and Lockhart (1972, see Chapter 2), which states that information that has been processed for meaning will be remembered better than information that has not. In order to do this, we might present all of our participants with the same list of nouns and then ask them to provide free recall 30 minutes later. Half of them might be asked to think of adjectives to go with the nouns (processing of meaning or semantic processing), whereas the other half are asked to think of rhyming words (non-semantic processing). In such a study, the main *aim* is to investigate levels of processing theory. In more general terms, the aim is to see whether long-term memory is influenced by the kind of processing that occurs at the time of learning. The *hypothesis* is more specific: "free recall from long-term memory is higher when there is semantic processing at the time of learning than when there is non-semantic processing".

Common sense recommends a quiet rather than a noisy place for study—but to test the hypothesis that noise interferes with learning requires an experimental design.

Hypotheses

Most experimental research starts with someone thinking of an **experimental hypothesis** (also known as the **alternative hypothesis**). This is simply a prediction or expectation of what will happen in a given situation. We all form hypotheses all the time, such as "My football team will win today" or "Women are more caring than men". Psychologists state their hypothesis so that they will be clear about what they aim to prove or disprove in their research. For example, if we return to our example of investigating the effects of noise (the research aim), our experimental hypothesis might be that "loud noise will have an effect on people's ability to learn the information in a chapter of an introductory psychology textbook".

In what way are research aims and hypotheses different?

The null hypothesis

The experimental hypothesis consists of the predicted effect of the independent variable on the dependent variable. This can be contrasted with the **null hypothesis**. The null hypothesis simply states that the independent variable will have no effect on the dependent variable. In terms of our example, a suitable null hypothesis would be as follows: "loud noise will have no effect on people's ability to learn the information contained in the chapter of the textbook". In a sense, the purpose of most studies using the experimental method is to decide between the merits of the experimental hypothesis and those of the null hypothesis.

Why do we need a null hypothesis when what we are interested in is the experimental hypothesis? The key reasons are because the null hypothesis is much more precise than the experimental hypothesis, and because you can never *prove* something—it can only be disproved.

In terms of precision, consider the null hypothesis that loud noise will have no effect on people's learning ability. This is precise because it leads to a prediction that the single most likely outcome is that performance will be equal in the loud noise and no noise conditions. Failing that there will probably only be a small difference between the two conditions, with the difference being equally likely to go in either direction. In contrast, consider the experimental hypothesis that loud noise will reduce people's learning ability. This hypothesis is very imprecise, because it does not indicate how much learning will be impaired. This lack of precision makes it impossible to decide the *exact* extent to which the findings support or fail to support the experimental hypothesis.

In terms of the issue of proof, consider the case of tossing a coin. If every time I toss the coin it comes down heads, then we might form the hypothesis that there are heads on both sides of the coin. But how do we prove this? We can't. The more heads we see, the more likely it would appear that the hypothesis is correct. However, if on one occasion we see tails, then we have disproved the hypothesis. It is possible to disprove something but not to prove it. Therefore, we propose a null hypothesis which can be *disproved* (or rejected) and this implies that we can accept the alternative hypothesis. The issues of precision and proof are aspects of the same thing: being able to reject the null hypothesis.

Variables

Experimental hypotheses predict that some aspect of the situation (in this case, the presence of loud noise) will have an effect on the participants' behaviour (in this case, their learning of the information in the chapter). The experimental hypothesis refers to an **independent variable**, which as you may remember is the aspect of the experimental situation that is manipulated by the experimenter. In our example, the presence versus absence of loud noise is the independent variable. The hypothesis also refers to a **dependent variable**, which is some aspect of the participants' behaviour that is measured or assessed by the experimenter. In our example, some measure of learning would be used to assess the dependent variable.

In a nutshell, most experimental hypotheses predict that a given independent variable will have some specified effect on a given dependent variable.

Non-experimental research

In non-experimental research (e.g. correlations, interviews, and observations), it is still useful to have hypotheses but these will not identify a potentially causal relationship. For example, the aim of an observational study might be "to study the feeding behaviour of geese". The researcher may have a number of hypotheses,

---

■ Activity: In order to confirm that you do understand what independent (IV) and dependent (DV) variables are, try identifying them in the following examples. The answers are given below (don't peek!)

Remember:

- The DV depends on the IV.
- The IV is manipulated by the experimenter or varies naturally.
- The DV is the one we measure.

1. Long-term separation affects emotional development more than short-term separation. (The two variables are length of separation and emotional development.)

2. Participants conform more when the model is someone they respect. (The two variables are extent of conformity and degree of respect for the model.)

3. Participants remember more words before lunch than after lunch. (The two variables are number of words remembered and whether the test is before or after lunch.)

4. Boys are better than girls at throwing a ball. (The two variables are gender and ability to throw a ball.)

5. Physical attractiveness makes a person more likeable. (The two variables are the attractiveness of a person's photograph and whether they are rated as more or less likeable.)

Answers: 1. IV=length of separation, DV=emotional development. 2. IV=degree of respect for model, DV=degree of conformity. 3. IV=whether test is before or after lunch, DV=number of words recalled. 4. IV=gender, DV=ability to throw a ball. 5. IV=attractiveness, DV=rating for likeability.

such as "one goose always acts as the lookout" and "geese work systematically through the field". Such hypotheses will be important in determining the categories used for the observations and for focusing the observations that are made, i.e. the process of designing research.

One-tailed or two-tailed?

Let us return to experimental research. It should be noted at this point that there are two types of experimental hypothesis: one-tailed and two-tailed hypotheses. A **one-tailed**, or **directional**, **hypothesis** predicts the *nature* of the effect of the independent variable on the dependent variable. In terms of our example of a possible study, a directional hypothesis might be as follows: "loud noise will *reduce* a person's ability to learn the information contained in the chapter of a textbook". In contrast a **two-tailed,** or **non-directional**, **hypothesis** predicts that the independent variable will have an effect on the dependent variable, but the *direction* of the effect is not specified. In terms of our example, a non-directional hypothesis would be as follows: "loud noise will have *an effect on* a person's ability to learn the information contained in the chapter of a textbook". This latter hypothesis allows for the possibility that loud noise might actually improve learning. So, a one-tailed hypothesis states that the independent variable will lead to either an increase or decrease in the dependent variable, whereas a two-tailed hypothesis just predicts a change—but doesn't give the direction of that change.

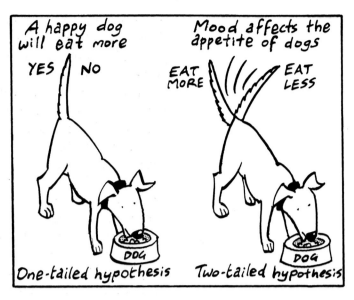

One-tailed hypothesis   Two-tailed hypothesis

■ Activity: Generating a hypothesis

1. Generate a hypothesis for each of these questions:
   • What are "football hooligans" really like?
   • Do children play differently at different ages?
   • What are the effects of caffeine on attention and concentration?
2. Identify the independent variable (IV) and dependable variable (DV) from each hypothesis.
3. Identify whether your hypotheses are one-tailed or two-tailed (remember, a one-tailed hypothesis predicts the direction of the effect of the IV on the DV, whereas a two-tailed hypothesis does not).
4. Write a null hypothesis for each of the experimental hypotheses.

Research Designs

After deciding on your aims and hypotheses, the next stage in the research process is to identify an appropriate design. We will consider experimental design, as well as some issues related to the design of qualitative research methods.

Experimental designs

If we wish to compare two groups with respect to a given independent variable, it is essential to make sure that the two groups do not differ in any other important way. This general rule is important when it comes to selecting participants to take part in an experiment. Suppose all the least able participants received the loud noise, and all the most able participants received no noise. We would not know whether it was the loud noise or the low ability level of the participants causing poor learning performance. How should we select our participants so as to avoid this problem? There are three main types of experimental design:

*   *Independent design*: each participant is selected for only one group (no noise or loud noise).

- *Matched participants design*: each participant is selected for only one group, but the participants in the two groups are matched for some relevant factor or factors (e.g. ability, sex, age).
- *Repeated measures design*: each participant appears in both groups, so that there are exactly the same participants in each group.

Independent design

With the independent design, the most common way of deciding which participants go into which group is by means of randomisation. In our example, this could involve using a random process such as tossing a coin to decide whether a participant is exposed to loud noise or to no noise. In other words, you toss a coin for participant 1 and this determines whether he or she is placed in condition 1 or condition 2, and this continues for all participants. Alternatively you could let all participants draw slips of paper, numbered 1 and 2, from a hat. This is called **random allocation**. It is possible with random allocation for all the most able participants to still end up in the same group. However, what happens in the great majority of cases is that the participants in the two groups do end up equivalent in terms of ability, age, and so on.

Matched participants design

With the matched participants design, we make use of information about the participants to decide which group each participant should join. In our example, we might have information about the participants' ability levels. We could then use this information to make sure that the two groups were matched in terms of range of ability.

Repeated measures design

With the repeated measures design, every participant is in both groups. In our example, that would mean that each participant learns the chapter in the loud noise condition, and that they also learn the chapter in no noise condition. The great

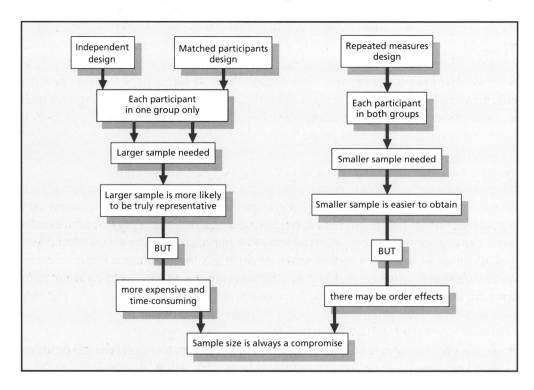

advantage of the repeated measures design is that we do not need to worry about the participants in one group being cleverer than those in the other group; as the same participants appear in both groups, so the ability level (and all other individual characteristics) must be identical in the two groups!

The main problem with the repeated measures design is that there may well be **order effects**. Participants' experiences during the experiment may change them in various ways. They may perform better when they appear in the second group because they have gained useful information about the experiment or about the task. On the other hand, they may perform less well on the second occasion because of tiredness or boredom. It would be hard to use a repeated measures design in our example: participants are almost certain to show better learning of the chapter the second time they read it, regardless of whether they are exposed to loud noise. However, there is a way around this, using counterbalancing.

Counterbalancing

Suppose we used a repeated measures design in which all of the participants first learned the chapter in loud noise and then learned it in no noise. We would expect the participants to show better learning in no noise simply because of order effects. A better procedure would be to have half the participants learn the chapter first in loud noise and then in no noise, while the other half learn the chapter first in no noise and then in loud noise. In that way, any order effects would be balanced out. This approach is known as **counterbalancing**. It is the best way of preventing order effects from disrupting the findings from an experiment.

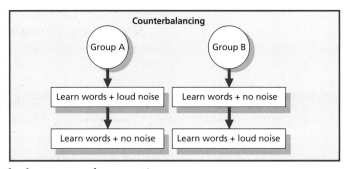

Experimental and control groups

We have discussed the issue of the control of confounding variables in experimental situations. The concept of "control" is also applied to establishing a baseline in some experiments. In the example of the noise and learning experiment one group receives the **experimental treatment** (noise) where the other receives nothing (no noise). This latter group serves as a **control group**. Their behaviour informs us about how people behave when they are not exposed to the experimental treatment so that we can make comparisons. The group who have the noise are called the **experimental group**.

If a repeated measures design is used, then we have two different *conditions*: a control condition and an experimental condition.

Design of qualitative research methods

Questionnaire surveys and interviews

Some of the important factors in the design of questionnaire surveys and interviews have already been discussed in the last chapter. In practical terms a researcher needs guidance on writing good questions which will avoid problems such as social desirability bias. The case study on the following page provides guidance in constructing good questions.

Designing naturalistic observations

It is usual to find that a huge amount of data is generated from the observation of others' behaviour. How can observers avoid being overloaded in their

Imagine that you are going to conduct an observation of children in a playgroup with two other researchers. To what extent do you think that you will all record the same behaviours? How might you cope with any disagreements?

attempts to record this behaviour? One approach is to focus only on actions or events that are of particular interest to the researcher, this is known as **event sampling**. Another approach is known as **time sampling**, in which observations are only made during specified time periods (e.g. the first 10 minutes of each hour). A third approach is **point sampling**, in which one individual is observed in order to categorise their current behaviour, after which a second individual is observed, and so on.

In considering the data obtained from naturalistic observation, it is important to distinguish between recording and interpretation (coding). For example, an observer may *record* that the participant has moved forwards, and *interpret* that movement as an aggressive action. In practice, however, observers typically only focus on interpreting the participants' behaviour. For example, Bales (1950) developed the interaction process analysis, which allows observers to watch groups of people talking together or interacting. The observers record inferred meanings for the forms of behaviour shown by members of a group (e.g. they might record "offers suggestion" when one participant speaks or "gives information").

There have been various attempts to develop ways of categorising people's behaviour in naturalistic observation without interpreting it. For example, McGrew (1972) devised a detailed and comprehensive recording system to place the social

---

CASE STUDY: *Questionnaire Construction*

The first step is to generate as many ideas as possible that might be relevant to the questionnaire. Then discard those ideas that seem of little relevance, working on the basis (Dyer, 1995, p.114) that: "It is better to ask carefully designed and quite detailed questions about a few precisely defined issues than the same number on a very wide range of topics."

Closed and open questions

There is an important distinction between closed and open questions. Closed questions invite the respondent to select from various possible answers (e.g. yes or no; yes, unsure, or no; putting different answers in rank order), whereas open questions allow respondents to answer in whatever way they prefer. Most questionnaires use closed questions, because the answers are easy to score and to analyse. Open questions have the disadvantage of being much harder to analyse, but they can be more informative than closed questions.

Ambiguity and bias

Questions that are ambiguous or are likely to be interpreted in various ways should be avoided. Questions that are very long or complicated should also be avoided, because they are likely to be misunderstood. Emotive questions should be avoided because they make people defensive and result in answers that are not true. Finally, questions that are biased should be avoided. Here is an example of a biased question: "In view of the superiority of Britain, why should we consider further political integration with the rest of Europe?"

Attitude scale construction

One of the most common ways to construct an attitude scale is to use the Likert procedure. Initially various statements are collected together, and the participants' task is to indicate their level of agreement on a 5-point scale running from "strongly disagree" at one end to "strongly agree" at the other end. For positive statements (e.g. "Most Hollywood stars are outstanding actors"), strongly disagree is scored as 1 and strongly agree as 5, with intermediate points being scored 2, 3, or 4. For negative statements (e.g. "Most Hollywood stars are not outstanding actors"), the scoring is reversed so that strongly disagree is scored as 5 and strongly agree as 1.

■ Activity: Construct your own questionnaire

1. Select an area of study from the work you are doing in class.

2. Research the topic to gain ideas about the possible questions to ask.

3. Develop sub-topics to investigate. It may be best to generate questions with a group of people because more varied ideas are produced (brainstorming). Each group member should put forward ideas which are received uncritically by the group. Later, the group can select the best questions.

4. Write the questions. It may help to include some irrelevant "filler" questions to mislead the respondent as to the main purpose of the survey.

5. Decide on a sequence for the questions. It is best to start with easy ones.

6. Write standardised instructions, which must include guidance regarding respondents' ethical rights.

7. Conduct a pilot run and redraft your questionnaire in response to areas of confusion or difficulty.

8. After you have conducted your questionnaire, analyse the results using descriptive data (see next section, "Data Analysis").

9. Debrief participants and advise them of your findings.

Question styles: A survey on chocolate

Closed question: Do you like chocolate? (tick one)

YES   NO   NOT SURE

Open question: Why do you like or dislike chocolate?

Ambiguous question: Is chocolate likely to do you more harm than a diet that consists mainly of junk food?

Biased question: Plain chocolate is a more sophisticated taste than milk chocolate. Which type do you prefer?

interactions of children at nursery school into 110 categories.

Factors Associated With Research Design

In order for a study to be designed and carried out successfully, there are several considerations that the researcher needs to bear in mind. Some of the main considerations apply to all kinds of research, whereas others are specific to experiments. We will consider them all together.

When conducting observational studies, psychologists need to categorise behaviour. When McGrew (1972) studied the interactions of nursery school children he used an observational rating system with 110 categories.

Standardised instructions and procedures

In order to carry out an experiment successfully, it is very important that every participant in a given condition is treated in the same way. In other words, it is necessary to use standardised procedures. For example, consider the instructions that are given to the participants. In order to ensure that all of the participants get precisely the same instructions, the experimenter should write down a set of **standardised instructions**. He or she should then either read them to the participants, or ask the participants to read them to themselves. An example is given in the box below.

In similar fashion, **standardised procedures** should be used for the collection of data. This applies to all research, not just experiments. Suppose we want to assess the effects of loud noise on learning from a book chapter. We might ask the participants to write down everything they could remember about the chapter. However, it would be very hard to compare the recalls of different participants with any precision. A standardised procedure would be to ask all of the participants the same set of, say, 20 questions relating to the chapter. Each participant then obtains a score between 0 and 20 as a measure of what he or she has learned.

Is it easy to make sure that standardised procedures are being used? No, it is not. Most experiments or other kinds of study can be thought of as social encounters between the researcher and the participant, and it is customary to behave in different ways towards different people. Rosenthal (1966) studied some of the ways in which researchers fall short of standardised procedures. He found, for example, that male researchers were more pleasant, friendly, honest, encouraging, and relaxed when their participants were female than when they were male. This led him to conclude: "Male and female [participants] may, psychologically, simply not be in the same experiment at all", i.e. conditions are so different for each gender that the results would not be comparable.

If an experimenter used different wording in the instructions to different participants, how might this affect the results of the study?

Control of variables

We have previously discussed the control of **confounding variables**. These are variables that may

---

A set of standardised instructions

Kelley (1950) conducted a field experiment to see whether class members would form different impressions of a lecturer if he was described as "warm" or as "cold". The standardised instructions for the experiment were:

"Your regular instructor is out of town today, and since we of Economics 70 are interested in the general problem of how various classes react to different instructors, we're going to have an instructor today you've never had before, Mr _____. Then, at the end of the period, I want you to fill out some forms about him. In order to give you some idea of what he's like, we've had a person who knows him write up a little biographical note about him. I'll pass this out now and you can read it before he arrives. Please read these to yourselves and don't talk about this among yourselves until the class is over so he won't get wind of what's going on."

The participants were then given the biographical note with the word "warm" or "cold" inserted. Incidentally, Kelley found that the "warm" lecturer was rated more positively.

mask the effect of the independent variable. If we consider our study on how noise affects learning, imagine that the no-noise group studied at midday, whereas the group exposed to a lot of noise did their work in the evening. If we find that the latter group learns less well than the former group, we would not know whether this was because of the loud noise or because they did their learning late at night when they were very tired. In this example, time of day is a confounding variable and noise is the independent variable.

Confounding variables are a form of constant error. **Constant error** is present when the effects of any unwanted variable on the dependent variable differ between conditions. There are numerous types of constant error. The participants in one condition may be more tired than those in another condition, or they may be more intelligent, or they may be more motivated.

Controlled variables

How do we avoid having any confounding variables? One useful approach is to turn them into **controlled variables**, which are variables that are held constant or controlled. Suppose that we want to study the effects of noise on learning, and we are concerned that the time of day may have an effect. We could make time of day into a controlled variable by testing all of our participants at a given time of day, such as late morning or early evening. If we did this, we would know that time of day could not distort our findings.

Operationalisation

Psychologists carry out studies to test hypotheses, such as "anxiety impairs performance" or "maternal deprivation leads to maladjustment". There is an immediate problem with designing a study to test such hypotheses: there is little or no agreement on the best way to measure psychological concepts or variables such as "anxiety", "performance", "maternal deprivation", or "maladjustment". The most common approach to this problem is to make use of **operationalisation**. This involves defining each variable of interest in terms of the operations taken to measure it. Such a definition is referred to as an operational definition. For example, anxiety might be defined as the score on the trait anxiety scale of Spielberger's State-Trait Anxiety Inventory, and performance might be defined as the number of five-letter anagrams that can be solved in five minutes. Maternal deprivation might be defined in terms of the number of months during which a child was separated from its main caregiver.

Operationalisation has the great advantage that it generally provides a clear and objective definition of even complex variables. However, there are various limitations associated with the use of operational definitions. First, operational definitions are entirely circular. As Stretch (1994, p.1076) pointed out:

> *A psychological construct is defined in terms of the operations necessary to measure it, and the measurements are defined to be measures of the psychological construct.*

Second, an operational definition typically only covers part of the meaning of the variable or concept. For example, defining anxiety in terms of the score on a self-report questionnaire largely ignores physiological and behavioural aspects of anxiety, and no-one believes that performance can *only* be assessed in terms of rate of anagram solution.

In spite of these important limitations with operational definitions, it is hard to carry out research without using them. Stretch (1994, p.1076) argued that operational definitions should be used in a careful fashion:

It might be said that the operational definition of "intelligence" is "that which is measured by intelligence tests". What is the main weakness of this definition?

What might be an operational definition of fatigue, or hunger?

A useful rule of thumb is to consider many different ways of measuring the psychological construct of interest and determine the extent to which each method could yield different experimental results. If you find that the measurement techniques radically affect the results that emerge, this should indicate that more work is needed on developing the underlying psychological and measurement models to explain these effects.

Pilot studies

An important consideration in designing good studies is to try out your planned procedures in a small-scale trial run, called a **pilot study**. Such a preliminary study makes it possible to check out standardised procedures and general design before investing time and money in the major study. Any problems can then be adjusted. If you have ever tried to conduct some research you will realise that invariably there are things you would have changed in your procedures. A trial run would have given you the opportunity to do this.

Improving and Measuring Reliability

One of the main goals of research is to design and carry out studies in such a way that *replication* or repetition of one's findings is possible. In order to achieve that goal, it is important that the measures we use should possess good **reliability** or consistency. As Coolican (1994, p.50) pointed out:

Any measure we use in life should be reliable, otherwise it's useless. You wouldn't want your car speedometer or a thermometer to give you different readings for the same values on different occasions. This applies to psychological measures as much as any other.

Determining the reliability of observations

Problems relating to reliability are likely to arise when a researcher is trying to code the complex behaviour of participants using a manageable number of categories (remember that even in experiments the DV may require observation as a means of "measurement"). For example, a study might require a record to be made of the number of aggressive acts performed by an individual. However, it may be hard to define those events with enough precision to produce reliable results. If only one person observes the behaviour this would produce a rather subjective judgement, and so usually two (or more) judges are asked to provide ratings of a behaviour. The ratings can then be compared to provide a measure of inter-observer or **inter-judge reliability** (observer reliability was also discussed earlier).

Determining the reliability of psychological tests

Reliability is established on psychological tests by using the **test–retest** method where the same test is given to participants on two separate occasions to see if their scores remain relatively similar. The interval between testings must be long enough to prevent a **practice effect** occurring.

When practising psychologists rely on evidence from psychological research, such as clinical psychologists or those giving advice to air traffic controllers, it is vital that the research is as reliable and valid as possible, as inaccuracies may put lives at risk.

This measuring instrument would be of little value unless it was reliable, i.e. gave consistent readings on all occasions.

Internal and external reliability

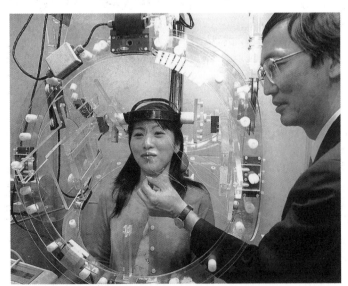

Internal reliability = consistency within the method of measurement. For instance, a ruler should be measuring the same distance between 0 and 5 centimetres as between 5 and 10 centimetres.

External reliability = consistency between uses of the method of measurement. For instance, the ruler should measure the same on a Monday as it does on a Friday.

- Reliability = consistent and stable
- Validity = measuring what is intended
- Standardisation = comparisons can be made between studies and samples

---

■ Activity: Construct a brief outline for each of the following:

- An experiment that should show high internal validity.
- An experiment that will be unlikely to show high internal validity.
- An experiment that is unlikely to show high ecological validity.

A second method of establishing reliability is called the **split-half technique**. Items from a test are randomly assigned to two sub-tests and then scores compared on both tests in the same way as on the test–retest method. The same person does both sub-tests simultaneously.

Improving and Measuring Validity

One of the key requirements of research is that any findings obtained are valid, in the sense that they are genuine and provide us with useful information about the phenomenon being studied (valid means "true"). Campbell and Stanley (1966) drew a distinction between internal validity and external validity. **Internal validity** refers to the issue of whether the effects observed are genuine and are caused by the independent variable. In contrast, **external validity** refers to the extent to which the findings of a study can be generalised to situations and samples other than those used in the study. This distinction between two kinds of validity is an important one: many experiments possess internal validity while lacking external validity. Note that validity was also discussed elsewhere in this book, in Chapter 6, Section 17.

The distinction between internal and external validity is especially relevant to experiments and quasi-experiments because of their potential artificiality, therefore we will focus on experimental research.

Internal validity

We will shortly consider some of the reasons why an experiment may lack external validity, but what are some of the main threats to the internal validity of an experiment? Coolican (1994) pointed out that there are many such threats, most of which were discussed earlier in this chapter. For example, the existence of any confounding factors threatens internal validity, as does the use of unreliable or inconsistent measures. Problems with internal validity can also arise if an experiment is designed without careful attention being paid to issues such as standardisation and randomisation. Other threats to internal validity include **experimenter effects**, **demand characteristics**, and **participant reactivity**, which are all discussed later in this chapter.

In a nutshell, virtually all of the principles of experimental design are intended to enhance internal validity, and failures to apply these principles threaten internal validity. If internal validity is high, then there are good prospects for being able to replicate the findings. If it is low, then replication is likely to be difficult or impossible.

Many laboratory-based experiments in psychology show low external (ecological) validity—that is, their findings do not translate reliably to behaviour outside the laboratory.

External validity and generalisability

What about external validity? There are close links between external validity and **generalisability**, because both are concerned with the issue of whether the findings of an experiment or study are applicable to other situations (also called **ecological validity**). More specifically, Coolican (1994) argued that there are four main aspects to external validity or generalisability, which we consider in turn:

- *Populations*: do the findings obtained from a given sample of individuals generalise to a larger population from which the sample was selected?
- *Locations*: do the findings of the study generalise to other settings or situations? If the findings generalise to various real-life settings, then the study is said to possess ecological validity. Silverman (1977, p.108) was sceptical about the ecological validity of laboratory experiments: "the conclusions we draw from our laboratory studies pertain to the behaviour of organisms in conditions of their own confinement and control and are probably generalisable only to similar situations (institutions, perhaps, such as schools or prisons or hospitals)."
- *Measures or constructs*: do the findings of the experiment or study generalise to other measures of the variables used? For example, suppose we find that people who are high on the personality dimension of trait anxiety as assessed by Spielberger's State-Trait Anxiety Inventory have worse long-term memory measured by recall than those low in trait anxiety. Would we obtain the same findings if trait anxiety were assessed by a different questionnaire or if we used a recognition test of long-term memory?
- *Times*: do the findings generalise to the past and to the future? For example, it could be argued that sweeping changes in many cultures in recent decades have affected conformity behaviour as studied by Asch, and obedience to authority as studied by Milgram (see Chapter 6).

What can we do to maximise the external validity of an experiment? Unfortunately, there is no easy answer to that question. What usually happens is that the external validity of an experiment only becomes clear when other researchers try to generalise the findings to other samples or populations, locations, measures, and times. It might be thought that the findings of field experiments are more likely than those of laboratory experiments to generalise to other real-life locations or settings, but that is not necessarily so.

Meta-analyses

One way of trying to determine whether certain findings generalise is to carry out what is known as a **meta-analysis**. What is done in a meta-analysis is to combine all of the findings from many studies designed to test a given hypothesis into a single analysis. If the meta-analysis indicates that some finding has been obtained consistently, this suggests that it generalises across populations, locations, measures, and times. For example, Smith and Bond (1993) carried out a meta-analysis on 133 Asch-type studies drawn from 17 countries. They claimed that the combined data "revealed significant relationships confirming the general hypothesis that conformity would be higher in collectivistic cultures than in individualistic cultures."

The greatest limitation of meta-analyses is that differences in the quality of individual studies are often ignored. This can lead to the situation in which a finding

Our culture today is different from the culture of the 1950s. This means that research conducted then, for example surveying women's attitudes towards domestic work, may not generalise to women's attitudes today.

is accepted as genuine when it has been obtained in several poorly designed studies but not in a smaller number of well-designed studies. Another problem is that it is often hard to know which studies to include and which to exclude. For example, the studies reviewed by Bond and Smith probably did not use identical procedures and therefore they are not directly comparable. It is also quite possible that the task did not have the same meaning for people in different cultures.

Ethics

We should finally consider the fact that good research design involves ethics. All research strives to satisfy the requirements of the psychologists' code of ethics. The details of this are discussed in Chapter 6, Section 18.

The Selection of Participants

Studies in psychology rarely involve more than about 100 participants. However, researchers generally want their findings to apply to a much larger group of people than those acting as participants. In technical terms, the participants selected for a study form a **sample**. This sample is taken from some larger **population** (called the target or sample population), which consists of all the members of the group from which the sample has been drawn. For example, we might select a sample of 20 children aged 5 for a study. The target population would consist of all the 5-year-olds living in England or the population might be the 5-year-olds in a particular primary school, depending on where we selected our sample.

The questions in an examination aim to sample your knowledge. You will feel unhappy if that sample doesn't touch on what you know!

When we carry out a study, we want the findings obtained from our sample to be true of the population from which they were drawn. In order to achieve this, we must use a **representative sample**, i.e. participants who are representative or typical of the population in question. Only if we have a representative sample can we generalise from the behaviour of our sample to the target population in general. In other words, as in the example, we can only make statements about all 5-year olds in the population studied, i.e. those in England or in the school, not those in the rest of the world. Many studies actually have non-representative samples. Such studies are said to have a **sampling bias**. Coolican (1994, p.36) was pessimistic about the chances of truly selecting a representative sample:

> *The simple truth is that a truly representative sample is an abstract ideal unachievable in practice. The practical goal we can set ourselves is to remove as much sampling bias as possible.*

■ Activity: Target populations

Identify an appropriate target population for each project below. You would select your research sample from this population.

- To discover whether there are enough youth facilities in your community.
- To discover whether cats like dried or tinned cat food.
- To discover whether children aged between 5 and 11 watch too much violent television.
- To discover the causes of anxiety experienced by participants in research studies.

Random sampling

To return to our earlier example, let us consider studying the effects of loud noise on learning in students preparing for a psychology exam. The best way of obtaining a representative sample from that population (students) would be to make use of **random sampling**. We could obtain lists of names of all the students due to sit the psychology exam in a given year. After that we could use some random method to select our sample. This could be done by picking names out of a hat.

Another approach is to assign a number to everyone in the population from which the sample is to be selected. After that, a computer can be used to generate a series of random numbers which are then used to select the sample. Alternatively, random number tables can be used in a similar way to produce the sample.

If we wanted to have a representative sample of the entire adult population, then we could apply one of the methods of random selection just described to the electoral roll. However, even that would be an imperfect procedure because several groups of people, including the homeless, illegal immigrants, and prisoners, are not included in the electoral roll.

As Cardwell, Clark, and Meldrum (1996) pointed out, there is a modified version of random sampling that is easier to use. This is **systematic sampling**. It involves selecting the participants by a quasi-random procedure. For example, if we have a list of all the members of the population, we could select every hundredth name from that list as participants. This procedure is not as effective as random sampling because it cannot be claimed that every member of the population is equally likely to be selected.

> Systematic sampling is not as effective as random sampling, but it does help to overcome the biases of the researcher. If we select every hundredth name on the list, we avoid missing out names that we cannot pronounce, or do not like the look of.

Evaluation of random sampling

Random sampling typically fails to produce a truly representative sample, because it is actually very hard for an experimenter to obtain a random sample. There are various reasons for this. First, it may not be possible to identify all of the members of the larger population from which the sample is to be selected.

Second, it may not be possible to contact all those who have been selected randomly to appear in the sample. For instance, you might identify a random sample for a questionnaire but some of the people may have moved house, or might be away on holiday. You would end up with a sample that is definitely not random.

Third, some of those who are selected to be in the sample are likely to refuse to take part in the study. This might not matter if those who agreed to take part in research were very similar in every way to those who did not. However, there is considerable evidence that volunteers differ in various ways from non-volunteers. This is called a **volunteer bias**. Manstead and Semin (1996, p.93) discussed some of the evidence, and concluded, "there *are* systematic personality differences between volunteers and non-volunteers." Volunteers tend to be more sensitive to demand characteristics (cues used by participants to work out what a study is about), and they are also more likely to comply with those demand characteristics.

In sum, it is worth bearing in mind what Coolican (1998, p.720) had to say about random samples: "Many students write that their sample was 'randomly selected'. In fact, research samples are very rarely selected at random." Usually students and many psychologists actually use opportunity sampling.

Why do you think volunteers are more likely than non-volunteers to be sensitive to the demand characteristics of a study?

Opportunity sampling

Random sampling is often expensive and time-consuming. As a result, many researchers use **opportunity sampling**. This involves selecting participants on the basis of their availability rather than by any other method. Opportunity sampling is often used by students carrying out experiments, and it is also very common in natural experiments.

Evaluation of opportunity sampling

Opportunity sampling is the easiest method to use. However, it has the severe disadvantage that the participants may be nothing like a representative sample. For

Ideally, psychological experiments should select a random sample of the population, although true randomness can be hard to achieve.

Consider the total number of participants to be included...

example, students who are friends of the student carrying out a study may be more likely to take part than students who are not. Opportunity sampling also gives the illusion of being drawn from a large population whereas it generally is from a very small sample, such as people who shop in the centre of town on a weekday.

Sample size

One of the issues that anyone carrying out a piece of research has to consider is the total number of participants to be included. What is the ideal number of participants in each condition? There is no definite answer to that question, but here are some of the relevant factors:

- It is generally expensive and time-consuming to make use of large samples running into hundreds of participants.
- If we use very small samples (fewer than 10 participants in each condition), then this reduces the chances of obtaining a meaningful effect.
- In general terms, sampling bias is likely to be greater with small samples than with large ones.
- You should also remember that the size of the sample population matters. If a relatively large sample is drawn from a small population, it will be very biased.

If there is a golden rule that applies to deciding on sample size, it is the following:

> *The smaller the likely effect being studied, the larger the sample size needed to demonstrate it.*

Would you need to use more participants in an independent measures design than a repeated measures design?

For most purposes, however, having about 15 participants in each condition is a reasonable number.

The Relationship Between Researchers and Participants

In most experimental research (and some non-experimental research), the researcher and the participants interact with each other. This can produce various kinds of problems. The way in which researchers behave and talk may influence the behaviour of the participants in ways that have nothing to do with the independent variable or other variables being controlled. In addition, the participants may form mistaken ideas of what the study is about, and these mistaken ideas may affect their behaviour. Some of the main problems stemming from the relationship between the researcher and the participants are discussed next.

Participant reactivity

A weakness that is found in many studies is what is known as **participant reactivity**. This refers to a situation in which an independent variable has an effect on behaviour simply because the participants know that they are being observed or studied. Any measure of the participants' behaviour which could suffer from this effect is called a reactive measure, and reactivity is the term used to refer to the changes in behaviour produced in this way. The **Hawthorne effect** is a classic example of participant reactivity. This is described in the Key Study on the next page. Examples of participant reactivity include **evaluation apprehension** and demand characteristics.

The way in which experimenters behave and talk may influence the behaviour of the participant.

Demand characteristics

A common criticism of laboratory research is that the situation is so artificial that participants behave very differently from normal. Claxton (1980) discussed an amusing example of this. He considered a laboratory task, in which participants have to decide as rapidly as possible whether sentences such as "Can canaries fly?" are true or false. Under laboratory conditions, people perform this task uncomplainingly. However, as Claxton pointed out, "If someone asks me 'Can canaries fly?' in the pub I will suspect either that he is an idiot or that he is about to tell me a joke."

Why do people behave in unusual ways under laboratory conditions? We have already considered **demand characteristics**. They include "the rumours or campus scuttle-butt about the research, the information conveyed during the original situation, the person of the experimenter, and the setting of the laboratory, as well as all explicit and implicit communications during the experiment proper." (In case you are wondering, the word "scuttle-butt" means gossip.) Orne (1962) believed that most participants do their best to comply with what they perceive to be the demands of the experimental situation, so they try to guess what is expected using any available clues and these then become demand characteristics. Of course, their perceptions may often be inaccurate.

As Orne showed, the demand characteristics in an experiment are so powerful that the participants can often be persuaded to do some very strange things. He discussed one study in which the participants spent hours adding numbers on random number sheets, then tearing up each completed sheet into at least 32 pieces.

There is another problem with demand characteristics, which applies to participants who have previously taken part in an experiment in which they were deceived about the experimental purpose (remember that psychological research often relies on psychology students as participants, and they take part in a number of studies). As a result of being deceived, some participants tend thereafter to respond in the opposite direction to the one suggested by an experiment's demand characteristics. Why should this be so? Silverman, Shulman, and Wiesenthal (1970) explained this effect in the following way:

Deceived [participants] may have become so alerted to possible further deceptions that they tend to respond counter to any cues regarding the experimenter's hypothesis. An element of gamesmanship may enter the experimental situation in that [participants] become wary of "tricks" underlying the obvious, and do not want to be caught in them.

The Hawthorne effect

In order to clarify the meaning of participant reactivity, we can consider a series of studies carried out at the Hawthorne Western Electric plant in Chicago (Roethlisberger & Dickson, 1939). They found that the workers became more productive when the amount of lighting was increased, suggesting that work rate increases when the working conditions become easier. However, they also found that *decreasing* the amount of lighting also led to increased productivity!

In general, it was found that productivity increased when *any* changes were made to the working conditions, whether these changes were to wages, length of the working day, or to rest. Productivity even improved when there was a return to the original working conditions. Presumably what was happening was that the workers responded to the interest being shown in them, rather than to the specific changes in their working environment.

KEY STUDY EVALUATION — The Hawthorne effect

Examining human relations in the workplace grew out of Roethlisberger and Dickson's (1939) study, which aimed to consider the relationship between working conditions and productivity. The initial emphasis was on the extrinsic rewards the worker received, and it was found that there was no relationship between extrinsic rewards and productivity. What became apparent was that intrinsic rewards had a greater effect. These intrinsic rewards derived from the workers' own attitudes towards their work both individually and as part of an informal group. The human need to be part of a social group and to be accepted within it determines attitudes to work and the motivation needed to perform successfully far more than financial rewards. From the Hawthorne study new research was stimulated, which examined the range of needs experienced by the workforce. To increase productivity it was found that social needs had to be met, such as friendship, group support, acceptance, approval, recognition, status, and the need for "self-actualisation", which involves the development of an individual's talents, creativity, and personality to the full.

The term "**Hawthorne effect**" came to be used to refer to changes produced because people know they are being studied, although the same phenomenon is now generally referred to as **participant reactivity**.

There are several published findings that may have been influenced by participant reactivity. For example, Klaus and Kennell (1976) reported that mothers who were allowed to interact for several hours a day with their newborn babies developed a closer relationship with them than did mothers who spent less time with their babies (see Chapter 3). The extra-contact mothers were mostly unmarried teenagers, and it has been argued that this effect was due to the interest shown in them by the hospital workers rather than to the extra contact itself. This interpretation is supported by the fact that this finding has generally not been replicated in studies of mothers who are less likely to be flattered at being the centre of attention (Durkin, 1995).

Participant reactivity or the Hawthorne effect is a serious problem, because it can lead us to misinterpret our findings. How can we decide whether some effect is due to participant reactivity? In essence, we need to make sure that participant reactivity is the same in both conditions, by making it equally clear to both groups that they are being studied and that their behaviour is of interest. If the effect is still found, then it cannot have been due to participant reactivity. For example, if extra contact of mothers and babies was still associated with a closer relationship even when equal interest was shown in the mothers given only routine contact, then it would be reasonable to conclude that it was the contact itself that produced the effect.

Discussion points

1. How much of a problem is participant reactivity in research?

2. When would you not expect to find evidence of participant reactivity?

Reducing demand characteristics

Information about the demand characteristics in any given experimental setting can be obtained by asking the participants afterwards to describe in detail what they felt the experiment was about. Armed with this information, the experimenter can take steps to make sure that the results of future experiments are not adversely affected by demand characteristics.

Some (but not all) of the problems of demand characteristics can be reduced by the **single blind** procedure, in which the participants are not informed of the

Ethical issues: Is honesty the best policy? Would demand characteristics be reduced if both participants and experimenters knew the true aims of the experiment?

condition in which they have been placed. Instead, they are usually given a false account of the purpose of the experiment so that they will not seek for cues about the nature of the research. However, this raises ethical issues, because full informed consent cannot be obtained in such circumstances.

Investigator effects

The ideal experimenter is someone who behaves in exactly the same mildly positive way with every participant, and who does not allow his or her expectations and experimental hypotheses to influence the conduct of a study. In reality, the experimenter's expectations, personal characteristics, and so on often have an effect on the participants' behaviour. These are known as **investigator (experimenter) effects**.

Experimenter expectancy

One of the most important investigator effects is **experimenter expectancy**, in which the experimenter's expectations have a systematic effect on the performance of the participants. Perhaps the first systematic demonstration of experimenter expectancy involved a horse known as Clever Hans. The horse was apparently able to count, tapping its hoof the right number of times when asked a simple mathematical question (e.g. 8 + 6). Pfungst (1911) studied Clever Hans. He found that Clever Hans could not produce the correct answer when the horse was blindfolded. What happened normally was that the experimenter made slight movements when the horse had tapped out the correct number, and Clever Hans was simply using these movements as the cue to stop tapping. Rosenthal (1966) experimentally demonstrated the power of unconscious cues in a studies with flatworms and rats (see Key Study on the following page).

Greenspoon (1955) found that he could alter participants' responses by saying "mm-hmm" or "uh-huh" at strategic moments. In what way is this "Greenspoon effect" an example of experimenter expectancy?

Other investigator effects

Barber (1976) argued that there are numerous ways in which the experimenter can influence the findings obtained. In addition to experimenter expectancy, he identified several other kinds of experimenter effects (summarised in Coolican, 1994). Some of these effects are listed here. In this list, a distinction is drawn between the investigator (the person *directing* the research) and the experimenter (the person actually *carrying out* the experiment). For example, an academic psychologist will often be the investigator, whereas an undergraduate or postgraduate student is the experimenter. So far as the studies carried out by A-level or undergraduate students are concerned, the investigator and the experimenter will typically be the same person.

Clever Hans, the "counting" horse who was in reality responding to unconscious cues from his trainer. In the same way, experimenters can unconsciously communicate cues to their participants.

- *Investigator experimental design effect*: for example, if an investigator wanted to show that a learning programme for disadvantaged children was not effective, he or she could arrange for the programme to last for a very short period of time to reduce the chances that there would be any noticeable effects.

Rosenthal's research has also been taken as a demonstration of the self-fulfilling prophecy: events turn out as expected simply because they were expected.

Rosenthal's research with flatworms

One of the best-known studies on experimenter effects was reported by Rosenthal (1966). He asked student experimenters to count the number of head turns and body contractions made by flatworms. Before the experiment started, the students were told that they should expect a lot of activity from half of the worms, but very little activity from the others. In fact, worms were assigned at random to the two groups, so there was no reason for assuming that they would actually differ in activity level.

KEY STUDY EVALUATION — Rosenthal

Coolican (1994) reported that at least 40 experiments that were designed specifically to test for the expectancy effect have found no evidence of it. There is evidence that the behaviour of human participants, especially those high in need for approval, can be influenced by the experimenter's behaviour. However, it seems less likely that flatworms would respond to a smile or a frown from the experimenter!

What do you think Rosenthal found? Somewhat surprisingly, the experimenters reported twice as many head turns and three times as many body contractions in the worms that were allegedly "highly active" as in the "inactive" ones! Rosenthal argued that this was an experimenter expectancy effect, but it is more likely that it was due to the experimenters failing to follow the proper procedures and/or misrecording of the data.

In a later experiment, Rosenthal and Fode (1963) demonstrated an expectancy effect when students were working with rats. The students were told that their experimental rats had been specially bred for high intelligence and could learn mazes very quickly. Another group of students were told that their rats had been bred for dullness. The rats were actually randomly assigned to the students, who trained the rats to perform certain maze-learning tasks. It was found that the "maze-bright" rats actually performed the maze tasks significantly faster than the "maze-dull" rats. It would seem that the students had in some way communicated their expectations to their rats, an example of an experimenter effect or **experimenter bias**.

Could the results of Rosenthal and Fode's experiment be explained in terms of deviation from the standardised procedure rather than the expectancy effect?

Discussion points

1. Are you surprised that it has proved hard to replicate Rosenthal's findings on flatworms?

2. In what circumstances would you expect to find experimenter effects?

- *Investigator loose procedure effect*: if the instructions and other aspects of the procedure are not clearly specified, there is more scope for the results to be influenced by the investigator.
- *Investigator fudging effect*: there is evidence that Burt (1955), who believed strongly that intelligence depends on heredity, fudged (or faked) some of his twin data.
- *Experimenter fudging effect*: the experimenter may fudge the data to please the investigator or to obtain good marks for his or her study.

It may be hard to believe that psychologists might engage in such dishonest practices—but they are only human!

Reducing investigator effects

What steps can be taken to minimise investigator effects? One approach is to use a **double blind** procedure, in which neither the investigator working with the participants nor the participants know the research hypothesis (or hypotheses) being tested. The double blind procedure reduces the possibility of investigator bias, but it is often too expensive and impractical to use. However, the incidence of investigator effects is probably less than it used to be, for the simple reason that more and more studies involve participants interacting with computers rather than with human investigators. In addition, data are increasingly stored directly in computers, making it harder to misrecord the information obtained from participants.

Why is double blind sometimes used instead of single blind (or vice versa)?

SECTION 21
Data Analysis

The data obtained from a study may or may not be in numerical or quantitative form, that is, in the form of numbers. If the data are not in numerical form, then we can still carry out *qualitative* analyses based on the experiences of the individual participants. If the data are in numerical form, then we typically start by working out some descriptive statistics to summarise the pattern of findings. These **descriptive statistics** include measures of central tendency within a sample (e.g. mean) and measures of the spread of scores within a sample (e.g. range). Another useful way of summarising the findings is through the use of graphs. Several such ways of summarising quantitative data are discussed later in this section. First we are going to consider the qualitative analysis of data.

Qualitative Analysis of Data

There is an important distinction between quantitative research and qualitative research. In **quantitative** research, the information obtained from the participants is expressed in numerical form. Studies in which we record the number of items recalled, reaction times, or the number of aggressive acts are all examples of quantitative research. In **qualitative** research, on the other hand, the information obtained from participants is *not* expressed in numerical form. The emphasis is on the stated experiences of the participants and on the stated meanings they attach to themselves, to other people, and to their environment. Those carrying out qualitative research sometimes make use of direct quotations from their participants, arguing that such quotations are often very revealing.

There has been rapid growth in the use of qualitative methods since the mid-1980s. This is due in part to increased dissatisfaction with the quantitative or scientific approach that has dominated psychology for the past 100 years. Reason and Rowan (1981) said:

Orthodox research produces results which are statistically significant but humanly insignificant. In human inquiry it is much better to be deeply interesting than accurately boring.

Many experimental psychologists would regard this statement as being clearly an exaggeration. "Orthodox (traditional) research" with its use of the experimental method has transformed our understanding of attention, perception, learning, memory, reasoning, and so on. However, qualitative research is of clear usefulness within some areas of social psychology, and it can shed much light on the

The mean height of these children is 132 cm. Stating the mean is a way of describing the data (in this case height).

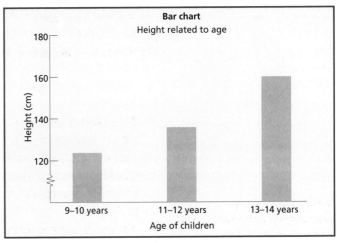

Another way to describe data is to represent them graphically.

Quantitative research would measure, for example, the number of aggressive acts witnessed. Qualitative research might try to explain why the aggressive acts occurred.

motivations and values of individuals. As a result, investigators using questionnaire surveys, interviews, or observations often make use of qualitative data, although they do not always do so.

Principles of qualitative analysis

Investigators who collect qualitative data use several different kinds of analysis but a few general principles can be described. The first step is to fully consider the categories spontaneously used by the participants *before* the investigators develop their own categories. This is a way of avoiding investigator bias. An investigator starts by gathering together all the information obtained from the participants. This stage is not always entirely straightforward. For example, if we simply transcribe tape recordings of what our participants have said, we may be losing valuable information. Details about which words are emphasised, where the speaker pauses, and when the speaker speeds up or slows down should also be recorded, so that we can understand fully what he or she is trying to communicate.

The investigator then arranges the items of information (e.g. statements) into various groups in a preliminary way. If a given item seems of relevance to several groups, then it is included in all of them. Frequently, the next step is to take account of the categories or groupings suggested by the participants themselves.

The final step is for the investigator to form a set of categories based on the information obtained from the previous steps. However, the investigator is likely to change some of the categories if additional information comes to light.

Qualitative investigators might be interested in the number of items or statements falling into each category (which is a *quantitative* approach) but their major concern is usually in the variety of meanings, attitudes, and interpretations found within each category. For example, an investigator might study attitudes towards A-level psychology by carrying out interviews with several A-level students. One of the categories into which their statements are then placed might be "negative attitudes towards statistics". A consideration of the various statements in this category might reveal numerous reasons why A-level psychology students dislike statistics!

When qualitative researchers report their findings, they will often include some raw data (e.g. direct quotations from participants) as well as analyses of the data based on categories. This gives greater depth and meaning to the data presented. For example, the report would quote the comments made by students, such as "Why study statistics when all you have to do is type the numbers into a computer?" Quotations bring the data to life. An example of this approach is shown in the study by Griffiths (1993, see Key Study below and opposite) which uses qualitative data to describe the behaviour of one individual. This is called a **case study**.

Qualitative researchers start with research aims and hypotheses, as in any research. At the end of the study, they often indicate how their hypotheses changed during the course of the investigation.

A qualitative analysis of gambling behaviour

Griffiths (1993) used the case study approach to investigate gambling behaviour, chronicling one teenage boy's descent into pathological gambling and his subsequent recovery. Most of the data were collected in separate interviews with "David" and his mother, although some was collected retrospectively in correspondence.

David had one younger sister and grew up in a seaside town. Up to the age of 14, in his mother's words, he was "a lovely, lively boy, clever at school and good at sports … someone I could be proud of." During the next four years he became "a miserable, withdrawn and rebellious son."

The beginning of the problem

David's swimming club and his school reported to his parents that he was often late and didn't appear interested in anything. At that stage his parents put his problems down to "adolescence", though his mother said that "He seemed to have completely lost respect for us." They thought he might be involved with drugs, but once his mother followed him and found that he went to an amusement arcade. It seemed he was just occupied with "harmless fun". Then his mother and sister began to find money missing.

David's story

David first used fruit machines on family holidays, and there were also machines where he went swimming and at his work place, a restaurant. He realised he had become compulsive but didn't think there was anything serious about it. He only worried where he was going to get money. He earned £60 a week in the restaurant but spent it immediately. There was one period when he managed to save £100 towards the cost of a motorbike. This was followed, however, by a series of family rows, and he returned to gambling full-time. He sold the motorbike and spent the £400 proceeds in one day. The more rows David had with his parents, the more he shut himself away and continued gambling—which led to more rows.

Why did he continue?

"I always got the feeling of being 'high' or 'stoned' … Although winning money was the first thing that attracted me to playing fruit machines, this gradually converted to light, sounds and excitement … I was always very upset about losing all my money and I returned many times to try to win back my losses … The only time I found it possible to think about giving up was after leaving the arcade at closing time and [vowing] never to return … Whenever I felt depressed (which was practically all the time) or rejected, the urge to play machines became even bigger. Whenever I had to make a slight effort in my life, I needed to counteract it by gambling." For example, at one time David did a paper round but then had to go immediately to the arcade to cope with the stress created by the job.

At first David enjoyed showing off his skills to his friends, but in time he started to gamble alone, and then his skills only mattered as a means of stretching out his money. His mother said: "He couldn't wait for the doors of the arcade to open in the mornings. He hammered on them in frustration … He was unable to concentrate on anything except his need to be there." His personality changed—he became evasive, withdrawn and argumentative. His appearance changed too—he didn't wash and went to school in smelly clothes.

Recovery

When David's mother was able to finally admit to herself how much David had been spending and the seriousness of the problem, she confronted him and he told her everything. "That was the first massive step towards reaching the light at the end of the tunnel." David's mother got in touch with Gamblers Anonymous and David said, "It was marvellous … there are people there who I can talk to who know exactly how I feel." This meant that David was able to accept that he had a problem. "I was able to talk … instead of playing the machines and [it] enabled me to GIVE UP. There was no method, just sheer will power and the fact that I wanted to give up." He also practised yoga, to relax when he felt the pull to gamble again, and he stayed well away from fruit machines.

Discussion points

1. Many of the data in this study were retrospective. How do you feel this may have affected the results?

2. To what extent do you think that a study such as this one affords greater understanding of gambling addiction than a survey-type study?

KEY STUDY EVALUATION — Griffiths

It is hazardous to generalise from a case study, but the data collected do highlight important issues, which may be overlooked in quantitative analyses. The data showed how gambling can be explained in terms of sociological and psychological factors. In this case study an important sociological factor was the easy access to gambling machines. As for psychological factors, initial motivations included winning money, displaying skill and having fun. Motivation to continue was almost entirely escapist, created by feelings of depression, confusion and rejection. What had been a primary motivator (money) became a means to an end. One of the key themes in the study was the lack of family communication and support.

Qualitative research is important in identifying areas for further research. For example in this study the role of depression has been identified as an antecedent of gambling. Such research can also offer useful insights that might help therapists relate better to their clients.

■ Activity: Investigating conformity quantitatively and qualitatively

One way to investigate conformity is to stand near a traffic light and observe how many cars go through the red light, i.e. the drivers do not conform to our traffic regulations. The results of such a study would involve a frequency count of the number of people who did this. You could distinguish between male and female drivers, and people who are on their own or with passengers.

A qualitative approach would be to interview individuals about their driving habits and consider the reasons given as to why people do not always conform to traffic signals.

Which approach would provide "better" or more useful information?

Evaluation of qualitative analysis

Qualitative analysis is often less influenced than quantitative analysis by the biases and theoretical assumptions of the investigator because these biases are recognised and incorporated in the research process. In addition, it offers the prospect of understanding the participants in a study as rounded individuals in a social context. This contrasts with quantitative analysis, in which the focus is often on rather narrow aspects of behaviour.

The greatest limitation of the qualitative approach is that the findings that are reported tend to be unreliable and hard to replicate. Why is this so? The qualitative approach is subjective and impressionistic, and so the ways in which the information is categorised and then interpreted often differ considerably from one investigator to another.

There are various ways in which qualitative researchers try to show that their findings are reliable (Coolican, 1994). Probably the most satisfactory approach is to see whether the findings obtained from a qualitative analysis can be replicated. This can be done by comparing the findings from an interview study with those from an observational study. Alternatively, two different qualitative researchers can conduct independent analyses of the same qualitative data, and then compare their findings, a kind of "inter-investigator" reliability.

Qualitative researchers argue that the fact that they typically go through the "research cycle" more than once helps to increase reliability. Thus, for example, the initial assumptions and categories of the researcher are checked against the data, and may then be changed. After that, the new assumptions and categories are checked against the data. Repeating the research cycle is of value in some ways, but it does not *ensure* that the findings will have high reliability.

Is it possible to demonstrate reliability in qualitative research?

Qualitative analysis of questionnaire surveys and interviews

We have already discussed the advantages and weaknesses of these kinds of research. Here we will consider the interpretation of such studies. Questionnaire studies and interviews vary considerably in terms of their degree of structure. In general terms, unstructured interviews (e.g. non-directive or informal) lend themselves to qualitative analyses, whereas structured interviews lend themselves to quantitative analysis. As Coolican (1994) pointed out, there are various skills that interviewers need in order to obtain valuable data. These skills involve establishing a good understanding with the person being interviewed, adopting a non-judgemental approach, and developing effective listening skills.

Cardwell et al. (1996) illustrated the value of the interview approach by discussing the work of Reicher and Potter (1985) on a riot in the St. Paul's area of Bristol in April 1980. Many of the media reports on the riot were based on the assumption that those involved in the riot were behaving in a primitive and excessively emotional way. Unstructured interviews with many of the participants indicated that in fact they had good reasons for their actions. They argued that they were defending their area against the police, and they experienced strong feelings of solidarity and community spirit. This interpretation was supported by the fact that very little of the damage affected private homes in the area.

Evaluation: Interpreting interviews

There are various problems involved in interpreting interview information. First, there is the problem of **social desirability bias**. Most people want to present themselves in the best possible light, so they may provide socially desirable rather than honest answers to personal questions. This problem can be handled by the interviewer asking additional questions to establish the truth.

Second, the data obtained from an interviewer may reveal more about the social interaction processes between the interviewer and the person being interviewed (the interviewee) than about the interviewee's thought processes and attitudes.

Third, account needs to be taken of the **self-fulfilling prophecy**. This is the tendency for someone's expectations about another person to lead to the fulfillment of those expectations. For example, suppose that a therapist expects his or her patient to behave very anxiously. This expectation may cause the therapist to treat the patient in such a way that the patient starts to behave in the expected fashion. **Experimenter bias** is an example of the self-fulfilling prophecy.

Reicher and Potter argued that the St. Paul's crowd saw themselves as a legitimate presence and the police as an illegitimate presence. Each group attached a different meaning to their actions. This is an example of qualitative data.

Nelson (1973) studied the way children acquire their vocabulary by asking caregivers to keep a record of all the words their young children used, and the circumstances surrounding the speech. This enabled both quantitative and qualitative analyses to be conducted.

Observations

As was discussed in Section 19, there are numerous kinds of observational studies, and the data obtained may be either quantitative or qualitative. We will consider issues relating to interpreting the data from observational studies by focusing on a concrete example.

Nelson (1973) conducted a study of language acquisition in children aged between 1 and 2 years old. Caregivers were asked to record any of the words that the child used. This enabled Nelson to identify the kind of words that children first used, which were names for objects (such as "ball") rather than non-objects (such as "up") and also tended to be quite specific ("Daniel" rather than "boy"). Nelson also asked caregivers to note whether the word was used as an imitation of someone or was used spontaneously by the child. All of these observations could be analysed quantitatively and represented using, for example, bar charts. In addition, Nelson also collected comments on what else was going on, such as where the child was, what he or she was doing, and what kind of mood the child was in. All of this data would be harder to quantify because there were so many variations but it could be presented as qualitative data, and might lead to ideas for later research. It also gives a richness to the data collected.

How can an experiment tell us more about "why" a behaviour has occurred than an observational study?

Evaluation of observational studies

Observational research does not really tell us *why* a behaviour has occurred but it does give us information on what happens. It is often very hard to interpret or make sense of the data obtained from observational studies, because we can only speculate on the reasons why the participants are behaving in the ways that we observe. Observations produce data that may lead to hypotheses which can then be tested in experiments.

Quantitative Analysis: Descriptive Statistics

Suppose that we have carried out an experiment on the effects of noise on learning with three groups of nine participants each. One group was exposed to very loud noise, another group to moderately loud noise, and the third group was not exposed to noise at all. What they had learned from a book chapter was assessed by giving them a set of questions, producing a score between 0 and 20.

What is to be done with the **raw scores**? There are two key types of measures that can be taken whenever we have a set of scores from participants in a given condition. First, there are **measures of central tendency**, which provide some indication of the size of average or typical scores. Second, there are **measures of dispersion**, which indicate the extent to which the scores cluster around the average or are spread out. Various measures of central tendency and of dispersion are considered next.

Measures of central tendency

Measures of central tendency describe how the data cluster together around a central point. There are three main measures of central tendency: the mean, the median, and the mode.

Mean

The **mean** in each group or condition is calculated by adding up all the scores in a given condition, and then dividing by the number of participants in that condition. Suppose that the scores of the nine participants in the no-noise condition are as follows: 1, 2, 4, 5, 7, 9, 9, 9, 17. The mean is given by the total, which is 63, divided by the number of participants, which is 9. Thus, the mean is 7 (see top box to the left).

The main advantage of the mean is the fact that it takes all the scores into account. This generally makes it a **sensitive** measure of central tendency, especially if the scores resemble the **normal distribution**, which is a bell-shaped distribution in which most scores cluster fairly close to the mean.

However, the mean can be very misleading if the distribution differs markedly from the normal distribution and there are one or two extreme scores in one direction. Suppose that eight people complete one lap of a track in go-karts. For seven of them, the times taken (in seconds) are as follows: 25, 27, 28, 29, 34, 39, and 42. The eighth person's go-kart breaks down, and so the driver has to push it around the track. This person takes 288 seconds to complete the lap. This produces an overall mean of 64 seconds. This is

Mean		
Scores	Number of scores	
1	1	
2	2	
4	3	
5	4	
7	5	
9	6	
9	7	
9	8	
17	9	
63	9	Total
63 ÷ 9		= 7

Example of a misleading mean
Scores
25
27
28
29
34
39
42
288
512 ÷ 8 = 64

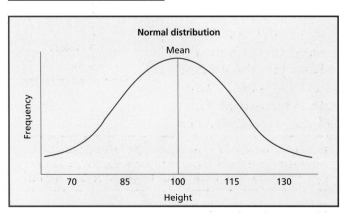

This is a normal distribution. It could represent the height of people in your class or the *x*-axis could be the "life-time" of a light bulb, given in weeks. Most of the scores will be clustered around the mean. The further away from the mean you get, the fewer cases there are.

LAP: 10 | TOTAL TIME: 20m 15 sec | FASTEST LAP: 1m 58 sec | THIS LAP: 2m 30 sec↑ | MEAN LAP: 2m 15 sec↑

An unexpected breakdown would cause the mean lap time to be very misleading.

clearly misleading, because no-one took even close to 64 seconds to complete one lap (see middle box on previous page).

The term "average" is rather vague. The mean, median, and mode are all averages.

Median

Another way of describing the general level of performance in each condition is known as the **median**. If there is an odd number of scores, then the median is simply the middle score, having an equal number of scores higher and lower than it. In the example with nine scores in the no-noise condition (1, 2, 4, 5, 7, 9, 9, 9, 17), the median is 7 (see box on the right). Matters are slightly more complex if there is an even number of scores. In that case, we take the two central values and work out their mean. For example, suppose that we have the following scores in size order: 2, 5, 5, 7, 8, 9. The two central values are 5 and 7, and so the median is (5 + 7) / 2 = 6.

The main advantage of the median is that it is unaffected by a few extreme scores, because it focuses only on scores in the middle of the distribution. In the case of our go-kart data the median would be 31.5, a more accurate "average" in this case than the mean. The median also has the advantage that it tends to be easier to work out than the mean.

The main limitation of the median is that it ignores most of the scores, and so it is often less sensitive than the mean. In addition, it is not always representative of the scores obtained, especially if there are only a few scores.

Scores
1
2
4
5
7   = Median
9
9
9
17

Mode

The final measure of central tendency is the **mode**. This is simply the most frequently occurring score. In the example of the nine scores in the no-noise condition, this is 9 (see box on the right).

The main advantages of the mode are that it is unaffected by one or two extreme scores, and that it is the easiest measure of central tendency to work out. In addition, it can still be worked out even when some of the extreme scores are not known.

However, its limitations generally outweigh these advantages. The greatest limitation is that the mode tends to be unreliable. For example, suppose we have the following scores: 4, 4, 6, 7, 8, 8, 12, 12, 12. The mode of these scores is 12. If just one score changed (a 12 becoming a 4), the mode would change to 4! Another limitation is that information about the exact values of the scores obtained is ignored in working out the mode. This makes it a less sensitive measure than the mean.

Scores
1
2
4
5
7
9
9   = Mode
9
17

The mode is useful where other measures of central tendency are meaningless, for example when calculating the number of children in the average family. It would be unusual to have 0.4 or 0.6 of a child!

A final consideration is that it is possible for there to be more than one mode. In the case of the following scores 4, 4, 4, 4, 5, 6, 6, 8, 8, 8, 8 there are two modes (4 and 8) and the scores are therefore called **bimodal**. And some sets of data have no mode, as in our go-kart data.

If we report the scores of these competitors in terms of how many points they scored this would be at the interval/ratio level of measurement, because each added unit represents an equal increase. For example, someone who gets a score of 100 has done twice as well as someone who gets 50. If we just give the scores in order of merit, i.e. who came 1st, 2nd and so on, then this would be at the ordinal level of measurement. Finally if we decide that everyone who scores over 50 is a winner and the rest are losers, then we are using categories or a nominal level of measurement.

Nominal

Interval

Ordinal

Ratio

Levels of measurement

From what has been said so far, we have seen that the mean is the most generally useful measure of central tendency, whereas the mode is the least useful. However, we need to take account of the **level of measurement** when deciding which measure of central tendency to use. There are four levels, here listed in order of increasing precision or sensitivity:

- **Nominal**: the data consist of the numbers of participants falling into various categories (e.g. fat, thin; men, women).
- **Ordinal**: the data can be ordered from lowest to highest (e.g. the finishing positions of athletes in a race).
- **Interval**: the data differ from ordinal data, because the units of measurement are fixed throughout the range. For example, there is the same "distance" between a height of 1.58 metres and 1.70 metres as between 1.70 metres and 1.82 metres (i.e. 0.12 metres), whereas on an ordinal scale the gap between each score (1st, 2nd, 3rd, and so on) will not be the same.
- **Ratio**: the data have the same characteristics as interval data, with the exception that they have a meaningful zero point. For example, time measurements provide ratio data because the notion of zero time is meaningful, and 10 seconds is twice as long as 5 seconds. The similarities between interval and ratio data are so great that they are sometimes combined and referred to as interval/ratio data.

The mean should only be used when the scores are at the interval level of measurement. The median can be used when the data are at the interval or ordinal level. The mode can be used when the data are at any of the three levels. It is the only one of the three measures of central tendency that can be used with nominal data.

Measures of dispersion

In addition to having an estimate of central tendency, it is also useful to work out what are known as measures of dispersion, such as the range and standard deviation. These measures indicate whether the scores in a given condition are similar to each other or whether they are spread out.

Range

The simplest of these measures is the **range**, which can be defined as the difference between the highest and the lowest score in any condition. In the case of the following numbers: 4, 5, 5, 7, 9, 9, 9, 17, the range is calculated as follows: highest number – lowest number, or 17 – 4 = 13.

In fact, it is preferable to calculate the range in a slightly different way (Coolican, 1994). The revised formula (when we are dealing with whole numbers) is as follows: (highest score – lowest score) + 1. Thus, in our example, the range is (17 – 4) + 1 = 14. This formula is preferable because it takes account of the fact that the scores were rounded to whole numbers. In our sample data, a score of 17 stands for all values between 16.5 and 17.5, and a score of 4 represents a value between 3.5 and 4.5. If we take the range as the interval between the highest possible value (17.5) and the lowest possible value (3.5), this gives us a range of 14, which is precisely the figure produced by the formula.

What has been said so far about the range applies only to whole numbers. Suppose that we measure the time taken to perform a task to the nearest one-tenth of a second, with the fastest time being 21.3 seconds and the slowest time being 36.8 seconds. The figure of 21.3 represents a value between 21.25 and 21.35, and 36.8 represents a value between 36.75 and 36.85. As a result, the range is 36.85 – 21.25, which is 15.6 seconds, whereas 36.8 – 21.3 = 15.5.

> **If the data are:**
> 4, 5, 5, 7, 9, 9, 9, 17
> the range is 13
>
> **If the data were:**
> 4, 5, 5, 7, 9, 9, 9, 10
> the range becomes 6, a drastic change due to one extreme value in the first set of data

Advantages and disadvantages of using the range. The main advantages of the range as a measure of dispersion are that it is easy to calculate and that it takes full account of extreme values. The main weakness of the range is that it can be greatly influenced by one score that is very different from all of the others. In the example above, the inclusion of the participant scoring 17 increases the range from 9 to 17. The other important weakness of the range is that it ignores all but two of the scores, and so is likely to provide an inadequate measure of the general spread or dispersion of the scores around the mean or median.

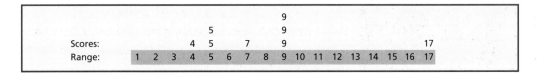

Standard deviation

The most generally useful measure of dispersion is the **standard deviation**. It is harder to calculate than the range, but generally provides a more accurate measure of the spread of scores. However, you will be pleased to learn that many calculators allow the standard deviation to be worked out rapidly and effortlessly. To calculate the standard deviation manually, follow these steps (also illustrated in the worked example on the next page):

1. The first step is to work out the mean of the sample. This is given by the total of all of the participants' scores $\sum x = 130$ (the symbol $\sum$ means "the sum of") divided by the number of participants (N = 13). Thus, the mean ($\bar{x}$) is 10.
2. The second step is to subtract the mean in turn from each score ($x - \bar{x}$). The calculations are shown in the fourth column.
3. The third step is to square each of the scores in the fourth column ($x - \bar{x}$)^2.
4. The fourth step is to work out the total of all the squared scores, $\sum(x - \bar{x})^2$. This comes to 136.

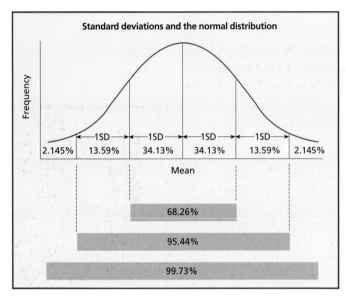

Standard deviations and the normal distribution

2.145%	13.59%	34.13%	34.13%	13.59%	2.145%

68.26%

95.44%

99.73%

Two-thirds of a normally distributed population (or 68.26%) are located within one standard deviation of the mean, 95.44% fall within two standard deviations, and 99.73% fall within three standard deviations.

Standard deviation: A worked example

Participant	Score (x)	Mean $(\bar{x})$	Deviation $(x - \bar{x})$	Deviation² $(x - \bar{x})^2$
1	13	10	3	9
2	6	10	−4	16
3	10	10	0	0
4	15	10	5	25
5	10	10	0	0
6	15	10	5	25
7	5	10	−5	25
8	9	10	−1	1
9	10	10	0	0
10	13	10	3	9
11	6	10	−4	16
12	11	10	1	1
13	7	10	−3	9
13	130	10		$\Sigma(x - \bar{x}) = 136$

Total of scores $(\Sigma x) = 130$

Number of participants (N) = 13

Mean $(\bar{x}) = \dfrac{\Sigma x}{N} = \dfrac{130}{13} = 10$

Σ means "the sum of"

$\bar{x}$ is the symbol for the mean

Variance $(s^2) = \dfrac{136}{13 - 1} = 11.33$

Standard deviation (SD) $= \sqrt{11.3} = 3.37$

5. The fifth step is to divide the result of the fourth step by one less than the number of participants, N − 1 = 12. This gives us 136 divided by 12, which equals 11.33. This is known as the **variance** (s^2), which is in squared units.

6. Finally, we use a calculator to take the square root of the variance. This produces a figure of 3.37. This is the standard deviation (SD).

The method for calculating the standard deviation that has just been described is used when we want to estimate the standard deviation of the population. If we want merely to describe the spread of scores in our sample, then the fifth step is to divide the result of the fourth step by N.

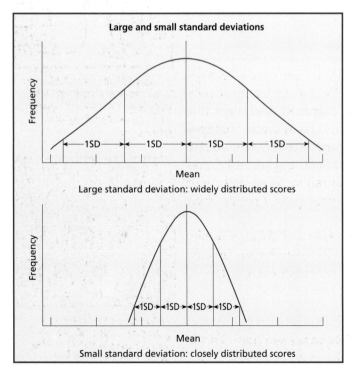

Large and small standard deviations

Large standard deviation: widely distributed scores

Small standard deviation: closely distributed scores

What does the standard deviation mean? Where data is normally distributed, about two-thirds of the scores in a sample should lie within one standard deviation of the mean. This is shown in the top graph on the left.

In our example, the mean of the sample is 10.0, one standard deviation above the mean will be 13.366 and one standard deviation below the mean will be 6.634. Eight out of the thirteen scores lie between these two values, which is 61.5%, which is only slightly below the expected percentage.

Advantages and disadvantages of using standard deviation. The standard deviation takes account of all of the scores and provides a sensitive measure of dispersion. As we have seen, it also has the advantage that it describes the spread of scores in a normal distribution with great precision. The most obvious disadvantage of the standard deviation is that it is much harder to work out than the other measures of dispersion.

The Nature of Correlations

In Section 19 we considered studies using correlational analysis. Strictly speaking correlation is not a research method but a method of analysing data. Therefore it is appropriate to consider correlation further in this section on data analysis.

Positive and negative correlation

If we study the IQs of pairs of twins, then we would expect their IQs to be quite similar. This is called a **positive correlation**, when two variables increase together. You can also have **negative correlation** when there is an inverse relationship between two variables—as one increases the other decreases (illustrations of positive and negative correlations are shown here). The co-variables still vary together, though in opposite directions. This can be seen in exposure to loud noise and hearing. As your exposure increases, in general your hearing abilities may decrease. The two variables are still correlated because there is a clear and predictable association, the co-variables vary systematically together.

A positive correlation: The taller the player, the higher the score.

Correlation coefficients

We assess the extent to which the co-variables are correlated using the **correlation coefficient**. A coefficient is a number that expresses the degree to which two things are related. If two variables are perfectly related then the coefficient is 1.0. Perfect positive correlation is +1.0 and perfect negative correlation is –1.0. Of course, perfect correlation is rare. A correlation coefficient of –0.75 would reflect a close inverse relationship between two variables. A correlation coefficient of –0.85 would suggest an even closer inverse relationship. A correlation coefficient of –0.25 or +0.25 would suggest a poor relationship between the two variables. A zero correlation coefficient (0.0) is a complete lack of relationship.

It is possible to calculate the correlation coefficient between co-variables using a statistical test, but this is not covered at AS level.

A negative correlation: The more time spent playing computer games, the less time spent studying.

Graphs and Charts

Measures of central tendency and of range are ways of summarising data. Perhaps it is even more helpful to use visual displays to summarise information and get a feel for what it means. If information is presented in a graph or chart, this may make it easier for people to understand what has been found, compared to simply presenting information about the central tendency and dispersion. We will shortly consider some examples. The key point to remember is that all graphs and charts should be clearly labelled and presented so that the reader can rapidly make sense of the information contained in them. It is also helpful to use squared paper when recording numbers and drawing graphs.

Suppose that we ask 25 male athletes to run 400 metres as rapidly as possible, and record their times (in seconds). Having worked out a table of frequencies (see the boxed example on page 286), there are several ways to present these data.

No correlation: Where there is no relationship, variables are uncorrelated.

Frequency polygon

One way of summarising these data is in the form of a **frequency polygon**. This is a simple form of chart in which the scores from low to high are indicated on the *x*

25 athletes running 400 metres

```
Raw data

Athlete    1    2    3    4    5    6    7    8    9
Speed     71   77   84   49   63   62   56   67   52

Athlete   10   11   12   13   14   15   16   17   18
Speed     61   63   59   48   61   65   68   54   61

Athlete   19   20   21   22   23   24   25
Speed     58   66   55   57   58   56   53
```

Table of frequencies (number of athletes obtaining each speed)

Speed	48	49	52	53	54	55	56	57	58	59	61	62	63	65	66	67	68	71	77	84
Athlete no.	13	4	9	25	17	21	7 24	22	19 23	12	10 14 18	6	5 11	15	20	8	16	1	2	3
Number	1	1	1	1	1	1	2	1	2	1	3	1	2	1	1	1	1	1	1	1

or horizontal axis and the frequencies of the various scores (in terms of the numbers of individuals obtaining each score) are indicated on the *y* or vertical axis. The points on a frequency polygon should only be joined up when the scores can be ordered from low to high. In order for a frequency polygon to be most useful, it should be constructed so that most of the frequencies are neither very high nor very low. The frequencies will be very high if the width of each class interval (the categories used to summarise frequencies) on the *x* axis is too broad (e.g. covering 20 seconds), and the frequencies will be very low if each class interval is too narrow (e.g. covering only 1 or 2 seconds). This is shown in the box to the left.

Histogram

A similar way of describing these data is by means of a **histogram** (see example on the next page). In a histogram, the scores are indicated on the horizontal axis and the frequencies are shown on the vertical axis. In contrast to a frequency polygon, however, the frequencies are indicated by rectangular columns. These columns are all the same width but vary in height in accordance with the corresponding frequencies. As with frequency polygons, it is important to make sure that the class intervals are not too broad or too narrow. All class intervals are represented, even if there are no scores in some of them. Class intervals are indicated by their mid-point at the centre of the columns.

Histograms are clearly rather similar to frequency polygons. However, frequency polygons are sometimes preferable when you want to compare two different frequency distributions.

The information contained in a histogram is interpreted in the same way as the information in a

Frequency polygons showing athletes' data

Class intervals are too large which makes it hard to interpret the data

Smaller class intervals permit easier interpretation

How should we interpret the findings shown in the frequency polygon? It is clear that most of the participants were able to run 400 metres in between about 53 and 67 seconds. Only a few of the athletes were able to better a time of 53 seconds, and there was a small number who took longer than 67 seconds.

frequency polygon. In the present example, the histogram indicates that most of the athletes ran 400 metres fairly quickly. Only a few had extreme times.

Bar chart

Frequency polygons and histograms are suitable when the scores obtained by the participants can be ordered from low to high. In more technical terms, the data should be either interval or ratio. However, there are many studies in which the scores are in the form of categories rather than ordered scores. In other words,

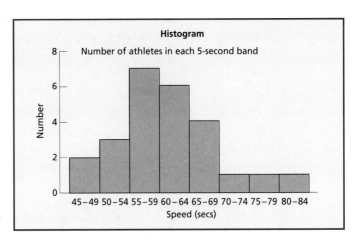

A histogram provides a means of summarising the data.

the data are nominal. For example, 50 people might be asked to indicate their favourite leisure activity. Suppose that 15 said going to a party, 12 said going to the pub, 9 said watching television, 8 said playing sport, and 6 said reading a good book.

These data can be displayed in the form of a **bar chart**. In a bar chart, the categories are shown along the horizontal axis, and the frequencies are indicated on the vertical axis, as in a histogram. However, in contrast to the data contained in histograms, the categories in bar charts cannot be ordered numerically in a meaningful way. However, they can be arranged in ascending (or descending) order of popularity. Another difference from histograms is that the rectangles in a bar chart do not usually touch each other.

The scale on the vertical axis of a bar chart normally starts at zero. However, it is sometimes convenient for presentational purposes to have it start at some higher value. If that is done, then it should be made clear in the bar chart that the lower part of the vertical scale is missing. The columns in a bar chart often represent frequencies. However, they can also represent means or percentages for different groups (Coolican, 1994).

Scattergraphs

In the case of correlational studies, the data are in the form of two measures of behaviour from each member of a single group of participants. These are called co-variables. These data can be presented in the form of a **scattergraph** (also known

A bar chart makes it easy to compare the popularity of different leisure activities. We can see at a glance that going to a party was the most popular leisure activity, whereas reading a good book was the least popular. The data in this chart are in nominal categories.

as a scattergram). It is given this name, because it shows the ways in which the scores of individuals are scattered.

Suppose that we have carried out a study on the relationship between the amount of television violence watched (co-variable A) and the amount of aggressive behaviour displayed (co-variable B). We could have a scale of the amount of television violence watched on the horizontal axis, and a scale of the amount of aggressive behaviour on the vertical axis. We could then put a dot for each participant indicating where he or she falls on these two dimensions. For example, suppose that one individual watched 17 hours of television and obtained a score of 8 for aggressive behaviour. We would put a dot at the point where the

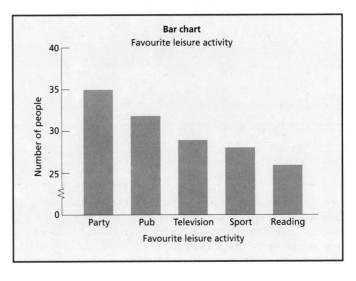

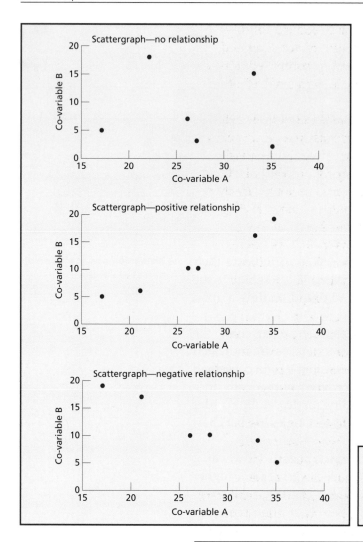

invisible vertical line from the 17 meets the invisible horizontal line from the 8.

How do we interpret the information contained in a scattergraph?

If there is a positive relationship between watching violence and aggression, then the dots should tend to form a pattern going from the bottom left of the scattergraph to the top right. If there is no relationship between the two variables, then the dots should be distributed in a fairly random way within the scattergraph. If there is a negative relationship between the two variables, then the dots will form a pattern going from the top left to the bottom right. In the case of television violence and aggression, a negative correlation would mean that watching a lot of television violence was associated with a *low* level of aggression, a negative correlation.

The scattergraph gives you a rough idea of the association between two variables. To be more precise you need to calculate an inferential statistic called a "correlation coefficient", but as we have said these statistics are not covered at AS level.

You have reached the end of the chapter on research methods in psychology. Research is fundamental to the status of psychology as a scientific subject. It enables us to be more than "armchair psychologists". We should be able to provide systematic, reliable, and valid evidence for our views.

CHAPTER SUMMARY

Quantitative and qualitative research methods

❖ All research is scientific. The scientific method involves collecting data, formulating theories that generate hypotheses, testing the hypotheses by designing research, and then collecting data, and finally revising the theory in line with the new data.

❖ The key principle of the experimental method is that an independent variable is manipulated (with all confounding variables controlled) in order to observe its effect on a dependent variable. Participants should be randomly allocated to conditions to further rule out confounding variables. The experimental method is used in laboratory and field experiments.

❖ Use of the experimental method allows us to infer causality, and it aims to be replicable.

❖ Laboratory experiments permit greater control of confounding variables and more detailed data collection, but they tend to be artificial (lack external validity and mundane realism). This artificiality can be compensated for by increased experimental realism (internal validity). Other concerns include the problems arising from knowing you are being observed (demand characteristics and evaluation apprehension) and ethical issues such as being obedient to authority and the right to withdraw.

❖ Field experiments are less artificial (higher external or ecological validity) than laboratory experiments, and suffer less from factors such as demand characteristics and evaluation apprehension. They are less controlled (lower internal validity), and they do create ethical problems in terms of lack of informed consent.

❖ Quasi-experiments fall short of true experiments because the experimenter has not manipulated the independent variable and because the participants are not allocated at random to conditions. Natural experiments are quasi-experiments involving some naturally occurring independent variable. One advantage of natural experiments is that the participants are not aware they are taking part in an experiment, which prevents demand characteristics. Natural experiments also permit the study of variables that could not be ethically manipulated by an experimenter. Limitations include problems of interpreting the findings due to a lack of randomisation. There is also an ethical concern about taking advantage of people at a time of high stress.

❖ Investigations using correlational analysis are inferior to experimental designs, because they do not permit inferences about causality. However, many issues can only be studied by assessing correlations or associations between variables. Correlational studies determine the extent that co-variables vary together, and offer the possibility of obtaining large amounts of data very rapidly. In terms of ethical concerns we should be wary of misinterpretations of correlational evidence.

❖ Naturalistic observation involves the use of methods designed to assess behaviour without the experimenter interfering in any way. Naturalistic observation can provide rich and full information from people who are unaware that they are being observed. It is especially suitable for some situations (e.g. workplace studies) and some kinds of participant (e.g. children). However, the experimenter has essentially no control over the situation, the participants are often aware they are being observed, and there can be problems with reliability and replication, as well as ethical concerns such as lack of informed consent. Participant observation may raise ethical objections.

❖ There are several types of interview ranging from the unstructured to the totally structured. Unstructured interviews are responsive to the personality, interests, and motivations of the interviewee and therefore tend to produce more qualitative data, although the data obtained tend to be unreliable. In contrast, structured interviews permit comparisons among interviewees, and they tend to be fairly reliable, but what the interviewee says can be constrained and artificial and the data collected tend to be more quantitative. Questionnaire surveys are written, highly structured interviews which permit large amounts of data to be collected but are not suitable for all participants. All types of interviews can produce problems due to social desirability bias, and interviewees can only provide information of which they are consciously aware. Ethically we might be concerned with the issue of confidentiality.

❖ The first stage in designing a study is to decide on its aims and hypotheses. Aims tell us why, and hypotheses tell us what. The null hypothesis is a statement of no effect. It increases precision. One can prove (accept) the alternative hypothesis by rejecting the null hypothesis. The experimental hypothesis may be directional or one-tailed, or it may be non-directional and two-tailed. Non-experimental research may also have aims and hypotheses.

Research design and implementation

❖ There are three main types of experimental design: independent design, matched participants design, and repeated measures design. With an independent design, random allocation is generally used to distribute participants to groups. The aim is to ensure that both groups are equivalent. Repeated measures compensates for any participant variation because the participants in both conditions are the same. However there is the problem of order effects, which may be overcome using counterbalancing. In an independent design there may be an experimental and a control *group*. In repeated measures there may be an experimental and a control *condition*. Matched participant design uses independent groups of participants who are similar. Control groups/conditions provide a baseline measure.

❖ The design of qualitative research concerns how to construct questionnaires and interviews, and the choice of various observational methods. Methods of data collection include event sampling, time sampling, and point sampling. We should distinguish between data recording and interpretation.

❖ Factors in research design that are important to "good practice" include the use standardised instructions and procedures. It is also important to avoid confounding variables and other forms of constant error by turning them into controlled variables. Operationalisation is useful, but operational definitions typically cover only part of the meaning of the variable in question. Pilot studies are important for testing the extent to which the design works in practice, before committing time and money to a full-scale study.

❖ Reliability and validity are also part of good research design. The measures used in a study should possess good reliability or consistency. If they do not, then they are inadequate measures of the variables in question, and it will be hard to replicate or repeat any findings obtained. Reliability can be determined by calculating inter-observer reliability, test–retest, and split-half measures. A study should also have internal validity, meaning that the findings are genuine and caused by the independent variable, and external validity, which refers to the extent to which the findings of a study can be generalised. It is important to be able to make generalisations about populations, locations, measures, and historical times. Information about the generalisability of any particular findings can be obtained by means of a meta-analysis. Finally, ethics are an key consideration for good practice.

❖ The participants selected for a study represent a sample from some target population. They should form a representative sample and be selected to avoid sampling bias. The best approach is random sampling, but this is difficult to achieve in practice because of problems identifying whole populations, finding all participants, and obtaining responses from them. Opportunity sampling is the easiest but least satisfactory method. The ideal sample size depends on the likely size of the effect being studied. Fifteen participants in each experimental condition is a reasonable size.

❖ Most research involves interactions between the researcher and the participants. This can introduce various systematic biases, which can be divided into participant reactivity and investigator effects. Examples of participant reactivity include the Hawthorne effect and demand characteristics. Demand characteristics involve the participants responding on the basis of their beliefs about the research hypothesis or hypotheses. These can be minimised using a single blind experimental design. Investigator effects include experimenter expectancy (e.g. Clever Hans), investigator loose procedure effect, and experimenter fudging. Double blind is one way to overcome these effects.

❖ Qualitative research is concerned with the experiences of the participants, and with the meanings they attach to themselves and their lives. A key principle of qualitative analysis is that theoretical understanding emerges from the data, and is not imposed by the researcher. Qualitative researchers typically categorise the data after taking account of all of the data and of the participants' own categories. However, findings based on qualitative data tend to be unreliable and hard to replicate.

❖ Investigators using questionnaire surveys, interviews, or observations often (but not always) make use of qualitative data. It can be hard to interpret the information obtained from questionnaire surveys and interviews because of social desirability bias, complex interactional processes, and the self-fulfilling prophecy. The findings of observational studies can be interpreted using both quantitative and qualitative analyses. One drawback is that such studies are often difficult to interpret because it is not clear why the participants are behaving as they are.

❖ The correlations between two variables can be positive (variables increase together) or negative (variables change in an inverse fashion). The extent to which the co-variables are related is expressed by a correlation coefficient. Perfect correlation is +1.0 or –1.0 for positive or negative correlation respectively.

❖ When we have obtained scores from a group of participants, we can summarise our data by working out a measure of central tendency (average) and a measure of dispersion or spread of scores around the central tendency. The mean is the most generally useful measure of central tendency because it takes all the scores into account, but other measures include the median and mode. The median is less affected by extreme values and the mode is used for nominal data. The standard deviation is the most useful and precise measure of dispersion, but the range is a much simpler figure to calculate, although it is affected by extreme scores.

❖ Summary data from a study can be presented in the form of a figure, so that it is easy to observe general trends. Among the possible ways of presenting the data in a figure are the following: table of frequencies, frequency polygon, histogram, bar chart, and scattergraph. Frequency polygons and histograms are used when the scores can be ordered from low to high, whereas bar charts are used when the scores are in the form of categories (nominal data). The data from correlational studies are presented in a scattergraph where the scores on two co-variables are recorded from every participant as a dot.

FURTHER READING

A book that covers most research methods in an accessible way is H. Coolican (1994) *Research methods and statistics in psychology* (London: Hodder & Stoughton). A shorter version of the Coolican (1994) textbook is H. Coolican (1995) *Introduction to research methods and statistics in psychology* (London: Hodder & Stoughton). A good student book that is reasonably priced is by A. Searle (1999) *Introducing research and data in psychology* (London: Routledge). Another useful textbook is J.J. Foster and J. Parker (1995) *Carrying out investigations in psychology: Methods and statistics* (Leicester, UK: BPS Books). The various forms of non-experimental study are described in C. Dyer (1995) *Beginning research in psychology* (Oxford, UK: Blackwell).

Revision Questions

The examination questions aim to sample the material in this whole chapter. For advice on how to answer such questions, refer to Chapter 1, Section 3. In this section of the AQA examination all questions are compulsory. You would have approximately 45 minutes in which to do both questions.

Question 1

A psychology student decides to conduct her coursework study on conformity. She plans to stop people in the street and ask them to estimate the number of jelly beans in a jar. To test participants' conformity she will ask them to respond on a sheet of paper that has the answers of other participants. Some participants will be shown sheet 1, which has answers that are high estimates. These participants would belong to the "high estimate group". Other participants (the "low estimate group") will be shown sheet 2, which has low estimates. The student prepares 30 sheets, 15 for each condition and hands these out in a random order to participants.

The student's initial hypothesis was that participants would conform to the norm established by the answers on the sheet. The "high estimate" group should produce a set of higher estimates than the "low estimate" group.

a. Name the method used in this study.   (1 mark)
b. Give *one* advantage and *one* disadvantage of this method.   (2 marks + 2 marks)
c. State a suitable hypothesis for this study.   (2 marks)
d. What would be a suitable measure of central tendency for the estimates given
   by each participant?   (2 marks)
e. Why would it be important to test participants individually?   (2 marks)
f. Why was it important that all participants were given the same instruction?   (2 marks)
g. Identify *one* ethical problem that may have arisen in this study.   (2 marks)

Question 2

Imagine that you have been asked to carry out a questionnaire study to assess the effects that stress has on physical and psychological health. Explain how you would carry out such a study.

a. Suggest a suitable hypothesis for this study.   (2 marks)
b. How would you select respondents to take part in your study?   (2 marks)
c. Why would you choose this particular method of selecting respondents?   (2 marks)
d. Suggest *one* kind of question you might use in this study.   (2 marks)
e. For this kind of question, identify *one* advantage and *one* disadvantage.   (2 marks + 2 marks)
f. How would you try to ensure that respondents answered the questions truthfully?   (3 marks)

References

Abernethy, E.M. (1940). The effect of changed environmental conditions upon the results of college examinations. *Journal of Psychology, 10,* 293–301.

Adams, P.R., & Adams, G.R. (1984). Mount Saint Helen's ashfall: Evidence for a disaster stress reaction. *American Psychologist, 39,* 252–260.

Adorno, T.W., Frenkel-Brunswik, E., Levinson, D., & Sanford, R. (1950). *The authoritarian personality.* New York: Harper.

Ainsworth, M.D.S. (1982). Infant–mother attachment. *American Psychologist, 34,* 932–937.

Ainsworth, M.D.S., & Bell, S.M. (1970). Attachment, exploration and separation: Illustrated by the behaviour of one-year-olds in a strange situation. *Child Development, 41,* 49–67.

Ainsworth, M.D.S., Bell, S.M., & Stayton, D.J. (1971). Individual differences in strange situation behaviour of one-year-olds. In H.R. Schaffer (Ed.), *The origins of human social relations.* London: Academic Press.

Ainsworth, M.D.S., Bell, S.M., & Stayton, D.J. (1974). Infant/mother attachment and social development as a product of reciprocal responsiveness to signals. In M.P.M. Richards (Ed.), *The integration of the child into a social world.* Cambridge, UK: Cambridge University Press.

Ainsworth, M.D.S., Blehar, M.C., Waters, E., & Wall, S. (1978). *Patterns of attachment: A psychological study of the strange situation,* Hillsdale, NJ: Lawrence Erlbaum Associates Inc.

Allport, G.W., & Postman, L. (1947). *The psychology of rumour.* New York: Holt, Rinehart & Winston.

Anderson, J. (1972). Attachment out of doors. In N. Blurton-Jones (Ed.), *Ethological studies of child behaviour.* Cambridge, UK: Cambridge University Press.

Andersson, B.-E. (1992). Effects of daycare on cognitive and socioemotional competence of thirteen-year-old Swedish schoolchildren. *Child Development, 63,* 20–36.

Arendt, H. (1963). *Eichmann in Jerusalem: A report on the banality of evil.* New York: Viking Press.

Aronson, E. (1988). *The social animal* (5th Edn.). New York: Freeman.

Asch, S.E. (1951). Effects of group pressure on the modification and distortion of judgements. In H. Guetzkow (Ed.), *Groups, leadership and men.* Pittsburgh, PA: Carnegie.

Asch, S.E. (1955). Opinions and social pressure. *Scientific American, 193,* 31–35.

Asch, S.E. (1956). Studies of independence and conformity: A minority of one against a unanimous majority. *Psychological Monographs, 70*(Whole no. 416).

Ashton, H. (1997). Benzodiazepine dependency. In A. Baum, S. Newman, J. Weinman, R. West, & C. McManus (Eds.), *Cambridge handbook of psychology, health and medicine.* Cambridge, UK: Cambridge University Press.

Atkinson, R.C., & Shiffrin, R.M. (1968). Human memory: A proposed system and its control processes. In K.W. Spence & J.T. Spence (Eds.), *The psychology of learning and motivation, Vol. 2.* London: Academic Press.

Attanasio, V., Andrasik, F., Burke, E.J., Blake, D.D., Kabela, E., & McCarran, M.S. (1985). Clinical issues in utilizing biofeedback with children. *Clinical Biofeedback and Health, 8,* 134–141.

Ayllon, T., & Azrin, N.H. (1968). *The token economy: A motivational system for therapy and rehabilitation.* New York: Appleton-Century-Crofts.

Bachen, E., Cohen, S., & Marsland, A.L. (1997). Psychoimmunology. In A. Baum, S. Newman, J. Weinman, R. West, & C. McManus (Eds.), *Cambridge handbook of psychology, health, and medicine.* Cambridge, UK: Cambridge University Press.

Baddeley, A.D. (1966). The influence of acoustic and semantic similarity on long-term memory for word sequences. *Quarterly Journal of Experimental Psychology, 18,* 302–309.

Baddeley, A.D., & Hitch, G.J. (1974). Working memory. In G.H. Bower (Ed.), *The psychology of learning and motivation, Vol. 8.* London: Academic Press.

Baddeley, A.D., & Lewis, V.J. (1981). Inner active processes in reading: The inner voice, the inner ear and the inner eye. In A.M. Lesgold & C.A. Perfetti (Eds.), *Interactive processes in reading.* Hillsdale, NJ: Lawrence Erlbaum Associates Inc.

Baddeley, A.D., Thomson, N., & Buchanan, M. (1975). Word length and the structure of short-term memory. *Journal of Verbal Learning and Verbal Behavior, 14,* 575–589.

Bahrick, H.P., Bahrick, P.O., & Wittinger, R.P. (1975). Fifty years of memory for names and faces: A cross-sectional approach. *Journal of Experimental Psychology: General, 104,* 54–75.

Bales, R.F. (1950). *Interaction process analysis: A method for the study of small groups*. Reading, MA: Addison-Wesley.

Bandura, A. (1965). Influences of models' reinforcement contingencies on the acquisition of initiative responses. *Journal of Personality and Social Psychology, 1,* 589–593.

Bandura, A. (1986). *Social foundations of thought and action: A social cognitive theory*. Englewood Cliffs, NJ: Prentice-Hall.

Bandura, A., Blanchard, E., & Ritter, B. (1969) Relative efficacy of desensitization and modeling approaches for inducing behavioural, affective and attitudinal changes. *Journal of Personality and Social Psychology, 13,* 173–199.

Bandura, A., Ross, D., & Ross, S.A. (1961). Transmission of aggression through imitation of aggressive models. *Journal of Abnormal and Social Psychology, 63,* 575–582.

Banuazizi, A., & Mohavedi, S. (1973). Interpersonal dynamics in a simulated prison: A methodological analysis. *American Psychologist, 30,* 152–160.

Banyard, P., & Hayes, N. (1994). *Psychology: Theory and application*. London: Chapman & Hall.

Barber, T.X. (1976). *Pitfalls in human research*. Oxford, UK: Pergamon.

Barlow, D.H., & Durand, V.M. (1995). *Abnormal psychology: An integrative approach*. New York: Brooks/Cole.

Baron, R.A., & Ransberger, V.M. (1978). Ambient temperature and the occurrence of collective violence: The "long hot summer" revisited. *Journal of Personality and Social Psychology, 36,* 351–360.

Barr, C.E., Mednick, S.A., & Munk-Jorgenson, P. (1990). Exposure to influenza epidemics during gestation and adult schizophrenia: A forty-year study. *Archives of General psychiatry, 47,* 869–874.

Barrett, H. (1997). How young children cope with separation: Toward a new conceptualization. *British Journal of Medical Psychology, 70,* 339–358.

Bartlett, F.C. (1932). *Remembering: A study in experimental and social psychology*. Cambridge, UK: Cambridge University Press.

Bates, J.E., Maslin, C.A., & Frankel, K.A. (1985). Attachment security, mother–child interaction, and temperament as predictors of behaviour-problem ratings at age three years. In I. Bretherton & E. Waters (Eds.), Growing points of attachment theory and research. *Monographs of the Society for Research in Child Development, 50*(Whole no. 209).

Baumrind, D. (1964). Some thoughts on ethics of research: After reading Milgram's behavioural study of obedience. *American Psychologist, 19,* 421–423.

Baumrind, D. (1975). Metaethical and normative considerations governing the treatment of human subjects in the behavioural sciences. In E.C. Kennedy (Ed.), *Human rights and psychological research: A debate on psychology and ethics*. New York: Thomas Y. Crowell.

Beck, A.T. (1976). *Cognitive therapy of the emotional disorders*. New York: New American Library.

Beck, A.T., & Clark, D.A. (1988). Anxiety and depression: An information processing perspective. *Anxiety Research, 1,* 23–36.

Beck, A.T., Rush, A.J., Shaw, B.F., & Emery, G. (1979). *Cognitive therapy of depression*. New York: Guilford Press.

Beck, A.T., & Weishaar, M.E. (1989). Cognitive therapy. In R.J. Corsini & D. Wedding (Eds.), *Current psychotherapies*. Itacca, IL: Peacock.

Belsky, J., & Rovine, M. (1987). Temperament and attachment security in the Strange Situation: A rapprochement. *Child Development, 58,* 787–795.

Belsky, J., & Rovine, M.J. (1988). Nonmaternal care in the first year of life and the security of parent–infant attachment. *Child Development, 59,* 157–167.

Berkun, M.M., Bialek, H.M., Kern, R.P., & Yagi, K. (1962). Experimental studies of psychological stress in man. *Psychological Monographs, 76*(Whole no. 15).

Bickman, L. (1974). Clothes make the person. *Psychology Today, 8*(4), 48–51.

Blos, P. (1967). The second individuation process of adolescence. *Psychoanalytic Study of the Child, 22,* 162–186.

Bogdonoff, M.D., Klein, E.J., Shaw, D.M., & Back, K.W. (1961). The modifying effect of conforming behaviour upon lipi responses accompanying CNS arousal. *Clinical Research, 9,* 135.

Bower, G.H., Black, J.B., & Turner, T.J. (1979). Scripts in memory for text. *Cognitive Psychology, 11,* 177–220.

Bowlby, J. (1946). *Forty-four juvenile thieves*. London: Bailliere, Tindall & Cox.

Bowlby, J. (1951). *Maternal care and mental health*. Geneva, Switzerland: World Health Organisation.

Bowlby, J. (1953). *Child care and the growth of love*. Harmondsworth, UK: Penguin.

Bowlby, J. (1958). The nature of the child's tie to his mother. *International Journal of Psycho-Analysis, 39,* 350–373.

Bowlby, J. (1969). *Attachment and love, Vol. 1: Attachment*. London: Hogarth.

Bowlby, J. (1988). *A secure base: Clinical applications of attachment theory*. London: Routledge.

Bowlby, J., Ainsworth, M., Boston, M., & Rosenbluth, D. (1956). The effects of mother–child separation: A follow-up study. *British Journal of Medical Psychology, 29,* 211–247.

Brady, J.V. (1958). Ulcers in executive monkeys. *Scientific American, 199,* 95–100.

Bransford, J.D., & Johnson, M.K. (1972). Contextual prerequisites for understanding: Some investigations of comprehension and recall. *Journal of Verbal Learning and Verbal Behavior, 11,* 717–726.

Breier, A., Albus, M., Pickar, D., & Zahn, T.P. (1987). Contollable and uncontrollable stress in humans: Alterations in mood and neuroendocrine and psychophysiological function. *American Journal of Psychiatry, 144*(11), 1419–1425.

Brewin, C.R., Andrews, B., & Gotlib, I.H. (1993). Psychopathology and early experience: A reappraisal of retrospective reports. *Psychological Bulletin, 113,* 82–98.

British Psychological Society. (1993). *Code of conduct, ethical principles and guidelines*. Leicester, UK: British Psychological Society.

Broberg, G., Wessels, H., Lamb, M.E., & Hwang, C.P. (1997). Effects of daycare on the development of cognitive abilities in 8-year-olds: A longitudinal study. *Developmental Psychology, 33,* 62–69.

Bronfenbrenner, U. (1979). *The ecology of human development: Experiments by nature and design*. Cambridge, MA: Cambridge University Press.

Brown, G.W., & Harris, T. (1978). *Social origins of depression*. London: Tavistock.

Brown, J. (1991). Staying fit and staying well: Physical fitness as a moderator of life stress. *Journal of Personality and Social Psychology, 60,* 555–561.

Brown, R. (1986). *Social psychology: The second edition.* New York: The Free Press.

Brown, R., & Kulik, J. (1977). Flashbulb memories. *Cognition, 5,* 73–99.

Bruce, V., & Valentine, T. (1988). When a nod's as good as a wink: The role of dynamic information in face recognition. In M.M. Gruneberg, P.E. Morris, & R.N. Sykes (Eds.), *Practical aspects of memory: Current research and issues (Vol. 1).* Chichester, UK: John Wiley.

Bruce, V., & Young, A.W. (1986). Understanding face recognition. *British Journal of Psychology, 77,* 305–327.

Bruch, H. (1971). Family transactions in eating disorders. *Comprehensive Psychiatry, 12(3),* 238–248.

Bryant, B., Harris, M., & Newton, D. (1980). *Children and minders.* London: Grant McIntyre

Budzynski, T.H., Stoyva, J.M., Adler, C.S., & Mullaney, D.J. (1973). EMG feedback and tension headache: A controlled outcome study. *Psychosomatic Medicine, 35,* 484–496.

Buehler, R., Griffin, D., & Ross, M. (1994). Exploring the "planning fallacy": Why people underestimate their task completion times. *Journal of Personality and Social Psychology, 67,* 366–381.

Burchinal, M., Lee, M., & Ramey, C. (1989). Type of daycare and preschool intellectual development in disadvantaged children. *Child Development, 60,* 128–137.

Burger, J.M., & Cooper, H.M. (1979). The desirability of control. *Motivation and emotion, 3,* 381–393.

Burt, C. (1955). The evidence for the concept of intelligence. *British Journal of Psychology, 25,* 158–177.

Bus, A.G., & van IJzendoorn, M.H. (1988). Attachment and early reading: A longitudinal study. *Journal of Genetic Psychology, 149(2),* 199–210.

Bushnell, I.W.R., Sai, F., & Mullin, J.T. (1989). Neonatal recognition of the mother's face. *British Journal of Developmental Psychology, 7,* 3–13.

Cahill, L., & McGaugh, J.L. (1998). Mechanisms of emotional arousal and lasting declarative memory. *Trends in Neuroscience, 21,* 294–299.

Calhoun, J.B. (1962). Population density and social pathology. *Scientific American, 206(2),* 139–148.

Campbell, D.T., & Stanley, J.C. (1966). *Experimental and quasi-experimental designs for research.* Chicago: Rand McNally.

Cardwell, M., Clark, L., & Meldrum, C. (1996). *Psychology for A level.* London: Collins Educational.

Carey, M.P., Kalra, D.L., Carey, K.B., Halperin, S., & Richard, C.S. (1993). Stress and unaided smoking cessation: A prospective investigation. *Journal of Consulting and Clinical Psychology, 61,* 831–838.

Carlsmith, H., Ellsworth, P., & Aronson, E. (1976). *Methods of research in social psychology.* Reading, MA: Addison-Wesley.

Carlson, N.R. (1994). *Physiology of behavior (5th Edn.).* Boston: Allyn & Bacon.

Carmichael, L.C., Hogan, H.P., & Walters, A.A. (1932). An experimental study of the effect of language on the reproduction of visually perceived form. *Journal of Experimental Psychology, 15,* 73–86.

Carpenter, G. (1975). Mother's face and the newborn. In R. Lewin (Ed.), *Child alive.* London: Temple Smith.

Carroll, D. (1992). *Health psychology: Stress, behaviour and disease.* London: The Falmer Press.

Case, R. (1974). Structures and strictures: Some functional limitations on the course of cognitive growth. *Cognitive Psychology, 6,* 544–573.

Claparède, E. (1911). Recognition et moitié. *Archives de Psychologie, 11,* 75–90.

Clarke, A.D.B., & Clarke, A.M. (1979). Early experience: Its limited effect upon later development. In D. Shaffer & J. Dunn (Eds.), *The first year of life.* Chichester, UK: John Wiley.

Clarke, A.M., & Clarke, A.D.B. (1976). *Early experience: Myth and evidence.* New York: Free Press.

Clarke, A.M., & Clarke, A.D.B. (1998). Early experience and the life path. *The Psychologist, 11(9),* 433–436

Clarke-Stewart, K.A., Gruber, C.P., & Fitzgerald, L.M. (1994). *Children at home and in day care.* Hillsdale, NJ: Lawrence Erlbaum Associates Inc.

Claxton, G. (1980). Cognitive psychology: A suitable case for what sort of treatment? In G. Claxton (Ed.), *Cognitive psychology: New directions.* London: Routledge & Kegan Paul.

Cobb, S., & Rose, R.M. (1973). Hypertension, peptic ulcer, and diabetes in air traffic controllers. *Journal of the American Medical Association, 224,* 489–492.

Cockett, M., & Tripp, J. (1994). Children living in disordered families. *Social policy research findings: 45.* Joseph Rowntree Foundation.

Cohen, C.E. (1981). Person categories and social perception: Testing some boundaries of the processing effects of prior knowledge. *Journal of Personality and Social Psychology, 40,* 441–452.

Cohen, G. (1983). *The psychology of cognition (2nd Edn.).* London: Academic Press.

Cohen, N.J., & Squire, L.R. (1980). Preserved learning and retention of pattern-analysing skill in amnesia using perceptual learning. *Cortex, 17,* 273–278.

Cohen, S., Tyrrell, D.A.J., & Smith, A.P. (1991). Psychological stress and susceptibility to the common cold. *New England Journal of Medicine, 325,* 606–612.

Cohen, S., Tyrrell, D.A.J., & Smith, A.P. (1997). Psychological stress in humans and susceptibility to the common cold. *International Universities Press Stress and Health Series, Monograph, 7,* 217–235.

Cohen, S., & Williamson, G.M. (1991). Stress and infectious disease in humans. *Psychological Bulletin, 109,* 5–24.

Collins, B.E. (1970). *Social psychology.* Reading, MA: Addison-Wesley.

Conrad, R. (1964). Acoustic confusions in immediate memory. *British Journal of Psychology, 55,* 75–84.

Conway, M.A., Anderson, S.J., Larsen, S.F., Donnelly, C.M., McDaniel, M.A., McClelland, A.G.R., & Rawles, R.E. (1994). The formation of flashbulb memories. *Memory and Cognition, 22,* 326–343.

Coolican, H. (1990). *Research methods and statistics in psychology.* London: Hodder & Stoughton.

Coolican, H. (1994). *Research methods and statistics in psychology (2nd Edn.).* London: Hodder & Stoughton.

Coolican, H. (1996). *Introduction to research methods and statistics in psychology.* London: Hodder & Stoughton.

Coolican, H. (1998). Research methods. In M.W. Eysenck (Ed.), *Psychology: An integrated approach.* London: Addison–Wesley Longman.

Cooper, P.J. (1994). Eating disorders. In A.M. Coleman (Ed.), *Companion encyclopaedia of psychology, Vol. 2.* London: Routledge.

Cooper, P.J., & Taylor, M.J. (1988). Body image disturbance in bulimia nervosa. *British Journal of Psychiatry, 153,* 32–36.

Cox, T. (1978). *Stress.* London: Macmillan Press.

Craik, F.I.M. (1973). A "levels of analysis" view of memory. In P. Pliner, L. Krames, & T.M. Alloway (Eds.), *Communication and affect: Language and thought*. London: Academic Press.

Craik, F.I.M., & Lockhart, R.S. (1972). Levels of processing: A framework for memory research. *Journal of Verbal Learning and Verbal Behavior, 11*, 671–684.

Craik, F.I.M., & Tulving, E. (1975). Depth of processing and the retention of words in episodic memory. *Journal of Experimental Psychology, 104*, 268–294.

Crowne, D.P., & Marlowe, D. (1964). *The approval motive: Studies in evaluative dependence*. New York: Wiley.

Cumberbatch, G. (1990). *Television advertising and sex role stereotyping: A content analysis* (Working paper IV for the Broadcasting Standards Council), Communications Research Group, Aston University, Birmingham, UK.

Curtis, A. (2000). *Psychology and health*. London: Routledge.

Curtiss, S. (1989). The independence and task-specificity of language. In M.H. Bornstein & J.S. Bruner (Eds.), *Interaction in human development*. Hillsdale, NJ: Lawrence Erlbaum Associates Inc.

Czeisler, C.A., Moore-Ede, M.C., & Coleman, R.M. (1982). Rotating shift work schedules that disrupt sleep are improved by applying circadian principles. *Science, 217*(4558), 460–463.

Dane, F.C. (1994). Survey methods, naturalistic observations, and case-studies. In A.M. Colman (Ed.), *Companion encyclopaedia of psychology, Vol. 2*. London: Routledge.

Darley, J.M., & Latané, B. (1968). Bystander intervention in emergencies: Diffusion of responsibility. *Journal of Personality and Social Psychology, 8*, 377–383.

Davison, G.C., & Neale, J.M. (1996). *Abnormal psychology (rev. 6th Edn.)*. New York: Wiley.

de Chateau P., & Wiberg B. (1977). Long-term effect on mother–infant behavior of extra contact during the first hour post-partum: I. First observation at 36 hours. *Acta Paediatrica Scandinavica, 66*, 137–144.

DeLongis, A., Coyne, J.C., Dakof, G., Folkman, S., & Lazarus, R.S. (1982). The impact of daily hassles, uplifts and major life events to health status. *Health Psychology, 1*, 119–136.

DeLongis, A., Folkman, S., & Lazarus, R.S. (1988). The impact of daily stress on health and mood: Psychological and social resources as mediators. *Journal of Personality and Social Psychology, 54*, 486–495.

DeRenzi, E. (1986). Current issues in prosopagnosia. In H.D. Ellis, M.A. Jeeves, F. Newcombe, & A. Young (Eds.), *Aspects of face processing*. Dordrecht, The Netherlands: Martinus Nijhoff.

Deutsch, M., & Gerard, H.B. (1955). A study of normative and informational influence upon individual judgement. *Journal of Abnormal and Social Psychology, 51*, 629–636.

Devlin, P. (1976). *Report to the Secretary of State for the Home Department of the Departmental Committee on evidence of identification in criminal cases*. London: Her Majesty's Stationary Office.

Diener, E., & Crandall, R. (1978). *Ethics in social and behavioural research*. Chicago: The University of Chicago Press.

DiNardo, P.A., Guzy, L.T., Jenkins, J.A., Bak, R.M., Tomasi, S.F., & Copland, M. (1988). Aetiology and maintenance of dog fears. *Behaviour Research and Therapy, 26*, 241–244.

Dollard, J., & Miller, N.E. (1950). *Personality and psychotherapy*. New York: McGraw-Hill.

Douglas, J.W.B. (1975) Early hospital admissions and later disturbances of behaviour and learning. *Developmental Medical Child Neurology, 17*, 456–480.

Durkin, K. (1995). *Developmental social psychology: From infancy to old age*. Oxford, UK: Blackwell.

Dworkin, B.R., & Dworkin, S. (1988). The treatment of scoliosis by continuous automated postural feedback. In R. Ader, R. Weiner, & A. Baum (Eds.), *Experimental foundations of behavioural medicine: Conditioning approaches*. Hillsdale, NJ: Lawrence Erlbaum Associates Inc.

Dworkin, B.R., & Miller, N.E. (1986). Failure to replicate visceral learning in the acute curarized rat preparation. *Behavioural Neuroscience, 100*, 299–314.

Dyer, C. (1995). *Beginning research in psychology*. Oxford, UK: Blackwell.

Eagly, A.H. (1978). Sex differences in influenceability. *Psychological Bulletin, 85*, 86–116.

Eagly, A.H., & Carli, L. (1981). Sex of researchers and sex-typed communications as determinants of sex differences in influenceability: A meta-analysis of social influence studies. *Psychological Bulletin, 90*, 1–20.

Ebbinghaus, H. (1885/1913). *Uber das Gedachtnis*. Leipzig: Dunker. (Trans. H. Ruyer & C.E. Bussenius). In *Memory*. New York: Teachers College, Columbia University. (Original work published 1885.)

Egeland, B., & Hiester, M. (1995). The long-term consequences of infant day-care and mother–infant attachment. *Child Development, 66*, 474–485.

Eibl-Eibesfeldt, I. (1995). The evolution of family and its consequences. *Futura, 10*(4), 253–264.

Endler, N.S., & Parker, J.D.A. (1990). Multidimensional assessment of coping: A critical evaluation. *Journal of Personality and Social Psychology, 58*, 844–854.

Erikson, M. (1968). The inhumanity of ordinary people. *International Journal of Psychiatry, 6*, 278–279.

Evans, P., Clow, A., & Hucklebridge, F. (1997). Stress and the immune system. *The Psychologist, 10*(7), 303–307.

Eysenck, M.W. (1990). *Happiness: Facts and myths*. Hove, UK: Psychology Press.

Eysenck, M.W. (1994). *Individual differences: Normal and abnormal*. Hove, UK: Psychology Press.

Eysenck, M.W., & Eysenck, M.C. (1980). Effects of processing depth, distinctiveness, and word frequency on retention. *British Journal of Psychology, 71*, 263–274.

Fallon, A.E., & Rozin, P. (1985). Sex differences in perceptions of desirable body shape. *Journal of Abnormal Psychology, 94*, 102–105.

Fava, M., Copeland, P.M., Schweiger, U., & Herzog, D.B. (1989). Neurochemical abnormalities of anorexia and bulimia nervosa. *American Journal of Psychiatry, 47*, 213–219.

Fischhoff, B. (1977). Perceived informativeness of facts. *Journal of Experimental Psychology: Human Perception and Performance, 3*, 349–358.

Fischhoff, B., & Beyth, R. (1975). "I knew it would happen": Remembered probabilities of once-future things. *Organizational Behaviour and Human Performance, 13*, 1–16.

Fisher, R.P., Geiselman, R.E., Raymond, D.S., Jurkevich, L.M., & Warhaftig, M.L. (1987). Enhancing enhanced eyewitness memory: Refining the cognitive interview. *Journal of Police Science and Administration, 15*, 291–297.

Forman, R.F., & McCauley, C. (1986). Validity of the positive control polygraph test using the field practice model. *Journal of Applied Psychology, 71*, 691–698.

Fox, N. (1977). Attachment of Kibbutz infants to mother and metapelet. *Child Development, 48,* 1228–1239.

Franzoi, S.L. (1996). *Social psychology.* Madison, WI: Brown & Benchmark.

Freedman, J.L. (1969). Role playing: Psychology by consensus. *Journal of Personality and Social Psychology, 13,* 107–114.

Freedman, J.L., Heshka, S., & Levy, A. (1975). Population density and pathology: Is there a relationship? *Journal of Experimental Social Psychology, 11*(6), 539–552.

Freud, A., & Dann, S. (1951). An experiment in group upbringing. *Psychoanalytic Study of the Child, 6,* 127–168.

Freud, S. (1910). The origin and development of psychoanalysis. *American Journal of Psychology, 21,* 181–218.

Freud, S. (1915). Repression. In *Freud's collected papers, Vol. IV.* London: Hogarth.

Freud, S. (1917). Introductory lectures on psychoanalysis. In J. Strachey (Ed.), *The complete psychological works, Vol. 16.* New York: Norton.

Freud, S. (1924). *A general introduction to psychoanalysis.* New York: Washington Square Press.

Friedman, M., & Rosenman, R.H. (1959). Association of specific overt behaviour pattern with blood and cardiovascular findings. *Journal of the American Medical Association, 96,* 1286–1296.

Friedman, M., & Rosenman, R.H. (1974). *Type A behaviour and your heart.* New York: Knopf.

Friedman, M.I., Tordoff, M.G., & Ramirez, I. (1986). Integrated metabolic control of food intake. *Brain Research Bulletin, 17,* 855–859.

Fruzzetti, A.E., Toland, K., Teller, S.A., & Loftus, E.F. (1992). Memory and eyewitness testimony. In M. Gruneberg & P. Morris (Eds.), *Aspects of memory: The practical aspects.* London: Routledge.

Funk, S.C. (1992) Hardiness: A review of theory and research. *Health Psychology, 11,* 335–345.

Gale, A. (1995). Ethical issues in psychological research. In A.M. Coleman (Ed.), *Psychological research methods and statistics.* London: Longman.

Gamson, W.B., Fireman, B., & Rytina, S. (1982). *Encounters with unjust authority.* Homewood, IL: Dorsey Press.

Ganster, D.C., Schaubroeck, J., Sime, W.E., & Mayes, B.T. (1991). The nomological validity of the Type A personality among employed adults. *Journal of Applied Psychology, 76,* 143–168.

Gardner, G.A. (1978). The effects of human subject regulations on data obtained in environmental stressor research. *Journal of Personality and Social Psychology, 36,* 317–349.

Garfinkel, P.E., & Garner, D.M. (1982). *Anorexia nervosa: A multidimensional perspective.* New York: Basic Books.

Garner, D.M., & Fairburn, C.G. (1988). Relationship between anorexia nervosa and bulimia nervosa: Diagnostic implications. In D.M. Garner & P.E. Garfinkel (Eds.), *Diagnostic issues in anorexia nervosa and bulimia nervosa.* New York: Brunner/Mazel.

Gatchel, R. (1997). Biofeedback. In A. Baum, S. Newman, J. Weinman, R. West, & C. McManus (Eds.), *Cambridge handbook of psychology, health, and medicine.* Cambridge, UK: Cambridge University Press.

Geiselman, R.E., Fisher, R.P., MacKinnon, D.P., & Holland, H.L. (1985). Eyewitness memory enhancement in police interview: Cognitive retrieval mnemonics versus hypnosis. *Journal of Applied Psychology, 70,* 401–412.

Glanzer, M., & Cunitz, A.R. (1966). Two storage mechanisms in free recall. *Journal of Verbal Learning and Verbal Behavior, 5,* 351–360.

Glass, D.C., Singer, J.E., & Friedman, L.W. (1969). Psychic cost of adaptation to an environmental stressor. *Journal of Personality and Social Psychology, 12,* 200–210.

Gleitman, H. (1986). *Psychology* (2nd Edn.). London: Norton.

Goa, K.L., & Ward, A.(1986). Buspirone: A preliminary review of its pharmacological properties and therapeutic efficacy as an anxiolytic. *Drugs, 32,* 114–129.

Goldfarb, W. (1947). Variations in adolescent adjustment of institutionally reared children. *American Journal of Orthopsychiatry, 17,* 499–557.

Goleman, D. (1991). Doctors find comfort is a potent medicine. *The New York Times,* November 26.

Graf, P., & Schachter, D.L. (1985). Implicit and explicit memory for new associations in normal and amnesic subjects. *Journal of Experimental Psychology: Learning, Memory, and Cognition, 11,* 501–518.

Greenspoon, J. (1995). The reinforcing of two spoken sounds on the frequency of responses. *American Journal of Psychology, 68,* 409–416.

Griffiths, M.D. (1993). Fruit machine addiction in adolescence: A case study. *Journal of Gambling Studies, 9*(4), 387–399.

Gross, R. (1999). *Key studies in psychology* (3rd Edn.). London: Hodder & Stoughton.

Grossman, K., Grossman, K.E., Spangler, S., Suess, G., & Uzner, L. (1985). Maternal sensitivity and newborn responses as related to quality of attachment in Northern Germany. In J. Bretherton & E. Waters (Eds.), Growing points of attachment theory. *Monographs of the Society for Research in Child Development, 50,* No. 209.

Grossmann, K.E., & Grossmann, K. (1991). Attachment quality as an organizer of emotional and behavioural responses in a longitudinal perspective. In C.M. Parkes, J. Stevenson-Hinde, & P. Marris (Eds.), *Attachment across the life cycle.* London: Tavistock/Routledge.

Guiton, P. (1966). Early experience and sexual object choice in the brown leghorn. *Animal Behaviour, 14,* 534–538.

Hailman, J. (1992). The necessity of a "show-me" attitude in science. In J. W. Grier & T. Burk (Eds.), *Biology of animal behaviour* (2nd Edn.). Dubuque, IO: W.C. Brown.

Hallstein, E.A. (1965). Adolescent anorexia nervosa treated by desensitization. *Behaviour Research and Therapy, 3*(2), 87–91.

Harlow, H.F. (1959). Love in infant monkeys. *Scientific American, 200,* 68–74.

Harlow, H.F., & Harlow, M.K. (1962). Social deprivation in monkeys. *Scientific American, 207*(5), 136–146.

Harris, J.R. (1998). *The nurture assumption.* London: Bloomsbury.

Harris, T.O. (1997). Adult attachment processes and psychotherapy: A commentary on Bartholomew and Birtschnell. *British Journal of Medical Psychology, 70,* 281–290.

Hastrup, J.L., Light, K.C., & Obrist, P.A. (1980). Relationship of cardiovascular stress response to parental history of hypertension and to sex differences. *Psychophysiology, 17,* 317–318.

Hay, D.F., & Vespo, J.E. (1988). Social learning perspectives on the development of the mother–child relationship. In B. Birns & D.F. Hay (Eds.), *The different faces of motherhood.* New York: Plenum Press.

Haynes, S.G., Feinleib, M., & Kannel, W.B. (1980). The relationship of psychosocial factors to coronary heart disease in the Framingham Study: III. Eight-year incidence of coronary heart disease. *American Journal of Epidemiology, 111*, 37–58.

Hazan, C., & Shaver, P.R. (1987). Romantic love conceptualised as an attachment process. *Journal of Personality and Social Psychology, 52*, 511–524.

Heather, N. (1976). *Radical perspectives in psychology*. London: Methuen.

Henderson, J. (1999) *Memory and forgetting*. London: Routledge.

Herman, J.L., & Schatzow, E. (1987). Recovery and verification of memories of childhood sexual trauma. *Psychoanalytic Psychology, 4*, 1–14.

Hitch, G., & Baddeley, A.D. (1976). Verbal reasoning and working memory. *Quarterly Journal of Experimental Psychology, 28*, 603–621.

Hockey, G.R.J., Davies, S., & Gray, M.M. (1972). Forgetting as a function of sleep at different times of day. *Quarterly Journal of Experimental Psychology, 24*, 386–393.

Hodges, J., & Tizard, B. (1989). Social and family relationships of ex-institutional adolescents. *Journal of Child Psychology and Psychiatry, 30*, 77–97.

Hofling, K.C., Brotzman, E., Dalrymple, S., Graves, N., & Pierce, C.M. (1966). An experimental study in the nurse–physician relationship. *Journal of Nervous and Mental Disorders, 143*, 171–180.

Holland, A.J., Sicotte, N., & Treasure, J. (1988). Anorexia nervosa: Evidence for a genetic basis. *Journal of Psychosomatic Research, 32*, 561–572.

Holmes, D.S. (1990). The evidence for repression: An examination of sixty years of research. In J. Singer (Ed.), *Repression and dissociation: Implications for personality theory, psychopathology, and health*. Chicago: University of Chicago Press.

Holmes, J. (1993). *John Bowlby and attachment theory*. London: Routledge.

Holmes, T.H., & Rahe, R.H. (1967). The social readjustment rating scale. *Journal of Psychosomatic Research, 11*, 213–218.

Homan, R. (1991). *The ethics of social research*. London: Longman.

Howes, C., Galinsky, E., & Kontos, S. (1998). Caregiver sensitivity and attachment. *Social Development, 7*(1), 25–36.

Howes, C., Matheson, C.C., & Hamilton, C.E. (1994). Maternal, teacher, and child care correlates of children's relationships with peers. *Child Development, 65*(1), 264–273.

Hsu, L.K. (1990). *Eating disorders*. New York: Guilford Press.

Humphrey, L.L., Apple, R.F., & Kirschenbaum, D.S. (1986). Differentiating bulimic-anorexic from normal families using interpersonal and behavioural observational systems. *Journal of Consulting and Clinical Psychology, 54*, 190–195.

Hyde, T.S., & Jenkins, J.J. (1973). Recall for words as a function of semantic, graphic, and syntactic orienting tasks. *Journal of Verbal Learning and Verbal Behavior, 12*, 471–480.

Immelmann, K. (1972). Sexual and other long-term aspects of imprinting in birds and other species. In D.S. Lehrmann, R.A. Hinde, & E. Shaw (Eds.), *Advances in the study of behaviour, Vol. 4*. New York: Academic Press.

Isabella, R.A., Belsky, J., & Von Eye, A. (1989). Origins of infant–mother attachment: An examination of interactional synchrony during the infant's first year. *Developmental Psychology, 25*, 12–21.

Jacobs, K.C., & Campbell, D.T. (1961). The perpetuation of an arbitrary tradition through several generations of a laboratory microculture. *Journal of Abnormal and Social Psychology, 62*, 649–658.

Jacobson, J.L., & Wille, D.E. (1986). The influence of attachment pattern on developmental changes in peer interaction from the toddler to the preschool period. *Child Development, 57*, 338–347.

Jahoda, M. (1958). *Current concepts of positive mental health*. New York: Basic Books.

Janis, I. (1972). *Victims of groupthink: A psychological study of foreign-policy decisions and fiascos*. Boston, MA: Houghton-Mifflin.

Jenkins, J.G., & Dallenbach, K.M. (1924). Obliviscence during sleep and waking. *American Journal of Psychology, 35*, 605–612.

Jenness, A. (1932). The role of discussion in changing opinion regarding matter of fact. *Journal of Abnormal and Social Psychology, 27*, 279–296.

Johnson, C., & Scott, B. (1978). *Eyewitness testimony and suspect identification as a function of arousal, sex of witness, and scheduling of interrogation*. Paper presented at the meeting of the American Psychological Association, Washington, DC.

Johnson, R.D., & Downing, L.L. (1979). Deindividuation and valence of cues: Effects on prosocial and antisocial behaviour. *Journal of Personality and Social Psychology, 39*, 1532–1538.

Jones, D.N., Pickett, J., Oates, M.R., & Barbor, P. (1987). *Understanding child abuse* (2nd Edn.). London: Macmillan.

Kagan, J. (1984). *The nature of the child*. New York: Basic Books.

Kagan, J., Kearsley, R.B., & Zelazo, P.R. (1980). *Infancy: Its place in human development*. Cambridge, MA: Harvard University Press.

Kahneman, D., & Tversky, A. (1979). Intuitive prediction: Biases and corrective procedures. *TIMS Studies in Management Science, 12*, 313–327.

Kalucy, R.S., Crisp, A.H., & Harding, B. (1977). A study of 56 families with anorexia nervosa. *British Journal of Medical Psychology, 50*, 381–395.

Karasek, R.A., Swartz, J., & Theorell, T. (1982) *Job characteristics, occupation and coronary heart disease* (Final report no. R–01–0H00906). Cincinnati, OH: National Institute for Occupational Safety and Health.

Kelley, H.H. (1950). The warm–cold variable in first impressions of people. *Journal of Personality, 18*, 431–439.

Kelley, H.H. (1967). Attribution theory in social psychology. In D. Levine (Ed.), *Nebraska symposium on motivation*. Lincoln, NE: University of Nebraska Press.

Kelman, H., & Lawrence, L. (1972). Assignment of responsibility in the case of Lt. Calley: Preliminary report on a national survey. *Journal of Social Issues, 28*, 177–212.

Kelman, H.C. (1958). Compliance, identification and internalisation: Three processes of attitude change. *Journal of Conflict Resolution, 2*, 51–60.

Kelman, H.C. (1972). The rights of the subject in social research: An analysis in terms of relative power and legitimacy. *American Psychologist, 27*, 989–1016.

Kendler, K.S., Maclean, C., Neale, M., Kessler, R., Heath, A., & Eaves, L. (1991). The genetic epidemiology of bulimia nervosa. *American Journal of Psychiatry, 148,* 1627–1637.

Kendler, K.S., Masterson, C.C., & Davis, K.L. (1985). Psychiatric illness in first degree relatives of patients with paranoid psychosis, schizophrenia and medical controls. *British Journal of Psychiatry, 147,* 524–531.

Kettlewell, H.B.D. (1955). Selection experiments on industrial melanism in the Lepidoptera. *Heredity, 9,* 323–342.

Khan, F., & Patel, P. (1996). A study of the impact of hassles versus life events on health outcome measures in students and the general population. *Proceedings of the British Psychological Society, 4*(1), 32.

Kiecolt-Glaser, J,K., Garner, W., Speicher, C.E., Penn, G.M., Holliday, J., & Glaser, R. (1984). Psychosocial modifiers of immunocompetence in medical students. *Psychosomatic Medicine, 46,* 7–14.

Kilham, W., & Mann, L. (1974). Level of destructive obedience as a function of transmitter and expectant roles in the Milgram obedience paradigm. *Journal of Personality and Social Psychology, 29,* 696–702.

Kimmel, A.J. (1996). *Ethical issues in behavioural research.* Oxford, UK: Blackwell.

Klaus, M.H., & Kennell, J.H. (1976). *Parent–infant bonding.* St. Louis: Mosby.

Klaus, M.H., & Kennell, J.H. (1982). *Parent–infant bonding.* St. Louis: Mosby.

Kobasa, S.C. (1979). Stressful events, personality, and health: An inquiry into hardiness. *Journal of Personality and Social Psychology, 37,* 1–11.

Kobasa, S.C. (1986). How much stress can you survive? In M.G. Walraven & H.E. Fitzgerald (Eds.), *Annual editions: Human development 86/87.* Guilford, CT: Dushkin.

Kobasa, S.C., Maddi, S.R., & Puccetti, M.C. (1982). Personality and exercise as buffers in the stress-illness relationship. *Journal of Behavioural Medicine, 5,* 391–404.

Kobasa, S.C., Maddi, S.R., Puccetti, M.C., & Zola, M.A. (1985). Effectiveness of hardiness, exercise and social support as resources against illness. *Journal of Psychosomatic Research, 29,* 525–533.

Koluchová , J. (1976). The further development of twins after severe and prolonged deprivation: A second report. *Journal of Child Psychology and Psychiatry, 17,* 181–188.

Koluchová, J. (1991). Severely deprived twins after twenty-two years' observation. *Studia Psychologica, 33,* 23–28.

Kovacs, M., & Beck, A.T. (1978). Maladaptive cognitive structures in depression. *American Journal of Psychiatry, 135,* 525–533.

Langer, E.J., & Rodin, J. (1976). The effects of choice and enhanced personal responsibility for the aged. *Journal of Personality and Social Psychology, 34,* 191–198.

Latané, B., & Wolf, S. (1981). The social impact of majorities and minorities. *Psychological Review, 88,* 438–453.

Laudenslager, M.L., Ryan, S.M., Drugan, R.C., Hyson, R.L., & Maier, S.R. (1983). Coping and immunosuppression: Inescapable but not escapable shock suppresses lymphocyte proliferation. *Science, 221,* 568–571.

Lazar, I., & Darlington, R. (1982). Lasting effects of early education: A report from the Consortium of Longitudinal Studies. *Monographs for the Society for Research in Child Development, 47*(2–3; Serial No. 195).

Lazarus, R.S., & Folkman, S. (1984). *Stress, appraisal and coping.* New York: Springer.

Leach, P. (1985). *Baby and child.* Harmondsworth, UK: Penguin.

Lee, S., Hsu, L.K.G., & Wing, Y.K. (1992). Bulimia nervosa in Hong Kong Chinese patients. *British Journal of Psychiatry, 161,* 545–551.

Leitenberg, H., Agras, W.S., & Thomson, L.E. (1968). A sequential analysis of the effect of selective positive reinforcement in modifying anorexia nervosa. *Behaviour Research and Therapy, 6,* 211–218.

Leon, G.R. (1984). Case histories of deviant behaviour (*3rd Edn.*). Boston, MA: Allyn & Bacon.

Lewinsohn, P.M. (1974). A behavioural approach to depression. In R.J. Friedman & M.M. Katz (Eds.), *The psychology of depression: Contemporary theory and research.* Washington, DC: Winston-Wiley.

Lewis, M., Feiring, C., McGuffog, C., & Jaskir, J. (1984). Predicting psychopathy in six-year-olds from early social relations. *Child Development, 55,* 123–136.

Lindsay, D.S. (1990). Misleading suggestions can impair eyewitnesses' ability to remember event details. *Journal of Experimental Psychology: Learning, Memory, and Cognition, 16,* 1077–1083.

Locke, E.A. (1968). Toward a theory of task motivation and incentives. *Organizational Behavior and Human Performance, 3,* 157–189.

Loehlin, J.C., & Nichols, R.C. (1976). *Heredity, environment and personality.* Austin, TX: University of Texas Press.

Loftus, E. (1979). *Eyewitness testimony.* Cambridge, MA: Harvard University Press.

Loftus, E.F., & Palmer, J.C. (1974). Reconstruction of automobile destruction: An example of the interaction between language and memory. *Journal of Verbal Learning and Verbal Behavior, 13,* 585–589.

Loftus, E.F., & Zanni, G. (1975). Eyewitness testimony: The influence of the wording of a question. *Bulletin of the Psychonomic Society, 5,* 86–88.

Lozoff, B. (1983). Birth and "bonding" in non-industrial societies. *Developmental Medicine and Child Neurology, 25,* 595–600.

Lynch, M., & Roberts, J. (1982). *Consequences of child abuse.* London: Academic Press.

Maccoby, E.E. (1980). *Social development: Psychological growth and the parent–child relationship.* San Diego: Harcourt Brace Jovanovich.

Maher, B.A. (1966). *Principles of psychopathology: An experimental approach.* New York: McGraw-Hill.

Main, M., Kaplan, N., & Cassidy, J. (1985). Security in infancy: A move to a level of representation. In I. Bretherton & E. Waters (Eds.), Growing points of attachment theory and research. *Monographs of the Society for Research in Child Development, 50*(1–2; Serial no. 209).

Main, M., & Soloman, J. (1986). Discovery of a disorganised disoriented attachment pattern. In T.B. Brazelton & M.W. Yogman (Eds.), *Affective development in infancy.* Borwood, NJ: Ablex.

Main, M., & Weston, D.R. (1981). The quality of the toddler's relationship to mother and father: Related to conflict behaviour and the readiness to establish new relationships. *Child Development, 52,* 932–940.

Mandler, G. (1967). Organisation and memory. In K.W. Spence & J.T. Spence (Eds.), *The psychology of learning and motivation: Advances in research and theory, Vol. 1.* London: Academic Press.

Manstead, A.S.R., & Semin, G.R. (1996). Methodology in social psychology: Putting ideas to the test. In M.

Hewstone, W. Stroebe, & G.M. Stephenson (Eds.), *Introduction to social psychology* (2nd Edn.). Oxford, UK: Blackwell.

Margolis, B., & Kroes, W. (1974). Work and the health of man. In J. O'Toole (Ed.), *Work and the quality of life.* Cambridge, MA: MIT Press.

Marmot, M., Ryff, C.C., Bumpass, L.L., & Shipley, M. (1997). Social inequalities in health: Next questions and converging evidence. *Social Science and Medicine, 44*(6), 901–910.

Marshall, B.J., McGechie, D.B., Rogers, P.A., & Glancy, R.J. (1985). Pyloric Campylobacter infection and gastroduodenal disease. *The Medical Journal of Australia, 142*(8), 439–444.

Martin, R.A. (1989). Techniques for data acquisition and analysis in field investigations of stress. In R.W.J. Neufeld (Ed.), *Advances in the investigation of psychological stress.* New York: Wiley.

Maslach, C., & Jackson, S.E. (1982). Burnout in health professions: A social psychological analysis. In G.S. Sanders & J. Suls (Eds.), *Social psychology of health and illness.* Hillsdale, NJ: Lawrence Erlbaum Associates Inc.

Maslow, A.H. (1954). *Motivation and personality.* New York: Harper.

Mason, J.W. (1975). A historical view of the stress field. *Journal of Human Stress, 1*, 22–36.

Matteson, M., & Ivancevich, J.M. (1982). The how, what and why of stress management training. *Personnel Journal, 61*(10), 768–774.

Matthews, K.A., Glass, D.C., Rosenman, R.H., & Bortner, R.W. (1977). Competitive drive, Pattern A, and coronary heart disease: A further analysis of some data from the Western Collaborative Group. *Journal of Chronic Diseases, 30*, 489–498.

Maurer, D., & Maurer, C. (1989). *The world of the newborn.* London, UK: Viking.

Mayall, B., & Petrie, P. (1983). *Childminding and day nurseries: What kind of care?* London: Heinemann Educational Books.

McCloskey, M., Wible, C.G., & Cohen, N.J. (1988). Is there a special flash-bulb memory mechanism? *Journal of Experimental Psychology: General, 117*, 171–181.

McGrew, W.C. (1972). *An ethological study of children's behaviour.* New York: Academic Press.

Meeus, W.H.J., & Raaijmakers, Q.A.W. (1995). Obedience in modern society: The Utrecht studies. *Journal of Social Issues, 51*(3), 155–175.

Meichenbaum, D. (1977). *Cognitive-behaviour modification: An integrative approach.* New York: Plenum Press.

Meichenbaum, D. (1985). *Stress inoculation training.* New York: Pergamon.

Melhuish, E.C. (1993). Behaviour measures: A measure of love? An overview of the assessment of attachment. *ACPP Review and Newsletter, 15*(6), 269–275.

Memon, A., & Wright, D.B. (1999). Eyewitness testimony and the Oklahoma bombing. *The Psychologist, 12*(6), 292–295.

Menges, R.J. (1973). Openness and honesty versus coercion and deception in psychological research. *American Psychologist, 28*, 1030–1034.

Menzies, R.G., & Clarke, J.C. (1993). The aetiology of childhood water phobia. *Behaviour Research and Therapy, 31*, 499–501.

Milgram, S. (1974). *Obedience to authority: An experimental view.* New York: Harper & Row.

Milgram, S. (1992). *The individual in a social world* (2nd Edn.). New York: McGraw-Hill.

Miller, G.A. (1956). The magic number seven, plus or minus two: Some limits on our capacity for processing information. *Psychological Review, 63*, 81–93.

Miller, N., & DiCara, L. (1967). Instrumental learning of heart rate changes in curarised rats: Shaping and specificity to discriminative stimulus. *Journal of Comparative and Physiological Psychology, 63*, 12–19.

Miller, T.Q., Turner, C.W., Tindale, R.S., Posavac, E.J., & Dugoni, B.L. (1991). Reasons for the trend toward null findings in research on Type A behaviour. *Psychological Bulletin, 110*, 469–485.

Mineka, S., Davidson, M., Cook, M., & Kuir, R. (1984). Observational conditioning of snake fear in rhesus monkeys. *Journal of Abnormal Psychology, 93*, 355–372.

Minuchin, S., Roseman, B.L., & Baker, L. (1978). *Psychosomatic families: Anorexia nervosa in context.* Cambridge, MA: Harvard University Press.

Moniz, E. (1937). Prefrontal leucotomy in the treatment of mental disorders. *American Journal of Psychiatry, 93*, 1379–1385.

Morris, C.D., Bransford, J.D., & Franks, J.J. (1977). Levels of processing versus transfer appropriate processing. *Journal of Verbal Learning and Verbal Behavior, 16*, 519–533.

Morris, P.E. (1979). Strategies for learning and recall. In M.M. Gruneberg & P.E. Morris (Eds.), *Applied problems in memory.* London: Academic Press.

Morris, T., Greer, S., Pettingale, R.W., & Watson, M. (1981). Patterns of expression of anger and their psychological correlates in women with breast cancer. *Journal of Psychosomatic Research, 25*, 111–117.

Moscovici, S. (1976). *Social influence and social change.* London: Academic Press.

Moscovici, S. (1980). Toward a theory of conversion behaviour. In L. Berkowitz (Ed.), *Advances in experimental social psychology, Vol. 13.* New York: Academic Press.

Moscovici, S. (1985). Social influence and conformity. In G. Lindzey & E. Aronson (Eds.), *Handbook of social psychology* (3rd Edn.). New York: Random House.

Moscovici, S., Lage, E., & Naffrenchoux, M. (1969). Influence of a consistent minority on the responses of a majority in a colour perception task. *Sociometry, 32*, 365–380.

Moscovitz, S. (1983). *Love despite hate: Child survivors of the Holocaust and their adult lives.* New York: Schocken.

Mowrer, O.H. (1947). On the dual nature of learning: A re-interpretation of "conditioning" and "problem-solving". *Harvard Educational Review, 17*, 102–148.

Myers, L.B., & Brewin, C.R. (1994). Recall of early experiences and the repressive coping style. *Journal of Abnormal Psychology, 103*, 288–292.

Nasser, M. (1986). Eating disorders: The cultural dimension. *Social Psychiatry and Psychiatric Epidemiology, 23*, 184–187.

Neisser, U. (1964). Visual search. *Scientific American, 210*, 94–102.

Nelson, K. (1973). Structure and strategy in learning to talk. *Monographs of the Society for Research in Child Development, 38*(Serial no. 149).

Nemeth, C., Swedlund, M., & Kanki, G. (1974). Patterning of the minority's responses and their influence on the majority. *European Journal of Social Psychology, 4*, 53–64.

NICHD Early Child Care Research Network. (1997). The effects of infant child care on infant–mother attachment security: Results of the NICHD study of early child care. *Child Development, 68*(5), 860–879.

Nisbett, R.E., & Wilson, T.D. (1977). Telling more than we can know: Verbal reports on mental processes. *Psychological Review, 84*, 231–259.

Nobles, W.W. (1976). Extended self: Rethinking the so-called Negro self-concept. *Journal of Black Psychology, 2*, 99–105.

Nuckolls, K.B., Cassel, J., & Kaplan, B.H. (1972). Psychological assets, life crisis and the prognosis of pregnancy. *American Journal of Epidemiology, 95*, 431–441.

Ogden, J. (1996). *Health psychology: A textbook*. Milton Keynes, UK. Open University Press.

Orne, M.T. (1962). On the social psychology of the psychological experiment: With particular reference to demand characteristics and their implications. *American Psychologist, 17*, 776–783.

Orne, M.T., & Holland, C.C. (1968). On the ecological validity of laboratory deceptions. *International Journal of Psychitary, 6*(4), 282–293.

Palmblad, J., Petrini, B., Wasserman, J., & Akerstedt, T. (1979). Lymphocyte and granulocyte reactions during sleep deprivation. *Psychosomatic Medicine, 41*(4), 273–278.

Park, R.J., Lawrie, J.M., & Freeman, C.P. (1995). Post-viral onset of anorexia nervosa. *British Journal of Psychology, 166*, 386–389.

Parke, R.D. (1981). *Fathers*. Cambridge, MA: Harvard University Press.

Pennebaker, J.W., Hendler, C.S., Durrett, M.E., & Richards, P. (1981). Social factors influencing absenteeism due to illness in nursery school children. *Child Development, 52*, 692–700.

Perrin, S., & Spencer, C. (1980). The Asch effect: A child of its time. *Bulletin of the British Psychological Society, 33*, 405–406.

Peterson, C., Seligman, M.E., & Valliant, G.E. (1988). Pessimistic explanatory style is a risk factor for physical illness: A thirty-five year longitudinal study. *Journal of Personality and Social Psychology, 55*(1), 23–27.

Peterson, L.R., & Peterson, M.J. (1959). Short-term retention of individual verbal items. *Journal of Experimental Psychology, 58*, 193–198.

Pfungst, O. (1911). *Clever Hans, the horse of Mr. von Osten*. New York: Holt, Rinehart, & Winston.

Piaget, J. (1970). Piaget's theory. In J. Mussen (Ed.), *Carmichael's manual of child psychology, Vol. 1*. New York: Basic Books.

Piliavin, I.M., Rodin, J., & Piliavin, J.A. (1969). Good samaritanism: An underground phenomenon? *Journal of Personality and Social Psychology, 13*, 289–299.

Pinel, J.P.J. (1997). *Biopsychology* (3rd Edn.). Boston: Allyn & Bacon.

Posner, M.I. (1969). Abstraction and the process of recognition. In J.T. Spence & G.H. Bower (Eds.), *The psychology of learning and motivation: Advances in learning and motivation, Vol. 3*. New York: Academic Press.

Putnam, B. (1979). Hypnosis and distortions in eyewitness memory. *International Journal of Clinical and Experimental Hypnosis, 27*, 437–448.

Quinton, D., & Rutter, M. (1976). Early hospital admissions and later disturbance of behaviour: An attempted replication of Douglas's findings. *Developmental Medicine and Child Neurology, 18*, 447–459.

Quinton, D., Rutter, M., & Liddle, C. (1985). Institutional rearing, parenting difficulties, and marital support. *Annual Progress in Child Psychiatry and Child Development*, 173–206.

Rahe, R.H., & Arthur, R.J. (1977). Life change patterns surrounding illness experience. In A. Monat & R.S. Lazarus (Eds.), *Stress and coping*. New York: Columbia University Press.

Rahe, R.H., Mahan, J., & Arthur, R. (1970). Prediction of near-future health-change from subjects' preceding life changes. *Journal of Psychosomatic Research, 14*, 401–406.

Rank, S.G., & Jacobsen, C.K. (1977). Hospital nurses' compliance with medication overdose orders: A failure to replicate. *Journal of Health and Social Behaviour, 18*, 188–193.

Raulin, M.L., & Graziano, A.M. (1994). Quasi-experiments and correlational studies. In A.M. Colman (Ed.), *Companion encyclopaedia of psychology, Vol. 2*. London: Routledge.

Reason, J.T., & Rowan, J. (Eds.). (1981). *Human enquiry: A sourcebook in new paradigm research*. Chichester, UK: Wiley.

Reicher, S.D., & Potter, J. (1985). Psychological theory as intergroup perspective: A comparative analysis of "scientific" and "lay" accounts of crowd events. *Human Relations, 38*, 167–189.

Reitman, J.S. (1971). Mechanisms of forgetting in short-term memory. *Cognitive Psychology, 2*, 185–195.

Riley, V. (1981). Psychoneuroendocrine influence on immuno-competence and neoplasia. *Science, 212*, 1100–1109.

Robertson, J., & Bowlby, J. (1952). Responses of young children to separation from their mothers. *Courier Centre International de l'Enfance, 2*, 131–142.

Robertson, J., & Robertson, J. (1971). Young children in brief separation. *Psychoanalytic Study of the Child, 26*, 264–315.

Rodin, J., & Langer, E.J. (1977). Long-term effects of a control-relevant intervention with the institutionalized aged. *Journal of Personality and Social Psychology, 35*, 897–902.

Roethlisberger, F.J., & Dickson, W.J. (1939). *Management and the worker*. Cambridge, MA: Harvard University Press.

Rogers, C.R. (1959). A theory of therapy, personality, and interpersonal relationships as developed in the client-centred framework. In S. Koch (Ed.), *Psychology: A study of a science*. New York: McGraw-Hill.

Roggman, L.A., Langlois, J.H., Hubbs-Tait, L., & Rieser-Danner, L.A. (1994). Infant daycare, attachment and the "file-drawer" problem. *Child Development, 65*, 1429–1443.

Rosen, J.C., & Leitenberg, H. (1985). Exposure plus response prevention treatment of bulimia. In D.M. Garner & P.E. Garfinkel (Eds.), *Handbook of psychotherapy for anorexia nervosa and bulimia*. New York: Guilford Press.

Rosenberg, M.J. (1965). When dissonance fails: On eliminating evaluation apprehension from attitude measurement. *Journal of Personality and Social Psychology, 1*, 28–42.

Rosenhan, D. (1969). Some origins of concern for others. In P. Mussen, J. Langer, & M. Covington (Eds.), *Trends and issues in developmental psychology*. New York: Holt, Rinehart & Winston.

Rosenhan, D.L., & Seligman, M.E.P. (1989). *Abnormal psychology* (2nd Edn.). New York: Norton.

Rosenthal, A.M. (1964). *Thirty-eight witnesses*. New York: McGraw-Hill.

Rosenthal, R. (1966). *Experimenter effects in behavioural research*. New York: Appleton-Century-Crofts.

Rosenthal, R., & Fode, K.L. (1963). The effect of experimenter bias on the performance of the albino rat. *Behavioural Science, 8*(3), 183–189.

Roy, D.F. (1991). Improving recall by eyewitnesses through the cognitive interview: Practical applications and implications for the police service. *The Psychologist: Bulletin of the British Psychological Society, 4*, 398–400.

Rundus, D., & Atkinson, R.C. (1970). Rehearsal processes in free recall. A procedure for direct observation. *Journal of Verbal Learning and Verbal Behavior, 9*, 99–105.

Russell, G.F. (1972). Premenstrual tension and "psychogenic" amenorrhoea: Psycho-physical interactions. *Journal of Psychosomatic Research, 16*(4), 279–287.

Rutter, M. (1972). *Maternal deprivation reassessed (1st Edn.)*. Harmondsworth, UK: Penguin.

Rutter, M. (1981). *Maternal deprivation reassessed (2nd Edn.)*. Harmondsworth, UK: Penguin.

Rutter, M., Graham, P., Chadwick, D.F.D., & Yule, W. (1976). Adolescent turmoil: Fact or fiction. *Journal of Child Psychology and Psychiatry, 17*, 35–56.

Rutter, M., & The ERA Study Team. (1998). Developmental catch-up and deficit following adoption after severe early privation. *Journal of Child Psychology and Psychiatry, 39*, 465–476.

Ryle, G. (1949). *The concept of mind*. London: Hutchinson.

Rymer, R. (1993). *Genie: Escape from a silent childhood*. London: Michael Joseph.

Sagi, A., van IJzendoorn, M.H., & Koren-Karie, N. (1991). Primary appraisal of the Strange Situation: A cross-cultural analysis of the pre-separation episodes. *Developmental Psychology, 27*, 587–596.

Sarafino, E.P. (1990) *Health psychology: Biosocial interactions*. New York: John Wiley & Sons.

Savin, H.B. (1973). Professors and psychological researchers: Conflicting values in conflicting roles. *Cognition, 2*, 147–149.

Schaefer, C., Coyne, J.C., & Lazarus, R.S. (1981). The health-related functions of social support. *Journal of Behavioral Medicine, 4*, 381–406.

Schaffer, H.R. (1998) *Making decisions about children*. Oxford, UK: Blackwell.

Schaffer, H.R., & Emerson, P.E. (1964). The development of social attachments in infancy. *Monographs of the Society for Research on Child Development*(Whole no. 29).

Schliefer, S.J., Keller, S.E., Camerino, M., Thornton, J.C., & Stein, M. (1983). Suppression of lymphocyte stimulation following bereavement. *Journal of the American Medical Association, 250*, 374–377.

Schulz, R. (1976). Effects of control and predictability on the physical and psychological well-being of the institutionalized aged. *Journal of Personality and Social Psychology, 33*, 563–573.

Selye, H. (1936). A syndrome produced by diverse nocuous agents. *Nature, 138*, 32.

Selye, H. (1950). *Stress*. Montreal, Canada: Acta.

Selye, H. (1980). The stress concept today. In I.L. Kutash (Ed.), *Handbook on stress and anxiety*. San Francisco: Jossey Bass.

Shaffer, D.R. (1993). *Developmental psychology*. Pacific Grove, CA: Brooks/Cole.

Shallice, T., & Warrington, E.K. (1970). Independent functioning of verbal memory stores: A neuropsychological study. *Quarterly Journal of Experimental Psychology, 22*, 261–273.

Shallice, T., & Warrington, E.K. (1974). The dissociation between long-term retention of meaningful sounds and verbal material. *Neuropsychologia, 12*, 553–555.

Shea, J.D.C. (1981). Changes in interpersonal distances and categories of play behaviour in the early weeks of preschool. *Developmental Psychology, 17*, 417–425.

Sheingold, K., & Tenney, Y.J. (1982). Memory for a salient childhood event. In U. Neisser (Ed.), *Memory observed*. San Francisco: W.H. Freeman.

Shepard, R.N. (1967). Recognition memory for words, sentences and pictures. *Journal of Verbal Learning and Verbal Behavior, 6*, 156–163.

Sherif, M. (1935). A study of some factors in perception. *Archives of Psychology, 27*, 187.

Sherrington, R., Brynjolfsson, J., Petursson, H., Dudleston, K., Barraclough, B., Wasmuth, J., Dobbs, M., & Gurling, H. (1988). Localisation of a susceptibility locus for schizophrenia on chromosome 5. *Nature, 336*, 164–167.

Shirom, A. (1989). Burnout in work organisations. In C.L. Cooper & I. Robertson (Eds.), *International review of industrial and organisational psychology*. Chichester, UK: Wiley.

Shotland, R.L., & Straw, M.K. (1976). Bystander response to an assault: When a man attacks a woman. *Journal of Personality and Social Psychology, 34*, 990–999.

Sigall, H., Aronson, E., & Van Hoose, T. (1970). The co-operative subject: Myth or reality? *Journal of Experimental Social Psychology, 6*, 1–10.

Silverman, I. (1977). *The human subject in the psychological laboratory*. Oxford, UK: Pergamon.

Silverman, I., Shulman, A.D., & Wiesenthal, D. (1970). Effects of deceiving and debriefing psychological subjects on performance in later experiments. *Journal of Personality and Social Psychology, 21*, 219–227.

Simon, H.A. (1974). How big is a chunk? *Science, 183*, 482–488.

Skinner, B.F. (1938). *The behaviour of organisms*. New York: Appleton-Century-Crofts.

Slovic, P., & Fischhoff, B. (1977). On the psychology of experimental surprises. *Journal of Experimental Psychology: Human Perception and Performance, 3*, 544–551.

Smith, P., & Bond, M.H. (1993). *Social psychology across cultures: Analysis and perspectives*. New York: Harvester Wheatsheaf.

Solso, R.L. (1991). *Cognitive psychology (3rd Edn.)*. London: Allyn & Bacon.

Spangler, G. (1990). Mother, child, and situational correlates of toddlers' social competence. *Infant Behavior and Development, 13*, 405–419.

Spencer, C., & Perrin, S. (1998). Innovation and conformity. *Psychology Review, 5*(2), 23–26.

Spitz, R.A. (1945). Hospitalism: An inquiry into the genesis of psychiatric conditions in early childhood. *Psychoanalytic Study of the Child, 1*, 113–117.

Spitz, R.A., & Wolf, K.M. (1946). Anaclitic depression. *Psychoanalytic Study of the Child, 2*, 313–342.

Squire, L.R., Ojemann, J.G., Miezin, F.M., Petersen, S.E., Videen, T.O., & Raichle, M.E. (1992). Activation of the hippocampus in normal humans: A functional anatomical study of memory. *Proceedings of the National Academy of Science, USA, 89*, 1837–1841.

Sroufe, L.A. (1983). Individual papers of adaption from infancy to preschool. In M. Perlmutter (Ed.), *Minnesota Symposium on child psychology*. Hillsdale, NJ: Lawrence Erlbaum Associates Inc..

Stang, D.J. (1972). Conformity, ability, and self-esteem. *Representative Research in Social Psychology, 3*, 97–103.

Stirling, J.D., & Hellewell, J.S.E. (1999). *Psychopathology.* London: Routledge.

Stone, S.V., Dembroski, T.M., Costa, P.T., Jr., & McDougall, J.M. (1990). Gender differences in cardiovascular reactivity. *Journal of Behavioural Medicine, 13*, 137–157.

Stoney, C.M., David, M.C., & Matthews, K.A. (1987). Sex differences in physiological responses to stress and in coronary heart disease: A casual link? *Psychophysiology, 24*, 127–131.

Stretch, D.D. (1994). Experimental design. In A.M. Colman (Ed.), *Companion encyclopedia of psychology, Vol. 2.* London: Routledge.

Strober, M., & Humphrey, L.L. (1987). Familial contributions to the aetiology and course of anorexia nervosa and bulimia. *Journal of Consulting and Clinical Psychology, 55*, 654–659.

Sue, D., Sue, D., & Sue, S. (1994). *Understanding abnormal behaviour.* Boston, MA: Houghton Mifflin.

Sulin, R.A., & Dooling, D.J. (1974). Intrusion of a thematic idea in retention of prose. *Journal of Experimental Psychology, 103*, 255–262.

Symington, T., Currie, A.R., Curran, R.S., & Davidson, J. (1955). The reaction of the adrenal cortex in conditions of stress. *Ciba Foundations Colloquia on Endocrinology, 20*, 156–164.

Szasz, T.S. (1960). *The myth of mental illness.* London: Paladin.

Tache, J., Selye, H., & Day, S. (1979). *Cancer, stress, and death.* New York: Plenum Press.

Tavris, C. (1974). The frozen world of the familiar stranger. *Psychology Today, June*, 71–80.

Thomas, C.B., & Duszynski, K.R. (1974). Closeness to parents and the family constellation in a prospective study of five disease states: Suicide, mental illness, malignant tumour, hypertension and coronary heart disease. *Johns Hopkins Medical Journal, 134*, 251–270.

Thomas, L.K. (1998). *Multicultural aspects of attachment.* http://www.bereavement.demon.co.uk/lbn/attachment/lennox.html. [See also Thomas, L.K. (1995). Psychotherapy in the context of race and culture. In S. Fernando (Ed.), *Mental health in a multi-ethnic society.* London: Routledge.]

Tizard, B. (1977). *Adoption: A second chance.* London: Open Books.

Tizard, B. (1979). Language at home and at school. In C.B. Cazden & D. Harvey (Eds.), *Language in early childhood education.* Washington, DC: National Association for the Education of Young Children.

Tizard, B., & Hodges, J. (1978). The effect of early institutional rearing on the development of eight-year-old children. *Journal of Child Psychology and Psychiatry, 19*, 99–118.

Tizard, B., & Rees, J. (1975). A comparison of the effects of adoption, restoration to the natural mother, and continued institutionalisation on the cognitive development of 4-year-old children. *Child Development, 45*, 92–99.

Trevarthan, C. (1979). Communication and cooperation in early infancy: A description of primary intersubjectivity. In M. Bullowa (Ed.), *Before speech: The beginning of interpersonal communication.* Cambridge, UK: Cambridge University Press.

Tronick, E.Z., Morelli, G.A., & Ivey, P.K. (1992). The Efe forager infant and toddler's pattern of social relationships: Multiple and simultaneous. *Developmental Psychology, 28*, 568–577.

Tulving, E. (1972). Episodic and semantic memory. In E. Tulving & W. Donaldson (Eds.), *Organisation of memory.* Hillsdale, NJ: Lawrence Erlbaum Associates Inc.

Tulving, E. (1979). Relation between encoding specificity and levels of processing. In L.S. Cermak & F.I.M. Craik (Eds.), *Levels of processing in human memory.* Hillsdale, NJ: Lawrence Erlbaum Associates Inc.

Tulving, E. (1989). Memory: Performance, knowledge, and experience. *European Journal of Cognitive Psychology, 1*, 3–26.

Tulving, E., & Psotka, J. (1971). Retroactive inhibition in free recall: Inaccessibility of information available in the memory store. *Journal of Experimental Psychology, 87*, 1–8.

Tulving, E., Schachter, D.L., & Stark, H.A. (1982). Priming effects in word-fragment completion are independent of recognition memory. *Journal of Experimental Psychology: Learning, Memory, and Cognition, 17*, 595–617.

Turner, L.H., & Solomon, R.L. (1962). Human traumatic avoidance learning: Theory and experiments on the operant–respondent distinction and failures to learn. *Psychological Monographs, 76*(40; Whole no. 559).

Tyrell, J.B., & Baxter, J.D. (1981). Glucocorticoid therapy. In P. Felig, J.D. Baxter, A.E. Broadus, & L.A. Frohman (Eds.), *Endocrinology and metabolism.* New York: McGraw-Hill.

Ucros, C.G. (1989). Mood state-dependent memory: A meta-analysis. *Cognition and Emotion, 3*, 139–167.

Underwood, B.J., & Postman, L. (1960). Extra-experimental sources of interference in forgetting. *Psychological Review, 67*, 73–95.

US Congress, Office of Technology Assessment. (1991). *Biological rhythms: Implications for the worker* (OTA-BA-463). Washington, DC: US Government Printing Office.

van Avermaet, E. (1988). Social influence in small groups. In M. Hewstone, W. Stroebe, J.-P. Codol, & G.M. Stephenson (Eds.), *Introduction to social psychology: A European perspective.* Oxford, UK: Blackwell.

van Avermaet, E. (1996). Social influence in small groups. In M. Hewstone, W. Stroebe, & G.M. Stephenson (Eds.), *Introduction to social psychology* (2nd Edn.). Oxford, UK: Blackwell.

Vandell, D.L., & Corasaniti, M.A. (1990). *Variations in early child care: Do they predict subsequent social, emotional, and cognitive differences?* Unpublished manuscript, University of Wisconsin, Madison. [Noted in Andersson, B.-E. (1992). Effects of daycare on cognitive and socioemotional competence of thirteen-year-old Swedish schoolchildren. *Child Development, 63*, 20–36.]

Van IJzendoorn, M.H., & Kroonenberg, P.M. (1988). Cross-cultural patterns of attachment: A meta-analysis of the Strange Situation. *Child Development, 59*, 147–156.

Venkatesan, M. (1966). Consumer behaviour: Conformity and independence. *Journal of Marketing Research, 3.*

Vidich, A.J., & Bensman, J. (1958). *Small town in mass society.* Princeton, NJ: Princeton University Press.

Wade, C., & Tavris, C. (1993). *Psychology.* New York: HarperCollins.

Warren, R., & Zgourides, G.D. (1991). *Anxiety disorders: A rational–emotive perspective.* New York: Pergamon Press.

Warrington, E.K., & Shallice, T. (1972). Neuropsychological evidence of visual storage in short-term memory tasks. *Quarterly Journal of Experimental Psychology, 24*, 30–40.

Watkins, M.J., Watkins, O.C., Craik, F.I.M., & Mazauryk, G. (1973). Effect of nonverbal distraction on short-term storage. *Journal of Experimental Psychology, 101*, 296–300.

Watson, J.B. (1928). *Psychological care of infant and child.* New York: Norton.

Watson, J.B., & Rayner, R. (1920). Conditioned emotional reactions. *Journal of Experimental Psychology, 3*, 1–14.

Weiner, H., Thaler, M., Reiser, M.F., & Mirsky, I.A. (1957). Etiology of duodenal ulcer: I. Relation to specific psychological characteristics to rate of gastric secretion (serum pepsinogen). *Psychosomatic Medicine, 19*, 1–10.

Wells, G.L., Liepe, M.R., & Ostrom, T.M. (1979). Guidelines for empirically assessing the fairness of a lineup. *Law and Human Behaviour, 3*, 285–293.

Westen, D. (1996). *Psychology: Mind, brain, and culture.* New York: Wiley.

Whyte, W.F. (1943). *Street corner society: The social structure of an Italian slum.* Chicago: University of Chicago Press.

Widdowson, E.M. (1951). Mental contentment and physical growth. *Lancet, 1*, 1316–1318.

Williams, J.H. (1987). *Psychology of women* (3rd Edn.). London: W.W. Norton & Co.

Williams, T.M. (Ed.). (1986). *The impact of television: A national experiment in three communities.* New York: Academic Press.

Williams, T.P., & Sogon, S. (1984). Group composition and conforming behaviour in Japanese students. *Japanese Psychological Research, 26*, 231–234.

Wills, T.A. (1985). Supportive function of interpersonal relationships. In S. Cohen & S.L. Syme (Eds.), *Social support and health.* Orlando, FL: Academic Press.

Yin, R.K. (1969). Looking at upside-down faces. *Journal of Experimental Psychology, 81*, 141–145.

Young, A.W., Hellawell, D., & Hay, D.C. (1987). Configural information in face perception. *Perception, 16*, 747–759.

Zegoib, L.E., Arnold, S., & Forehand, R. (1975). An examination of observer effects in parent–child interactions. *Child Development, 46*, 509–512.

Zimbardo, P. (1969). The human choice: Individuation, reason, and order versus deindividuation, impulse, and chaos. In W.J. Arnold & D. Levine (Eds.), *Nebraska Symposium on Motivation, 17.* Lincoln, NE: University of Nebraska Press.

Zimbardo, P.G. (1973). On the ethics of intervention in human psychological research: With special reference to the Stanford prison experiment. *Cognition, 2*, 243–256.

Glossary

Abnormal or **atypical psychology**: the study of individuals who differ from the norm, such as those with mental disorders.

Abnormality: deviation from a norm or standard. The problem lies in determining the standard.

Adaptive: the extent to which a behaviour increases the reproductive potential of an individual and survival of its genes.

Adrenal glands: the endocrine glands that are located adjacent to and covering the upper part of the kidneys.

Adrenaline and **noradrenaline**: hormones produced by the adrenal gland which increase arousal by activating the sympathetic nervous system and reducing activity in the parasympathetic system.

Adrenocorticotrophic hormone (ACTH): a hormone produced by the anterior pituitary gland which stimulates the adrenal cortex.

Affectionless psychopathy: a condition where individuals appear to experience little guilt or emotion, lack normal affection, and are unable to form permanent relationships.

Agentic state: a state of feeling controlled by an authority figure, and therefore lacking a sense of personal responsibility.

Aims: the purpose of a research study.

Alternative hypothesis: another term for the experimental hypothesis. The experimental hypothesis is the *alternative* to the null hypothesis.

Altruism: helping someone else at a risk to one's own life.

Amnesia: a partial loss of long-term memory, usually as a result of brain damage.

Anaclitic depression: a severe form of depression in infants who experience prolonged separations from their mothers, The term "anaclitic" means "arising from emotional dependency on another".

Animal behaviour: the study of non-human animals in their own right.

Anorexia nervosa: an eating disorder in which the individual has an intense fear of becoming fat despite being seriously underweight due to gross undereating.

Antibodies: protein molecules that attach themselves to invaders, marking them out for subsequent destruction.

Antigens: foreign bodies such as viruses.

Articulatory-phonological loop: the part of working memory that holds information for a short period of time in a phonological (sound) or speech-based form.

Attachment: a strong emotional tie that develops over time between an infant and its primary caregiver(s) and results in a desire to maintain proximity.

Attribution theory: an account of what caused one's own or another person's behaviour.

Atypical psychology: see abnormal psychology.

Authoritarian personality: identified by Adorno et al. as someone who is more likely to be obedient. They tend to hold rigid beliefs, be hostile towards other groups, and submissive to authority.

Autokinetic effect: a visual illusion where a small spot of light in a darkened room appears to be moving when in fact it is stationary.

Autonomic nervous system: that part of the nervous system that controls vital body functions, which is self-regulating and needs no conscious control (automatic).

Autonomous state: being aware of the consequences of our actions and therefore taking voluntary control of our behaviour.

Aversion therapy: a form of treatment in which undesirable behaviour is eliminated by associating it with severe punishment.

Avoidant attachment (type A): an insecure attachment of an infant to its mother. The child avoids contact on reunion.

Barbiturates: drugs that used to be widely used to treat anxiety disorders.

Bar chart: like a histogram, a representation of frequency data but the categories do not have to be continuous; used for nominal data.

Benzodiazepines: anti-anxiety drugs such as Valium and Librium. They work by reducing serotonin levels and are more effective than barbiturates.

Bimodal: a distribution with two modes.

Biochemistry: the study of the chemical processes of living organisms.

Biofeedback: a technique that aims to control involuntary (autonomic) muscles through the use of feedback about current physiological functioning. Relaxation is an important aspect of its success.

Black box: the term used by behaviourists to refer to the mind. Their focus was on what goes in (a stimulus) and what comes out (a response).

Bond disruption: when a child is deprived of their main attachment object, in the short or long term.

Bonding: the process of forming close ties with another.

Bulimia nervosa: an eating disorder in which excessive (binge) eating is followed by compensatory behaviour such as self-induced vomiting or misuse of laxatives.

305

Burnout: physical and/or emotional exhaustion produced especially by stress.

Buspirone: a more recent anti-anxiety drug, which increases the production of serotonin and has fewer side effects than benzodiazepines.

Capacity: a measurement of how much is held in memory.

Caregiving sensitivity hypothesis: secure attachments are due to a caregiver's sensitivity and responsiveness, which creates independence in the infant.

Case study: detailed study of a single individual, event, or group.

Central executive: the key component of working memory. It is a modality-free system (i.e. not visual or auditory) of limited capacity and similar to "paying attention" to something.

Chunks: integrated units of information.

Classical conditioning: learning through association; a neutral stimulus becomes associated with a known stimulus–reflex response.

Client-centred therapy: a form of humanistic therapy introduced by Rogers and designed to increase the client's self-esteem and reduce incongruence between self and ideal self.

Clinician (or clinical psychologist): a person who works in clinical psychology, concerned with the diagnosis and treatment of abnormal behaviour.

Cognitive interview: an interview technique that is based on our knowledge about the way human memory works, paying attention, for example, to the use of retrieval cues.

Cognitive restructuring: the technique used by cognitive therapists to make distorted and irrational beliefs more rational.

Cognitive therapies: a form of treatment that involves attempts to change or restructure the client's thoughts and beliefs.

Cognitive triad: negative thoughts about the self, the world, and the future, found in depressed clients.

Collectivistic: a culture where individuals share tasks, belongings, and income. The people may live in large family groups and value interdependence.

Comparative psychology: the study of non-human animals in order to gain insights into human behaviour by making comparisons.

Compliance: the influence of a majority or minority, based on its power. The influence is more on public than private behaviour.

Concordance rates: the extent to which two measures are in agreement, such as if one twin has a condition and so does the other.

Conditioning: when one response is made dependent on another.

Confederate: a colleague of the experimenter who acts a part during the experiment unknown to the real participant(s) who are unaware of the confederate's relationship with the experimenter.

Confidentiality: the requirement for ethical research that information provided by participants in research is not made available to other people.

Conformity: yielding publicly to group pressure, and sometimes yielding privately as well.

Confounding variables: variables that are mistakenly manipulated or allowed to vary along with the independent variable and therefore affect the dependent variable.

Constant error: any unwanted variable that has a systematically different effect on the dependent variable in different conditions.

Control group: the group of participants who receive no treatment and act as a comparison to the experimental group to study any effects of the treatment.

Controlled variables: variables, not of interest to the experimenter, that are held constant or controlled.

Conversion: the influence of the minority on the majority. This is likely to effect private beliefs more than public behaviour.

Correlation: an association that is found between two variables.

Correlation coefficient: a number that expresses the extent to which two variables are related or vary together.

Cortisol: a hormone produced by the adrenal gland which elevates blood sugar and is important in digestion, especially at times of stress.

Cost–benefit analysis: a comparison between the costs of something and the related benefits, in order to decide on a course of action.

Counselling: client-centred therapy where the counsellor actively listens to the client and, by means of positive unconditional regard, allows the client to achieve self-acceptance and eventually self-actualisation.

Counterbalancing: used with repeated measures design to overcome the problems of practice and order effects, and involves ensuring that each condition is equally likely to be used first and second by participants.

Counterconditioning: the substitution of a relaxation response for the fear response to a threatening stimulus in systematic desensitisation.

Co-variables: the variables involved in a correlational study that may vary together (co-vary).

Critical period: a biologically determined period of time during which an animal is exclusively receptive to certain changes.

Cross-cultural evidence: data collected from different cultures.

Cue-dependent forgetting: forgetting that occurs because of the absence of a suitable retrieval cue.

Cued recall: after presenting the material to be learned, cues are provided to help recall.

Cultural relativism: the view that one cannot judge a behaviour properly unless it is viewed in the context of culture in which it originates.

Cultures: groups of people who are bound by the same rules, morals, and methods of interaction.

Debriefing: attempts by the experimenter at the end of a study to provide detailed information for the participants about the study and to reduce any distress they might have felt.

Declarative knowledge: knowledge related to "knowing that", including episodic and semantic memory.

Defence mechanisms: strategies used by the ego to defend itself against anxiety.

Deindividuation: losing one's sense of personal identity.

Demand characteristics: features of an experiment that help participants to work out what is expected of them, and lead them to behave in certain predictable ways.

Dependent variable: an aspect of the participant's behaviour that is measured in the study.

Deprivation: to lose something, such as the care of an attachment figure for a period of time.

Deprivation dwarfism: physical underdevelopment found in children reared in isolation or in institutions. Thought to be an effect of the stress associated with emotional deprivation.

Depth of processing: the extent to which something is processed, not in terms of how much processing is done (as in repetition) but in terms of how much meaning is extracted.

Descriptive statistics: a diagram or numbers used to describe research data.

Diathesis–stress model: the notion that psychological disorders occur when there is a genetically determined vulnerability (diathesis) and relevant stressful conditions.

Directional hypothesis: see one-tailed hypothesis.

Disorganised attachment (type D): the infant shows no set pattern of behaviour at separation or reunion (thus "disorganised"). This kind of behaviour is associated with abused children or those whose mothers are chronically depressed.

Dizygotic (DZ) twins: non-identical twins formed from two eggs (ova). Genetically as similar as any pair of siblings.

Double blind: a procedure where neither the participant nor the experimenter knows the precise aims of the study. This reduces experimenter effects.

DSM-IV: the most recent version of the *Diagnostic and Statistical Manual of Mental Disorders* published by the American Psychiatric Association, provides a means of classifying and diagnosing mental disorders.

Duration: a measurement of how long a memory lasts.

Ecological or **external validity**: the validity of an experiment outside the research situation itself; the extent to which the findings of a research study are applicable to other situations, especially "everyday" situations.

Ego: the conscious, rational part of the mind which is guided by the reality principle.

Ego defence: strategies used by the ego to defend itself against anxiety.

Elaboration of processing: a form of deep processing, achieved by engaging in complex processing.

Electra complex: a process in girls similar to the Oedipus complex in boys, which is also resolved by identifying with the same-sex parent.

Electroconvulsive shock therapy: brief shocks are applied to a person's non-dominant hemisphere to relieve the symptoms of a mental disorder.

Encoding: putting something into code; creating a memory trace.

Encoding specificity principle: the notion that memory is best when there is a large overlap between the information available at the time of retrieval and the information in the memory trace.

Endocrine system: a system of a number of ductless glands located throughout the body which produce the body's chemical messengers, called hormones.

Endorphins: naturally occurring opiate substances that reduce pain.

Enmeshment: a situation in which all of the members of a family lack a clear sense of their own personal identity.

Episodic memory: long-term memory for autobiographical or personal events, usually including information about the time and place of an episode or event.

et al.: Latin, meaning "and others".

Ethical committees: a committee of psychologists and lay individuals who consider all research proposals from the perspective of the rights and dignity of the participants.

Ethics: a set of moral principles used to guide human behaviour.

Ethologists: individuals who study animal behaviour in its natural environment, focusing on the importance of innate capacities and the functions of behaviours.

Evaluation apprehension: concern felt by research participants that their performance is being judged.

Event sampling: a technique for collecting data in an observational study. The observer focuses only on actions or events that are of particular interest to the study.

Experiment: a procedure undertaken to make a discovery about causal relationships. The experimenter manipulates one variable to see its effect on another variable.

Experimental group: the group receiving the experimental treatment.

Experimental hypothesis: the hypothesis written prior to conducting an experiment, it usually specifies the independent and dependent variables.

Experimental realism: the use of an artificial situation in which participants become so involved that they are fooled into thinking the set-up is real rather than artificial.

Experimental treatment: the alteration of the independent variable.

Experimental or **internal validity**: the validity of an experiment in terms of the context in which it is carried out. Concerns events within the experiment as distinct from external validity.

Experimenter bias: the effect that the experimenter's expectations have on the participants and therefore the results of the study.

Experimenter effects: see investigator effects.

Experimenter expectancy: the systematic effects that an experimenter's expectations have on the performance of the participants.

Expert witnesses: a person who offers testimony in a trial in relation to their professional knowledge, such as a medical expert or an expert on hypnosis.

Explicit memory: memory based on conscious recollection.

External validity: see ecological validity.

F (Fascism) Scale: a test of tendencies towards fascism. High scorers are prejudiced and racist.

False memory syndrome: a condition where an adult "recovers" apparently repressed memories. In fact the memories are for events that did not happen, thus "false memory".

Field experiment: a study in which the experimental method is used in a more naturalistic situation.

Fixation: in Freudian terms, spending a long time at a given stage of development because of over- or under-gratification.

Flashbulb memory: accurate and long-lasting memories formed by significant public or personal events.

Forgetting: the inability to recall or recognise information that was previously learned or placed in memory.

Free association: a method used in psychoanalysis to access the unconscious mind by asking the client to say the first thing that comes into his or her mind.

Frequency polygon: a graph showing the frequencies with which different scores are obtained by participants in a study.

Fundamental attribution error: the tendency to explain the causes of another person's behaviour in terms of dispositional rather than situational factors.

GABA: a neurotransmitter that is produced at times of stress.

Gene: a unit of inheritance that forms part of a chromosome. Some characteristics are determined by one gene whereas for others many genes are involved.

Gene-mapping: determining the effect of a particular gene on physical or psychological characteristics.

General Adaptation Syndrome (GAS): the response to stress that enables the body initially to cope (adapt) but, when prolonged, leads to depletion of resources. There are three stages: alarm reaction, resistance, and exhaustion.

Generalisability: the extent to which the findings of a study can be applied to other settings, populations, times, and measures.

Generalisation: the tendency to transfer a response from one stimulus to another that is quite similar.

Genetic: information from genes, the units of inheritance.

Genetic vulnerability: an inherited susceptibility to a particular condition or characteristic.

Glucose: a form of sugar that is one of the main sources of energy for the brain.

Hardiness: a cluster of traits possessed by those people best able to cope with stress.

Hawthorne effect: the changes that take place to participants' behaviour as a result of knowing that they are being observed.

Hindsight bias: the tendency to be wise after the event, using the benefit of hindsight.

Histogram: a graph in which the frequencies of scores in each category are represented by a vertical column; data on the *y*-axis must be continuous with a true zero.

Homeostasis: the process of maintaining a reasonably constant environment.

Hormones: chemical substances produced by the body.

Humanistic psychologists: an approach to psychology that focuses on higher motivation, self-development, and on each individual as unique.

Hypermnesia: an enhanced ability to remember information, claimed to be found in hypnotised individuals.

Hypertension: a condition associated with very high blood pressure.

Hypothalamus: the part of the brain that integrates the activity of the autonomic nervous system. Involved with emotion, stress, motivation, and hunger.

Hypothesis: a statement of what you believe to be true.

Id: in Freudian theory, that part of the mind, motivated by the pleasure principle and sexual instincts.

Identification: conforming to the demands of a given role because of a desire to be like a particular person in that role.

Immune system: a system of cells within the body that is concerned with fighting disease.

Implicit memory: memory not based on conscious recollection.

Imposed etic: the use of a technique developed in one culture to study another culture.

Imprinting: a kind of restricted form of learning that takes place rapidly and has both short-term effects (e.g. a following response) and long-lasting effects (e.g. choice of reproductive partner).

Incidental learning: learning that occurs without any intention to learn, such as in the absence of any instructions that there will subsequently be a memory test.

Independent behaviour: resisting the pressures to conform or to obey authority.

Independent measures design: a research design where different participants are used for each condition in the experiment. For example they might each learn only one list of words.

Independent variable: some aspect of the research situation that is manipulated by the researcher in order to observe whether a change occurs in another variable.

Individual differences: the characteristics that vary from one individual to another.

Individualistic: a culture that emphasises individuality, individual needs, and independence. People tend to live in small nuclear families.

Informational social influence: this occurs when someone conforms because others are thought to possess more knowledge.

Informed consent: the requirement for ethical research that participants agree to take part after they have been informed of what they will be asked to do.

Innate: inborn, a product of genetic factors.

Instrumental learning: see operant conditioning.

Interference: one set of information competes with another, causing it to be "overwritten" or physically destroyed.

Inter-judge reliability: the extent to which ratings from two judges are consistent.

Internalisation: conformity behaviour where the individual has completely accepted the views of the majority.

Internal validity: see experimental validity.

Internal working model: a mental model of the world which enables individuals to predict, control, and manipulate their environment. The infant has many of these, some of which will be related to relationships.

Inter-observer reliability: the extent to which the ratings from two observers are consistent, or in agreement.

Interval: data with equal units of measurement throughout the scale but without a true zero.

Interviewer bias: the effects of an interviewer's expectations on the responses made by an interviewee.

Introspection: the process by which a person considers their inner thoughts as a means of understanding how the mind works.

Investigator (experimenter) effects: the various ways that investigators' expectancies, personal characteristics, misrecordings of data, and so on, can influence the findings of a study.

Learning: a relatively permanent change in behaviour, which is not due to maturation.

Learning theory: the explanation of behaviour using the principles of classical and operant conditioning; the view that all behaviour is learned.

Leucocytes: white blood cells that find and destroy antigens.

Level of measurement: the way that the data are measured in terms of the amount of information represented; the higher the level of measurement, the greater the amount of information represented.

Levels of processing theory: the view that long-term memories are created through depth of processing rather than a repeated number of analyses.

Lie scale: a set of questions in an interview to determine the extent to which a respondent is telling the truth.

Life events: events that are common to many people that involve change from a steady state.

Long-term memory: relatively permanent storage which has unlimited capacity.

Maladaptive: the extent to which a behaviour is not adaptive.

Maternal deprivation hypothesis: the view that separation from a primary caregiver (maternal deprivation) leads to the breaking of attachment bonds and long-term effects on emotional development.

Mean: an average worked out by dividing the total of participants' scores by the number of participants.

Measures of central tendency: any means of representing the mid-point of a set of data, such as the mean, median, and mode.

Measures of dispersion: any means of expressing the spread of the data, such as range or standard deviation.

Median: the middle score out of all the participants' scores.

Memory: refers to (1) the mental function of retaining information, (2) the storage system that holds that data, and (3) the data that are retained.

Memory trace: the physical record or "trace" of the memory, presumably a chemical change in the brain cells.

Meta-analysis: a form of analysis in which the data from several related studies are combined to obtain an overall estimate.

Metabolism: all the chemical processes within the living organism.

Mode: the most frequently occurring score among participants' scores in a given condition.

Model: a simplified description of a system that is intended to assist in predicting behaviour.

Modelling: a form of therapy based on observing a model and imitating that behaviour.

Monotropy hypothesis: the notion that infants have an innate tendency to form strong bonds with one caregiver, usually their mother.

Monozygotic (MZ) twins: identical twins formed from the same egg (zygote).

Mood-state-dependent memory: memory is better when a person is in the same mood when trying to retrieve a memory as they were at the time of learning.

Multi-store model: the concept that memory is divided into several kinds of store (sensory, short- and long-term) and data are passed from one to the other because of verbal rehearsal.

Mundane realism: the use of an artifical situation that closely resembles a natural situation.

Mutations: a genetic change that can then be inherited by any offspring.

Natural experiment: a type of experiment where use is made of some naturally occurring variable(s).

Naturalistic observation: an unobtrusive observational study conducted in a natural setting.

Natural killer cells: a type of leucocyte that destroys certain kinds of tumour cells and cells infected with viruses.

Natural selection: the process by which individuals are selected because they are best adapted to their environment.

Nature and nurture: nature is that which is inherited and genetic, as distinct from nurture which refers to all influences after conception, i.e. experience.

Negative correlation: as one co-variable increases the other decreases. They still vary in a constant relationship.

Neuroanatomy: the anatomy of the nervous system, i.e. the study of its structure and function.

Neurotransmitters: biochemical substances that facilitate or block communication between nerves.

Nominal: data consisting of the number of items falling into qualitatively different categories.

Non-directional hypothesis: see two-tailed hypothesis.

Nonsense syllables: meaningless sets of letters.

Noradrenaline: see adrenalin.

Normal distribution: a bell-shaped distribution in which most of the scores are close to the mean. This characteristic shape is produced when measuring many psychological and biological variables, such as IQ and height.

Normative social influence: this occurs when someone conforms in order to gain liking or respect from others.

Norms: cultural expectations, standards of behaviour.

Null hypothesis: the hypothesis that the independent variable will have no effect on the dependent variable.

Nurture: see nature and nurture.

Obedience: behaving as instructed, usually in response to individual rather than group pressure. Unlikely to involve a change of private opinion.

Observational learning: learning through imitating or copying the behaviour of others.

Oedipus complex: Freud's explanation of how a boy resolves his love for his mother and feelings of rivalry towards his father by identifying with his father.

One-tailed or **directional hypothesis**: a prediction that there will be a difference or correlation between two variables *and* statement of the direction of this difference.

Operant conditioning: learning through reinforcement; a behaviour becomes more likely because the outcome is reinforced. Learning that is contingent on the response.

Operationalisation: defining all variables in such a way that it is easy to measure them.

Opportunity sampling: participants are selected because they are available, not because they are representative of a population.

Order effects: participants' performance on two conditions may be affected by the order in which they are performed, e.g. because of being bored or having more practice.

Ordinal: data that can be ordered from smallest to largest.

Paired-associate learning: participants are given word pairs to learn and then tested by presenting them with one of the words and asking them to recall the other word.

Parasympathetic branch: the part of the autonomic nervous system that monitors the relaxed state, conserving resources, and promoting digestion and metabolism.

Participant observer: an observer who is also taking part in the activity being observed.

Participant reactivity: the situation in which an independent variable has an effect on participants merely because they know they are being observed.

Pathogens: agents that cause physical illness.

Phonemic processing: processing material by attending to the sounds of the words (phonemes are sounds).

Physiological: concerning the study of living organisms and their parts.

Pilot study: a smaller, preliminary study that makes it possible to check out standardised procedures and general design before investing time and money in the major study.

Pituitary gland: an endocrine gland located in the brain. Called the "master gland" because it directs much of the activity of the endocrine system.

Planning fallacy: the false belief that a plan will succeed even though past experience suggests it won't.

Pleasure principle: the drive to do things that produce pleasure or gratification.

Point sampling: a technique used in an observational study. One individual is observed in order to categorise their current behaviour, after which a second individual is observed.

Population: the total number of cases about which a specific statement can be made. This in itself may be unrepresentative.

Positive correlation: when two co-variables increase at the same time.

Practice effect: an improvement in performance as a result of doing the task before.

Presumptive consent: a substitute for voluntary informed consent, it is presumed that if one set of people regard an experimental procedure as acceptable this applies to all people, including the experimental participants whose consent has not been obtained.

Primacy effect: high level of free recall of the first items in a list; depends mainly on extra rehearsal.

Prior general consent: obtaining apparent consent from research participants by arranging for them to agree in general to taking part in certain kinds of research before enlisting their involvement in an experiment.

Privation: the lack of any attachments as distinct from the loss of attachments.

Proactive interference: current learning and memory being disrupted by previous learning.

Procedural knowledge: knowledge related to "knowing how", including motor skills.

Processing: changing the form or structure of something.

Projection: attributing one's undesirable characteristics to others, as a means of coping with emotionally threatening information and protecting the ego.

Psychiatrist: a medically trained person who specialises in the diagnosis and treatment of mental disorders.

Psychoanalysis: the form of therapy derived from psychoanalytic theory.

Psychoanalytic theory: Freud's explanation of how adult personality develops based on biological (sexual) drives in interaction with early experience.

Psychoneuroimmunology (PNI): the study of the effects of both stress and other psychological factors on the immune system.

Psychosexual development: Freud's stages in personality development based on the child's changing focus on different parts of the body (e.g. the mouth and the anal region). "Sexual" is roughly equivalent to "physical pleasure".

Psychosurgery: sections of the brain are removed or lesions are made to treat a psychological condition.

Psychotherapy: any psychological form of treatment of a mental disorder or illness, as distinct from medical forms of treatment.

Qualitative: concerned with how things are expressed, what it feels like, meanings or explanations; the quality.

Quantitative: concerned with how much. Data is presented in numerical terms.

Quasi-experiment: research that is similar to an experiment but certain key features are lacking, such as the direct manipulation of the independent variable by the experimenter and random allocation of participants to conditions.

Random allocation: placing participants in different experimental conditions using random methods to ensure no differences between the groups.

Random sampling: selecting participants on some random basis (e.g. numbers out of a hat). Every member of the population has an equal chance of being selected.

Randomisation: the allocation of participants to conditions on a random basis, i.e. totally unbiased distribution.

Range: the difference between the highest and lowest score in any condition.

Ratio: as for interval data but with a true zero.

Raw scores: the data before they have been summarised in some way.

Reactance: reacting against attempts to control or restrict one's personal choices.

Reality principle: the drive to accommodate to the demands of the environment.

Recency effect: free recall of the last few items in a list, where higher performance is due to the information being in short-term store.

Reductionist: an argument or theory that reduces complex factors to a set of simple principles.

Regression: in Freudian terms, returning to an earlier stage of development as a means of coping with anxiety.

Reinforced: a behaviour is more likely to re-occur because the response was agreeable.

Reliability: the extent to which a method of measurement or test produces consistent findings.

Repeated measures design: a research design where the same participants are used for all conditions in the experiment.

Replication: the ability to repeat the methods used in a study and achieve the same findings.

Representative sample: the notion that the sample *is* representative of the whole population from which it is drawn.

Repression: Freud's concept that material that is anxiety-provoking is kept out of conscious awareness.

Research: the process of gaining knowledge and understanding via either theory or empirical data collection.

Research hypothesis: a statement put forward at the beginning of a study stating what you expect to happen, generated by a theory.

Resistant attachment (type C): an insecure attachment of an infant to its mother. The child resists contact on reunion.

Retrieval: recovering stored information. Essentially, remembering it.

Retroactive interference: subsequent learning disrupting memory for previous learning.

Right to privacy: the requirement for ethical research that no participants are observed in situations that would be considered as private.

Right to withdraw: the basic right of participants in a research study to stop their involvement at any point.

Role conflict: when the demands of various jobs or roles produce opposing requirements.

Role-playing experiments: studies in which participants are asked to imagine how they would behave in certain situations.

Sample: a part of a population selected such that it is considered to be representative of the population as a whole.

Sampling bias: some people have a greater or lesser chance of being selected than they should be, given their frequency in the population.

Scattergraph (scattergram): two-dimensional representation of all the participants' scores in a correlational study.

Schema: an "organised" packet of information that is stored in long-term memory.

Schema theory: the view that memory is affected by schemas.

Science: a branch of knowledge conducted on objective principles. It is both an activity and an organised body of knowledge.

Secondary reinforcer: a reinforcer that has no natural properties of reinforcement but, through association with a primary reinforcer, becomes a reinforcer, i.e. it is learned.

Secure attachment (type B): a strong and contented attachment of an infant to its mother. The child is distressed on separation but easily comforted on reunion.

Self-actualisation: fulfilling one's potential in the broadest sense.

Self-esteem: the feelings that an individual has about himself or herself.

Self-fulfilling prophecy: the tendency for someone's expectations about another person to lead to a fulfilment of those expectations.

Semantic memory: organised knowledge about the world and about language, stored in long-term memory.

Semantic processing: processing material according to its meaning.

Sensitive: in the context of statistics, "sensitive" means more precise, able to reflect small differences or changes

Sensitive period: a looser interpretation of the concept of a critical period—changes are more likely during the period of time rather than being exclusive to it.

Separation anxiety: the sense of concern felt by a child when separated from their attachment figure.

Separation protest: the infant's behaviour when separated—crying or holding out their arms. Some insecurely attached infants show no protest when left by their attachment figure, whereas securely attached children do.

Serotonin: a neurotransmitter that is associated with lower arousal, sleepiness, and reduced anxiety.

Shallow processing: a minimal amount of processing, such as in the physical analysis of information.

Shaping: using a system of progressive reinforcement to produce responses that are closer and closer to the desired behaviour.

Short-term memory: a temporary place for storing data where they receive minimal processing. Short-term memory has a very limited capacity and short duration, unless it is maintained through rehearsal.

Single blind: a procedure in which the participants are not informed of the condition in which they have been placed.

Skill AO1: one aspect of the assessment procedure, which rewards knowledge and understanding.

Skill AO2: the other assessment criterion, which rewards analysis and evaluation.

Sociability: the tendency to seek and enjoy the company of others.

Social desirability bias: the tendency to provide socially desirable rather than honest answers on questionnaires or in interviews.

Social impact theory: a way of explaining social influence in terms of cumulative factors, such as the number and status of people present, the consistency of the message, and closeness to the influencer.

Social influence: the effects one person or group has on the attitudes or behaviour of another.

Social learning theory: the view that behaviour can be explained in terms of direct and indirect reinforcement, through imitation, identification, and modelling.

Social releasers: a social behaviour or characteristic that elicits a caregiving reaction. Bowlby suggested that these were innate and critical in the process of forming attachments.

Sociopaths: individuals who lack a conscience and empathy for others, making it likely that they will commit crimes and have difficulty forming relationships.

Span measure: a measurement of how large something is, such as the span of your fingers.

Split-half technique: a technique used to establish reliability by assigning items from one test randomly to two sub-tests (split-halves). The same person does both sub-tests simultaneously and their scores are compared to see if they are similar, which would suggest that the test items are reliable.

SQ3R: five strategies for effective reading: Survey, Question, Read, Recite, Review.

S–R link: an abbreviation for stimulus–response link.

Standard deviation: a measure of the spread of the scores around the mean. It is the square root of the variance and takes account of every measurement.

Standardised instructions: instructions given to each participant which are kept identical to help to prevent experimenter bias.

Standardised procedures: the same procedures are used on every trial of an experiment to ensure that no confounding variables affect the dependent variable.

Stereotype: a social perception of an individual in terms of some readily available feature, such as skin colour or gender, rather than their actual personal attributes.

Storage: storing a memory for a period of time so that it can be used later.

Strange Situation: an experimental procedure used to test the security of a child's attachment to a caregiver. The key features are what the child does when it is left by the caregiver and the child's behaviour at reunion, as well as responses to a stranger.

Stranger anxiety: the distress experienced by a child when approached by a stranger.

Stress: a state of psychological tension and physiological arousal produced by a stressor.

Stress inoculation training: a technique to reduce stress through the use of stress-management techniques and self-statements that aim to restructure the way the client thinks.

Stressors: events that throw the body out of balance and force it to respond.

Superego: the part of the mind that embodies one's conscience. It is formed through identification with the same-sex parent.

Sympathetic branch: the part of the autonomic nervous system that activates internal organs.

Synapses: the extremely small gaps between neighbouring neurons (nerves).

Systematic desensitisation: a form of treatment for phobias, in which the fear response to a threatening stimulus is replaced by a different response such as relaxation.

Systematic sampling: a modified version of random sampling in which the participants are selected in a quasi-random way (e.g. every 100th name from a population list).

TEE approach: an approach to studying and understanding: theory (T), evidence (E), evaluation (E).

Temperament: innate and characteristic modes of emotional response, such as sociability.

Temperament hypothesis: the view that a child's temperament is responsible for the quality of attachment between the child and its caregiver, as opposed to the view that experience is more important.

Test–retest: a technique used to establish reliability, by giving the same test to participants on two separate occasions to see if their scores remain relatively similar.

Theory: a general explanation of a set of findings. It is used to produce an experimental hypothesis.

Theory of evolution: an explanation for the diversity of living species. Darwin's theory was based on the principle of natural selection.

Time sampling: a technique used in observational studies. Observations are only made during specified time periods (e.g. the first 10 minutes of each hour).

Token economy: institution-based therapy based on the principles of operant conditioning. Desirable behaviours are encouraged by the use of selective reinforcements.

Trace decay theory: the view that forgetting is due to the physical disappearance of the memory trace.

Transactional model: an explanation for behaviour which focuses on the interaction between various factors. The transactional model of stress explains stress in terms of the interaction between the demands of the environment and the individual's ability to cope.

True experiment: research where an independent variable is manipulated to observe its effects on a dependent variable and so determine a cause-and-effect relationship.

Two-tailed or **non-directional hypothesis**: a prediction that there will be a difference or correlation between two variables, but no statement about the direction of this difference.

Type A: in biopsychology, a personality type who is typically impatient, competitive, time pressured, and hostile.

Undisclosed observation: an observational study where the participants have not been informed that it is taking place.

Validity: the soundness of the measurement tool, the extent to which it is measuring something that is real or valid.

Variables: things that vary or change.

Variance: the extent of variation of the scores around the mean.

Vicarious reinforcement: receiving reinforcement through another person.

Visuo-spatial sketch pad: a system within working memory designed for spatial and/or visual coding.

Volunteer bias: the systematic difference between volunteers and non-volunteers.

Working memory system: the concept that short-term (or working) memory can be subdivided into other stores which handle different modalities (sound and visual data).

Author Index

Abernethy, E.M. 56
Adams, G.R. 247, 248
Adams, P.R. 247, 248
Adler, C.S. 145
Adorno, T.W. 211, 220, 221
Agras, W.S. 190
Ainsworth, M. 100
Ainsworth, M.D.S. 86, 87, 88, 90
Akerstedt, T. 128
Albus, M. 151
Allport, G.W. 60
Anderson, J. 251
Anderson, S.J. 52, 59
Andersson, B.-E. 107, 108, 109
Andrasik, F. 147
Andrews, B. 57
Apple, R.F. 189
Arendt, H. 221
Arnold, S. 243, 244
Aronson, E. 215, 220, 227, 244
Arthur, R.J. 132, 133
Asch, S.E. 201, 202, 203, 205, 208, 209,
  226
Ashton, H. 148
Atkinson, R.C. 34, 42, 44
Attanasio, V. 147
Ayllon, T. 179
Azrin, N.H. 179

Bachen, E. 129
Back, K.W. 202
Baddeley, A.D. 35, 36, 44, 45
Bahrick, H.P. 38, 67
Bahrick, P.O. 38, 67
Bak, R.M. 178
Baker, L. 189
Bales, R.F. 262
Bandura, A. 15, 16, 177, 179
Banuazizi, A. 204
Banyard, P. 15
Barber, T.X. 273
Barbor, P. 86
Barlow, D.H. 175, 183, 188, 191
Baron, R.A. 135

Barr, C.E. 168
Barraclough, B. 169
Barrett, H. 97
Bartlett, F.C. 60, 61, 62
Bates, J.E. 87
Baumrind, D. 217, 233
Baxter, J.D. 122
Beck, A.T. 181, 182
Bell, S.M. 86, 87, 88, 90
Belsky, J. 86, 89, 109
Bensman, J. 256
Berkun, M.M. 229
Beyth, R. 5, 6
Bialek, H.M. 229
Bickman, L. 216, 227
Black, J.B. 60
Blake, D.D. 147
Blanchard, E. 179
Blehar, M.C. 88
Blos, P. 189
Bogdonoff, M.D. 202
Bond, M.H. 209, 217, 267
Bortner, R.W. 141
Boston, M. 100
Bower, G.H. 60
Bowlby, J. 75, 77, 81, 83, 94, 97, 98, 99,
  100, 104, 105
Brady, J.V. 122, 124, 126, 151
Bransford, J.D. 47, 49, 62
Breier, A. 151
Brewin, C.R. 57
British Psychological Society 230, 231
Broberg, G. 109
Bronfenbrenner, U. 88
Brotzman, E. 216
Brown, G.W. 104, 112, 151
Brown, J. 129
Brown, R. 57, 58, 59, 218
Bruce, V. 67
Bruch, H. 185, 190
Bryant, B. 107
Brynjolfsson, J. 169
Buchanan, M. 44

Budzynski, T.H. 145
Buehler, R. 22
Bumpass, L.L. 137
Burchinal, M. 109
Burger, J.M. 211, 223
Burke, E.J. 147
Burt, C. 274
Bus, A.G. 95
Bushnell, I.W.R. 79

Cahill, L. 58
Calhoun, J.B. 134
Camerino, M. 128
Campbell, D.T. 201, 266
Cardwell, M. 269, 278
Carey, K.B. 129
Carey, M.P. 129
Carli, L. 211, 223
Carlsmith, H. 215, 244
Carlson, N.R. 120
Carmichael, L.C. 65
Carpenter, G. 78
Carroll, D. 143
Case, R. 34
Cassel, J. 152
Cassidy, J. 87, 89
Chadwick, D.F.D. 104
Claparède, E. 41
Clark, D.A. 182
Clark, L. 269, 278
Clarke, A.D.B. 100, 103, 105
Clarke, A.M. 100, 103, 105
Clarke, J.C. 178
Clarke-Stewart, K.A. 108, 109, 110
Claxton, G. 271
Clow, A. 129
Cobb, S. 126
Cockett, M. 104
Cohen, C.E. 62
Cohen, G. 132
Cohen, N.J. 25, 41, 58, 126
Cohen, S. 129, 136, 152
Coleman, R.M. 138
Collins, B.E. 200

Subject Index

Illustration Credits